MW01002371

FROM MY

P.3 Enquiry (Herodotos) but most of all,
  Thucyd.
Rejection of To muthodes

gp [540 - 6873186

  Blake Land senses -
    - Installation of
                2900

Guthrie
Kirk Raven Schofield
Barnes, the Pre Soc hit upon that special
  way of looking at the world which is
  the sci or rational way.

Verant
grof - T. most rational

            - Lemos
            - Carlos
            - Marathon
            - JFK

From Myth to Reason?

Studies in the Development of
Greek Thought

Edited by

RICHARD BUXTON

OXFORD
UNIVERSITY PRESS

Elements of bluff & exaggeration in scholars' arg.s

Vernant

fundamental shift

7-8- different forms of rationality
— rationality of myth, sophism (?)
1 thesis of the "from to" model

M D — contrast sophist persuasion w/ to Plt.

2- Guthrie — dev. from mythopoeic to a
rational view (his standard bearer is Thales)

Reason involves generality & system

* quote - p. 4

661 - 3669

7- WS towards an interest in how, w/m
specific competitive intellectual
social contexts partic. groups or indiv
... Vernant - intellec, artistic & tech develop
[?] the in Greece against background of socio-pol.
illegal change

aims & practices

OXFORD
UNIVERSITY PRESS

Great Clarendon Street, Oxford OX2 6DP

Oxford University Press is a department of the University of Oxford.
It furthers the University's objective of excellence in research, scholarship,
and education by publishing worldwide in

Oxford New York

Athens Auckland Bangkok Bogotá Buenos Aires Cape Town
Chennai Dar es Salaam Delhi Florence Hong Kong Istanbul Karachi
Kolkata Kuala Lumpur Madrid Melbourne Mexico City Mumbai Nairobi
Paris São Paulo Shanghai Singapore Taipei Tokyo Toronto Warsaw

with associated companies in Berlin Ibadan

Oxford is a registered trade mark of Oxford University Press
in the UK and in certain other countries

Published in the United States
by Oxford University Press Inc., New York

© Oxford University Press 1999

The moral rights of the author have been asserted
Database right Oxford University Press (maker)

First published 1999
First published in paperback 2001

All rights reserved. No part of this publication may be reproduced,
stored in a retrieval system, or transmitted, in any form or by any means,
without the prior permission in writing of Oxford University Press,
or as expressly permitted by law, or under terms agreed with the appropriate
reprographics rights organization. Enquiries concerning reproduction
outside the scope of the above should be sent to the Rights Department,
Oxford University Press, at the address above

You must not circulate this book in any other binding or cover
and you must impose this same condition on any acquirer

British Library Cataloguing in Publication Data

Data available

Library of Congress Cataloging in Publication Data

From myth to reason? : studies in the development of
Greek thought / edited by Richard Buxton.
Includes bibliographical references and index.
1. Mythology, Greek. 2. Philosophy, Ancient.
I. Buxton, R. G. A.
BL782.F76   1999   180—dc21   98-50450
ISBN 0-19-815234-5 (Hbk)
ISBN 0-19-924752-8 (Pbk)

1 3 5 7 9 10 8 6 4 2

Typeset in Bembo
by Best-set Typesetter Ltd., Hong Kong
Printed in Great Britain
on acid-free paper by
Bookcraft (Bath) Ltd., Midsomer Norton

Preface

FIRST of all, my thanks are due to the contributors to this volume; fortunate indeed is the editor who, like the present one, has to deal with colleagues whose learning is matched by their willingness to co-operate good-humouredly in the process of revision. Then, contributors and editor alike are indebted to the various bodies whose sponsorship made possible the Bristol Myth Colloquium of 1996, viz. (in alphabetical order) the British Academy, the Classical Association, the Hellenic Foundation, the Leventis Foundation, the Society for the Promotion of Hellenic Studies, and the University of Bristol. Next, the editor acknowledges the invaluable assistance given by Michael Howarth, Pantelis Michelakis, and Glenn Moodie in the preparation of this volume; Mr Howarth also translated two of the papers. Last but not least, Hilary O'Shea, of Oxford University Press, has patiently and carefully overseen this project from its inception; to her, too, much gratitude is owed.

The book is dedicated to 'the helpers'—Robert Benton, Pauline Hambling, Jo Kear, Rachel McNally, Irene Plant, Manolis Psarros, Spiros Siropoulos, Maria-Elena Springsted, and Pippa Sturt—that band of stalwarts whose friendly efficiency did so much to make the 1996 Colloquium memorable.

R.G.A.B.

Bristol
April 1998

022   in a Presocratic poet,
the exposition of doctrine is
presented as a mythos -
1) from a deity
2) to which addressee is
invited to listen

a discourse compared to a
multiple progression &
articulated in the act of
legein; unspoken oral discourse
expressly presented my the
pragmatic, if not performatic

Contents

viii   *Contents*

Notes on the Contributors

Note. Several of the books cited below have been translated into English from other languages; the dates of publication recorded here apply to the translations.

MIREILLE BÉLIS has written a thesis, under the direction of Pierre Vidal-Naquet, on aspects of purple in Greek, Roman, and Jewish antiquity. Her present research is devoted to the textiles found at Qumran, a subject on which she has published two articles.

JAN N. BREMMER is Professor of the History and Science of Religion at the Rijksuniversiteit Groningen. In addition to many articles on the religions of the Greeks and Romans and their reception in modern times, he is the author of *The Early Greek Concept of the Soul* (1983) and *Greek Religion* (1994); co-author of *Roman Myth and Mythography* (1987); editor of *Interpretations of Greek Mythology* (1987), *From Sappho to de Sade: Moments in the History of Sexuality* (1989), *The Apocryphal Acts of John* (1995), *The Apocryphal Acts of Paul and Thecla* (1996), and *The Apocryphal Acts of Peter* (1998); and co-editor of *A Cultural History of Gesture* (1991), *Between Poverty and the Pyre: Moments in the History of Widowhood* (1995), and *A Cultural History of Humour* (1997).

WALTER BURKERT was until 1996 Professor of Classics at the University of Zürich. His principal scholarly interests are the study of Greek religion from an anthropological perspective, Greek philosophy, and Greek–oriental interrelations. His books include *Lore and Science in Ancient Pythagoreanism* (1972), *Structure and History in Greek Mythology and Ritual* (1979), *Homo Necans: The Anthropology of Ancient Greek Sacrificial Ritual and Myth* (1983), *Greek Religion, Archaic and Classical* (1985), *The Orientalizing Revolution* (1992), and *Creation of the Sacred* (1996).

RICHARD BUXTON is Professor of Greek Language and Literature at the University of Bristol. In addition to articles on Greek tragedy, religion, and mythology, he has written *Persuasion in Greek Tragedy* (1982), *Sophocles* (2nd edn. 1995), and *Imaginary Greece* (1994). He is currently editing *Oxford Readings in Greek Religion*, and working on a book provisionally entitled *The Greeks and the Sacred*.

CLAUDE CALAME is Professor of Greek Language and Literature at the University of Lausanne. Thanks to his interest in modes of poetic enunciation and in anthropology, he has devoted particular attention to the ritual and symbolic aspects of Greek literature. Amongst his publications are *Choruses of Young Women in Ancient Greece* (1997), *The Craft of Poetic Speech in Ancient Greece* (1995), *Thésée et l'imaginaire athénien* (2nd edn. 1996), *I Greci e l'eros* (1992), and *Mythe et histoire dans l'Antiquité grecque* (1996). In addition he has edited several collective volumes, including *L'amore in Grecia* (1984), *Métamorphoses du mythe en Grèce antique* (1988), and *Figures grecques de l'intermédiaire* (1992).

JOHN GOULD retired from the H. O. Wills Chair of Greek at the University of Bristol in 1991. He is the author of *The Development of Plato's Ethics* (1955), *Herodotus* (1989), and co-editor, with D. M. Lewis, of the revised edition of Sir A. Pickard-Cambridge's *Dramatic Festivals of Athens* (1968). He has also published essays on Herodotus and Plato, on Greek tragedy, and on Greek religion and society.

FRITZ GRAF is Professor of Latin Philology and Religions of the Ancient Mediterranean at the University of Basel. His main area of research relates to Greek and Roman rituals and festivals. Among his monographs are *Nordionische Kulte: Religionsgeschichtliche und epigraphische Untersuchungen zu den Kulten von Chios, Erythrai, Klazomenai und Phokaia* (1985), *Greek Mythology: An Introduction* (1993), and *Magic in the Ancient World* (1997). He has also edited *Mythos in mythenloser Gesellschaft: Das Paradigma Roms* (1993).

ALAN GRIFFITHS is Senior Lecturer in Greek and Latin at University College London. He is the editor of *Stage Directions: Essays in Ancient Drama in Honour of E. W. Handley* (1995), and has also published in the areas of Archaic and Hellenistic poetry and Greek vase-painting; but his main field of interest is the typological study of Greek accounts of the mythical and historical past. He is preparing an edition of Herodotus Book 3, and a book on Herodotean narrative, provisionally titled *Herodotos His Stories*.

FRANÇOIS HARTOG is Professor of Ancient and Modern Historiography at the École des Hautes Études en Sciences Sociales, Paris. Amongst his books are *The Mirror of Herodotus: The Representation of the Other in the Writing of History* (1980; new French edn. 1991), *Le XIXe Siècle et l'histoire: Le Cas Fustel de Coulanges* (1988), and *Mémoire d'Ulysse: Récits sur la frontière en Grèce ancienne* (1996).

ALBERT HENRICHS is Eliot Professor of Greek Literature at Harvard University. He is the author of *Die Götter Griechenlands: Ihr Bild im Wandel der Religionswissenschaft* (1987), *Warum soll ich denn tanzen? Dionysisches im Chor der griechischen Tragödie* (1996), and the forthcoming version of his 1990 Sather Lectures *Playing God, Performing Ritual: Dramatizations of Religion in Greek Tragedy*. He has written numerous articles on Greek literature, religion, and myth, and has recently prepared a new edition of Wilamowitz's *Geschichte der Philologie* (1998).

THOMAS K. JOHANSEN is Lecturer in Ancient Philosophy and Classics at the University of Bristol. He is the author of *Aristotle on the Sense-Organs* (1997), and is currently working on a book on Plato's philosophy of Nature.

DOMINIQUE LENFANT is Maître de Conférences in Greek History at the University of Strasbourg. She is author of a forthcoming edition of and commentary on the fragments of Ctesias of Cnidus, and has published several articles on Greek conceptions of ethnicity and alien peoples.

Sir GEOFFREY LLOYD is Master of Darwin College, Cambridge; since 1983 he has also been Professor of Ancient Philosophy and Science in the University of Cambridge, and since 1992 Chairman of the East Asian History of Science Trust. He has published extensively in the field of Greek philosophy and science, and more recently also in areas of ancient Chinese thought. His most recent books are *Demystifying Mentalities* (1990), *Methods and Problems in Greek Science* (1991), *Aristotelian Explorations*, and *Adversaries and Authorities* (both 1996). He is co-editor of *Le Savoir grec* (1996).

GLENN W. MOST is Professor of Classics at the University of Heidelberg, and Professor of Social Thought and Classics at the University of Chicago. He has edited and published books and articles on Greek and Latin poetry, on ancient and modern philosophy, and on the history of the classical tradition, including *The Measures of Praise: Structure and Function in Pindar's Second Pythian and Seventh Nemean Odes* (1985), *Theophrastus' Metaphysics* (co-edited with André Laks (1993)), *Collecting Fragments—Fragmente sammeln* (1997), and *Studies on the Derveni Papyrus* (co-edited with André Laks (1997)). He is the area editor responsible for the articles on Greek literature in *Der Neue Pauly*, and is co-editor of Friedrich Nietzsche's philological writings within the Colli–Montinari critical edition of his collected works.

PENELOPE MURRAY is Senior Lecturer in Classics at the University of Warwick. She has written on a variety of topics in ancient literature and is particularly interested in poetics. She has edited *Genius: The History of an Idea* (1989), and is the author of *Plato on Poetry* (1996). She is currently working on a book on the Muses.

CHRISTOPHER ROWE is Professor of Greek at the University of Durham. His publications include translations of, and commentaries on, Plato's *Phaedrus* (1986), *Statesman* (1995), and *Symposium* (1998), a commentary on Plato's *Phaedo* (1993), and an edited volume of essays on the *Statesman* (*Reading the Statesman: Proceedings of the Third Symposium Platonicum* (1995)). He is currently co-editing (with Malcolm Schofield) *The Cambridge History of Greek and Roman Political Thought*, and is joint editor of *Phronesis*.

JACOB STERN is Professor of Classics in the Graduate School at the City University of New York. He is the author of articles on Pindar, Bacchylides, Herodotus, Theocritus, Herodas, and other Hellenistic poets, and co-editor (with W. M. Calder III) of *Pindaros und Bakchylides* (1970). In recent years he has translated (with introduction and commentary) Parthenius, *Erotika Pathemata* (1992) and Palaephatus, *ΠΕΡΙ ΑΠΙΣΤΩΝ: On Unbelievable Tales* (1996).

SITTA VON REDEN is Lecturer in Classics and Ancient History at the University of Bristol. She is the author of *Exchange in Ancient Greece* (1995), and is currently working on a book on *Money in Classical Antiquity*.

Abbreviations

A&A	*Antike und Abendland*
AAWM	*Abhandlungen der Akademie der Wissenschaften in Mainz, geistes- und sozialwissenschaftliche Klasse*
ABG	*Archiv für Begriffsgeschichte*
AION (filol.)	*Annali dell'Istituto Universitario Orientale di Napoli. Dipartimento di Studi del mondo classico e del Mediterraneo antico, Sezione filologico-letteraria*
AJP	*American Journal of Philology*
AKG	*Archiv für Kulturgeschichte*
AncSoc	*Ancient Society*
ANET	J. B. Pritchard (ed.), *Ancient Near Eastern Texts Relating to the Old Testament*, 3rd edn. with Supplement (Princeton, 1969)
ARW	*Archiv für Religionswissenschaft*
ASNP	*Annali della Scuola Normale Superiore di Pisa, Classe di Lettere e Filosofia*
BASO	*Bulletin of the American Schools of Oriental Research in Jerusalem and Baghdad*
BICS	*Bulletin of the Institute of Classical Studies*
CH	*Cahiers d'histoire*
ChHist	*Church History*
CJ	*The Classical Journal*
ClAnt	*Classical Antiquity*
C&M	*Classica et Mediaevalia*
CPh	*Classical Philology*
CQ	*Classical Quarterly*
CSCA	*California Studies in Classical Antiquity*
CW	*The Classical World*
DK	H. Diels and W. Kranz, *Die Fragmente der Vorsokratiker*, 6th edn. (Berlin, 1952)
EL	*Études de lettres: Bulletin de la Faculté des Lettres de l'Université de Lausanne et de la Société des Études de Lettres*

FGrHist	F. Jacoby, *Die Fragmente der griechischen Historiker* (Berlin and Leipzig, 1923–58)
G&R	*Greece and Rome*
HR	*History of Religions*
HSCP	*Harvard Studies in Classical Philology*
IG	*Inscriptiones Graecae*
Inscr. Cret.	M. Guarducci (ed.), *Inscriptiones Creticae* (Rome, 1935–50)
JBL	*Journal of Biblical Literature*
JHS	*Journal of Hellenic Studies*
JWI	*Journal of the Warburg and Courtauld Institutes*
LEC	*Les Études classiques*
LIMC	*Lexicon Iconographicum Mythologiae Classicae* (Zürich, 1981–)
LSJ	*Greek–English Lexicon,* compiled by H. G. Liddell and R. Scott, revised by H. S. Jones, 9th edn. (Oxford, 1940); revised Supplement by P. G. W. Glare (1996)
MDAI (A)	*Mitteilungen des Deutschen Archäologischen Instituts (Athenische Abteilung)*
MH	*Museum Helveticum*
PCG	R. Kassel and C. Austin (eds.), *Poetae Comici Graeci* (Berlin, 1983–)
PCPhS	*Proceedings of the Cambridge Philological Society*
PEG	A. Bernabé (ed.), *Poetarum Epicorum Graecorum testimonia et fragmenta,* i (Leipzig, 1987)
PLF	E. Lobel and D. L. Page (eds.), *Poetarum Lesbiorum Fragmenta* (Oxford, 1955)
PMG	D. L. Page (ed.), *Poetae Melici Graeci* (Oxford, 1962)
PP	*La parola del passato*
RE	Pauly–Wissowa, *Real-Encyclopädie der classischen Altertumswissenchaft* (Stuttgart, 1894–)
REA	*Revue des études anciennes*
REG	*Revue des études grecques*
RhM	*Rheinisches Museum*
RIPh	*Revue Internationale de Philosophie*
SEG	*Supplementum Epigraphicum Graecum*
SIG^3	W. Dittenberger, *Sylloge Inscriptionum Graecarum*^{3} (Leipzig, 1915–24)

TAPhA	*Transactions of the American Philological Association*
THES	*Times Higher Education Supplement*
TrGF	*Tragicorum Graecorum Fragmenta*, ed. B. Snell *et al.* (Göttingen, 1971–)
WSt	*Wiener Studien*
YCS	*Yale Classical Studies*
ZPE	*Zeitschrift für Papyrologie und Epigraphik*
ZVS	*Zeitschrift für vergleichende Sprachforschung*

QUOTATIONS FROM GREEK

In the main text, all Greek is transliterated. In the footnotes, Greek script has been retained in certain cases, especially where the language of a particular passage is the subject of detailed comment.

Introduction

RICHARD BUXTON

It has often been maintained, and it is still widely held, that the civilization of ancient Greece underwent a development from myth to reason, or—to adopt the Greek-derived terms which have sometimes assumed talismanic status in relation to the debate—from Mythos to Logos.[1] Such a progress, embracing, among other areas, philosophy, historiography, medicine, technology, and various sciences, has frequently been presented as a triumphal one. That may be why, at the beginning of volume 2 of the otherwise unillustrated *Die Fragmente der Vorsokratiker* by Diels–Kranz, we find an Ephesian coin on which the philosopher Heraclitus, one of Ephesus' most famous sons, is depicted, in the manner of Hera*cles*, brandishing a club.[2]

A slogan for the Rise of the Rational was provided by the title of Wilhelm Nestle's *Vom Mythos zum Logos*, a work to which more than one contributor to the present volume will critically return.[3] Bruno Snell—to take an altogether more substantial scholar than Nestle—in a chapter ('From Myth to Logic') of his significantly entitled *The Discovery of the Mind*, observed that 'the myth of the Homeric paradigm, and all myth in general, stands half way between the compulsive ideas of early magic mentality, and the problems and uncertainties of later empirical and

---

[1] The use of the collective singular (Mythos, myth) is noted by T. Hölscher, 'Mythen als Exempel der Geschichte', in Graf (1993*b*), 67–87, at 74–5 n. 23.

[2] The coin-type is 2nd–3rd cent. CE. What might have prompted the creation of the original image is another question. For the suggestion that the brandished club on the coin (perhaps an emblem of 'striking opinions') might have been a misunderstanding of an earlier statue representing the philosopher *leaning on a staff*, see Lippold (1911).

[3] On that work, and in particular on the significance of its place and date of publication (Stuttgart, 1940), see especially Most and Bremmer in this volume.

2   *Richard Buxton*

historical thought.'[4] Few have put the 'from . . . to . . .' case as uncompromisingly as W. K. C. Guthrie, in whose view Greek philosophical thought between 600 and 300 BCE exhibited a development 'from a mythopoeic to a rational view of the world'. The standard-bearer of Guthrie's enlightenment was Thales, who, 'so far as we can tell, had thrown off mythical expression, and was giving what he considered to be a purely rational account of the origin and nature of the universe'.[5] Equally authoritative is the voice of Kirk–Raven–Schofield in *The Presocratic Philosophers*. Thales once more has pride of place, since he 'evidently abandoned mythic formulations; this alone justifies the claim that he was the first philosopher, naïve though his thought still was.' But that naïvety was soon superseded by Anaximander, author of 'the first attempt of which we know to explain the origin of man, as well as of the world, rationally', and by Heraclitus, whose 'relation of the soul to the world was more credible than that of Pythagoras, since it was more rational'.[6] Neither Guthrie nor Kirk–Raven–Schofield argues that there occurred a *wholesale replacement* of myth by reason: Guthrie concedes that 'mythical thinking never dies out completely', while for Kirk–Raven–Schofield the contrast between Hesiod and the Milesian philosophers is only that between the '*mainly* mythical' and the '*mainly* rational'.[7] Yet the assumption that a fundamental shift towards rationality took place is not in question. In the same spirit Michael Frede prefaces an account of 'the notion of reason which we find in [Socrates, Plato, Aristotle, and the Stoics]' with 'the prehistory of this notion *as it slowly emerges in Greek thought*';[8] key players in that emergence are the Presocratics, who, in the words of Jonathan Barnes, 'hit upon that special way of looking at the world which is the scientific or rational way'.[9] Nor is this view confined to those whose angle of approach is from

---

[4] (1953), 207. The fault-lines in Snell's developmental approach to, in particular, concepts of the will and responsibility are exposed in Williams (1993), esp. 21–6; cf. Padel (1992), 44–8.

[5] Guthrie (1953), 5, 10.

[6] Kirk, Raven, and Schofield (1983), 99, 142, 212.

[7] Guthrie (1953), 7; Kirk, Raven, and Schofield (1983), 7 (my italics).

[8] Frede and Striker (1996), 5 (my italics).

[9] (1987), 16. Stephen R. L. Clark gives an altogether less Whiggish (his term) view, observing that '[t]he philosophic temperament, on the available evidence, is found throughout the world and may be assumed to have been present throughout the hundred thousand years of human being [*sic*] . . .' (Kenny (1994), 4; 'Whiggish': 5).

philosophy. Fritz Graf, one of the foremost contemporary interpreters of mythology, was in no doubt of the momentousness of
the shift from mythical to philosophical explanation when he
referred to 'the abandonment of the idea that cosmic events are
brought about by gods whose actions resemble those of human
beings, in favour of the assumption that underlying these events
are purely physical processes . . .'[10] For Graf, as for Guthrie, it was
Thales who first wielded the club.[11]

In the passage quoted above, Snell mentions historical thought,
and that serves as a reminder that the 'from . . . to . . . ' thesis has
been extended well beyond philosophy. In the opinion of many,
the rise of Greek historiography constituted an analogous move
away from traditional, mythical ways of conceiving the relationship between humans and their past. For Arnaldo Momigliano,
'The origin of Greek historiography lies in Ionic [i.e. early philo-
sophical] thought.'[12] Moses Finley, while explicitly denying that
the writing of history formed part of 'the step from *mythos* to
logos',[13] saw Herodotus as conducting an enquiry remarkable for
the extent to which it offered explanations that were systematic,
human, secular, and political, a methodological revolution carried
much further by Thucydides.[14] In fact, Thucydides' rejection of
to muthōdes ('the fabulous') is precisely the characteristic which
tempted Jean-Pierre Vernant to describe him as 'notwithstanding
Herodotus . . . the first true Greek historian'.[15] More explicit still
is Fritz Graf's remark that Thucydides is 'generally and rightly
regarded as the most rational of the Greek historians'.[16]

The notion that reason involves generality and system has led
scholars to see developments in medicine, too, in terms of
'from . . . to . . .'. Albrecht Dihle linked 'the rise of medicine to
the status of a science' with the name of Hippocrates;[17] a recent

---

[10] Graf (1993a), 98.

[11] 'What was being developed here [sc. by Thales] was a model of the world explained
on rational rather than mythical grounds' (Graf (1993a), 97).

[12] (1966), 211. The particular link explored by Momigliano is that between
Xenophanes and Hecataeus.

[13] 'that step was not mediated by history. It bypassed history altogether. It moved from
the timelessness of myth to the timelessness of metaphysics' (Finley (1975), 17).

[14] Ibid. 30 ff.

[15] (1980), 191; the quotation comes from a section entitled 'From myth to history and
philosophy'.

[16] (1993a), 122.

[17] (1994), 154.

French history of Greek literature speaks of a period when medicine, which had long been nothing more than a combination of magical therapeutic techniques and more natural remedies, 'became a rational art and attempted to define the rules of an empirical practice', a view echoed in the title and argument of James Longrigg's *Greek Rational Medicine*.[18] It would be easy to cite comparable observations in relation to other scientific domains. One example may stand for many: so astonishing is the achievement of Aristotelian zoology that Urs Dierauer is inclined to emphasize a fundamental difference between the pre-philosophical and philosophical conceptions of animals: in contradistinction to what went before, 'the philosopher attempts to discover general perspectives which are valid for all animals, and to compare and contrast the animal world *as a whole* with the world of humanity'.[19]

It is clear, then, that a great deal of distinguished scholarship can be cited in support of one or another variant of the 'from . . . to . . .' thesis. Yet it is equally clear that the idea of a heroic, progressive shift in Greek thought involves a nest of fearsome problems.

Suppose, firstly, we begin by focusing on the period between the sixth and fourth centuries BCE (the period covered by Nestle, and singled out also by Guthrie and many others). Of course, startling intellectual developments took place then (the Presocratics, Plato, Aristotle; Herodotus, Thucydides; the Hippocratics); but it would seem evident that, before any global generalizations can be hazarded, these developments must first be differentiated in the light of the disparate situations obtaining in philosophy, historiography, medicine, etc., *vis-à-vis* the various traditional pasts which they were inheriting and modifying.

Secondly, there is a need also for *sociological* differentiation. What, for example, of the woman working with her husband in the fields on the island of Chios; or the Arcadian goatherd tending his flock in the valley of the Neda; or the slave, physically destroyed and mentally numb, toiling in the Laurium silver-

[18] Saïd, Trédé, and Le Boulluec (1997), 114; Longrigg (1993), on which see the criticisms of Dale B. Martin, 'Hellenistic superstition: the problems of defining a vice', in Bilde *et al.* (1997), 110–27, at 111.
[19] (1977), 6 (my italics).

mines? In what sense, if any, were *they* a part of the intellectual developments just mentioned?

Thirdly, even if we can properly describe certain areas of *thought* in developmental terms, we are faced with the intractable problem of relating such changes to the *practices* of everyday life—in the agora, on a battlefield, before an altar, in the bedroom. Did these practices, too, develop 'from . . . to . . .'?[20]

Fourthly, if we decide that we do want to make claims about a process of change—whether general or particular, whether throughout society or at just one level within it, whether in discourse or in practice—the explanation for that process is going to be extremely problematic. Are we to relate the genesis of 'rational' modes of thinking to the growth of the polis?[21] Or to the demand for general rules, for example in law, and then also in relation to mathematical proof, as a consequence of disputes within Archaic elites?[22] Or to the growth of literacy or coinage?[23] Or to all, or some, or none of these factors?

But even that does not begin to exhaust the difficulties. What of the periods before and after the sixth-to-the-fourth centuries? What, for instance, of the third century BCE? That century witnessed the framing of what some have regarded as the apogee of the rational, namely Euclid's set of postulates.[24] Yet the same century witnessed Apollonius' making of a poem in which Medea dissolved the bronze giant Talos by fixing him with the Evil Eye; and in that episode, as a recent critic has persuasively argued, the echoes of scientific (specifically, Democritean) theory in Apollonius' narrative serve to enhance rather than to undermine the horror: there is no *opposition* between rationality and magic.[25] Would it not then be preferable, instead of speaking of a 'shift', to think in terms of a constant to-ing and fro-ing between the mythical and the rational? After all—a point driven

---

[20] The same question may be put, *mutatis mutandis*, in relation to other intellectual movements, such as the Scientific Revolution in 17th-cent. Europe; cf. Shapin (1996), 6.

[21] See e.g. Vernant (1982), 119–29; cf. G. E. R. Lloyd (1987), 78–83. On historiography: 'The new impulse came from the classical polis, and in particular the Athenian polis' (Finley (1975), 30).

[22] Osborne (1996), 316.

[23] Literacy: see the discussion, with extensive bibliography, in G. E. R. Lloyd (1987), 70–8. Coinage: Seaford (1994), 222 ff., on Heraclitus.

[24] Cf. Heath (1926), i. 202–20; Sarton (1959), 39. Euclid's genius is hardly diminished by the subsequent discovery of non-Euclidean geometries.

[25] Dickie (1990).

home often enough by E. R. Dodds[26]—myths, and the religious
structure they were embedded in, were not simply *superseded*.
Long after Anaximander, Aristotle, and Archimedes, people—
thoughtful people, not just Theophrastus' Superstitious Man—
still sacrificed, still sang hymns to the gods, still felt uneasy at
crossroads, in case Hecate was on the prowl.[27]

But even 'to-ing and fro-ing' implies the independent and
identifiably separable existence of the terms between which the
alleged oscillation takes place. In other words, it confers respect-
ability on 'the mythical' and 'the rational' as analytical tools. But
how far *are* they respectable? If we acquiesce in their adoption,
have we not already begged one of the central questions which
any investigation into the ancient Hellenic world ought to regard
as problematic? Could there, then, be a case for setting the frame
of the argument at yet one more remove further back?

Given all these difficulties, it is hardly surprising that some
Hellenists have come to feel uneasy with various aspects of the
'from . . . to . . .' model, or even to recommend its wholesale
abolition. It may be useful to review some of the strategies they
have adopted.

1. One strategy moves the focus from observers' to actors' categories, by asking whether there were concepts which *for the
Greeks themselves* occupied a similar place to 'mythical' and 'rational'. How, for example, were those notoriously slippery words
muthos and *logos* deployed? To address these questions is to leave
the mist-enshrouded, time-free contours of Mythos and Logos
for a messier, more immediate, and more pragmatic world of
semantic skirmishing, where, amid a methodological hubbub,
disputants in various fields staked out their own territories by
defining them against their rivals. *Muthos* and *logos*, aggressively
and by no means consistently delimited, came readily to hand in
these conflicts. Enquiries into these matters, in particular by

[26] Dodds (1951), on which see G. E. R. Lloyd (1979: 4–5) and Dale B. Martin in Bilde
et al. (1997: 110–27).
[27] On Theophrastus, see Martin (n. 26 above). For good measure, we may add that the
complex power of Greek stories has *still* not been 'superseded', either for the opera-lover
enraptured by Monteverdi's *Il ritorno d'Ulisse in patria*, or for the child who, after switching
off an episode of the futuristic cartoon *Ulysses 31*, settles down with *Labyrinth of Time*, a
computer game in which 'it's up to you to overcome the awesome power of Minos'. The
most important element in the title of this volume is the question mark.

Geoffrey Lloyd, have had the effect of deflecting the debate away
from a search for the intrinsic properties of 'myth' and 'reason',
towards an interest in how, within specific competitive intellectual and social contexts, particular groups or individuals defined
the aims and content of their ideas and practices. Thus the author
of the Hippocratic treatise *On the Sacred Disease* castigates as
'charlatans' and 'magicians' those who regard epilepsy as demoni-
cally caused; nevertheless, for all his rhetoric, he himself holds
views (e.g. about the role of bile and phlegm blocking the veins)
which are, in Lloyd's words, 'very largely a product of his
imagination'.[28] To register the prevalence of this kind of rhetoric
is not to deny the possibility of progress in scientific understanding (cf. Lloyd's remarks on *advances* in the understanding of
anatomy and in the application of mathematics to physical problems).[29] The argument, rather, is that our (observers') assessments
of the 'success' of ancient investigations have to take account of
the elements of bluff and exaggeration which might have characterized the rhetorical context within which the original claims
were made.

2. A second strategy has been to pluralize the notion of Greek
reason. The emergence of this pluralizing trend can be seen
clearly in successive stages in the work of one of the most
influential of modern Hellenists, Jean-Pierre Vernant.[30] In the
1960s and at the beginning of the 1970s Vernant was concerned
to locate intellectual, artistic, and technical developments in
Greece against a background of socio-political and legal change:
such was the programme of the first volume of *Mythe et tragédie
en Grèce ancienne* (written with Pierre Vidal-Naquet),[31] as it had
been of *Mythe et pensée chez les Grecs*[32] and *Les Origines de la pensée
grecque*,[33] in which Vernant related the geometricization of intellectual space to analogous developments in the political arena.
Like Louis Gernet before him, Vernant rejected the idea of a

[28] G. E. R. Lloyd (1990), 50–2.
[29] Ibid. 56.
[30] Anyone wishing to trace this scholar's intellectual career can now take advantage of Riccardo di Donato's extensive edition of some of Vernant's less well-known publications (Vernant (1995)).
[31] See Vernant and Vidal-Naquet (1988), a trans. which combines *Mythe et tragédie*, i–ii; the Fr. orig. of vol. i appeared in 1972.
[32] Vernant (1983); the Fr. orig. appeared in 1965.
[33] Vernant (1982); the Fr. orig. appeared in 1962.

Greek Miracle;[34] yet he stressed that a fundamental shift towards rational thought did indeed take place, a shift describable as 'secularization' or 'laicization'.[35] In 1972 Vernant could still decisively maintain: 'The birth of the City and of law; the arrival of a rational kind of thought; the creation of new artistic forms . . . These innovations marked a change in *mentalité* so fundamental that it has been possible to see in it the very birth of Western man.'[36] Yet by 1984 the same scholar was freely conceding 'the fact that there are different forms of rationality', a position which he spelled out in 1987 under the significantly plural heading of 'Forms of belief and of rationality in ancient Greece'.[37] There was, Vernant now argued, a rationality of myth, a rationality of the sophists (linked to victory by persuasion), and a rationality whose model was that of Euclidean mathematics; there were even different types of rationality amongst doctors.[38]

3. A third modification of the 'from . . . to . . .' model has been generated by detailed studies of Greek myth and religion. Greek mythical narratives had *their own*, often rich and complex logic(s).[39] Some of the work leading to this conclusion has concentrated on 'the signified'—the content or 'thought' present in myths. In his analysis of the morphology of the Greek hero, Angelo Brelich demonstrated how the bewildering data about this religious phenomenon may be induced to make sense on the basis of quite a small number of schemata.[40] From a different perspective, structuralists highlighted how the Greek pantheon, especially the forms of action typical of each divinity, formed an intricate and far-from-random network; the extreme example of this approach was Marcel Detienne's still extraordinary *tour de force*, *Les Jardins d'Adonis*, a committed, Lévi-Straussian account of

---

[34] Gernet (1983).
[35] See von Reden in this volume. Lévêque and Vidal-Naquet (1964), an analysis of the reforms of Cleisthenes, is another example of an approach in terms of geometricization-cum-laicization. Regarding this approach, one should not underestimate the role played, as an implicit model, by the French Revolution, with its moves towards a secularization of space and time.
[36] Vernant (1995), i. 140.
[37] Ibid. 155, 282–94.
[38] Ibid. 292–3, 303.
[39] Merely to entertain the possibility of a multiplicity of logics is of course to tread on ground which some philosophers will consider lethally mined. At the outset of a volume such as this it seems prudent to beg as few questions as possible; hence the brackets.
[40] Brelich (1958).

the role of spices and perfume in 'mythical thought'.[41] More recently, attention has turned to 'the signifier'. Myths have been shown to exhibit *narrative* logic, a logic of tale-telling. This is an emphasis common to both Walter Burkert and Claude Calame, scholars whose approaches in other respects exhibit major differences, Burkert being keen to link tale-types with ritual and ultimately with biological 'programs of action', as against Calame's stress on 'contexts of enunciation'.[42]

There is in fact still much scope for further analysis of mythical logic. I take the example of Hesiod. On the grounds that he seems not to be doing philosophy, and not to be doing history either, Hesiod is often taken to be, on both counts, a prime candidate for the 'from . . .' end of the 'from . . . to . . .' polarity. However, his text is richer and deeper than is sometimes acknowledged. Consider his use of time. Scholars have relentlessly picked over line 175 from *Works and Days*, in which Hesiod expresses the wish, in relation to the men of the Iron Race, that he had either died before them or been born afterwards. Does this line—it has been repeatedly asked—imply a cyclic conception of time, or is the polar expression it contains just a way of saying 'not now'? Before trying to ascribe relative weights to signifier and signified in this single line, however, we should look at the wider picture. Like any aetiologist, Hesiod sees traces of the past in the present, but because of the subject-matter the nature of this presence is actually quite intricate. In the *Theogony*, Heracles kills the eagle which is tormenting Prometheus (526 ff.), and yet a few verses later (616) the Titan is still in bonds—as if, just as Zeus' power still persists, so the punishment of those who oppose him 'still' continues. Again, the *Theogony* is about a *sequence* of divinities, but it is also about figures who—precisely because they are divinities—*persist* in time even though superseded in power. That is why the *Theogony* centrally concerns not killing, but castration and swallowing: divine power can be curtailed or incorporated, but not abolished. Time in the *Works and Days* is no less complex. Pandora was the first woman, yet she is also Everywoman: the past in the present. Yet the myth of the Races stresses that things now are, from another point of

[41] Detienne (1977); the Fr. orig. appeared in 1972.
[42] Cf. Burkert (1979), 5 ff., about the inheritance of Propp, and Calame (1995), 32–5.

view, *not* as they once were: iron is not gold. And yet (again), the sequence of Races exhibits, albeit in different blends, the same, recurring traits: aggressive violence, and righteousness. Linear and/or cyclic: given that Hesiod is trying to narrate both the time of humans and the time of gods, it is no surprise that his stories cannot be mapped on to a simple chronological chart.

Work of this kind, on mythical logic, meshes in with recently revised perspectives on the nature of Greek religion. Developing the ideas of the American anthropologist Clifford Geertz, John Gould has made a powerful case for seeing Greek myth and ritual as constituting 'a language for dealing with the world', and as 'modes of religious response to experience in a world in which "chaos", the threat posed by events which seem to be unintelligible or which outrage moral feeling, is always close'.[43] The nature of this 'coping' is by no means simple, since, on Gould's model, both myth and ritual importantly involve the notion of ambiguity: divinity both is and is not intelligible, is and is not analogous to the world of human behaviour. Yet, amid all the interpretative complexity, there is discernible, in Gould's placing of religion as in Geertz's, a clear sense of logical priority. First comes the felt inadequacy of other modes of apprehending the world; subsequently, religion steps in to attempt to cope—a stark contrast with the 'religion superseded by reason' thesis which achieved its culmination in the work of J. G. Frazer. Myth-telling, with its expressive and semantic logic(s), has a significant part to play in the process of coping.

4. As a representative of the fourth and most radical strategy for circumventing the 'from . . . to . . .' model we may take the most recent work of Claude Calame. In his opinion, asking questions about the relative scope of 'the mythical' and 'the rational' amounts to the illegitimate imposition of modern criteria on ancient data; the very existence of 'myth' as a meaningful category should be seen as a product of Western anthropological thought, or in other words as 'universitaire'.[44] That leaves us with a conceptual toolbox, if not empty, then at least only very austerely furnished: at the bottom lie just 'des représentations symboliques narratives, ou tout simplement

---

[43] J. Gould, 'On Making Sense of Greek Religion', in Easterling and Muir (1985), 1–33, at 5, 8–9.
[44] (1996a) 22, 46. Calame is here developing the thesis of Detienne (1981).

discursives'.[45] Combining this approach with Geoffrey Lloyd's recent comparative studies of Greek and Chinese thought—studies which call into question the universality of such categories as science, magic, myth, and reason[46]—we might seem to have reached a point where not only does 'the Greek achievement' have about it more of the mirage than the miracle, but where we are actually left *without a vocabulary* for describing the events which were once thought to constitute that achievement.

BEYOND GREECE

The 'from . . . to . . .' debate is not taking place within a Hellenic vacuum. We shall now take a brief look at the wider picture.

'Not emotion'? 'Not faith'? 'Not madness'? 'Not myth'? Contrastive definitions of 'the rational' depend on the position of the definer (whether they depend *only* on that position is one of the hottest intellectual potatoes at the time of writing). Within the scope of this Introduction it would be futile to attempt even to scratch the surface of the history of the debate about reason: merely to mention the names of Aquinas, Descartes, and Kant is enough to rule *that* out of court. Even if we confine ourselves to the twentieth century, strategies have varied hugely, from the work of Max Weber, especially on economic rationality, to the self-positioning (or not) of Jacques Derrida *vis-à-vis* the Cartesian tradition. The 1970s and 1980s saw a particularly vigorous debate amongst Anglo-American scholars, about rationality as contrasted with, or as complementary to, supposedly irrational beliefs such as that in witchcraft. The arguments deployed at that time raised fascinating issues, even if now they have in one respect a slightly dated feel to them, perhaps owing to the fact that, under the enormous weight of Evans-Pritchard's authority, the beliefs and practices of the Azande and the Nuer—'his' peoples—received disproportionate attention.[47] Yet the problems aired in that debate about rationality have not gone away; indeed, attacks on the

---

[45] Calame (1996a) 54.

[46] e.g. G. E. R. Lloyd (1996).

[47] Some important participants in the debate: Wilson (1970), Horton and Finnegan (1973), Hollis and Lukes (1982); cf. Tambiah (1990). See also Hollis (1996), a collection of essays many of which appeared originally in the 1980s or earlier.

viability of the concept of the rational have become even more
assertive.

Whose reason is it anyway? That of Westerners? Robin Horton
was in no doubt that 'if the West has done nothing else of
indisputable worth, it *has* succeeded in creating an institutional
framework that has generated forms of explanation, prediction and
control of a power hitherto unrivalled in any time or place'.[48] Some
such assumption has underpinned many an investigation into the
history of science, like A. C. Crombie's account of developments
in Europe at the end of the thirteenth century: the invention of the
mechanical clock meant that 'organic' time came to be replaced by
abstract, mathematical time, the symbolic *mappa mundi* by abstract
cartography, and hierarchical representation by perspective.[49] But
which scientists, and what kind of science, are we to take as
representatives of reason? Isaac Newton, who devoted himself with
such energy to the study of alchemy? Ideas of what it is to do
science do not remain static, and the ripples caused by Thomas
Kuhn's notion of a 'paradigm shift' have certainly not ceased;
indeed, *The Structure of Scientific Revolutions* has been appropriated—
in spite of its author—to justify the most radical relativizations of
truth and objectivity.[50] Being found lacking in conclusiveness at
levels ranging from the subatomic to the intergalactic, modern
physics has, it has been argued, come to resemble just one more,
more-or-less plausible story about the world.[51]

More generally, the latter part of the twentieth century has
seen the notion of reason subjected to all kinds of criticism, aimed
variously at redefining, undermining, pillorying, or abolishing it.
The metahistorian Hayden White has described historical narra-

---

[48] Horton and Finnegan (1973), 294; italics in original.

[49] Crombie (1979), 190. On 'the emergence of the arithmetical mentality' in medieval
Europe, see A. Murray (1978), ch. 7.

[50] Kuhn (1962). Kuhn himself decisively rejected the extreme 'social construction is all
there is' (SCIATI) view of science: '"[T]he strong program" [sc. SCIATI] has been
widely understood as claiming that power and interest are all there are. Nature itself,
whatever that may be, has seemed to have no part in the development of beliefs about it.
Talk of evidence, or the rationality of claims drawn from it, and of the truth or probability
of those claims has been seen as simply the rhetoric behind which the victorious party
cloaks its power. What passes for scientific knowledge becomes, then, simply the belief of
the winners. I am among those who have found the claims of the strong program absurd:
an example of deconstruction gone mad' (Thomas S. Kuhn, Rothschild Lecture 1992,
cited by Stephen Cole in Gross, Levitt, and Lewis (1997) 276).

[51] On the unattainability of the ideal of scientific/philosophical verification, cf.
Biderman and Scharfstein (1989), pp. xi–xii.

tives as 'verbal fictions, the contents of which are as much *invented* as *found*'.[52] A number of advocates of feminist epistemology have concluded that reason is gendered male; it may even be the case (some have suggested) that the grounds for preferring one theory of knowledge to another should be political.[53] As regards scientific rationality, it has become common in the contemporary United States to speak of 'science wars': attacks on the dominant scientific establishment have provoked a vehement counter-attack against 'the flight from science and reason'.[54] It is impossible, in the space available here, to do justice to the complexity of the political and intellectual issues involved: suffice it to say that the prevailing climate is one of sharp and bitter disagreement.

Or ought one rather to say: the prevailing *academic* climate (that which Calame would call 'universitaire')? For one must ask the identical question regarding the contemporary Western world as one must ask about ancient Greece: the question, namely, about the place of reason *in practice*. The world's most scientifically and technologically advanced society, that of the United States, has been exhibiting, especially since the 1970s, a number of marked trends involving beliefs which, from the point of view of central scientific orthodoxy, might be termed 'superstitious' or 'paranormal', ranging from 'alternative' medicine and astrology to belief in reincarnation and in the widespread occurrence of abduction by aliens.[55] It would, once more, be begging crucial questions to call those beliefs 'irrational'; but it is at any rate clear that discontent with orthodox views about the progression of knowledge extends far beyond the sometimes rarefied atmosphere of the university campus. One thing is certain: we are even more aware now than was the case twenty years ago of the hidden agendas lurking beneath any enquiry into 'reason'.

---

[52] (1978), 82; italics in original.

[53] '[F]eminist epistemologies must be tested by their effects on . . . practical political struggles' (Alcoff and Potter (1993), 14). On the link between maleness and concepts of reason, see Genevieve Lloyd (1984), with the bibliographical essay at pp. 123–33. However, for a sustained onslaught on the whole notion of feminist epistemology, see the essays (by feminist philosophers and feminist scientists) in Gross, Levitt, and Lewis (1997), 383–441.

[54] See the barrage in Gross, Levitt, and Lewis (1997).

[55] It has been alleged that 'several hundred thousand to several million Americans may have had abduction [sc. by aliens] or abduction-related experiences' (Mack (1994), 15; cited by Vyse (1997), 15).

THE SCOPE OF THIS VOLUME

One way of taking forward our understanding of these fundamental issues is to reflect on them in the broadest and most
general terms: and indeed, studies of myth and rationality, or
investigations into the very possibility of entertaining such concepts, are not in short supply. There is, however, an alternative
strategy, advocated by W. H. Whitely: 'It is, I believe, only by
building up detailed accounts of particular aspects of thinking
in specific societies that one can acquire the necessary foundation
for answering the broader comparative question in more realistic
terms.'[56] That is the intention with which this volume was
conceived.

   Over a period of five days in July 1996, around 150 scholars
from several continents came together in Bristol, England, to
attend a Colloquium entitled 'Myth into Logos?' Its aim was to
reconsider some of the issues raised earlier in this Introduction,
issues which have not only constituted for Hellenists a problem
of recurrent concern, but which might even be felt to imply
a definition of what it is to *be* a Hellenist—or of why it *matters*
to be a Hellenist. It would have been too much to hope that
all these issues could have been adequately addressed, much less
resolved, at the Bristol Colloquium. Nevertheless, in a relaxed
and genial atmosphere, some remarkable contributions were
made to the understanding of the topic under analysis. The aim
of the present volume is to put these contributions before a wider
public.

   The genre of the-book-of-the-conference runs all kinds of
risks: that which soars in a lecture hall may flop in print (though
if that happens, it is the editor's fault). It is for others to judge
the present project. I will simply say that (1) all the contributors
have taken the opportunity to revise, in most cases very
extensively, and in a few cases out of all recognition; (2)
the collection includes only about four-fifths of the total
number of orally delivered papers; the main reason for this
was to achieve a greater degree of thematic focus—
though emphatically not identity of approach—than might
otherwise have been the case; (3) one paper (Lloyd's) was not

---

[56] In Horton and Finnegan (1973), 145.

presented orally, being specially commissioned for the written volume.

The decision about how to order the papers was not an easy one, and the result has something of the arbitrary about it. Eventually, it seemed appropriate to group the contributions into small sections, each with its own distinctive thematic emphasis; but the reader will easily be able to think of alternative possibilities. In any case, the virtue of unity can be over-praised, and one of the notable features of the present volume is the way it reflects a diversity of voices and approaches between sophisticated and knowledgeable critics. Anyone wanting to learn about a single consensual view had better stop reading now.

We start (Section I) with a paper which gives historical depth to the 'from . . . to . . .' question. Glenn Most's point of departure is the still-influential position adopted by Nestle, but the burden of his paper consists of a discussion of relevant, mainly German-language scholarship from the eighteenth till the mid-twentieth century. Most argues that the eighteenth century marked a decisive turning point, away from a consensus that Mythos never put Logos into question, towards a view (e.g. that of Nietzsche) that Logos could be criticized in the name of Mythos. Though Most is well aware of difficult problems posed by a Mythos/Logos polarity, he is less ready than some of the other contributors to jettison that polarity altogether.

In Section II, Sitta von Reden and Jan Bremmer continue Most's engagement with the history of the 'from . . . to . . .' question, in that each reconsiders a particular, influential, earlier scholar in the field: von Reden looks at Louis Gernet, Bremmer at Max Weber. But both von Reden and Bremmer then go on to apply their respective dialogues to current debates about Greek social practice, whether economic (von Reden) or religious (Bremmer). The papers differ in many respects. Von Reden investigates what the implications are for our placing of myth and rational thought if we regard the relationship between gift exchange and money as being one not of chronological sequence, but of ideological opposition. Bremmer, for his part, asks how far it makes sense to talk of the beliefs and behaviour of whole social groups—in this case, Orphics and Pythagoreans—in terms of a move 'towards rationality'. Yet, in spite of differences in approach, von Reden and Bremmer agree on the need to look at

the myth/*logos* question against the background of specific socio-
historical developments in Archaic and Classical Greece.

   The papers paired in Section III ask how far we can get with
the 'from . . . to . . .' problem by looking at the logic of narratives
usually regarded as mythological. Towards the end of his contribution, Walter Burkert observes that something 'unique' took
place when the Greeks' work in philosophy and science took off;
but the bulk of his argument is encapsulated in the assertion that
'there is *logos* in cosmogonic myth from the start, so that no
simple change or progress "from *muthos* to *logos*" is to be observed.' Anticipating potential deconstructive criticism, he defends the viability of the notion of cosmogony as an analytical
tool for understanding a range of Near Eastern narratives about
beginnings. Burkert does make some suggestions about the possible social-contextual setting of such tales—myths 'in practice'—
but the main thrust of his analysis is directed at uncovering the
logic of narratives.

   John Gould too examines the logic of mythical narratives, this
time those presented by the tragedians. Alive both to the danger
of oversimplistically casting either the chorus or the heroes as
vehicles of *logos* (or, for that matter, as vehicles of myth), and to
the risks involved in any attempt to pigeon-hole experience as
either myth or reason, Gould asks what kind of rationality can be
found in tragic explorations of experience. By analysing the
conventions of tragic myth-telling, he shows how 'myth is deployed to reinforce or support reasoned (and yet often conflicting) interpretations of human experience'. Tragic myths are
simultaneously about narrated memory, about conflict, and about
reasoned explanation.

   The next two papers (Section IV) take scepticism about the
viability of the myth/*logos* polarity one stage further. Like several
other contributors, Claude Calame emphasizes that what we call
'Greek myths'[57] exhibit *narrative* logic. But after a detailed analysis
of the stories embedded in Isocratean prose texts, he goes on to
argue, not only that 'Greek myths' were examples of *logoi*—
discourse—but that 'they do not seem to be markedly differentiated from other types of discourse in which we, by contrast,
would perceive the operation of reason.'

[57] In order to do justice to Calame's argument, the quotation marks are here
unavoidable.

This position gains added resonance when set beside that taken up by Geoffrey Lloyd. Lloyd juxtaposes Greece with China. He is just as wary as Calame is about the myth/*logos* polarity. But, whereas Calame seeks to dissolve such a polarity *within* the Greek world, Lloyd is struck, rather, by the way in which, while in Greece some variant or other of such a dichotomy *is* used in a range of intellectual debates, in China, on the other hand, no comparable effort was devoted to the drawing of such boundaries. That difference, if established, calls for explanation, and Lloyd's suggestions about contrasts between the two societies take us back into the socio-political territory opened up (albeit in very different ways) by von Reden and Bremmer.

The five papers in Section V (Griffiths, Hartog, Lenfant, Stern, Henrichs) raise matters which may broadly be described as historical. But of course, one of the key issues which crops up explicitly or implicitly in those papers is: *are* they 'historical' matters—as opposed, for instance, to 'mythical'?

Alan Griffiths makes a similar point about Herodotus to one which Lloyd makes about certain Chinese texts: that there can be a movement between registers (in shorthand: between *muthos* and *logos*) even within one and the same passage. But Griffiths puts his own spin on this observation: Herodotus, he argues, was perfectly well aware of what he was doing in effecting these shifts—as were his audience. Like several contributors, then, Griffiths highlights the extent to which our reading of the myth/reason issue must depend on how we assess the narrative strategies at work.

Like Griffiths, François Hartog focuses on Herodotus, who must occupy a pivotal position in any debate about a movement 'towards rationality' in Greek historiography. After noting just how fluid Herodotus' own terminology is over *muthos*/*logos*, Hartog turns to examine how we place this historian. Story-teller? Half-way from myth to reason? Taking as an example the role of oracles in the Croesus episode, Hartog addresses the problem by analysing the stance of the narrator of stories. Like Griffiths, Hartog stresses the polyphony of Herodotean narrative, but his way into this polyphony is very different. The key word is *sēmainein*, 'to signify', which has to do both with oracular divination and with the craft of the knowledgeable historian. It is by attending to the kind of signifying which Herodotus practises, rather than by locating him somewhere between myth and reason, that Hartog seeks to define the nature of the historian's craft.

Such is the breadth of source material covered in Dominique Lenfant's piece on monsters that it was hard to know where to locate it (appropriately enough, since it deals so much with boundary-crossing). Lenfant's discussion of how the Greeks actually treated monstrosity links her to those contributors who analyse myth/reason in practice; on the other hand, her discussion of Aristotle points to a connection with Johansen's paper (see below). Eventually, it seemed useful to juxtapose her account with those of Griffiths and Hartog, since Lenfant too sees Herodotus as a key figure through whom critically to reappraise the 'from . . . to . . .' theory. At all events, the placement of her paper is less important than its content, which is essentially double. First, Lenfant argues that the evidence about the way in which monstrous births in Greece were perceived will *not* sustain the view that the Hippocratics and Aristotle stood to conventional opinion as reason to superstition. Secondly, she shows how, in the works of historian-ethnographers such as Herodotus and Ctesias, monsters were 'good to think with'. So history/ethnography resembled mythology: yet another dent in the myth/reason polarity.

It is only too easy to write the history of the myth-versus-reason debate in terms only of the contributions of intellects of the stature of Parmenides, Herodotus, and Plato. Yet, as Jacob Stern argues, that would be a mistake. In fact Palaephatus, the obscure post-Aristotelian figure whose writings Stern analyses, practised a kind of naïve rationalization of myths which was to prove extremely durable. Palaephatus' strategy for negotiating the myth/history boundary was devastatingly uncomplicated: he reclaimed the heroes for history by reducing their superhuman exploits to that which was consistent with *logos*.

The last paper in the historians' section is that by Albert Henrichs, who brings the story down to the Hellenistic period by examining two more aspects of the fluidity of the myth/history boundary. The first aspect relates to tales of human sacrifice, a subject which Henrichs sees as peculiarly suited to the collapsing of myth into history: he interprets one piece of Hellenistic prose fiction on this subject as a return 'from *logos* to *muthos*'. The second aspect concerns the pattern whereby historical Hellenistic figures imitated mythical precedents—another illustration of fluidity.

Several of the papers already summarized touch on matters which for most modern observers would count as philosophical; but the contributors to Section VI focus on this area directly.

Penelope Murray and Christopher Rowe offer closely interrelated discussions of Plato. After drawing attention to terminological plurality in the Platonic use of *muthos/logos*, Murray tackles what are conventionally called 'Plato's myths'—Er in the *Republic*, and so forth. She notes how such passages are signposted within the text, an observation which recalls Griffiths' comments on changes of narrative register in Herodotus. But Murray then goes on to question the mythical/philosophical distinction more fundamentally, suggesting that the *whole* Platonic text can be seen as partaking of the nature of myth, for example in virtue of its use of imagery and dialogic story-telling.

Rowe aligns himself with the more radical of what he takes to be two possible readings of Murray's position, viz. that which holds that the fictionality of the dialogue form necessarily lends to *all* Plato's writings a sense of provisionality: 'human reason itself', as Rowe puts it, 'ineradicably displays some of the features we characteristically associate with story-telling.' Though, at the end, Rowe is still willing to accept a distinction between story-telling and 'those sorts of discourse which are—comparatively at least—lacking in an imaginative dimension', he gives us a Plato in whom the rational can become myth by being narrated, while the mythical may properly form part of the philosopher's armoury, even to the extent of having a role in dialectic. So, as often in these pages, it is narrative strategy, rather than delineated territories of 'thought', on which the spotlight falls.

In the final paper in this section, Thomas Johansen demonstrates that Aristotle is every bit as central to the 'from . . . to . . .' debate as Plato. Johansen begins with the points (following Lloyd) that for Aristotle, too, (1) to call a rival's account a *muthos* can be a way of dismissing it as fictional, as false, as not based on systematic observation and rational inference, and (2) such a dismissal may mask *continuities* between the allegedly myth-dominated dismissee and the allegedly empirico-rational dismisser. But Johansen further argues both that Aristotle himself employs *muthoi* in constructing his own theories, and that he does so in a way which makes good sense given Aristotelian presuppositions about philosophy and history.

The bulk of this volume is about the Archaic, Classical, and Hellenistic periods; but the issues raised by the myth/reason opposition are relevant to the whole of antiquity. So it is appropriate to end with two papers whose authors extend the discussion well beyond the Hellenistic period.

All the contributors confront in one way or another the question of whether and where certain boundaries should be drawn. The papers by Mireille Bélis and Fritz Graf are no exception. As Lenfant did with monstrosity, so Bélis (purple) and Graf (metallurgy) have chosen specific themes to enable them eventually to move on to general conclusions. The fact that these themes are of a kind not usually introduced into discussions of 'the emergence of reason' only enhances their interest.

Bélis's conclusion can be concisely stated: purple was thought to be magical—*and that was exactly why it was rational to use it.* Across a range of social contexts, from dyeing to cooking to the administration of aphrodisiacs to medicine (more boundary-crossing here), purple was used throughout antiquity in a manner which suggested the consistent presence of 'a rational form of mythic thinking'. Bélis's stress on mythical *terminology* and on the associated mode of *thinking*, rather than on the logic of mythical *narrative*, sets her apart from some of the other contributors; and her emphasis on the *persistence* of ways of using purple and (as she puts it) 'talking purple' forms a contrast with those papers which seek to locate aspects of the myth/reason debate within more specific historical situations. Yet her central argument echoes an opinion voiced from one end of this book to the other: that there are excellent reasons for being dissatisfied with the assumption that myth is one thing and reason quite another.

Like Bélis, Graf analyses a set of traditional notions which exhibited a remarkable degree of continuity throughout antiquity. He shows that, in parallel with obvious and well-known developments in the *practice* of metallurgy, there was a long tradition which linked metal-working with sorcery, wildness, and ambivalence. Although different writers—Greek and Roman, Jewish and Christian—had their own motives for preserving and retelling such tales, Graf detects a common concern, which ties in with the anxiety generated by yet another boundary: that between the natural and the artificial. In Graf's words, '[w]ithout doubt, all this is not *logos* supplanting *muthos*'. Rather, technological developments generated, by their very nature, certain traditional stories which accompanied them, and even called them into question.

Taken together, these papers represent, at the intersection of two millennia, a major reassessment of another intersection. It is hoped that the result will be found stimulating by historians, anthropologists, and philosophers, as well as by Hellenists.

I
History of a Polarity

I

From Logos to Mythos

GLENN W. MOST

SOME readers, perhaps, will be startled by my title. And under-
standably: after all, they will long have been familiar with the idea
that the development of mankind as a whole has tended to follow
a trajectory leading from Mythos to Logos, and will have learned
that a development of this sort not only took place in ancient
Greece but has also been one of the most important parts of the
legacy of the Classical world to Western civilization. Such an idea
is expounded in numerous works of scholarship and, even more,
in countless popular presentations;[1] and indeed there is much to
be said for it, not least that it enlists the Greeks in the service of
modern impulses towards Enlightenment whose benefits many
of us have come to count upon (and thereby legitimates at one
stroke both the ancients and the moderns). Hence my present
purpose is not to call into doubt the fact, and the value, of some
kind of evolution—in at least certain parts of the history of
Europe and of those countries influenced by Europe—away from
a traditional, narrative, anthropocentric view of the structure and
meaning of things (which I shall call here Mythos) and towards a
more progressive, logical, mechanical kind of account (let us call
this Logos)—indeed, even brief reflection upon the news reports
coming from those parts of our world today in which such an
evolution has been delayed, halted, or reversed is enough to make
one glad for its even sporadic appearances. Nor would I wish
to deny that, among the turbulent innovations characteristic of
Greek culture in the first millennium before Christ, there were
also a number of sustained critiques of traditional myths in the
name of something much like our own version of rationality—

---

[1] Three examples chosen not quite at random: Burkert (1985), 312; West (1986), e.g.
116; Wilamowitz-Moellendorff (1959), 40 f.

after all, considering how much delight the Greeks took in putting things into question, it would have been quite strange if it had not occurred to at least some of them to criticize their myths too.

Rather, I would like to suggest that more has been involved, both in this familiar evolution from Mythos to Logos in ancient Greece and above all in the discovery of this evolution by the modern historiography of ancient Greece, than a simple and self-evident movement of spiritual progress on the one hand—what Leopardi derided as 'dell'umana gente | Le magnifiche sorti e progressive'[2]—and its inevitable recognition by a value-free modern scholarship on the other. Matters were—matters always are—infinitely more complex, and hence more interesting. Perhaps the most convenient entrance into these unfamiliar complexities is provided by a book whose very title announces its programmatic adherence to these familiar notions: Wilhelm Nestle's *From Mythos to Logos: The Self-Development of Greek Thought from Homer to the Sophists and Socrates.*[3] For widespread though these notions may be, Nestle's version of them remains one of their most eloquent, and stubbornly influential, formulations; and below the superficial clarity and simplicity of his conception lie significant tensions and surprising paradoxes which can tell us much not only about this single scholar but also about this whole set of issues in modern scholarship.

Consider the following passage, taken from its very first page:

Just as the surface of the earth was originally completely covered by water, which only gradually withdrew and let islands and continents appear, so too for primitive man the world surrounding him and his own nature were covered over by a mythical layer of beliefs, which only over a long period of time gradually retreated enough for larger and larger areas to be uncovered and illuminated by rational thought.[4]

---

[2] G. Leopardi, 'La ginestra o il fiore del deserto', lines 50–1. The italicized words are a citation, as Leopardi himself indicates in an ironic note: 'Parole di un moderno, al quale è dovuta tutta la loro eleganza.' They come from his cousin, Terenzio Mamiani. As often, Leopardi deploys citationality in order to undermine facilely optimistic notions of human progress.

[3] W. Nestle (1940).

[4] Ibid. 1: 'Wie die Erdoberfläche ursprünglich ganz mit Wasser bedeckt war, das erst allmählich zurückwich und Inseln und Kontinente hervortreten ließ, so war auch dem

As mythical images go, this one is certainly quite striking; but what Nestle evidently intended was in fact to use it to illustrate the inevitable *decline* of Mythos. For this scholar, Mythos and Logos were above all two contradictory ways in which humans can establish meaning in their world: as he put it in the book's opening words,

Mythos and Logos—with these terms we denote the two poles between which man's mental life oscillates. *Mythic imagination* and logical thought are opposites. The former is imagistic and involuntary, and creates and forms on the basis of the unconscious, while the latter is conceptual and intentional, and analyses and synthesizes by means of consciousness.

Put in these terms, one might suppose that these two modes of consciousness could be connected with one another in any one of a number of ways, that they could operate simultaneously at different levels or upon different objects, or could follow upon one another in the one direction or the other at any time. But, at least for Nestle, this is far from being the case. He claims instead that a unidirectional, necessary sequence determines both modes temporally in such a way that at a first stage we find Mythos, and only at a second one, derived from it, Logos. In his eyes, the paradigmatic example of this fundamental process of human history is provided by ancient Greece, and above all by the sixth and fifth centuries BCE, when 'the mythic thought of the Greeks was replaced step by step by rational thought, one domain after another was conquered for natural explanation and research, and the consequences for practical life were drawn'.[6] To

primitiven Menschen die ihn umgebende Welt und sein eigenes Wesen von einer mythischen Vorstellungsschicht überdeckt, die erst in längeren Zeiträumen allmählich soweit zurücktrat, daß immer größere Gebiete vom denkenden Verstande bloßgelegt und erhellt wurden.'

[5] W. Nestle (1940), 1: 'Mythos und Logos—damit bezeichnen wir die zwei Pole, zwischen denen das menschliche Geistesleben schwingt. *Mythisches Vorstellen* und logisches Denken sind Gegensätze. Jenes ist—unwillkürlich und aus dem Unbewußten schaffend und gestaltend—bildhaft, dieses—absichtlich und bewußt zergliedernd und verbindend—begrifflich.' (Italics in original.)

[6] This is how Nestle (1940: p. v) defines the fundamental aim of his book: 'Denn das ist sein eigentliches Ziel: zu zeigen, wie in einer überraschend kurzer Zeitspanne, im 6. und 5. Jahrhundert v.Chr., das mythologische Denken der Griechen Schritt für Schritt durch das rationale Denken ersetzt, ein Gebiet um das andere für eine natürliche Erklärung und Erforschung erobert und daraus die Folgerungen für das praktische Leben gezogen wurden.'

linger for a moment upon Nestle's oceanic analogy: once upon a
time—let us say, at the time of Homer—reality was covered over
by mythical hallucinations as though by a primeval layer of water
and slime; but in the following centuries—let us say, by the time
of Plato—the blazing force of the sunlight of reason gradually
evaporated the oozy habitat of the imagination's insubstantial
creatures and allowed the contours of the real world to appear.
From the sixth century BCE to our own time, the mythic primal
ooze has apparently retreated even further—indeed, if only there
were no greenhouse effect to melt the polar ice, we might be
able to imagine it vanishing once and for all one day. It is only
on the basis of mythical notions like this that Nestle could ever
have come up with the title for his book, a title which may seem
innocuous at first glance, but which becomes more bizarre the
more one reflects upon it.

What is so problematic in this title and in the ideas underlying
it? Not so much that Nestle's interpretation distorts the meaning
of many individual texts and authors of earlier Greek literature—
after all, doing just this is our own profession and favourite
pastime. Nor is it simply that he has constructed a framework
which brightly illuminates some developments that may well
have been taking place in the period he is considering but which
leaves many others in the shadows—for such disadvantages are
the inevitable consequence of any approach, and no hermeneutics
can avoid thematizing some phenomena at the cost of turning
others into foil or context for them. Nor shall I insist here upon
the obvious objection that in the period of Greek literature
Nestle is investigating there is much of Logos in Mythos and
much of Mythos in Logos—for example, that already Homer
betrays unmistakable traces of familiarity with the rationalizing
allegorical interpretation of traditional legends[7] and attempts
wherever possible to suppress or play down the more monstrous
or irrational elements of Greek mythology, while Plato still introduces what he calls, and what we recognize, as myths, in order to
communicate what he says is incapable of being revealed by
logical means alone: for Nestle's teleological model, as he himself
points out,[8] is certainly flexible enough to be able to deal with
such hybrids.

---

[7] See Most (1993).   [8] e.g. (1940), 17–18, 21.

All the objections listed and, by *praeteritio*, not posed in these sentences, can, and indeed should, be directed against Nestle's project and against the many like it for which Nestle may be taken as a particularly helpful example. But here I should like instead to place the emphasis upon a feature of Nestle's approach which is much more fundamentally problematic than these particular issues or results and which resides, instead, in the basic structure of his model. What I have in mind is Nestle's basic premiss of a strict teleological development from Mythos to Logos, from a starting point measured as defective by unalterable criteria towards a necessary goal identified with the knowledge of an absolute and unchanging reality which must, inevitably, one day be attained. When we are asleep, says Heraclitus, everyone dreams his own world, but once we awaken we all share the same world;[9] Nestle replies that in Mythos the world is always distorted, and in a potentially infinite number of different ways, but that in Logos there is only one world and we all inhabit it. If this were not so, the Greek achievement could not claim any validity for us: for, in Nestle's view, the Mythos of the Greeks, entertaining as it is, must in the end remain foreign to us, while the Logos of the Greeks is identical with our Logos too. For Nestle, if the myths of Greek Mythos seem familiar to us, it is only because, and to the extent that, particular historical traditions have chosen, for whatever reasons, to transmit them to us; but the law of non-contradiction and the syllogism, towards which Nestle's book points at the horizon like an Aristotelian Promised Land which Plato could see but not yet enter, are ours not because of specific historical contingencies but because of the essential nature of our minds and of the reality surrounding us. Hence for Nestle the Greek development from Mythos to Logos in fact amounts to a process of dehellenization, a transformation which begins with the Greeks as being merely Greeks and ends up with the Greeks as being universal, unconditioned specimens of humanity in the abstract (a condition to which Germans, too, can aspire).

It should be clear by now that Nestle's concept of Logos is—within his very own terms—deeply implicated in Mythos: his fundamental construction of a necessary development from

---

[9] Heraclit. B 89 DK.

Mythos to Logos corresponds not to what he himself could ever
describe as Logos, but rather to impulses which he too would
have no choice but to assign to the realm of Mythos. Indeed,
there is scarcely a single symptom of Mythos listed by Nestle
which could not be diagnosed throughout his own text. Does
Mythos make rich use of personifications? But Nestle too per-
sonifies his two basic concepts and permits them to enter into
lively relations with one another and to become involved in
complicated dramatic plots, seemingly without the decisive contribution or the active participation of concrete human beings.
Does Mythos translate mental contents into reified material
terms? But Nestle too conceives the mental development he is
describing as being identical with the bodily maturation of a child
towards adulthood, as though the one process were just as continuous, irreversible, and natural as the other. Does Mythos
believe in the magical effect of cult practices? But Nestle too
ascribes to the great geniuses of human history supernatural capa-
bilities which are necessary for his model as the motors of historical evolution and which he emphatically indicates, but which in
the end he cannot explain, but only revere. And any lingering
traces of doubt about the status as Mythos (in Nestle's sense) of
Nestle's Logos can perhaps be banished by a sentence, a place,
and a date. The sentence reads:

To go on this path from Mythos to Logos, to grow up from the
immaturity of the mind to its maturity, seems to have been reserved
for the Aryan peoples since these are the ones that belong to the most
highly talented race, and among these there is in turn no other people
in whom this development can be traced so clearly as among the
Greeks.[10]

And the place and date: Stuttgart 1940, the city and year in which
Nestle's book was first published.

Nestle was apparently not at all a Nazi himself and seems to
have thought, oddly, that by means of this book he could help to
increase the amount of rationality in the troubled world around

---

[10] W. Nestle (1940), 6: 'Diesen Weg vom Mythos zum Logos zu gehen, aus der
Unmündigkeit zur Mündigkeit des Geistes emporzuwachsen, scheint den arischen
Völkern als denen der höchstbegabten Rasse vorbehalten geblieben zu sein, und unter
ihnen läßt sich wieder bei keinem diese Entwicklung so klar verfolgen wie bei den
Griechen.' The peculiar mixture, in this sentence, of the cosmopolitan language of Kant's
Enlightenment with the racist vocabulary of Hitler's Germany has a markedly distasteful
effect.

him.[11] But it is hard to work with pitch without blackening one's hands; and no pitch is blacker, or stickier, than the opposition between Mythos and Logos. It would not have been worth spending so much time on Nestle if he had been only a little confused, or if he had merely intended to secure for his book a greater success in the local markets of his day by introducing into it a few poetical interludes and topical remarks. On the contrary, Nestle's book is significant enough to justify my recalling, but at the same time revising, his title with my own. For it is not merely the case that his work is still widely known and astonishingly influential, above all, but not only, in Germany; what is more important is the evident fact that the teleological, developmental program formulated so strikingly in its title is familiar even today to many people who otherwise, when they hear the name Nestle, think only of chocolate.

So fascinated is this program by the questions (which I deliberately set aside here), whether, and if so for what reasons and in what ways, the Greeks actually did undergo some sort of development from Mythos to Logos in the sixth and fifth centuries BCE, that it seems entirely to fail to recognize the existence of another, no less important development, namely the decisive evolution since the eighteenth century in modern Western culture's understanding of rationality from Logos to Mythos— hence my title. During this latter period, philosophers have developed the concept of rationality in such a way that they have created from within it a new concept of the mythic which has put into question any simple opposition between Mythos and Logos and has revealed Mythos to be in fact nothing other than an especially interesting category of Logos. The momentous consequence of this process is that Logos itself, so far from remaining unaffected by this development, has been fundamentally altered by it, and has turned out not to be so completely different from Mythos as earlier generations had sometimes supposed. In other words: the concept of Logos presupposed by Nestle has been hopelessly out of date for over two centuries, and what has above all demonstrated its inadequacy has been precisely the modern study of myths, especially Greek myths.[12]

---

[11] Cf. (1940), p. vi.

[12] The secondary bibliography on the history of modern studies of ancient myth is enormous. I have found most useful the following general works: Bäumler (1926); Burkert

Until the eighteenth century, myths were understood entirely on the basis of the rational structure of a Logos which was itself not put into question by them. Whether this Logos was conceived as philosophical or religious, pagan, Jewish, or Christian, in antiquity, the Middle Ages, or the Renaissance, was of course of decisive importance for the specific results, but mattered surprisingly little for the methodological question of the way in which this Logos had to deal with those myths. The myths never put the Logos into question; only the Logos put the myths into question, and never failed to find the right answer for every question. This could happen in one or the other of two ways.

On the one hand, the Logos could simply exclude the myths, by demoting them to the status of being an error, a lie, a sacrilege, or a mere entertainment. Plato took over, extended systematically, and grounded philosophically Xenophanes' polemic claim that the myths of the poets had nothing to do with true religion;[13] the rest of Western culture went on to inherit as a central topos Plato's anguished contempt for the poets (but without Plato's anguish). When Plutarch writes, '*muthos* means a false *logos* similar to a true one',[14] or when Crates distinguishes *muthos* from historical truth (*historia*) and fiction (*plasma*) and defines it as 'a representation of what has not happened and is not true',[15] or when St Paul contrasts Jesus' message of salvation as the truth (*alētheia*) with the *muthoi* of the unbelieving heathens,[16] the Logos, whatever it happens to be in each case, remains untouched by the Mythos: the definitive rejection of the Mythos as insubstantial cathartically reinforces the Logos.

Or, on the other hand, the Mythos could be integrated into the Logos—but only according to the rules of Logos' game and only if the Mythos were thereby entirely denatured. For this purpose the indispensable tool for many centuries was allegorical interpretation; indeed, there are worse ways to define our own

---

(1980); Burkert and Horstmann (1984); Feldman and Richardson (1972); Fuhrmann (1971); Graf (1993*a*); Gruppe (1921); Horstmann (1979).

[13] Xenoph. B 11 DK; Pl. *Rep.* 377e–383c.

[14] Plu. *De glor. Ath.* 4 = *Mor.* 348a: ὁ δὲ μῦθος εἶναι βούλεται λόγος ψευδὴς ἐοικὼς ἀληθινῷ.

[15] Crates fr. 18 Mette = Sext. Emp. *Adv. math.* 1. 264: μῦθος δὲ πραγμάτων ἀγενήτων καὶ ψευδῶν ἔκθεσις.

[16] 2 Tim. 4: 4; Titus 1: 14; cf. also 1 Tim. 4: 7; 2 Pet. 1: 16.

modern age than to call it the first largely post-allegorical period. The duty and the achievement of allegorical interpretation was always to corroborate the Logos by demonstrating that the Mythos, which had at first seemed so alien to it, had in fact always already been entirely contained within it. Certainly, defending the Mythos, protecting it from total condemnation, was sometimes the allegorist's conscious intention, sometimes an unexpected by-product he readily welcomed; but the fundamental asymmetry of allegorical interpretation is immediately revealed by the fact that the allegorists never looked for traces of Mythos in their Logos, but only for traces of their Logos in the Mythos. Allegorical interpretation always started with a Logos and returned to it after a detour which passed through Mythos but which did not change the Logos in any way whatsoever.

In every regard, allegorical interpretation confirmed the correctness of the Logos and saved the Mythos only in so far as it proved that the latter's intelligibility rested upon its identification with the former. *Objectively* the doctrinal content of the Mythos was always unmasked at the end as being identical with the already quite familiar contents of whichever Logos was involved—whether these contents were historical or physical, moral or psychological, cosmological or medical, theological or astrological, seems to be of considerable interest to some modern historians of allegoresis but was in fact of no importance at all as far as the methodological principles themselves were concerned. There was no kind of doctrinal content whatsoever that could be transmitted *only* by means of myths: for each particular content, a purely conceptual version could readily be found that was both possible as a paraphrase and plausible as a premiss.

Subjectively the allegorist presupposed that the person who spoke in terms of Mythos was himself already entirely familiar with this Logos and had deposited it as his authentic message within the myths he invented—in other words, that he had cloaked the Logos in Mythos in order to protect it from the ignorant masses, or to guarantee that only a few elect would have access to it, or to save himself from being misunderstood, or to attract children and challenge the curious, or for whatever reason the allegorist could invent. In any case, the poet told the people myths, but at the same time he himself knew the Logos perfectly well: had he wished to, he would have been entirely capable of uttering forth the Logos unconcealed, like Protagoras in Plato's dialogue, who offers his listeners the choice whether they would prefer that he deliver his speech as a *muthos* or as a *logos*.[17] In this way the contrast between Logos and Mythos is distributed between the two opposite roles of the *sophos* and the *polloi*, the wise (male) individual and the ignorant masses: the trajectory of the Logos through the Mythos corresponds to a communicative path which begins with the author and finally reaches the allegorical interpreter unaltered, but only via the detour of the benighted masses, who, like an idiot entourage, surround the royal Logos in its intentionally transparent mythical incognito, celebrating its fame and completely misunderstanding its meaning. Even Nestle still locates the Logos in the endangered individual genius and the Mythos in the indolent, suspicious masses.[18] Hence allegorical exegesis cannot, strictly speaking, have any awareness of the kinds of historical problems modern hermeneutics was created to deal with, since the allegorist supposes that he is merely rediscovering a postulated identity: what he thinks he finds in the myths is the very same Logos which the wise author had concealed within them; the transparent community of a few enlightened individuals over the course of centuries provides a last instance and guarantee for the universal intelligibility and eternal self-identity of the Logos contained within the Mythos.

But there is always a fly in the allegorist's soup: for even if the *content* of the Mythos always reveals itself in the allegorist's hands to be nothing other than the Logos, none the less the *conversion mechanisms* which transform that Mythos into his Logos remain resolutely arbitrary and cannot themselves ever be successfully subsumed into the Logos. In other words, the soberly edifying content of the Logos remains the goal of allegorical interpretation, but in the capricious techniques of allegorical interpretation the Mythos' whimsical vivacity lives on to avenge itself on its dry, learned mockers. The whole rhetorical toolbox of tropes and figures of speech is emptied out and put to use so as to transform the characters of Mythos into the concepts of Logos, by metaphor and synecdoche, by metonymy and synonymy, by homonymy and antonymy, etc.: in the end even the dustiest philosophy is rescued by a suavely unscrupulous rhetoric, and

---

[17] Pl. *Prt.* 320c.   [18] (1940), 18.

however rational, expectable, and edifying the tenets finally revealed turn out to be, the means that had to be used in order to attain them are always irrational, astonishing, and entertaining. Consider Proclus' replies to Socrates' criticisms of some traditional Greek myths:

the ejection of Hephaestus from Olympus signifies the procession of the divine from the top down to the last creatures in the sensible world, a procession begun, ended, and guided by the Demiurge and the universal Father; the chaining of Cronos represents the union of all creation with the intellectual and paternal transcendence of Cronos; the castration of Ouranos suggests in hidden language the separation out of the Titanic chain from the order which maintains the whole...[19]

What I wish to emphasize here is not so much the evident discrepancy between the poets' colourful stories and the philosopher's technical doctrines, but rather the apparent lack of any sense on Proclus' part that he needs to explain to us just why he has chosen the specific figural transformations he has in order to create these philosophical meanings: for him, clearly, the doctrinal ends entirely justify the rhetorical means. *We*, who at long last have managed with some difficulty to take up a position outside the allegorical tradition, may well be able to enjoy such colourful feats of sleight of hand aesthetically, as a form of literary play within the Logos, by means of which the enchanting techniques of poetic texts manage to live on in the philosophical treatises which were supposed after all to demystify and replace them; but the conceptuality of the Logos, which was supposed to be guaranteed by allegorical interpretation, certainly ends up in the long run being undermined by it instead. How can the Logos possibly tolerate Proclus' frank admission, just a few lines later, that philosophical allegorical interpretation sometimes asserts the exegetical equivalence of something not only with what is similar to it, but even with what is exactly opposite to it?[20] It is hardly surprising that different allegorists—or indeed even the same one—can present a multiplicity of entirely different interpretations for the very same mythic story without almost ever comparing them, let alone criticizing or refuting them. A procedure which does not allow the rational instance of intersubjective

---

[19] Procl. *in Rem publ.* i, p. 82, 10–18 Kroll.
[20] Ibid. 20–3.

control to set any limit to the potentially infinite multiplication of mutually incompatible but not mutually competitive interpretations must sooner or later suffer a crisis. For allegorical interpretation, that crisis came in the eighteenth century.[21]

But scholars are stubborn, and many variants of the traditional allegorical approach to myths managed to survive well beyond the end of that century. Karl Philipp Moritz performed an aesthetic exclusion of Mythos from Logos,[22] Walter F. Otto an ontological one;[23] the unmasking of Mythos as an error in the name of Logos was the ambition of Max Müller, for whom myths were a childhood illness of language,[24] and of Jane Ellen Harrison, for whom they were ritual misunderstood.[25] And anyone who subscribes even today to a global hermeneutic strategy that prides itself on imagining that it is the science which holds the keys to all mysteries—so for example the Freudians, the Jungians, and the Marxists—inevitably ends up resurrecting old techniques in new forms.

But already in the eighteenth century, the foundation for a quite different approach to Mythos had been laid by Bernard le Bovier de Fontenelle,[26] Giambattista Vico,[27] Johann Gottfried Herder,[28] and above all Christian Gottlob Heyne, certainly the most important German classicist before the nineteenth century.[29] To be sure, in a number of ways all of these Enlightenment mythologists remain firmly rooted in the allegorical tradition. For

[21] I have discussed the crisis of allegorical interpretation in the 18th cent. in Most (1989).

[22] Moritz (1791).

[23] Otto (1929); (1955); (1963).

[24] See n. 61 below.

[25] (1890), pp. iii, xxxiii; (1903); (1912); (1921).

[26] 'Histoire des oracles' (1687) and 'De l'origine des fables' (1724), in Œuvres complètes, ed. G.-P. Depping (Geneva, 1968 = Paris, 1818), ii. 85–167 and 388–98.

[27] Principi di una scienza nuova (Naples, 1725), in La scienza nuova prima, ed. F. Nicolini (Bari, 1931); 3rd edn. (Naples, 1744), in Opere, ed. R. Parenti, ii (Naples, 1972).

[28] See esp. Sämtliche Werke, ed. B. Suphan (Berlin, 1877–1913), i. 426–49 ('Ueber die neuere Deutsche Litteratur' (1767), II); xi. 323 ff. ('Vom Geist der Ebräischen Poesie' (1782, 1787)); xiii. 387–95 ('Ideen zur Philosophie der Geschichte der Menschheit, Zweiter Teil' (1785), IX. v); xiv. 98–105 ('Ideen zur Philosophie der Geschichte der Menschheit, Dritter Teil' (1787), XIII. ii); xviii. 483–502 ('Iduna, oder der Apfel der Verjüngung' (1796)); xxiv. 311–18 ('Adrastea' (1804), X. vi); xxv. 313 ff. ('Volkslieder. Zweiter Theil' (1779)).

[29] Heyne's importance has long been unfairly overshadowed by that of his talented and ungrateful pupil, Friedrich August Wolf. Heyne's most important articles on the ancient myths are conveniently listed by Horstmann (1972), 61 n. 5.

example, they all start out from the idea that the Mythos is either originally an error or else began as truth but later became a myth by being misunderstood. Thus Fontenelle writes in the closing paragraph of his treatise, 'Let us therefore not look for anything else in fables than the history of the errors of the human spirit';[30] while Vico and Heyne equip their own primitive men with a boundlessly lively faculty of imagination that exaggerates everything and misunderstands much, in this way assuring for themselves the discrepancy between Mythos and Logos which they too regarded as being, at least in some ways, no less fundamental than their predecessors. And all relapse constantly, indeed systematically, into different versions of allegorical interpretation. For example, Heyne's distinction between historical and philosophical myths[31] is derived from the difference between ancient Euhemeristic accounts of the origin of the worship of the gods on the one hand and especially Stoic physical allegorical explanations on the other, and in the end is best understood as an attempt to deal with the basic fact of Greek literary history that at its beginning stand both Homer with his *Iliad* and *Odyssey* and Hesiod with his *Theogony* and *Works and Days*.

Yet despite their frequent recidivism, there can be no doubt that these thinkers stand at the threshold of a new era in the understanding of Mythos—indeed it is not accidental that Heyne is one of the first authors to substitute the Latinized Greek term '*mythus*' for the earlier Latin word '*fabula*'.[32] To be sure, they all

[30] Fontenelle (n. 26 above), 398: 'Ne cherchons donc autre chose dans les fables, que l'histoire des erreurs de l'esprit humain.'

[31] e.g. C. G. Heyne, 'Temporum mythicorum memoria a corruptelis nonnullis vindicata' (1763), in *Commentationes Societatis Regiae Scientiarum Gottingensis Antiquiores*, 8 (1785–6: Göttingen, 1787), 3–19, here 4, 6; 'Commentatio de Apollodori bibliotheca novaque eius recensione simulque universe de litteratura mythica', in *Apollodori bibliothecae libri tres et fragmenta* (Göttingen, 1783; 2nd edn. 1803), i, pp. xxv–lvi (in the 2nd edn., from which I cite here and below), here p. xxviii; 'Historiae scribendae inter Graecos primordia' (1799), in *Comm. Soc. Reg. Sci. Gott.* 14 (1798–9: Göttingen, 1800), *class. hist. et philol.* 14 (1797–8), 121–42, here 138–40; 'De opinionibus per mythos traditis tanquam altero, secundum historiam, mythorum genere', ibid. 143–9, here 143–6; 'De mythorum poeticorum natura origine et caussis', ibid. 149–55, here 149; 'Sermonis mythici seu symbolici interpretatio ad caussas et rationes ductasque inde regulas revocata' (1807), in *Comm. Soc. Reg. Sci. Gott.* 16 (1804–8: Göttingen, 1808), *class. hist. et philol.* 16 (1801–5), 285–323, here 301, 304.

[32] Heyne himself acknowledges his terminological preference: 'Commentatio de Apollodori bibliotheca' (n. 31 above), p. xxix. Cf. Heyne, 'De fide historica aetatis mythicae' (1798), in *Comm. Soc. Reg. Sci. Gott.* 14 (1798–9), 107–20, here 116–17.

tended to see myths as based upon error; however, to the extent
that all of them, but especially Heyne, ascribed the errors of
myths not to contingent, corrigible mistakes, but instead to a
specific, inevitable stage in the historical development of
mankind, they decisively undermined the millennial tradition of
allegorical interpretation: for the speaking voice which could be
heard in the myths was thereby shown to belong no longer to a
single wise man, but instead to the people as a whole, and the
mythic apparel was, in Heyne's words, no longer a *lusus ingenii*,
which dispensably cloaked a rational message unaffected thereby,
but rather a *necessitas*, the only adequate way under those unique
historical circumstances to express a meaningful statement about
the world.[33] Heyne is explicit that his views are incompatible
with the traditional allegorical approach to myths:

And it is not really correct to call this kind of philosophy or narrative
[viz. by fables] allegorical, since it was not so much covers for their
opinions that men were seeking in some kind of zeal for witticisms, as
rather that they had no other way to express their mind's meanings. The
difficulty and poverty of their language confined and compressed their
spirit, which was struggling almost to erupt forth, and their mind, struck
as it were by the inspiration of some divinity, boiling and rushing, since
neither it nor the community possessed the right words, toiled to show
the things themselves and to represent them visibly, to present deeds to
public inspection, and to put onto the stage, like a drama, what it had
thought up.[34]

[33] Heyne, 'De fide historica aetatis mythicae' (n. 32 above), 114: 'similisque esset
narratio ei, quam *symbolicam* appellamus, quamque, ut ab hac discernamus, *mythicam*
appellare praestat; quippe haec profecta est a necessitate, cum sermo idoneus deficeret; illa
altera ab ingenii lusu et acumine.' Cf. Heyne, 'Temporum mythicorum memoria' (n. 31
above), 3; 'De origine et caussis fabularum Homericarum' (1777), in *Novi Commentarii
Societatis Regiae Scientiarum Gottingensis. Commentationes historicae et philologicae*, 8 (1777:
Göttingen, 1778), 34–58, here 34; 'Vita antiquissimorum hominum Graeciae ex ferorum
et barbarorum populorum comparatione illustrata', Commentatio I, II, Epimetrum (1779),
in *Opuscula academica collecta et animadversionibus locupletata*, iii (Göttingen, 1788), 1–16, 17–
30, 31–8, here 26; 'De opinionibus per mythos traditis' (n. 31 above), 150–1; 'Sermonis
mythici seu symbolici interpretatio' (n. 31 above), 285, 290, 293–4.
[34] Heyne, 'De origine et caussis fabularum Homericarum' (n. 33 above), 38: 'Nec vero
hoc philosophandi aut narrandi genus recte satis appelletur allegoricum: cum non tam
sententiis involucra quaererent homines studio aliquo argutiarum, quam quod, animi
sensus quomodo aliter exponerent, non habebant. Angustabat enim et coarctabat spiritum,
quasi erumpere luctantem, orationis difficultas et inopia, percussusque tanquam numinis
alicujus afflatu animus, cum verba deficerent propria et sua et communia, aestuans et
abreptus, exhibere ipsas res et repraesentare oculis, facta in conspectu ponere, et, in
dramatis modum, in scenam proferre cogitata allaborabat.' For other passages in which

In effect, though without realizing it entirely, Heyne has already performed the fundamental step which separates the modern view of myths from the pre-Enlightenment one: that is, he has distinguished them from poetry, by analysing the transmitted poetic myths, like those found in the works of Homer and Hesiod, into two different components, an earlier, mythic content, and a later, poetic form.

Heyne's idea of an 'aetas mythica' in the 'infantia generis humani', when men knew how to speak no other language than a defective (and hence almost poetic) 'sermo mythicus',[35] may well have been influenced by recent anthropological reports from America and Africa, as his many references to apparent ethnographic parallels suggest.[36] But most likely the anthropological material, so far from playing a decisive role in shaping his views, served not as productive inspiration but as retroactive confirmation: only after the beloved myths of the Greeks had provided an incontrovertible example of an evolution of human reason over time, of a *diachronic* differentiation of the Logos, could the primitives scattered throughout the rest of Heyne's own world then supply further support by adding *synchronic* variants. Hence Heyne too insists that myths have a philosophical content—but for him its content is not that of *our* philosophy, but rather that of a quite different, more primitive stage of development:

Hence whenever we say that in Homer or other poets the philosophical doctrines of ancient men survive, the reader should think of the

---

Heyne distinguishes his own understanding of myths from the traditional allegorical approach, cf. ibid. 35, 58; 'Temporum mythicorum memoria' (n. 31 above), 8; 'De theogonia ab Hesiodo condita. Ad Herodoti lib. II. c. 52' (1779), in *Comm. Soc. Reg. Sci. Gott., hist. et philol. class.* 2 (1779: Göttingen, 1780), 125–54, here 135; 'Commentatio de Apollodori bibliotheca' (n. 31 above), pp. xxxix–xl; 'De opinionibus per mythos traditis' (n. 31 above), 150–1, 155; 'Sermonis mythici seu symbolici interpretatio' (n. 31 above), 290, 294.

[35] e.g. Heyne, 'Temporum mythicorum memoria' (n. 31 above), 4, 9–10, 14–15; 'Nonnulla ad quaestionem de caussis fabularum seu mythorum veterum physicis' (1764), in *Opuscula academica collecta*, i (Göttingen, 1785), 184–206, here 188 f., 190; 'De theogonia' (n. 34 above), 136; 'De fide historica aetatis mythicae' (n. 32 above), 109, 113–15; 'De opinionibus per mythos traditis' (n. 31 above), 144, 146; 'Praefatio', in *Apollodori bibliothecae libri* (n. 31 above), i, pp. vi–vii; 'Sermonis mythici seu symbolici interpretatio' (n. 31 above).

[36] e.g. 'Temporum mythicorum memoria' (n. 31 above), 10; 'Nonnulla ad quaestionem de caussis fabularum' (n. 35 above), 192, 196, 200; 'Vita antiquissimorum hominum Graeciae' (n. 33 above); *Apollodori bibliothecae libri* (n. 31 above), pp. viii–ix; 'Sermonis mythici' (n. 31 above), 307.

conception and common sense and intelligence of humans who are uncivilized or still lying in the cradle of wisdom.[37]

Suddenly there is no longer only the one Logos, timeless and spaceless, universally valid in every period and in every place for all creatures who deserve the title of human being; instead there are as many different forms of the Logos as there are conditions of humanity. Heyne and his followers tend to speak of myths as though they were *prelogical*; but in fact it would be more accurate to term their conception of them *heterological*, for the temporal priority of one form over another is in fact far less important than the pluralization of forms of Logos itself; and among these all, myths can then assume a privileged position as the sole remaining testimony to a childhood which we have all passed through and for which we have never ceased to yearn.

It was this discovery that led a number of important European philosophers in the centuries following the Enlightenment to recognize as one of their most important tasks the merciless criticism of Logos on the basis of a newly positive evaluation of Mythos. The critique of Logos in the name of Mythos has become one of the central traditions of German philosophy since the nineteenth century and has gone on to influence almost all significant strains of contemporary European and American thought. To be sure, even within modern German philosophy there have been a few important figures who had little or no interest in myths, like Kant or Husserl (who ignored them) or Hegel (who was willing to assign them a subordinate role in his aesthetics but categorically declared, 'From our history of philosophy, however, mythology must remain excluded'[38]); but they have been the exceptions. Among those other German philosophers who have used myths to criticize reason, perhaps the

---

[37] 'Nonnulla ad quaestionem de caussis fabularum' (n. 35 above), 197: 'Quoties itaque in Homero aliisue philosophemata superesse dicimus veterum hominum, de notione et sensu communi et acumine hominum incultorum aut in incunabulis sapientiae versantium cogitandum est.'

[38] G. W. F. Hegel, *Vorlesungen über die Ästhetik*, i = *Werke*, ed. E. Moldenhauer and K. M. Michel (Frankfurt a. M., 1970), xiii. 402–9, 505–6; *Vorlesungen über die Geschichte der Philosophie*, i = *Werke*, xviii. 104: 'Allein aus unserer Geschichte der Philosophie muß die Mythologie ausgeschlossen bleiben. Der Grund davon liegt darin, daß es uns in derselben nicht zu tun ist um Philosopheme überhaupt, um Gedanken, die nur implizite enthalten sind in irgendeiner Darstellung, sondern um Gedanken, die heraus sind, und nur insofern sie heraus sind, sofern solcher Inhalt, den die Religion hat, in der Form des Gedankens zum Bewußtsein gekommen ist.'

most important, and certainly the most influential, was Friedrich Nietzsche, who in his *Birth of Tragedy* reinvented polemically the Greek gods Dionysus and Apollo so as to counter the Socratic scientific rationality that had come to dominate the world after the fifth century BCE,[39] and who later went on to create his own personal myths, like Zarathustra and the eternal return of the same.[40] Nietzsche, like the German Romantics before him, argued that only a culture bounded by myths could achieve unity and identity, and that modern culture could be redeemed only if a new mythology could arise.[41] Nietzsche's vatic lucubrations on Mythos remain a high-water mark of its philosophical fortunes in Germany; but in this century, too, it has remained a favourite hammer to hit Logos with for thinkers both less serious than he was and more so. Among the latter, one thinks of Ernst Cassirer's extended analysis and justification of myths as an organ for under-standing reality in the second volume of his *Philosophy of Symbolic Forms*[42] and in other essays he wrote during the 1920s in co-operation with the Warburg Institute and in close collaboration with Aby Warburg's studies in anthropology and symbolism;[43] to a certain extent, of Martin Heidegger's critique of modern rational technology in the name of the mythic values of Greek and German poets, Presocratics, and local traditions (above all Alemannic ones);[44] of Horkheimer and Adorno's thesis in *The Dialectic of Enlightenment* that myths themselves already perform the work of enlightenment, while on the other hand the self-styled Enlightenment never succeeds in freeing itself from myths;[45] or of the massive recent tomes in which such contemporary German

[39] F. Nietzsche, *Die Geburt der Tragödie aus dem Geiste der Musik* (1872), in *Werke: Kritische Gesamtausgabe*, ed. G. Colli and M. Montinari, iii. 1 (Berlin, 1972), 3–152.

[40] See esp. *Also Sprach Zarathustra: Ein Buch für Alle und Keinen* (1883), in *Werke* (n. 39 above), vi. 1 (Berlin, 1968).

[41] *Die Geburt der Tragödie* (n. 39 above), § 23, pp. 141–5.

[42] Cassirer (1925).

[43] E. Cassirer, 'Die Begriffsform im mythischen Denken' (1922) and 'Sprache und Mythos' (1925), in Cassirer (1994), 1–70 and 71–158; cf. also Cassirer (1995), 19 f., 29 f., 65 f., 86–90.

[44] e.g. M. Heidegger, *Seminare*, ed. C. Ochwadt = *Gesamtausgabe*, i. 15 (Frankfurt a. M., 1986); *Die Grundbegriffe der antiken Philosophie* (Marburger Vorlesung, SS 1926), ed. F.-K. Blust = *Gesamtausgabe*, ii. 22 (Frankfurt a. M., 1993); *Parmenides* (Freiburger Vorlesung, WS 1942/3), ed. M. S. Frings = *Gesamtausgabe*, ii. 54 (Frankfurt a. M., 1982); *Heraklit* (Freiburger Vorlesung, SS 1943 and SS 1944), ed. M. S. Frings = *Gesamtausgabe*, ii. 55 (Frankfurt a. M., 1979).

[45] Horkheimer and Adorno (1947).

philosophers as Hans Blumenberg and Kurt Hübner ponderously defend the proposition that myths do indeed provide some relative degree of access to an important kind of truth.[46] It is obviously not my intention here to deny the many evident differences among these various thinkers. Rather, my point is that one thing unites them all, and not only them: the conviction that traditional Logos, the form of rationality we have inherited from our philosophical predecessors as being universal, inalterable, and perfect, is in fact radically defective and can only be improved if we restore to its proper place the neglected or repressed truth contained in myths. No longer does the Logos remain unaffected by the Mythos, no longer does the Mythos allow itself to be simply excluded or appropriated by the Logos. Instead, the Logos of philosophy develops from within itself, as its dialectical other, a concept of Mythos which is full of the elements and claims of Logos and has the dignity of a Quasi-Logos—and thereby the Logos fundamentally changes itself. In the course of its own development by a process of self-examination and self-criticism, the Logos leads eventually to a new idea of Mythos which is a recognizable, albeit an untraditional, form of Logos. We might term this process the mythification of the Logos.

The close and reciprocal relations between these philosophical tendencies on the one hand, and the contributions of psychoanalysis and anthropology towards questioning reason's claim for autonomy and rehabilitating myths and the so-called primitive mind on the other, are obvious. In terms of intellectual history, all these developments can be traced back directly or indirectly to the philosophy of Friedrich Wilhelm Joseph Schelling, whose œuvre probably represents the most serious philosophical examination of the myths, next to Plato's, in the whole Western tradition. In the winter of 1792–3, at the tender age of 17, Schelling wrote an essay entitled 'On Myths, Historical Legends and Philosophical Doctrines of the Most Ancient World';[47] here he followed Heyne's footsteps conscientiously but went far beyond his master in emphasizing the childish element in the ancient myths. Already three years later Schelling, Hölderlin, and

---

[46] Blumenberg (1979); Hübner (1985).

[47] 'Ueber Mythen, historische Sagen und Philosopheme der ältesten Welt' (1793), in *Werke: Historisch-Kritische Ausgabe*, i, ed. W. G. Jacobs, J. Jantzen, and W. Schieche (Stuttgart, 1976), 193–246.

Hegel collaborated to compose the so-called 'Oldest Systematic Program of German Idealism' as a token and monument of their youthful *symphilosophia*; here Schelling, whose ideas the text seems largely to reflect, called for a new mythology, a mythology this time of reason, which would make sure that reason and traditional forms of science would be transformed into art— astonishingly, in our eyes, it was precisely to myths that he assigned the task of helping reason transcend itself.[48] In Schelling's early *Lectures on the Philosophy of Art* of 1802–5 he defines the role of the myths in art quite traditionally, as a representation of the ideas of Logos—'The ideas in philosophy and the gods in art are one and the same'[49]—but then in his late *Lectures on the Philosophy of Mythology*, the very last text upon which he was working when he died, goes on, at enormous length and with an only rarely contagious enthusiasm, to explain the myths themselves, in their historical development towards monotheism, not, in his terms, allegorically (as meaning something other than what they say), but rather tautegorically (as meaning just what they say), as embodying a truth which is not just religious, but instead general.[50] Whoever, like myself, finds Schelling's philosophical style at times not to his taste, should perhaps think twice before measuring him by the traditional criteria of a Logos which he himself contributed decisively towards overcoming.

[48] '[. . .] wir müssen eine neue Mythologie haben, diese Mythologie aber muß im Dienste der Ideen stehen, sie muß eine Mythologie der *Vernunft* werden. Ehe wir die Ideen ästhetisch, d.h. mythologisch machen, haben sie für das *Volk* kein Interesse, und umgekehrt: ehe die Mythologie vernünftig ist, muß sich der Philosoph ihrer schämen. So müssen endlich Aufgeklärte und Unaufgeklärte sich die Hand reichen, die Mythologie muß philosophisch werden, um das Volk vernünftig, und die Philosophie muß mythologisch werden, um die Philosophen sinnlich zu machen. Dann herrscht ewige Einheit unter uns.' Cited from Hegel, *Frühe Schriften* = *Werke* (n. 38 above), i. 234–6, here 236.

[49] *Philosophie der Kunst*, in *Sämmtliche Werke*, ed. K. F. A. Schelling, i. 5 (Stuttgart–Augsburg, 1859), 401: 'Die Ideen in der Philosophie und die Götter in der Kunst sind ein und dasselbe, aber jedes ist für sich das, was es ist, jedes eine eigne Ansicht desselbigen, keines um des andern willen, oder um das andere zu bedeuten.'

[50] *Einleitung in die Philosophie der Mythologie*, in *Sämmtliche Werke*, ii. 1 (Stuttgart–Augsburg, 1856), 195–6 ('Die Mythologie ist nicht *allegorisch*, sie ist *tautegorisch*. Die Götter sind ihr wirklich existirende Wesen, die nicht etwas anderes *sind*, etwas anderes *bedeuten*, sondern *nur* das bedeuten, was sie sind.'); 216 ('Der mythologische Proceß hat also nicht bloß religiöse, er hat *allgemeine* Bedeutung, denn es ist der allgemeine Proceß, der sich in ihm wiederholt; demgemäß ist auch die Wahrheit, welche die Mythologie im Proceß hat, eine nichts ausschließende, universelle.'). The emphasis is, characteristically, Schelling's.

From our own disenchanted perspective, it seems evident that part of the fascination, and much of the danger, which Mythos posed for such thinkers has resided in its liminal position on the threshold between what could be known and what could only be imagined: for the term 'Mythos' or 'myth' could be understood either on the one hand as 'the *myths*', a transmitted body of stories, often poetic and individual, always at least in part freely invented and usually localizable in a particular historical context, or on the other hand as 'the *mythic*', a vanished numinous quality attributed to a lost people's religious sense, entirely unfree (since it was seen as the immediate expression of a whole people's identity, not just of an individual's) and necessarily prehistoric (for otherwise it would inevitably seem locally conditioned and arbitrary). The term 'Mythos' or 'myth' could play the two sides off against one another or create slippages between them and thereby unleash an extraordinary productivity, not only for dialectical differentiation, but also for sheer confusion. Unpacking the self-contradictions contained in that single term has taxed the strength of generations of thinkers.

All these last figures were philosophers, not classicists; and it is obvious that the reception of such philosophical discussions among professional Hellenists has been, with very few exceptions, at best rather hesitant. And yet it has been above all the Greek myths which all these thinkers exploited in order to reach a more complex and satisfactory concept of Logos. The philosophers' philhellenism is perhaps not surprising (at least to classicists)—but the philologists' silence is, or should be. Where were the Hellenists while the world was falling all over their myths?

They were indeed there, but for the most part they were standing on the sidelines. For the outcome of the controversy in the first decades of the nineteenth century centring on Friedrich Creuzer's *Symbolism and Mythology of the Ancient Peoples, Especially of the Greeks*[51] meant that for a long time the professional study of classical antiquity felt obliged to prove its scientific nature precisely by refraining strictly from any discussion of what the Greek myths could mean *for us*, and instead concentrated intensively and exclusively upon research into what the Greek myths could have

---

[51] Creuzer (1810–12). A good introduction and a brief selection of contemporary documents are provided by Howald (1926).

meant *for the Greeks*.[52] Creuzer himself blended in his own research into the myths Romantically irrational elements and traditionally rationalizing ones in a way hard to disentangle or sometimes even to understand: on the one hand he emphasized the symbols, which were not reducible to concepts and were accessible only to the intuition of those who were innately spiritually gifted with a sensitivity for them; but on the other hand he usually arrived at the contents of these symbols by applying traditional allegorical interpretations, especially those of the Neoplatonists of late antiquity. This inconsistency was so glaring that it permitted Gottfried Hermann on the one hand to attack his intuitionism and to recommend, as a mode of doing what he considered real historical research into the myths, a bizarre mixture of etymologies of divine names and a highly rationalistic allegorical exegesis of the natural philosophical doctrines allegedly contained in them,[53] and Christian August Lobeck on the other sharply to reject Creuzer's allegorism and to displace the philologists' attention on to *Quellenforschung*, the study of the sources of our evidence for the ancient Greeks' understanding of their myths.[54] Creuzer took over the ancient allegorists' notion that the speakers of myths were those few who truly understood them and who pronounced them as a deep mystery to the astonished populace[55]—a view by this time so outdated that Karl Otfried Müller could effectively demolish it by comparing it to missionaries giving sermons to Greenlanders.[56] But the central issue, as it was recognized especially by Lobeck and Ludwig Preller, was that of the scientific status of the new discipline of classical philology itself:[57] and the defeat of Creuzer meant that henceforth scientific seriousness could only be bought at the price of a rigorous refusal to make any claim to mediate the artistic or religious meaning of the Greek myths for our own time. Indeed,

---

[52] Part of the following argument overlaps with another study of mine in which I have examined the dynamics and the consequences of this controversy in the context of the series of scholarly disputes which marked German classics in the first third of the 19th cent.: see Most (1997).

[53] Hermann and Creuzer (1818); Hermann (1819); (1827).

[54] Lobeck (1829).

[55] Creuzer (1810–12), i, bk. 1, ch. 1, § 1–6 = Howald (1926), 46–51.

[56] K. O. Müller (1821), cited from Howald (1926), 143.

[57] Lobeck (1812), cited from Howald (1926), 84; Preller (1838), cited from Howald (1926), 146–9.

even in the twentieth century, it has been above all the great
artists and writers, as well as popularizers often ignored or scorned
by professional classicists,[58] who have dedicated themselves to the
task of mediation—with such great success that we can have little
doubt about the enormous popular thirst for it.

After Creuzer's defeat, classicists reverted to slightly altered but
still easily recognizable variants on the very same ways of dealing
with myths that had been systematized in the Hellenistic period
in the opposition between Epicurean Euhemerism and Stoic
physical allegoresis and that remained typical until the eighteenth
century:[59] first to a new Euhemerism, in Karl Otfried Müller's
explanation of the Greek myths as tribal legends which could
provide information about the early history of the various Greek
peoples;[60] and then to a new version of the old physical allegorical
explanation of the myths as references to natural phenomena, in
the Indo-European comparative mythology of the second half
of the nineteenth century[61]—a school of research that ended up
reducing the myths to what Lewis Farnell called 'highly figurative
conversation about the weather'.[62] It was therefore only to be
expected that when in the course of the twentieth century the
philological approach to myths has been revitalized, as it has been
over and over again, the impetus has come each time not from
within classical philology, but from without, through the adoption of stimuli from other disciplines—above all from anthropology, but also from psychology and structuralism. But it remains
an open question whether even exogamic unions like these will
long be able to help classics to strengthen the chances of its own
survival by playing once again, as it did until the early nineteenth
century, the role of mediator between the Greek myths and the
enormous potential audience which may not care very much
about their alleged philosophical truth but still insists upon
succumbing, obstinately and eagerly, to their seemingly irresistible
fascination. For the Greek myths provide an extraordinary
reservoir of easily intelligible and strikingly formulated codes and
models of moral (and immoral) behaviour and thought, and are

[58] Two examples of the latter: Graves (1957); Calasso (1988).
[59] So, aptly, Burkert (1980), 162.
[60] K. O. Müller (1820–4); (1825).
[61] e.g. M. Müller (1856); (1869); (1873); (1897).
[62] (1896), 9.

likely to remain for a long time an attractive intellectual substitute for more parochial religious systems to any one of which only some, but not all, can adhere.

Once upon a time, the phrase 'From Mythos to Logos' could be coined to designate an optimistic teleological program. The inversion of that phrase, 'From Logos to Mythos', certainly does not imply a message which is either optimistic or teleological. But the inversion itself is not symmetrical: the movement from Logos to Mythos traced here is marked by ruptures and lurches, its future course and destination are still unclear, it offers not only opportunities but also dangers. The triumph of Logos in Greece did not after all destroy Mythos for ever by the fourth century BCE: on the contrary, by a kind of macroscopic return of the repressed, Mythos has come back in the last two centuries to avenge itself on the Logos that had tried to efface it by transforming its nature in turn. Or, to revert to Nestle's mythic image cited earlier: the waters of the primeval flood may well have retreated; but only now have we begun to realize that they have left behind, upon the dry land and in our own hearts, creatures even more fabulous than those ever were that once swam around in the murky depths of the sea.

II

Myth and Reason in Practice

2

Re-evaluating Gernet: Value and Greek Myth

SITTA VON REDEN

ALMOST fifty years after its first publication, Louis Gernet's article 'La Notion mythique de la valeur en Grèce' is still widely read and frequently cited.[1] This is not only because no similar study has been devoted to the same subject again, but also because of Gernet's distinctive influence on the sixième section of the École Pratique des Hautes Études, on French structuralism, and especially on J.-P. Vernant.[2] Yet despite the enduring importance that his work has had through the 'Vernant school' in international scholarship, and quite in contrast to his book and papers on law, Gernet's article on value has been more frequently referred to than it has been engaged with in detail. This is all the more regrettable as its argument, to the extent that it concerns economic history, is far more radical than any advanced by Moses Finley, and anticipates a conceptual turn which is only now entering Anglo-American scholarship. More relevant still to this volume is the fact that the problem of value as Gernet poses it raises important questions about myth and *logos* in relation to the transformation of a premonetary to a monetary society in ancient Greece.

The way successive intellectual generations negotiate the relationship between myth and what might be termed 'rational

[1] Having appeared first in the *Journal de psychologie*, 41 (Oct./Dec. 1948), 415–62, the article was reprinted in Gernet (1968), 93–137, and translated at pp. 73–111 of the English version of that work. A further translation of the article appeared in Gordon (1981), 111–46. In the text I refer to the page numbers both of the 1968 French edition and of the translation in Gordon; thus 94/111 = 94 in original, 111 in Gordon. Translations are taken from Gordon, with my own modifications where I thought them appropriate.

[2] See Humphreys (1978), 80; R. Buxton in Gordon (1981), pp. xiii–xiv; Schlesier (1992), 98 ff.; and Vernant himself in his preface to Gernet (1968). Humphreys (1978) is still fundamental for a broader assessment of Gernet's work, his intellectual contexts, and full bibliography. See also Humphreys (1984), a review of the English trans. of Gernet (1968).

thought' has fundamental bearings on the content of their research.[3] Gernet was the first to acknowledge that the economy
was not an external reality which could best be represented in
terms of systematic analysis, but a mental activity which was
transformed alongside the historical transformation of modes of
thought (94/111; see n. 1). It was thus part of what he investigated in a more comprehensive project of 'psychologie
historique', which aimed at the historical reconstruction of
thought as it manifests itself in different but interrelated fields of
human activity such as law, economics, politics, religion, science,
etc.[4] In Archaic and early Classical Greece, these activities and
their respective institutions changed, in a dialectical relation with
the transformation of thought and its articulation in myth,
into what in French is vaguely circumscribed by the term 'la
pensée positive'.[5] Money, just like law, was such an institution
(and form of thought) which emerged in dialectical relationship
to 'positive' thought (95/112). Myth was the form of thought
related to the premonetary society of ancient Greece at particular
historical stages; but it was also a cross-cultural category for the
expression of thought in a particular way: it operated with
figurative signification and represented the world in a 'total'
way—that is, time, space, the physical world, relationships, morality, etc. are mapped on to each other (94/111).[6] In other
words, for Gernet myth is both a form of thought and the source
for an early mode of thinking about value before coinage had
made its impact on Greek society. In the overlap of a structural
and historical reading of myth I see a methodological fault which
can have been overlooked only because most people would a

[3] In the following I use 'rational/positive thought/argument', and 'pensée/raison positive' interchangeably (note, however, n. 5 below). The rather more complicated term *logos*
I use only in the ancient sense of 'more verifiable discourse' (Pl. *Rep.* 522a8: *alēthinōteroi
logoi*) or for prose argument discussed in a particular deliberative context (for which see
below). See Buxton (1994: 11–14) and Bruit Zaidman and Schmitt Pantel (1992: 143–5),
for a brief survey of the problems of defining the boundaries of *logos*.
[4] See Meyerson (1948); Vernant in 'Préface' to Gernet (1968), pp. i–v; Humphreys
(1978), 27. 'La psychologie historique' falls in English parlance normally, though slightly
incorrectly, into the general category of 'history of mentality'.
[5] According to Humphreys, Gernet regarded 'la pensée positive' as a society's capacity
to be conscious of itself and of its own structures. It was brought about by increasing social
complexity and 'le conflit et la synthèse entre les représentations qui émanent de groupes
différents ou répondent à des moments différents de la société'. See Humphreys (1978:
94), quoting from Gernet (1917).
[6] Cf. Meyerson (1948), 40–9.

priori accept Gernet's hypothesis of a historical development from 'symbolic' gift value to the 'functional' value of coin. It is my contention that Gernet's theoretical assumptions and structuralist methodology made him pay too little attention to the performative contexts of myths and *logos*, and also to the politics that lie behind differing representations of value in these different kinds of discourse. This in turn has important consequences for the conceptualization of the relationship between myth and *logos*.

1

'La Notion mythique' contains a substantive hypothesis which, if read regardless of the methodological point it wishes to make, might be summarized as follows. Taking his lead from Marcel Mauss's *Essai sur le don* (1925), Gernet identifies a number of qualities attached to precious objects (*agalmata*) and their representation in myth. *Agalmata* embodied aristocratic wealth, honour, and splendour. They were characteristically 'mobile' goods and their possession was transitory. *Agalmata*, moreover, were a particular class of objects produced by human labour: metalwork, statues, textiles, etc. In this they were quite different from 'standards of value', such as cattle, which were not normally exchanged and which acquired their status of being valuable through their use in religious ritual, sacrifice in particular. Typically, *agalmata* were acquired by a particular class of people in particular contexts: as booty in war, prizes in games, gifts on the occasion of marriage or in other situations of gift exchange, and they were never purchased from outsiders (97 f./113 f.). Thus they circulated in exclusive networks of exchange, were used, moreover, as offerings and dedications to gods, and never functioned as commodities in mercantile trade. Constantly crossing the boundary between sacred and profane, *agalmata* acquired a quality that was intrinsically different from that of other goods.

Mythical stories made explicit, and were implied in, the meaning of *agalmata*. At the time immediately before the invention of coinage, myths generated, and reflected, a more abstract notion of value by divorcing certain qualities from particular objects that used to embody them: very consciously, some myths seemed to

circumscribe the meaning of precious objects and thereby to
crystallize a generalized meaning of value. The tripod of the
Seven Sages was an object set out as a prize in a competition; it
was caught by a fisherman; its possession was transitory so that it
eventually became a dedication to a god; and, in some versions of
the tale, it was the object of a quarrel between cities (Plu. *Sol.*
4. 2) (100–4/115–19). Moreover, the tapestry in Aeschylus'
Agamemnon, and Eriphyle's necklace and *peplos*, were objects to
which fear and a potentially evil power were attached despite
their splendour. If used wrongly, or not passed on, they turned
into an evil spirit.[7] In some cases, a precious item had the power
to return unasked, as in the case of Polycrates' ring, and was then
a manifestation of *numen, nemesis* (105–119/123–31). In its positive capacity, an *agalma*, such as the fleece of the golden lamb of
the house of Atreus, had the power to confer the right to rule,
was the origin of prosperity, and served as a talisman for both the
king and his subjects (119–30/131–43). The source and destination of a precious item in myth was often the sea, which, as the
mediator between two worlds, intimated the double nature of
precious objects as belonging both to a particular class of humans
and to the gods, thereby confirming the privileged relationship
between the two.

Already in myth, Gernet argues, the idea of 'substitution'
emerged, as precious objects appear both as objects and as the
images of what they stand for. The golden fleece, a symbol of
agrarian wealth and royal investiture, is in Pindar represented as a
garment with golden tassels (*Pyth.* 4. 231). Just as mass-produced
anathēmata of cheaper material could replace *agalmata* as offerings,
and just as representations of sacrificial animals appear on coins, so
mythical representations of valuables play with the interchangeability of image and object, object and image. Gernet argues that
at this stage *agalmata* were valuable because they *represented* things
endowed with magical properties and might be compared to the
value of a talisman (cf. 128/139).[8] From here it was only a small
step to the invention of coinage. The magical quality of, and
gradual abstraction of value from, figurative 'substitutes' were the
presages of the invention of coinage and its value. Gernet
concludes:

[7] NB here Gernet's debt to Mauss (1924), repr. in Mauss (1968), iii. 46–51.
[8] See for this also Mauss (1914), repr. in Mauss (1968) ii. 106–12.

In the historical milieu in which sign value [i.e. coinage] first appeared, the religious, aristocratic and agonistic symbols stamped on its first specimens were attestations of origin: a mythical way of thinking endured right to the very moment at which the invention of coinage became possible. By which I mean to say that in 'value', and so in the sign that represents it, there is a core which cannot be reduced to what is commonly called 'rational thought' (137/146).

However, the transformation of value did not happen in a social and political vacuum. As Gernet suggests immediately before the remarks just quoted, external signs of wealth came to be no longer the exclusive possession of a privileged class within which the images of inherited mythical kingship and its symbols had flourished. Coin value, though stripped of many of the class-bound associations which had hitherto been related to value, imposed itself on the modes of thought of the elite. Already in Alcaeus (fr. 360 *PLF*) we find the saying '*chrēmat' anēr*' ('money makes the man'), which aims to confirm, but at the same time denies, that wealth implied the exclusive rights of a particular class.

2

Now Gernet's substantive hypothesis unfolded within a particular methodological framework, and was, moreover, by no means unrelated to political concerns. Gernet operated with a concept of thought, or mind, which was related to particular assumptions about the historical interdependence of thought and institutions. It therefore radically differed from the idealist notion of mind characteristic of the German humanist tradition, which had produced two publications just a few years previously. Wilhelm Nestle's *Vom Mythos zum Logos* had appeared in Nazi Germany in 1940, and Bruno Snell's *Die Entstehung des Geistes* was published, significantly, after the war in 1946. For Nestle *logos* ('Vernunft'), and Christian monotheism were different aspects of the same spirit which had grown from immaturity ('Unmündigkeit') to maturity ('Mündigkeit') in the course of Western (Aryan) history.[9] Snell, who wrote in quite a different intellectual context

---

[9] W. Nestle (1940), 1–20, esp. 6; see also Most in this volume.

from Nestle, was more cautious when claiming that the 'discovery of the mind' did not imply the discovery of a free spirit
outside and beyond history.[10] Yet he nevertheless distinguished
between two qualitative levels of human thought, and in the 1975
edition of his book he replied to Vernant that it was by no means
'classical arrogance' if we credited the Greeks with the discovery
of the 'primary functions of the mind, how it can be the origin
of knowledge, emotions and active participation in the world'.[11]
Gernet took a quite different view: however much his work
was shaped by cross-cultural categories of primitive thought or
mythology, *logos* among the Greeks was different from the reason
of today. Thus Vernant writes in the preface to his *Mythe et
pensée*:

The title of the last study in this book is 'From Myth to Reason'.
However, by this we do not claim to be considering mythical thought
in general, any more than we admit to the existence of rational thought
in an immutable form. On the contrary, in our closing remarks, we
emphasize that the Greeks did not invent reason as such, but a type of
rationality dependent on a historical context and different from that
today. Similarly, we believe that in what is known as mythical thought
there are diverse forms, multiple levels and different modes of organization, and types of logic.[12]

Gernet only hints at such a formulation—not least in the passage
quoted above—but the fact that his research was concerned
above all with a representation of pre-logical thought as a creative
energy bringing about positive thought suggests that his primary
concern lay with the former. His ideas about the nature of 'la
pensée positive', though conceptually clear, remained historically
less well explored than his ideas about myth.[13] From his extant
work it appears that he was interested above all in the historically
brief period of *transition* from mythical to positive thinking and
that it was socio-psychological process, rather than achievement,
that was on his political agenda.

The cultural anthropology of Gernet and his pupils also faced
opposition from another quarter. In 1966 there appeared Michel

[10] Snell (1953), p. vii.
[11] See p. 290 of the 4th German edn. (1975); cf. also G. E. R. Lloyd (1966), 4.
[12] (1983), p. xi. See also Vernant (1982); this book was, by the way, dedicated to Louis
Gernet.
[13] Gernet's only explicit statement about the nature of Athenian law during the
Classical period is represented by his 1917 Budé edition of Plato's *Laws*.

Foucault's *Les Mots et les choses*, which, to put it simply, proposed a history of discourse and power which radically denied that a collective consciousness could develop in a power-free space. Indeed, consciousness is a notion rather alien to the theory of Foucault. It has been argued that the collection of Gernet's articles which Vernant edited posthumously (Gernet (1968)) was a political response to a movement which—coming, it should be noted, from outside the established institutions of French academia—threatened the intellectual project of the humanities.[14] Thus in his preface to the volume Vernant emphasizes Gernet's contemporary concerns:

In the course of his precise and fine analysis of institutions, secondary sources, and original documents, the question that was constantly posed by Gernet concerned us directly—it put us at the very heart of things: why and how were these forms of social life constituted, these modes of thought where the West has its origins, where it believes it can recognize itself, and that today still serve as a reference point and justification for European civilization? From this perspective, what one traditionally calls 'humanism' finds its proper place, its correct historical context, and becomes something relative. Despoiled of its pretension to incarnate absolute Spirit/eternal Reason, the Greek experience recovers its color and full shape. It finds its full meaning only when confronted with great civilizations as different as those of the Near East, India, China, Africa, and pre-Columbian America; it appears as only one way among others in which human history has developed (pp. ii–iii = viii in Eng. trans.).

Perhaps this is mainly Vernant's own voice. Yet for both Vernant and Gernet it was the warning memory of German Fascism that prevented them from accepting any theory which relativized precisely those capacities of the human mind which had been violently disregarded in Nazi Germany. As Humphreys notes, the belief in a 'raison positive' integrated Gernet's research on Greek institutions with his commitment to socialism and sociology. Speaking to the Association Guillaume Budé in 1939, he contrasted collectivism with totalitarianism. If Fascist ancient historians emphasized the fact that the Greeks subordinated the individual to the collective, they concealed the fact that the Greeks did so only by allowing each citizen free speech and

---

[14] Schlesier (1992), 100.

discussion.[15] Human consciousness of themselves and their procedures, which developed in a climate of conflict and debate, was
potentially a guard against repression and inhumanity.

Reason was thus on the one hand relative to historical institutions and social practice; yet on the other hand it should not be
relativized and denied to the degree imposed by the new political
theory of discourse. To understand the strengths and weaknesses
of this path we have to turn to Gernet's methodological assumptions.

Let us begin by recalling that 'la psychologie historique' was
indebted in France to the work of Gernet's friend and colleague Ignace Meyerson, a psychologist at the Laboratoire de
Psychophysiologie de l'Institut de Psychologie de Paris;
Meyerson's *Les Fonctions psychologiques et les œuvres* appeared in the
same year as Gernet's 'La Notion mythique de la valeur en
Grèce'. As the name of Lévi-Strauss has so dominated theoretical
discussion about structuralism, the importance of Meyerson's
work for Gernet and Vernant may have been lost sight of.[16]
Especially for 'La Notion mythique', this work seems particularly
important. Meyerson started from the assumption that the human
mind creates (sometimes quite figuratively) forms of the world
around it, forms which pervade all specialized activities as a kind
of pattern.[17] These patterns or forms could be studied historically
by means of their representations in the form of *objectivations*. By
this term Meyerson referred to the process by which the human
mind mediates between itself and the physical and social world
surrounding it. Objectivations are expressed by the creation of
signs. Signs constituted the human reality of an apparently external world, as in the case of language, myth, religion, or mathematics.[18] Gernet adopted Meyerson's concept of the function of
the sign, as well as his distinction between sign and symbol. For
Meyerson, a symbol was on the one hand a more figurative sign
(e.g. religious symbols, paraphernalia of power, etc.), and on the

---

[15] Humphreys (1978), 94.

[16] Vernant, though, conceived his *Mythe et pensée chez les Grecs* as an application of
Meyerson's methodological framework to the field of ancient Greece, and dedicated the
volume to him; see p. 5 there (=p. ix in Eng. trans.), and Humphreys (1978), 27. The
influence was by no means one-sided, as one can see from the frequent references to
Gernet in Meyerson (1948). On Meyerson, see also Vernant (1995), i, esp. 3–47 (with
index, s.v. 'Meyerson, I.').

[17] Meyerson (1948), 31–2.   [18] Ibid. 74–82.

other a more complex sign that entailed precisely the operations that it implied and of which it was the object (e.g. mathematical symbols).[19] In a mythico-magical world the symbol (image) merged with what it represented: the god is present in the sacred object. Yet to the extent that human thought becomes more conscious of its operations, a greater distance develops between the symbol and what it represents. As a result, a symbol acquires an increasingly indirect relation to its origin, rendering it at the same time less precise and less figurative.[20]

Gernet applied Meyerson's theory of the sign to the transformation of value (and its representations) in Greek thought. Thus he writes with reference to Meyerson:

If we agree to distinguish between symbol and sign in such a way that the first remains charged with immediate affective meanings, whereas the significance of the 'sign' is limited, or apparently limited, entirely to its *function*, it is clear that what we mean by 'the origins of money' is the transition from symbol to sign (94–5/112).

The attempt to describe the transition from mythical value to money in semiotic terms is not accidental. It prefaces an exposition in which the attempt is made to relate social institutions to modes of representation (or signification) in historical perspective. Gernet is usually credited with being among the first to have applied structural linguistics to the interpretation of myth. If we see Gernet's article in the light of Meyerson's theory of 'objectivation', and its importance for 'la psychologie historique', we may see more clearly how well Saussurean linguistics tied in with Gernet's and Meyerson's intellectual project. In the notion of the *signifiant* they saw what was precisely the linguistic equivalent to collective thought and its representation not just in linguistic performance. Saussurean 'langage' was not only an analogy for myth but the very fabric of which myth was made. The historical psychologist thus had to proceed like a linguist in order to understand how thought was generated and developed within a collective. This was true for all kinds of thought, but comparatively easy to discern in myth, seen as a kind of language composed of narrative details:

The stories imply particular human attitudes: we should take them into consideration if we wish to read aright. The stories, moreover, are

---

[19] Ibid. 76–7.   [20] Ibid. 101–3.

interconnected . . . I need really be granted only one thing: that mythology is a special category of language ['une espèce de langue']. We know
the function of '*signifiants*' in a language; taking my cue from linguistics,
I would say that we have to take into account two kinds of connections.
First, those between the constituent elements or 'moments' of a single
tale . . . ; and second the associations by means of which one episode,
theme or image evokes a similar group. Such connections and associations will help our understanding (100/116).

To render this methodological programme less abstract, let us
look briefly at Gernet's analysis of the tripod of the Seven Sages
(101 f./117 f.). First he demonstrates how the significant object is
signified explicitly by details given in any particular rendition of
the story itself ('syntagmatic connections'): in Plutarch, for example, the tripod is conceived as a prize in a competition, and it
contributes to the fame of the combatants because of its circulation (*periodos*), its passing through all their hands (*dia pantōn
anakuklēsis*), and their 'mutual declining of it out of generous
good will' (*anthupeixis met' eumeneias philotimou genomenē*, Plu. *Sol.*
4. 1). But there are also elements in the story which describe
'value' by association with other mythical complexes which are
only alluded to in the story itself ('paradigmatic associations'): the
tripod has a history that goes back to the family of the Pelopidae,
it was originally a wedding gift from the gods, and it was passed
down through the family until it reached Helen (who alone is
mentioned in Plutarch's version). Helen throws the vessel into
the sea, which creates further associations connected with the sea
and valuable objects recovered from it. And in some versions of
the story of the tripod there are elements which presage, as
Gernet suggests, the use of golden vessels in contractual trade (for
example the fact that the competition in wisdom is organized by
the Lydian king at a time when mainland Greece was still poor
(Diog. Laert. 1. 29; cf. Lys. 19. 24–6; Gernet 102/119); one might
add that the pot is bought by the Milesians before it is set out as
a prize. Connections with other stories are created by the re-
appearance of details attached to significant objects, such as competition, conflict, religious awe, or, as already mentioned, their
recovery from the sea.

The search for paradigmatic associations leads Gernet through
several variants of related myths preserved in different literary
genres at different periods, such as epic, epinikion, tragedy,

historiography, Hellenistic biography, etc. The inevitable question arises whether these genres simply 'preserve' myth, and whether—since they clearly do not—their reworking of mythical material preserves a particular historical image of value. The problem has been discussed intensely with respect to Homer, over the issue of whether the *Iliad* and *Odyssey* preserve a faithful image of gift exchange as a past historical institution. Against Finley's seminal hypothesis that gift exchange in Homer reflected a social institution of the Dark Ages, many scholars nowadays are inclined, rather, to ask: in what ways did Homeric audiences engage with such images, and what function did they have at the time the epics were performed in their final version?[21] The same should be done, I think, with regard to images of value 'in myth': what was the function of these particular images *at the time the stories were used in any particular genre*? What were the politics behind these representations of value? Gernet's structural analysis seeks a *system* of symbols instead of looking at how the meaning of particular symbols was negotiated and renegotiated.

3

Gernet set *agalma* and coin in a relation of meaning and function, qualitative and quantitative value, as well as past and present. This is a distinction that has often been made.[22] But it is important to realize that it springs from the very idea which Gernet suggests hypothetically: that myth and *logos* have a different historical background related to a particular mode of signification. If one adopts a less essentialist distinction between coinage/money and *agalmata*/gifts so as to allow for the possibility that the representation of value is part of the politics of exchange, then a rather different picture emerges. Attention is drawn then, for example, to contexts in which *agalmata* continued to 'function' as a means of payment (such as dedications and penalty payments rendered to a temple[23]) or where their value was rather precisely

---

[21] For a summary of the discussion, see von Reden (1995), 13–18.

[22] See in particular the classical anthropological statement by Gregory (1982), with discussion by Appadurai (1986), 3–16.

[23] See, for example, the famous agrarian law of Naupactus (*IG* ix/1. 3² 609 B 22 ff.) dated to about 500 BCE: if the *damiourgoi* make more profit than was fixed, they must give

computed.[24] Conversely, there are situations in which the value
of money was represented in a highly symbolic, 'qualitative'
way.[25] There is a degree of anthropological romanticism implied
if one overemphasizes the affective value of gifts and dedications
as against their function and exchangeability.[26]

The difference between the representation of *agalmata* in terms
of gift exchange and that of coinage in terms of commerce is not
so much a matter of historical change as of ideological political
conflict. I have tried to show in my *Exchange in Ancient Greece*
(1995) how the redefinition of 'transactional orders' in the course
of the development of the polis created a new contrast between
the long-term order of exchange constituted by rituals which aim
at the reproduction of the community as a whole, and the short-
term order within which individuals strive for a living through
the acquisition of goods for consumption and storage. The terminology is borrowed from Parry and Bloch, who suggest that
many societies differentiate between two 'transactional orders'.
Though related through the metaphor of exchange and the valuables that circulate, communities distinguish a long-term order of
exchange from the short-term order in terms of the moral rules
applied to each of them. While wealth, prosperity, and gain are
in a long-term order cast into images of gift exchange, and are
morally accepted since they benefit the community as a whole,
they are castigated in a short-term order as they appear to benefit
individuals in an asocial, commercial sort of way.[27] With the
emergence of political institutions in the late Archaic polis, the
boundary between the two orders of exchange came to be con-
tested. Did the exchange rituals that ordered and maintained the
polis belong to the long-term order of communal benefit or did
they satisfy the 'commercial' needs of individuals in the short-
term? Did the payments made to the representatives of the polis

an *agalma* to Apollo after nine years, and the profit must not be credited. See also [Arist.]
Ath. Pol. 55. 5, where *diaitētai* are said to dedicate a golden statue if they take presents
thanks to their office.

[24] See esp. the Cleombrotus inscription from Sybaris (*Atti e Memorie della società Magna
Grecia*, 6 (1965), 14 ff.) where Cleombrotus, an Olympic victor, promises to dedicate a
statue of a certain size and thickness to Athena, 'as I vowed a tenth <of my prize> to the
goddess'. For bibliography, see Ebert (1975), 251–5.

[25] See Kurke (1993) and von Reden (1997), as well as the present paper.

[26] Strathern (1992), 171–2; Appadurai (1986), 13.

[27] Parry and Bloch (1989), 24 ff.

maintain the prosperity of all its members or just the self-interest of its leaders? Was coinage—which originated, arguably, in the polis itself rather than in a timeless past—the hallmark of a short-term order, or could it function in the long-term order just as *agalmata* did? How these questions were answered was an ideological matter, but the very discussion itself led to misrepresentations of coinage as a purely functional medium of exchange in an impersonal economic sphere of self-interested market exchange.

This thesis has, somewhat independently, found support in the work of Leslie Kurke, who has shown in a number of publications that coinage was part of what we may term, with Ian Morris, 'a conflict . . . over . . . legitimate culture' which marked the hostilities among the elite in Archaic poleis.[28] In her book on Pindar, Kurke (1991) investigated the relationship between images of traditional forms of wealth and generosity, on the one hand, and commercial and monetary images, on the other. Epinician poetry was composed at a time of profound political change. Traditional aristocratic values were confronted with a new civic ideology, the primacy of the *oikos* and intra-elite relationships were challenged by that of the polis, and the introduction of coinage questioned the privileges of wealth embodied in aristocratic possessions. Athletic victory, which in the rhetoric of praise was assimilated to mythical heroism, was celebrated in front of a civic community. Yet the heroization of individuals was arguably a positive value in civic communities. As a result, conflicting types of transaction clashed and merged in epinician poetry, rendering it a testimony to the implicit conflicts in the late Archaic polis. The entire spectrum of exchanges within the polis was put at stake in the public celebration of victory: gift exchange, sacrifice, hospitality, trade, and commerce. Modulating between civic and aristocratic ideologies,

---

[28] Kurke (1991), (1993), and (1995). For the quotation, see I. Morris (1996), 27. I have argued (in von Reden (1997)), against Kurke (1995: 42) that the polemics against coinage found in Archaic poetry are unlikely to be expressions of a split 'along class lines'. In an as yet unpublished response she has modified her position, arguing instead that coinage became a site of contestation within a broader political struggle between different ideological positions, not directly linked to social classes but coinciding with the split between the elitist and middling traditions which Morris identifies. I am fully persuaded by this modified position, and find compelling her argument that there are systematic correlations between Archaic Greek genre, performance context, and attitudes to money.

Pindar sets images of trade and commerce in contrast to the imagery of traditional social exchange symbolized by *xeniai* ('guest gifts'), *dōra* ('gifts'), *hedna* ('dowry'), and *apoina* ('wergeld'). Yet, rather than espousing the tension between conflicting spheres of exchange, he assimilates them. The beginning of *Isthmian* 2, in which Pindar contrasts the liberal Muse of old with the wage-labourer of his own day, is a critical reflection upon the effects of money; but in the course of the poem coinage is appropriated for the symbolic economy of the aristocracy, and monetary expenditure becomes a sign of their power and prestige.

Epinikion is only one genre in which the conflict over coinage found expression. As Kurke emphasizes, care must be taken that not all texts are located with a single, collective or class mentality. There is some indication that different attitudes to the new medium of exchange prevailed within different parts of the literate elite. Ian Morris has argued for an ideological opposition developing from the eighth century onwards and spanning most of the Greek-speaking world.[29] On the one hand there were those people who derived their authority from the emerging conception of the state as a community of citizens, and on the other those who opposed this development, arguing 'that authority lay outside these . . . communities, in an inter-polis aristocracy that had privileged links to the gods, the heroes, and the East'.[30] Following Mazzarino and Kurke, Morris maintains that these ideological positions were expressed in different poetic traditions and different contexts of performance. While iambus and elegy, publicly performed, dominated the 'political' (Morris calls it 'middling') tradition, the opposition (or 'elitist' tradition) is represented above all by monodic lyric performed within the aristocratic symposium. In choral lyric, as we saw above, the two positions were mediated and combined. Homer was championed by the elitist tradition while Hesiod was at the head of the middling voice.[31] We may begin to see that different ideological positions, and the exclusion or inclusion of coinage into particular constructions of value, were dependent on the place where these positions were expressed.

[29] I. Morris (1996).   [30] Ibid. 19.
[31] Ibid. 27; Mazzarino (1947); Kurke (1992).

4

It is generally agreed that the emergence of *logos*—in the sense of critical enquiry that could be questioned, tested, and argued about—was a product of the political culture of the Greek polis.[32] This is a complex proposition which has various aspects, each on its own being open to discussion. One of the aspects is, however, that the authority of argument and evidence—as opposed to the authority of wisdom, which relied on formal beauty of expression and the personal authority of the poet or sage—gained much support from the regular routines of political procedure. As Geoffrey Lloyd puts it, 'in the competitive situation that arose those who cultivated the art of speaking and who were prepared to put their case like statesmen before an Assembly, or like advocates in a court of law, were evidently more likely to succeed in persuading certain audiences'. *Logos* was a mode of thought and type of argument that was in a stronger position in front of a civic audience.[33]

Those who have, like Gernet, considered money in this context have done so in different, though related, ways. Vernant, building on Gernet's argument, contends that money allowed exchange to be seen for the first time as an independent, economic, category that was separated from the social and sacred connotations of *agalmata*, as well as from the bonds of dependence that the circulation of *agalmata* implied. The universal use of money led to a new, quantifiable, positive and abstract notion of value. Taking his cue from Aristotle, he argues furthermore that money as a common measure, agreed upon by convention, allowed the delineation of a secular sphere of pure *nomos*.[34] Seaford, who has offered perhaps the most complex recent argument about the interdependence of social practices and notions of

[32] Vernant (1983), 357–66; G. E. R. Lloyd (1979), 240–64.
[33] The quotation is from G. E. R. Lloyd (1979), 259. Lloyd is careful not to identify critical enquiry with democracy, but rather with polis culture more generally, regardless of constitution: 'The experience of deliberation on affairs of state was less widespread in the oligarchies . . . but such deliberation occurred' (261). The same holds true for coinage. Given the variety of constitutional backgrounds of poleis in which coinage emerged and was used, it can hardly be identified with democracy. Democratic Athens just happens to be the only polis where attitudes to coinage can be investigated from different perspectives. The question of how far democracies and money-use reinforced each other is, of course, another matter.
[34] Vernant (1983), 360–1.

exchange in the developing polis, suggests that money as a universal medium of exchange facilitated precise commensurability of what was exchanged. Commodity exchange based on the precise commensurability of goods replaced dependence between people, such as is created by gift exchange, with a more abstract dependence of people on the socially recognized power of money, and on the authority of law which guaranteed the legal status of purchase. This common experience, moreover, made a champion of *logos* like Heraclitus seek for an equally universal measure or formula that made possible the exchange or transformation of elements according to which all things happen. Money was an agent of positive cosmological thought, since it could be regarded as (*a*) universally valid and (*b*) a measure that was independent of its substance and context of exchange.[35] We may finally recall Humphreys's observation that 'the most precise and rational accounting and organisation of contracts was to be found in city finances, where record-keeping and the separation of public and private funds were taken for granted'.[36] Rationality is here not simply a matter of thought but of practice.

There is thus a broad spectrum within which a correlation between money and *logos* can be conceived. I am far from questioning the justification of any of these propositions. Nevertheless, I would like to confront them with another argument which brings the relation between politics, performance context, and constructions of value into play. It might help to see links between *logos*, money, and polis in a light different from the usual one.

Lisa Kallet-Marx has observed that financial knowledge and political power were intimately related in post-Periclean fifth-century Athens.[37] Asking how much the average Athenian male could and did know about public and imperial finance, she finds, first, that direct access to financial office was limited to members of the highest census group; secondly, that a good working knowledge of financial matters was confined to those who had

---

[35] Seaford (1994), 204 f., 220–3.   [36] (1983), 11.

[37] Kallet-Marx (1994); see also *ead.* (1993). In another article (forthcoming), the same scholar again investigates symbolic meanings of financial resources in Athenian discourse. The disaster at Mycalessus, she argues, was represented by Thucydides as forming an organic unity with Athens' financial ruin, with both being described in the imagery and language of the body affected by disease.

served in the *boulē* (Council) in the same or in the previous year; and, thirdly, that financial information on stone, though abundant, was not comprehensive enough for those who could read it to get a grasp of the city's overall financial status. It was thus left to the *rhētōr* with specialized knowledge to instruct (not simply to advise) a mass audience who was armed with little knowledge outside what they learned in the Pnyx. It is no coincidence that Aristotle names finance as the first of five general subjects on which people deliberate and on which deliberative orators give advice in public (*Rhet.* 1359^{b}8).

Turning to Pericles' speech to the Athenians in Thuc. 2. 13, Kallet-Marx argues that, although Pericles gives a detailed catalogue of the city's finances, nevertheless the purpose of his recording Athens' expenditure was not deliberative. Rather, it was designed to produce a particular emotional state, *tharsos* ('confidence'), one of the emotions Pericles was particularly adept at arousing in the *dēmos*. The authority of the speech was built on the particular rhetorical ability, financial knowledge, and pre-existing authority of the *rhētōr*. Conversely, the display of financial knowledge maintained and enhanced his authority. The *rhētōr* was in an immensely powerful position to shape public opinion on a largely inaccessible subject, and at the same time it was this position which stabilized his future authority.

Kallet-Marx then turns to the symbolic aspects of Athenian public finance which gained the status of rational argument against the background of traditional assumptions about wealth, power, and military strength. Thucydides makes Pericles encourage the Athenians on the eve of the war by noting that their strength lay in their good judgement (*gnōmē*) and financial resources (*chrēmatōn periousia*).[38] The combination of these two advantages recurs several times in Thucydides' work, as indeed in other texts of the time. The claim that financial resources are essential to successful warfare is nothing exceptional today, but it was still hypothetical in fifth-century Athens. Warfare was traditionally land warfare, with each hoplite equipping himself at his own expense. *Individual* wealth was always essential for military power, but the association of military strength with public funds was a transvaluation of traditional experience. Kallet-Marx

---

[38] Thuc. 2. 13. 2.

emphasizes the importance of expenditure (*dapanē*) within this rhetoric. *Dapanē* was endowed with pregnant associations, signifying power and superiority but also a kind of aristocratic generosity by which an individual sacrificed part of his private wealth to the whole community. In Pindar's victory odes it had expressed a particular kind of generosity by which the athletic victor reintegrated himself into the polis.[39] In Athenian public rhetoric it became an ideograph, laden with traditional beliefs, that confirmed the claim that Athens' strength lay in its monetary resources. It was a 'rhetorical formulation but it became a collective democratic belief'.[40]

Athenian *logos*, its performative contexts, and the value of money were thus inextricably linked. They formed a unity which confirmed and made sense of each of its constituents. Kallet-Marx rightly remarks that the citizens' direct experience of monetary exchange in both public and private spheres, through receipt of payment for participation in the democratic institutions, and through private commercial activity, predisposed them to be interested in and receptive to financial information, especially as this was tied to their welfare. In this respect the short-term transactional order for once helped to maintain the ideology of the long-term order of the polis. The way the value of money was communicated to the *dēmos* authenticated both the power structures of Athens and the value of money. Conversely, it was the deliberative institutions of Athens together with the common experience of market exchange which made the arguments of the *rhētores* plausible to a critical audience.

Seaford has observed incisively that money does not resolve dependency, but rather replaces personal dependence with a more abstract dependence, both on a collective that recognizes the value of coinage and on a government that guarantees the legal status of purchase.[41] The difference between *agalmata* and coinage, or gift exchange and commodity exchange, need not be conceived in terms of meaning (related to personalized experience) and function (related to the exchange of things). With

---

[39] See Kurke (1991), esp. 225–39.
[40] Kallet-Marx (1994), 241. With M. C. McGee, Kallet-Marx calls ideograph 'a term which in a particular context is a sort of "building block" of ideology or collective consciousness'. See also McGee (1980).
[41] (1994), 223.

Bourdieu one might suggest that the two exchange ideologies and their objects *conceal* different relationships and asymmetries.[42] While gifts often conceal a large array of asymmetries in personal relationships, economic function, and computation of equivalence, money lays these bare but conceals the dependence of citizens on a state, on its institutionalized political culture, its social practices, and politicians. In somewhat tautological fashion we might say that it was because money revealed and concealed certain dependencies that it was related to the particular forms of discourse and exchange ideologies of the polis.

One might arrive thus at a new approach to the relationship between conceptions of value and forms of discourse (*muthos/ logos*). If, as is assumed by many contributors to this volume, mythology is a category largely created by Western thought and anthropological scholarship, then an essentialist distinction between gift and money is equally so.[43] The cluster of qualities that Gernet identifies with *agalmata* in myth, on the one hand, and the functions implied in the economic conceptualization of coinage, on the other, coexist to a greater or lesser extent in every society. But they are concealed to varying degrees by different exchange ideologies. I have tried to introduce three considerations which might qualify Gernet's notion of 'value in myth'. First, we have to consider the politics that lie behind representations of value, gifts, and money in ancient texts. Secondly, we should be aware that representations of value are a function of the tension between two 'transactional orders', one of which is related to the timeless order of the community as a whole and is thus more likely to be associated with figurative notions of value typically attached to gifts. Thirdly, we should recognize that the performative contexts within which money or other objects of value were represented varied, privileging the one or the other. Rather than distinguishing chronologically between different concepts of value, we should more pertinently observe the coexistence and continuous conflict of the concepts. To the extent that *muthos* and *logos* were related to different but coexisting practices of social exchange, their ideologies of exchange and thus their conceptions of value differed. I do not attempt to resolve the

---

[42] (1977), 171–83.

[43] Detienne (1981) for the creation of mythology; Appadurai (1986: 3–16) and Strathern (1992) for the false dichotomy between gift and commodity.

problem implied by the question *From Myth to Reason?*; but I do suggest that the answer we give to that question will have to be differentiated, depending on how we conceive the relationship between gift exchange and monetary transactions at any particular place or period of time in the ancient Greek world.

3

Rationalization and Disenchantment in Ancient Greece: Max Weber among the Pythagoreans and Orphics?

JAN BREMMER

EVERY attempt at periodization in history carries the danger of dividing the flow of time into a strict before and after. Naturally, we would all claim to be aware of this problem, but experience teaches that it is hard to escape such easy categorizations. In any case, a certain truth can hardly be denied to important distinctions such as that represented by the concept of the Renaissance or, even more clearly, that of the Enlightenment. The opposition of *muthos* vs. *logos* is another of these well-known distinctions, popularized in particular by Wilhelm Nestle (1865–1959), who in his book *Vom Mythos zum Logos* attempted to sketch the process of rationalization in Greece.[1]

There is something ironic about the appearance of a book with this title in Germany in the year 1940. This is the more so, since Nestle, 'Oberstudiendirektor' at the Stuttgart Karlsgymnasium and 'Honorarprofessor' at the University of Tübingen, had been an early follower of the National Socialist movement.[2] He regularly published in its journal *Aus Unterricht und Forschung*,[3] his work was allowed to appear all through the Second World War, and he was active in attempts to promote the National Socialist

---

[1] W. Nestle (1940: 1) explains the two terms of his title as 'die zwei Pole, zwischen denen das menschliche Geistesleben schwingt. Mythisches Vorstellen und logisches Denken sind Gegensätze'. See also Most in this volume.

[2] This side of his career is not even alluded to in *Abschied von Wilhelm Nestle 16.4.1865–18.4.1959* (no place, no date). The pamphlet, which I owe to the kindness of Christoph Auffarth, contains the addresses spoken at his burial on 22 April 1959, a report on Nestle's last days, some of his poems, and a note on his scholarly legacy.

[3] From 1930 to 1942 Nestle reviewed for and contributed to *Aus Unterricht und Forschung: Wissenschaftliche Zeitschrift auf nationalsozialistischer Grundlage*, cf. R. Nestle (1965), who, perhaps not surprisingly, omits to mention the subtitle of the journal, which is still mentioned in his father's own bibliography in *Vom Mythos zum Logos*, 552–4. B. Lincoln (1996: esp. 2 n. 2) has clearly overlooked these references.

ideology in the field of classics.[4] His political sympathies are also evident from his introduction to *Vom Mythos zum Logos*, in which he notes that the transition expressed in his title seems to have been the privilege of 'the Aryan peoples as the most gifted race'.[5] Nestle's book is not profound, but it still remains a highly readable introduction to the theme of our present collection of studies.

Nestle's distinction is a typical 'etic' one, which is not found in the Greek sources, where historical periodization is absent before Polybius.[6] The distinction is not very popular either in recent books on Greek mythology. The valuable studies by Ken Dowden, Fritz Graf, and Richard Buxton do not have a lemma *muthos/logos* (or *mythos/logos*) in their indexes; neither do we find it in the standard history of Greek philosophy by W. K. C. Guthrie.[7] Apparently, the polarity evoked in the title of our collection seems already to have been quietly dumped by contemporary scholars.

This is not surprising. The gradual advance of philosophical and scientific thought in Greece has been well documented and accepted and, unless we would attempt a completely revisionist approach to the development of Greek culture, our task seems to be one of refinement rather than spectacular innovation. What we need now is a more careful analysis of the ways the *Greeks* contrasted and distinguished between *muthos* and *logos* (the 'emic' approach) and the ways *we* should analyse the advances and/or possible relapses of more rational ways of thought (the 'etic' approach).

With the famous German sociologist Max Weber (1846–1920), the most influential modern thinker on rationalization (whom we will meet again in these pages), I take it that life can be rationalized on the basis of very different premises and in very different directions.[8] Since a debate on the transition from *muthos* to *logos* can become rather slippery when there is no clear definition of

---

[4] See the revealing report (Losemann (1977: 94–102)) of an important meeting, in Würzburg in 1941, on the 'new duties in the field of the Greco-Roman world'; Nestle participated in this meeting in the company of other famous Hellenists, such as Hans Herter (1899–1984), Albin Lesky (1896–1981), and Wolfgang Schadewaldt (1900–74).

[5] (1940), 3 and 6, respectively.

[6] Diller and Schalk (1972); Aalders (1986). For the etic/emic opposition, see below. This distinction was coined by Kenneth Pike: cf. Pike (1967), 37 ff.

[7] Dowden (1992); Graf (1993a); Buxton (1994); Guthrie (1962–81).

[8] M. Weber (1920), 62.

rationalization, I accept as my point of departure the most prominent elements of the process as outlined by Weber, however
'overgeneralized and incompletely formulated' these may be:[9] 'the
increasing systematization of religious ideas and concepts, the
growth of ethical rationalism, and the progressive decline of ritual
and "magical" elements in religion';[10] I add the rationalization
and/or discarding of mythology, an aspect generally neglected by
Weber.

Rather paradoxically, Weber located the origins of rationalization within religion, specifically amongst the prophets of ancient
Israel.[11] It may therefore be worth while to concentrate our
investigation on two striking groups, which had put themselves at
the margin of the Greek polis on the basis of a religious criterion,
viz. by opposing conventional animal sacrifice: the Pythagoreans
and Orphics. The object of my brief *sondage* will be to investigate
to what extent we can find elements of disenchantment and
rationalization in the ideology and behaviour of these two
groups, which are often closely associated in modern scholarship.[12] It is one of Weber's merits that he called attention to
rational elements in behaviour, and I too will direct my attention
towards these aspects of the two groups, since they are usually
neglected in discussions of Greek rationality, as for example in
Nestle's book.

PYTHAGORAS AND THE *BIOS PYTHAGOREIOS*

Unfortunately, it is not easy to establish the facts either about the
beginnings of Pythagoreanism and Orphism, or about their mutual relationship. Let us start with Pythagoras.[13] The sage left
Samos around 530 BCE and established himself in Croton, where
he was well received by the local elite. Pythagoras himself probably derived from the Samian aristocracy, which in the sixth

---

[9] Geertz (1973), 171. I take the quotation from his '"Internal Conversion" in Contemporary Bali' (170–89), an inspiring essay which applies Weber's thoughts on rationalization to modern Bali.

[10] B. Morris (1987), 69.

[11] See especially Schluchter (1981).

[12] 'Disenchantment' is the standard translation of Weber's *Entzauberung*. For Weber's
term and idea, see Winckelmann (1980); Kippenberg (1991), 32–4.

[13] The standard study remains Burkert (1972); for some additions, see Bremmer (1995).
I have not yet seen Zhmud (1997).

century had been materially very well off, as we know from a
fragment of the local poet Asius, who described their 'snow-
white tunics', 'golden brooches', and 'cunningly worked brace-
lets'. Like theirs, Pythagoras' 'tresses', too, probably 'once waved
in the wind in golden bands' (fr. 13 *PEG*). This aristocratic origin
must be one reason why Pythagoras was heartily welcomed in
Croton, a south Italian city ruled by an oligarchy, the Thousand,
who were the descendants of the original colonists.[14] The city was
as rich as Samos, as the treasures excavated from the sanctuary of
Hera Lacinia, the most prominent sanctuary of the town, eloquently show.[15] In Croton, Pythagoras was politically active for a
long time, until he was exiled to Metapontum. During his
Crotoniate activities, as far as we can get behind the legends, he
was active in representing himself as somebody with a more than
normal human status, whether like a Spartan or Persian king or
through a close association with Demeter and Apollo.[16]

Pythagoras continued with this aristocratic performance even
in exile. At least, that is the conclusion we can draw on the basis
of the ascetic, closely-defined lifestyle he prescribed for his followers. His rules must have been hard to follow for people who
had to work for a living, since, as Burkert notes, the many
prohibitions and taboos, such as not to travel by the main road
and not to speak in the dark, meant 'an almost frightening
constriction of one's freedom'; moreover, the Pythagorean rule
always to wear white linen clothes could only have been realized
by really wealthy people.[17] In late antiquity, Iamblichus (*Life of
Pythagoras* 96–100) described this lifestyle as a kind of monastic
way of living—an interesting testimony to the instant pagan
fascination with this Christian ideal. However, the reality was
somewhat different. The old Pythagoreans retained their own
houses and private property, but did help one another when need
arose.[18] This *Brüderlichkeitsethik* confirms another of Weber's
insights, viz. that where people first come together on the basis of

---

[14] Giangiulio (1989), 3–50.

[15] Spadea (1994 [1996]) and (1996).

[16] King: Bremmer (1995), 66. Apollo: Burkert (1972), 91, 114, 141, 143, 178;
Giangiulio (1994); Demeter: Burkert (1972), 155, 159, 178–9.

[17] Burkert (1972), 165 (white clothes: add Iamblichus, *Life of Pythagoras* 149), 191
(taboos).

[18] For Pythagoras' stress on friendship and community of goods, see de Vogel (1966),
151–9; van der Horst and Mussies (1990), 141–2.

religious views, they are more closely associated with one another than with their 'normal' associates, such as relatives or neighbours, and thus will help each other in case of material needs.[19] On the other hand, the Pythagorean lifestyle did indeed show some resemblances to that of the earliest monks, but presumably more in characteristics such as vegetarianism, the lack of laughter, and the simplicity of life than in the attitude towards property.[20]

Can we notice rationalizing elements in Pythagoreanism? For our purpose I would like to stress here two aspects of this movement. First, it did not have a specific theogonic, cosmogonic, or anthropogonic mythology, as was the case in Orphism, although we can still detect cosmogonical traditions in Pythagorean number philosophy: the One becomes a Two as the Unlimited penetrates it. In other words, we have here the same separation as between Ouranos and Gaia.[21] Even when Pythagoreanism employed mythological terms, we are in for a surprise. Aristotle (fr. 196 Rose, quoted by Porphyry, *Life of Pythagoras* 41) relates that Pythagoras or early Pythagoreans called the sea 'the tears of Cronos', the Great and the Little Bear 'the hands of Rhea', the Pleiades 'the lyre of the Muses', and the planets 'Persephone's dogs'; less drastic, but equally innovative, was the elevation of the singing Sirens, who now produce the music of the spheres.[22] A striking aspect of these denominations is the deviation from traditional Greek mythology, where we never find the Pleiades or the planets associated with the Muses or Persephone. Apparently, Pythagoras used traditional names in completely untraditional roles. Especially intriguing is the mention of the Little Bear, the discovery of which was ascribed to Thales, which perhaps suggests that it was mentioned in the latter's *Nautical Astronomy* (if we can accept this work as authentically Thalesian). The interesting aspect, then, of this allegorical use is the employment of mythological concepts to order the world and draw it into the realm of the known and familiar. At the same time, though, the old system was abolished by a, so to speak, *bricolage*-like use of traditional mythology.[23] It seems, then,

---

[19] (1920), 536–73.   [20] Bremmer (1992) and (1997).
[21] Burkert (1972), 36–7.
[22] Ibid. 170–1, 187 (Sirens); Breglia Pulci Doria (1994).
[23] Burkert (1972), 170–1; Meijer (1981).

that we find in Pythagoras a clear step towards the disenchant-ment of the world.

If we can consider the discarding of traditional mythology by the Pythagoreans under the heading 'from *muthos* towards *logos*', can we do the same regarding the introduction of a *bios Pythagoreios*, our second aspect? Burkert has compared the Py-thagorean ascetic lifestyle with early modern Puritanism and Pietism.[24] This comparison seems perfectly acceptable, but Weber already saw that these Protestant movements combined a discipli-nary life with a more rational, calculating mentality.[25] Weber also made some useful distinctions regarding rationality. In the open-ing pages of his *Wirtschaft und Gesellschaft* he distinguished be-tween *Wertrationalität*, a 'conscious belief in the intrinsic value of acting in a certain way, regardless of the consequences of so acting', and *Zweckrationalität*, 'a consciously calculating attempt to achieve desired ends with appropriate means'.[26] In my view Pythagorean life can certainly be seen as *wertrational*, since the Pythagoreans broke with traditional habits and designed a new way of life. We are so used to new movements in the modern world that it is hard to appreciate now the magnitude of the innovation made by Pythagoras. To the best of my knowledge, this is the first major, conscious break with traditional life attested in our historical sources.

Can we call Pythagorean life also *zweckrational*? With some hesitation I am inclined to an affirmative answer, for two reasons. First, many elements of the *bios Pythagoreios* were not innovative at all, but traditional. This means that Pythagoras had made the rules of the tradition explicit and thus potential objects for fur-ther reflection.[27] Secondly, there will have been a connection between the conscious following of the Pythagorean lifestyle and the doctrine of metempsychosis. Unfortunately, our sources are not very rich regarding Pythagoras' views, which we only see through a glass darkly. One thing is certain, though. The doctrine was an 'attempt at consistent thinking, a groping for something like an eternal, imperishable Being'.[28]

[24] Burkert (1972), 190–1.
[25] On the so-called Weber thesis, see most recently van Dülmen (1988); Hudson (1988); Lehmann and Roth (1993); Valeri (1997).
[26] (1956), 12–13. I quote the summary by Brubaker (1984), 50. For other good introductions see Lemmen (1977); Schluchter (1979); Passeron (1994).
[27] For the Pythagorean lifestyle, see also Parker (1983), 291–307.
[28] Burkert (1972), 136.

II
Myth and Reason in Practice

Burkert has also noted that in the Pythagorean lifestyle there is 'a certain *logos*, a kind of "reflection"', even if in his opinion 'this does not imply a rationally constructed system'.[29] Now the most recent research into Pietism and Puritanism also stresses that irrationality, magic, and witchcraft had their part in this development; we may think here of Newton's involvement not only in the laws of gravity but also in alchemy.[30] For us the juxtaposition of *akousmata*, such as 'thunder is a noise to frighten souls in Tartarus', with 'good counsel is sacred', may look odd, but the advance of the rational over the non-rational has been so slow in Western history that we should not ask too much from the early Greeks.

There is also another interesting aspect to Pythagoras' doctrine, which again leads to Weber. With his doctrine Pythagoras had become a purveyor of salvation. The 'invention' of the transmigration of the soul is a complicated problem, but it is sufficient for us to note here that it originated in Greece at a time when the influence of the old aristocracy was diminishing. Whereas it had once been sufficient for an aristocrat to survive in the memory of the group through his 'eternal fame' (*kleos aphthiton*), it now became more attractive to survive in person.[31] In other words, Pythagoras had designed an *Erlösungsreligion*. Similar inventions, such as Christianity and Islam, are always the product of intellectuals, as Weber stressed.[32] It would of course be anachronistic to say that Pythagoras was an intellectual, but his erudition was already known to Heraclitus (B 40 DK) who reproached Pythagoras with *polymathīē*, and his questioning of the status quo surely brings Pythagoras close to the modern intellectual.

In Weber's vision, religions of salvation were the answer to the intellectuals' experience of the 'Irrationalität der Welt'. It may well be that Pythagoras' system and ideology were stimulated by his experience of exile after the fall from power in Croton. Pythagoras' speculative thought, however, cannot be reduced to this event, since it originated as part of the general rise of rational thought in Greece. This phenomenon is still an enigma of which the causes are not yet clear. Whereas Jack Goody has pointed to

---

[29] Ibid. 190.

[30] Hsia (1989); Roper (1994). Newton: Westfall (1980).

[31] I discuss this process in detail in my forthcoming *Inventing the Afterlife*, a book based on the Read Tuckwell Lectures given in Bristol in May 1995.

[32] (1956), 319–48; Kippenberg (1989).

the innovation of the Greek alphabet and the concomitant revolution in the technology of communication, Geoffrey Lloyd has
recently again stressed the oral nature of debate in Greece and the
importance of democracy and political debate.[33] Against Lloyd it
may be observed that (1) Pythagoras was already criticized in
writing by Xenophanes (B 7 DK) and reproached by Heraclitus
(B 129 DK) for having plundered many writings,[34] that (2) democracy was a latecomer in Greece, which did not flourish in
sixth-century Ionia or southern Italy,[35] and that (3) the development of Greek democracy itself is hardly imaginable without
literacy.[36] The debate is still open, it seems to me.

ORPHISM

If recent decades have not given us any new sources for Pythagoras, except for some new portraits of the sage,[37] the situation
is rather different for the other alternative lifestyle, Orphism.
Until 1960 our knowledge of early Orphism was very limited,
but since then we have had to keep on modifying our picture
of the Orphic movement because of a series of stunning
discoveries: the famous Derveni papyrus,[38] the Olbian bone-
tablets,[39] and the continuing publication of new Orphic gold
leaves.[40] It is especially in the latter area that we have been
constantly surprised. Even since Robert Parker's important study

[33] Goody (1977); G. E. R. Lloyd (1990), 36–7 (oral nature, democracy).
[34] Writing: Bremmer (1995), 69. Heraclitus: Burkert (1972), 130–1; Mansfeld (1990),
443–8; Riedweg (1997), esp. 78–87.
[35] One cannot escape the impression that Lloyd, admittedly in the good company of
many ancient historians, too closely associates the development of the polis with Athenian
democracy, cf. the objections by W. Eder, 'Die athenische Demokratie in 4. Jahrhundert
v. Chr. Krise oder Vollendung?', in Eder (1995), 11–28, at 15–16.
[36] Hedrick (1994); Thomas (1995).
[37] R. R. R. Smith (1991); Strocka (1992).
[38] I quote the translation (with the new numbering of the columns) from A. Laks and
G. W. Most, 'A Provisional Translation of the Derveni Papyrus', in *eid.* (1997), 9–22. The
only edition still remains the unauthorized publication in *ZPE* 47 (1982), after p. 300. For
new readings note especially K. Tsantsanoglou, 'The First Columns of the Derveni
Papyrus and their Religious Significance', in Laks and Most (1997), 93–128.
[39] The tablets have most recently been edited by Dubois (1996), 154f.
[40] See the beautiful publication by Pugliese Carratelli (1993); see now C. Riedweg,
'Initiation—Tod—Unterwelt: Beobachtungen zur Kommunikationssituation und
narrativen Technik der orphisch-bakchischen Goldblättchen', in Graf (1998), 359–98 at
389–98.

of 1995,[41] we have had two more full texts published,[42] and attention has been drawn to a series of small, Macedonian gold leaves, which stress the fact that the deceased is a *mystēs* and mention his or her name, which is not the case in the long texts.[43]

The larger gold leaves mention *bakchoi*, Bakchios, and Persephone and thus strongly suggest Bacchic mysteries, which are perhaps for the very first time alluded to by Heraclitus, who in one and the same fragment speaks of *bakchoi* and *mystēria* (B 14 DK). In fact, numerous sources associate Orpheus and Dionysiac mysteries and the connection now seems firmly established, although its exact nature is still not very clear.[44] Pindar's *Second Olympian* presupposes Orphic literature, and Empedocles (*c.*492– 432 BCE) was already influenced by Orphism.[45] These data point to the first quarter of the fifth century as the period of Orphic genesis, perhaps not accidentally just after the death of Pythagoras, when the absence of this towering figure must have created space for other views in his vicinity.

Antiquity and modern scholarship have closely associated Orphism and Pythagoreanism. There is much to say for this view, since both espouse metempsychosis and an ascetic lifestyle, such as vegetarianism, and both were prominent in southern Italy. On the other hand, there were also striking differences. Pythagoras is a historical figure, Orpheus a mythological personage. Pythagoras used prose, 'Orpheus' poetry. Pythagoreanism was a movement which isolated itself, Orphism remained more or less integrated in society. Pythagoreanism was a community without a text, Orphism all text and little community. Pythagoreanism stressed ethics, Orphism purifications. Pythagoreanism, unlike Orphism, displayed little interest in mythology, however modified, as we will see shortly. Pythagoras favoured Apollo (see above), Orphism Dionysus (see below). Finally, Orphism had a much more pessimistic view of the world than the earliest Pythagoreanism.

---

[41] The best modern survey is now Parker (1995), to which I am much indebted in the following; for the Orphic lifestyle, see also still Burkert (1982).

[42] Chrysostomou (1991), 372–98; *SEG* xliv. 750.

[43] Cf. Dickie (1995); Rossi (1996).

[44] Cf. F. Graf, 'Dionysian and Orphic Eschatology: New Texts and Old Questions', in Carpenter and Faraone (1993), 239–58.

[45] Riedweg (1995).

To what extent does Orphism reflect a transition towards a more rationalizing era? The question may seem out of place, since, if ever there was a movement with a strange mythology, it was Órphism. Isocrates could still get angry at Orpheus because he more than any other poet had 'told stories about the gods such as no-one would venture to tell about their enemies . . . eating of children and castration of fathers and intercourse with mothers' (*Busiris* 38–9). The passage proves that Isocrates already knew what we are told only by later testimonies, viz. that in the Orphic theogony Ouranos was castrated by Cronos, who ate his children, but was deposed by Zeus, who castrated his father and had intercourse with his mother Rhea and their daughter Persephone.[46] This mythological B-movie is not easy to understand, but it is clear that the author exaggerated. Jean Rudhardt has called the procedure 'sursacralisant',[47] which is undoubtedly true, but leaves the question of why still unexplained. The connection with mysteries, that is with secrecy, may have been a factor, but the Eleusinian Mysteries could do without such scandals. Or did the author simply overdo matters in stressing the particular nature of Dionysus? There is a problem here which still awaits its solution.

Given this embarrassment of scandalous details, it is rather surprising to observe that at the very same time Orphic mythology was not uninfluenced by contemporary philosophy and ideology. Unfortunately, the precise nature of the oldest Orphic theogony is hard to reconstruct. For our purpose it is important to note that according to Eudemus the theogony started with Night, who already occupied an important position in later parts of the *Iliad*.[48] The early evidence implies that Orphic genealogy had become rationalized in comparison with that of Hesiod, in which personal gods appear only after personified natural phenomena. Moreover, the Derveni papyrus mentions that Zeus 'devised' (*emēsato*) Oceanus and, probably, Achelous (col. 23, 4), which also looks more modern than the development sketched

[46] For a useful summary of events as described in the so-called Rhapsodic Theogony, see West (1983), 70–5. For a more detailed and convincing discussion of these late antique sources, see Brisson (1995); note also Burkert (1996), 70–1.

[47] Rudhardt (1982). Moreau (1997) has collected various examples of a pattern of transgression before the institution of a new order, but his examples, too, do not display the same number of transgressions.

[48] For the prominence of Night, see Bremmer (1994), 87.

by Hesiod. Finally, the Derveni papyrus mentions 'Zeus the king, Zeus the ruler of all, god of the bright bolt' (col. 19, 10), which reminds us of Xenophanes' striking fragment, 'One god is greatest among gods and men' (B 23 DK). Even though Dionysus was highly important, the Orphics do not seem to have ventured to dethrone Zeus from his pre-eminent position. To conclude, the Orphic poet still employed a traditional medium, poetry, and a traditional genre, genealogical mythology. In fact, in this respect there is a very clear contrast with Pythagoreanism (see above). On the other hand, he also rationalized his genealogy and shows the influence of the most advanced critic of traditional thought, Xenophanes. Apparently, he was unable to escape the influence of the rationalizing mentality that had become prevalent in public discourse.[49]

It is interesting that the gold leaves also contain mythology, but once again not in its traditional form. On a number of gold leaves, the initiate says: 'I am a child of Earth and starry Heaven, but I am of heavenly stock.' The expression is surprising for at least two reasons. First, it would traditionally have been impossible for a human to claim to be a child of Earth and Heaven.[50] Secondly, we are surprised by the stress on the divine nature, which was probably the final stage of the process of reincarnation.[51] Evidently in this respect Orphism had elaborated upon Pythagoreanism, which does not seem to have developed in detail its doctrine of metempsychosis.

What about Orphic lifestyle? Here, it is clear that the Orphic initiator, the Orpheotelestes, was far removed from the Pythagoreans. Plato has given us the picture of wandering priests, and it is likely that Empedocles modelled himself on their role, even though these priests do not seem to have dressed themselves as fashionably as the sage of Acragas, who went round with 'a purple robe and over it a golden girdle . . . and again slippers of bronze and a Delphic laurel wreath' (Diog. Laert. 8. 73). Orphic priests seem to have operated on their own and not to have

---

[49] This is not the place to discuss the concept of 'mentality', which has recently been rejected by G. E. R. Lloyd (1990), but let me just observe that Lloyd has neglected discussions of the concept in Germany and The Netherlands: there are more things in heaven and earth than England and France. For an excellent recent survey, see Kuhlemann (1996); note also Borgolte (1997).

[50] As is rightly observed by Sourvinou-Inwood (1995), 195.

[51] For Orphic ideas of metempsychosis, see Parker (1995), 500.

constituted an Orphic community. Except for their vegetarianism,[52] we have virtually no information about their lifestyle.

However, we do know something about their activities. They claimed to be able to heal, just like Empedocles,[53] and Plato tells us that they promise 'not just individuals but also cities that there are forms of release and purifications from wrongdoing through sacrifices and play, effective both during life and also after death; these they call initiations—they free us from evil there [in the underworld], but if we do not sacrifice a terrible fate awaits us' (*Rep.* 364e, trans. Parker); the Orpheotelestes may well have read out (part of) an Orphic theogony to the novice during an initiation.[54] What they do not insist upon—at least Plato does not mention it—is the obligation to become a vegetarian. It seems that the Orpheotelestai practised certain ascetic rules which they did not prescribe for their wealthy followers.

Plato most likely derived his information about the Orpheotelestai from everyday Athenian practice, but elsewhere it must also have been a rich, often female clientele who were interested in the so-called Orphic gold leaves, which have not yet been attested for Attica: *symbola* or 'passports', as they are called in the two most recently published ones (see note 42). (Incidentally, the prominence of women is clearly something Weber nowhere seems to imagine as possible in his reflections; his is still very much a man's world.) The wealth of the Orphic followers is illustrated by the material of the leaves and by the aristocratic nature of several of the graves in which they have been found.[55]

Compared to Pythagoreanism, Orphism can clearly lay much less claim to being 'rationalized', since it still considered mythology very important. Regarding its lifestyle, there seems to have been a difference between the Orpheotelestai and the 'normal' followers. The first group may have thought that the practice of vegetarianism would lead to reincarnation, and as such can lay claim to Weber's category of *zweckrational*. The followers, on the other hand, attached much value to ritual, and thus certainly do

<hr/>

[52] Eur. *Hipp.* 953–55; Aristoph. *Frogs* 1032; Pl. *Leg.* 782c.
[53] Orphics: Eur. *Alc.* 967, *Cyc.* 646. Empedocles: Kingsley (1995), 220.
[54] Cf. D. Obbink, 'Cosmology as Initiation vs. the Critique of Orphic Mysteries', in Laks and Most (1997), 39–54. The translation from Plato is at Parker (1995), 483–4.
[55] Bremmer (1994), 88.

not fit Weber's qualifications for rationality. Perhaps, Orphics and Pythagoreans were less similar than is often thought.

CONCLUSION

What can we conclude from these necessarily short observations?

1. The views of Max Weber deserve attention also in the area of Greek religion.[56]

2. Both Pythagoreans and Orphics found their followers among the social and/or political elites of ancient Greece.[57]

3. Although Pythagoreanism and Orphism put themselves into opposition with the rest of Greek society, they could not isolate themselves from the 'spirit of the time', that enigmatic phenomenon of the *Zeitgeist*.[58] They had rejected or rationalized mythology and, to a certain extent, accepted some of Xenophanes' criticism.

4. In early modern Europe the ascetic lifestyle of Puritans and Pietists was part of a general advance of a more rational mode of thought. Despite its strangeness and unfamiliarity, this was probably also the case in Greece with the new lifestyle of Pythagoreans and, to a more limited extent, Orphics.

5. The transition 'from *muthos* towards *logos*' needs to be investigated not only on the level of discourse, but also on that of social practices.[59]

---

[56] Finley (1985: 88) quotes with approval Alfred Heuss's observation that 'the special disciplines pertaining to antiquity have gone their way as if Max Weber had never lived', and this is still certainly true for Greek religion.

[57] This is also observed in connection with metempsychosis by Lorenz (1990).

[58] Kamerbeek (1964); Kossmann (1995), 32–46.

[59] In addition to discussions during the Bristol 1996 Colloquium, especially with Fritz Graf, I also greatly profited from the observations of our Groningen research group, 'Religious Symbols', on 16 June 1997. Richard Buxton kindly corrected my English.

III
Mythical Logic

4

The Logic of Cosmogony

WALTER BURKERT

I T has often been assumed that cosmogonic myth, i.e. tales about the origin of the universe, are the very centre or even the essence of mythology. Take the definition of myth in the recent *Encyclopedia of Religion*:[1] 'A myth is an expression of the sacred in words; it reports realities and events from the origin of the world that remain valid for the basis and purpose of all there is.' 'Origin of the world', in relation to 'all there is': these are the central concepts of cosmogony, which would thus become the general matrix of myth as such. I, for one, would leave the notion 'sacred' out of the definition of myth, and would rather take 'traditional tale' as a starting point: myths are traditional tales with special relevance, traditional tales with a secondary but important reference.[2] For illustration we may refer to collections such as Hesiod's *Theogony* and *Catalogues*, Apollodorus' *Library*, and Ovid's *Metamorphoses*. In these corpora, however, cosmogonical myths make up only a very small section of the whole—for example, only 84 lines out of the 15 books of the *Metamorphoses*. Other topics are far more common: myths about genealogies, migrations, foundations of cities, the establishment of culture, and the origins of rituals, especially initiation and sacrifice. This is a rough enumeration of the themes of myth with regard to the tales' reference, the *signifié*; if we try to make distinctions by the *signifiant*, the tale types, we shall find the great favourite to be the quest, taken as *the* form of narrative by Vladimir Propp and his followers. Its most thrilling variety is the combat tale; in addition, there are tales about sex and progeny, tales of deceit and deception, 'trickster' stories; migration tales too may be a separate type.[3] What is the status of cosmogony

---

[1] Kees W. Bolle, 'Myth: An Overview', in Eliade *et al.* (1987), 261–73, at 261.
[2] Burkert (1979), 1–34.   [3] On tale types, see Burkert (1996), 56–79.

in this context? It is evidently not a tale type in its own right, rather an assemblage of different tale types, complete or fragmentary, held together by the greatest subject, 'everything' or 'all there is', which is itself a problem rather than something definite.

In fact one might doubt whether it is possible to define cosmogony at a general, transcultural level. 'Kosmos' is an artificial concept which we see evolving at the beginning of Greek philosophy.[4] Archaic languages do not usually have a word for 'world'; it remains to enumerate the basic constituents, above all 'heaven and earth',[5] or else 'gods and men', 'gods, men, animals, and plants'. There will still be a concept of 'all', 'everything', 'universe', which we may take to constitute 'cosmology', but we must be aware that this is a logical concept, not mythical intuition. If this is combined with the notion of 'first', of 'beginning', a hybrid of logical postulate and mythical determination takes the lead. Still, cosmogonical myth is not the basis, but rather a problem for myth as such. It is true that there is a psychological approach which makes 'kosmos' a metaphor for the inner world, the self-experience of the individual, and hence makes 'cosmogony' a mirror of psychic development from embryo to adult.[6] This would provide a natural basis and direct source for cosmogonic myth. But this is still not a general theory of myth, rather a very special and selective one.

It is easy to see where the preference for cosmogonic myth, among the many varieties of traditional tales, comes from: it was, first, philosophy which focused on the problem of *archē*, and, later, Christianity which insisted on the one creator god. Plato, in his *Sophist* (242c), refers to his predecessors, whom we call Presocratics, with the words: 'Each of them appears to be telling a myth (*muthos*) to us, as if we were children . . .' (*muthon tina hekastos phainetai moi diēgeisthai paisin hōs ousin hēmin*), and he presents his own cosmology, his *Timaeus*, as a cosmogonic myth, *eikōs muthos* or *logos*. Aristotle, in the famous résumé of *archē*-philosophy given at *Metaphysics* A, mentions 'very old theologians' anticipating the theory of Thales (983[b]27); the reference is

---

[4] On the development of the Greek term κόσμος, see Kerschensteiner (1962).
[5] See Burkert (1992), 91 with n. 8, 93 f.
[6] See Bischof (1996).

to Oceanus and Tethys in Homer.[7] In another famous context, in the argument of *Metaphysics* Λ, Aristotle has Orpheus, who 'generates from Night', and Anaxagoras side by side.[8] Damascius, last head of the Neoplatonic Academy at Athens, includes in his treatise *On Principles* a vast survey of mythical cosmogonies, including Orphic and Phoenician texts and even the Babylonian *Enuma elish*.[9] Pagan defence of myth as against Christian attacks would concentrate on the interpretation of *Timaeus*.[10] In other words, wherever there is interest in myth, it is cosmogonical myth. As philosophy turned Christian, it was a lasting challenge to correlate *Timaeus* to Genesis; the problem grew to unprecedented dimensions with the advance of modern science which made it impossible to accept the literal sense of the Genesis text. But there was also the practical work of Christian missionaries to whom the seminal reports on so-called primitives are due. They found it an easy starting point for preaching Christianity to ask their hearers: Do you know who made this world?—imprinting, as it were, the gospel of the one creator god on the pre-existing conglomerate of native traditions. The *Popol Vuh* of the Quiché Maya was written by a convert, 'amid the preaching of God, in Christendom now', as the introduction says;[11] the *Gylfaginning* in the Prose Edda of Snorri Sturluson begins with the quotation of Genesis 1: 1.[12]

It would be in the post-modern spirit to conclude that cosmogony is a Western–Christian construct. But we may happily state that there are texts which are older and independent of these tendencies. If we leave out, for reasons of competence, the Old Indian texts—which anyhow are farther removed from antiquity—there may be agreement by now that there is a family of texts from the Near East, from Israel, and from Greece which should be considered together, since they are connected not only by similarity of structure and motifs but also, no doubt, by mutual influences; see the chapter of Damascius mentioned already. Classicists had difficulty in realizing the great advances in the

---

[7] Cf. Burkert (1992), 91–3.

[8] Arist. *Metaph.* 1071^{b}27.

[9] Damasc. *Princ.* 123–5 (=i. 316–24 Ruelle), partly deriving from Eudemus, fr. 150 Wehrli.

[10] A basic work is Proclus, *In Timaeum*; cf. Baltes (1976–8).

[11] Tedlock (1985), 71.   [12] Lorenz (1984), 43, 46, 50.

study of antiquity which occurred in the nineteenth century thanks to the decipherment of hieroglyphs and cuneiform, advances which have added to our cultural memory about 2,000 years of recorded history. Gradual change has come with the new discoveries made in the twentieth century, especially with the publication of the Hittite texts *Kingship in Heaven* (1946) and *Ullikummi* (1952). Their closeness to Hesiod was undeniable.[13]

It may be helpful to give a short survey of the relevant texts. The paradigm of oriental cosmogony is represented by the Babylonian text *Enuma elish*.[14] The date of composition has not been established definitely, but seems to lie in the second part of the second millennium; it was well known in the first millennium, when it was recited at the Babylonian New Year festival. There are other comparable Akkadian texts, but also much older Sumerian 'myths of origin'; these, however, usually concern special details, not 'everything', not the universe as such. In Egypt we do not find one representative text, in fact not even narrative texts in the full sense, but rather a system of notions about stages of 'creation', developed in the Old and Middle kingdoms, integrated in priestly theology;[15] how this state of the Egyptian evidence can be reconciled with the general concept of 'myth' is a problem which cannot be discussed here. In Hittite, we have the *Kumarbi* text, *Kingship in Heaven*, which is especially close to Hesiod in the sequence of the ruling gods and in the motif of the castration of 'Heaven'. In addition, there are the much longer, but lacunose, *Ullikummi* text and the *Illuyankash* text, both of which have relations to the Greek Typhoeus myths.[16] Ugaritic myth has generations and conflicts of gods, but not so far cosmogony in the full sense.[17] Phoenician cosmogonies, however, are referred to in various Greek sources, especially in the book of Philon of Byblos.[18] This is not to forget the beginning of our Bible, where, as is well known, cosmogony occurs in double form, Genesis chapters 1 and 2–3. The central Greek text is Hesiod's *Theogony*, but this is not unique; there are cosmogonical

---

[13] Cf. n. 16 below; Burkert (1991), 155–81.

[14] Cuneiform text: Lambert and Parker (1967). Translations: Heidel (1951), 18–60; Bottéro and Kramer (1989), 604–53; Dalley (1989), 233–77.

[15] Cf. Sauneron and Yoyotte (1959); Assmann (1977); Bickel (1994).

[16] *ANET* 120f., 121–5, 125f.; Hoffner and Beckman (1991), 40–3, 52–61, 10–14.

[17] See de Moor (1987); cf. n. 59 below.

[18] *FGrHist* 790; Baumgarten (1981); cf. West (1994).

allusions in the *Iliad*, especially in the context of the 'Deception of Zeus' (book 14),[19] and there are fragments of various parallel or competing texts, beginning with an epic *Titanomachia*.[20] Important details have become known from the theogony of Orpheus, in particular, through the Derveni papyrus.[21] In addition, the varying statements about the 'beginning' by the so-called Presocratic philosophers largely belong still to the same family.

All cosmogonic texts use the form of narrative in a naïve matter-of-fact way: these are typical 'just-so stories'—a term playfully introduced by Rudyard Kipling for children's stories and turned into a term of scorn for anthropologists by Evans-Pritchard.[22] The basic form is just a statement of sequence: 'In the beginning there was . . . then came . . . and then'—just so. Even the Presocratics did not disdain this form: 'Together were all the things,' Anaxagoras began, and then *Nous* began to move.[23] 'The earth was without form and void,' Genesis relates; . . . 'And God said: "Let there be light."' (1: 2–3). It is this form of narrative which makes cosmogony a myth—as stated already by Plato in the above-mentioned passage of the *Sophist*.

A speculative achievement still lingers in the concept of 'first', of 'beginning'. This is not the normal beginning of a tale, which is, 'Once upon a time, there was'. In Greek, this is *ēn pote* or *ēn chronos*;[24] in Akkadian, a tale just begins with 'When . . .'.[25] Thus the normal tale creates its own time; myth usually takes what has happened once as a model for what is now. Beyond this, in a more pointed way, cosmogony insists on a time which was the 'first' of all, the one beginning from which everything else is about to rise. 'In the beginning', *bereshit*, is the first word of the Bible; using the same word root, *Enuma elish* calls Apsu, the

[19] See Burkert (1992), 91–3.
[20] Davies (1988), 16–20.
[21] *ZPE* 47 (1982), appendix; West (1983).
[22] Evans-Pritchard (1965), 42, referring to Freud's *Totem and Taboo*; R. Kipling, *Just-So Stories for Little Children* (London, first pub. 1902).
[23] Anaxag. B 1 DK.
[24] Attested in Critias, *TrGF* 43 F 19, 1; Pl. *Prt.* 320c; Moschion, *TrGF* 97 F 6, 3; cf. *Amor and Psyche*, Apuleius, *Met.* 4. 28. 1; compare German 'es war einmal'.
[25] *Enuma elish* means 'when above'; same beginning in *Atrahasis*—and in Hammurapi's *Laws*, too. *Gilgamesh and Huwawa* (D. O. Edzard, 'Gilgameš und Huwawa A', *Zeitschrift für Assyriologie*, 80 (1990), 165–203, and 81 (1991), 165–233) starts: 'Do you know, how . . .'

watery Deep, 'the first one', *reshtu*;[26] later, the Presocratics spoke of *archē*, and changed the meaning of the word in the process, from 'beginning' to 'principle'.[27] Hesiod asks, 'Which of these came into being first?' and then starts: 'First of all . . .'[28] A dialectic of 'one' and 'many' is thus implicit from the start; but this is not at all made explicit in every exemplar of the family.

Further achievements of speculation are reversal and antithesis, a basic logical function. If you start to tell the tale about 'the beginning' of 'everything', you must first delete 'everything' from your mental view, i.e. our whole world of heaven and earth, sea and mountains, plants, animals, and humans: all this has to go. Thus the typical beginning of cosmogonic myth is performed by subtraction: there is a great and resounding 'Not Yet'. *Enuma elish* begins: 'When above skies were not named, nor earth below pronounced by name . . . (when nobody) had formed pastures nor discovered reed-beds, when no gods were manifest, nor names pronounced, nor destinies decreed . . .'[29] An Egyptian Pyramid Text says: 'When heaven had not yet been constructed, when earth had not yet come into being, when nothing yet had been constructed . . .'[30]—what was there then? 'Darkness brooding over the face of the abyss', the Bible tells us; or a yawning gap, *chaos*, as Hesiod has it; Night, the theogony of Orpheus said; the Infinite, Anaximander seems to have written. 'Together were all the things', we read in Anaxagoras (B 1 DK). An alternative answer is: there was god—as we read in Egypt.

The most common response, though, is: in the beginning there was Water. This is not limited to the ancient world: it is also reported from America, e.g. the *Popol Vuh* of the Quiché Maya.[31] The Egyptians developed water-cosmogonies in diverse variants, having the yearly flood of the Nile before their eyes; but *Enuma elish* too has ground water and salt water, Apsu the begetter and Tiamat who bore them all, as the first parents of everything. Surprisingly enough, this recurs in the midst of Homer's *Iliad* with Oceanus and Tethys, 'begetting of everything'; this may be direct influence. (It was William Ewart Gladstone, better known

---

[26] *Enuma elish* I 3 (Dalley (1989), 233).   [27] Lumpe (1955).

[28] Hes. *Th.* 115 f.

[29] *Enuma elish* I 1–8 (Dalley (1989), 233).

[30] Pyramid Text 1040 a–d, cf. 1466 b–d, Sauneron and Yoyotte (1959), 46.

[31] Tedlock (1985), 64.

as British Prime Minister, who first saw this connection.)[32] The Bible has the spirit of God hovering on the waters, and Thales, the *archēgetēs of archē*-philosophy according to Aristotle,[33] posited water as his first principle.

The primeval role of water has attracted the theories of psychologists who try to translate myth into their own systems of interpretation. The more realistic variants recall the embryo floating in uterine water; Jungians find worlds emerging from 'the Unconscious' *tout court*; others try to imagine the newborn's world as an indistinct 'oceanic' whole in which 'everything' is diluted and merging, to take shape later.[34] I find it difficult to verify any of these interpretations. In the whole family of cosmogonic myths, 'water' appears to be just one option among others. 'Night' should be granted equal status, with parallel opportunities for interpretation—be it uterine night, or the Unconscious; combinations of the two will do just as well: 'darkness' and 'water', as they appear in Genesis. The 'yawning gap' of Hesiod does not fit so well, nor the Egyptian 'god'. At any rate, each of these formulas appears already embedded in a contextual system which is spelt out linguistically in the respective texts. Neither 'the Unconscious' nor 'oceanic feelings' produce texts by themselves. But they may be factors favouring the selection and conservation of particular versions amidst a richer palette of possibilities.

Togetherness is bound to dissolve: differentiation must come out of the one beginning. Every cosmogonical tale is bound to proceed on these lines. The most grandiose idea is that heaven was lifted from earth at a secondary stage of creation, that the world *qua* 'heaven and earth' came into being by splitting apart. Even this idea is not a speciality of the ancient world: parallels have been adduced from Africa, Polynesia, and Japan.[35] The Hittites and Hesiod have the violent myth of the castration of Heaven. There are even two versions in Hittite: according to the *Ullikummi* text, it was done with an 'ancient bronze knife', whereas *Kingship in Heaven* introduces the much more primitive proceedings of castration by biting and

---

[32] Burkert (1992), 93 with n. 14.

[33] Thal. A 12 DK = Arist. *Metaph.* 983^{b}20. Cf. Hölscher (1953), revised and expanded in Hölscher (1968), 9–89.

[34] See Bischof (1996).   [35] Staudacher (1942).

swallowing.[36] Egyptians, though, have quite a peaceful development, as Shu, 'Air', lifts up the goddess of heaven, Nut, from
earth, Geb.[37] According to Anaximander, a sphere of fire grew
around the centre, which was apparently a form of slime; the
sphere then burst into pieces, which formed into wheels, carrying
openings of flames around the earth. This is still the separation of
heaven and earth, which also lingers on in the atomistic cosmogony of Leucippus.[38]

In Hesiod—but not in the Hittite version—the castration of
Heaven is made an act in a family drama: Cronos, son of
Ouranos, rebels against the oppressive sexual power of his father,
helped by his mother Gaia, Earth. It has been said that this is the
gist of Oedipal wish-fulfilment;[39] we are back to interpretations
on the basis of developmental psychology: separation of father
and mother, discovery of the sex differentiation, the Oedipal
phase which means the end of indistinct 'oceanic' experience.
But it is difficult to impose this interpretation on all the variants
of heaven–earth separation. Note that heaven is female in Egypt;
and there is no trace of father–son antagonism in the oldest text,
the Hittite *Kingship in Heaven*, where no family relationship is
stated between Alalu, Anu, and Kumarbi, who are kings in
heaven in this sequence. Note also the reference to cultural
evolution in Hesiod—Earth produces iron; and to ritual—Cronos
throws the severed parts behind his back in Hesiod's text; this
does not come from developmental psychology. There are other
myths which seem to insist on a 'Freudian' perspective, imple-
menting Oedipal motifs, especially one strange Akkadian text,
now called the *Theogony of Dunnu*.[40] Into a primeval sequence of
gods or powers this text routinely introduces father-killing and
mother–son incest: 'The Cattle-god married Earth his mother,
and killed Plough his father . . .' and so on. The motif is repeated
about five times; this is beyond developmental psychology.

For further developments in cosmogony, there are two narrative options, two models: one might be called biomorphic, the
other technomorphic. The biomorphic model introduces couples

[36] *Ullikummi*: ANET 125; Hoffner and Beckman (1991), 59. *Kumarbi*: ANET 120;
Hoffner and Beckman (1991), 40; cf. West (1966), 20–2; 211–13.
[37] Sauneron and Yoyotte (1959), 47 § 9.
[38] Anaximand. A 10 DK; Leucipp. A 1 § 32 DK.
[39] Hes. *Th.* 154–81; Dodds (1951), 61.
[40] ANET 517f.; Dalley (1989), 277–81.

of different sex, insemination, and birth; the technomorphic model presents a creator in the role of the clever craftsman. The first one follows the model of genealogical myth; the second means description rather than tale.

It is tempting to call the biomorphic model the Greek one, the technomorphic model the biblical one. It is true that Hesiod has fully opted for the biomorphic version, whereas Genesis is the 'book of creation': 'And God made . . .' and he carves Eve from a rib. Things are more complicated none the less: the second chapter of Genesis (2: 4) introduces the title *toledoth*, which means 'actions of birth', whereas Hesiod does resort to the technical process when Pandora the woman is fashioned.

Creation is in fact more rational, giving the author an opportunity to present objects in detail; description takes over, as against a dramatic tale. Listen to *Enuma elish*: Marduk

made the crescent of the moon appear, entrusted night to it . . . 'Go forth every month without fail in a corona, at the beginning of the month, to glow over the land; you shine with horns to mark out six days; on the seventh day the crown is half. The fifteenth day shall always be the mid-point, the half of each month. When Shamash looks at you from the horizon, gradually shed your visibility and begin to wane . . .'[41]

The Old Testament is much more cursory: Elohim 'made the two great lights, the greater to govern the day and the lesser to govern the night, and with them he made the stars.'[42] Least precise is Hesiod: 'Theia gave birth to great Helios and resplendent Selene, and also to Eos who shines for all on earth, overcome in love by Hyperion; . . . and Eos, mated to Astraios, . . . gave birth to the Morning Star, and to the brilliant stars.'[43] Nobody would say Hesiod is more rational than the orientals; he just gives names to the concepts of 'divine'—Theia—and 'walking above', Hyperion; he is absolutely unsystematic in separating the Morning Star from the other stars, and it is just tautology to make Astraios father of the stars. What can be expressed in both models is the feeling of 'wonder' at the complicated beauty of the cosmos: Marduk 'created marvels' according to *Enuma elish*; Elohim, looking at his creation, found that 'everything was very

[41] *Enuma elish* IV/V (Dalley (1989), 254 ff.).
[42] Gen. 1: 16.   [43] Hes. *Th.* 371–82.

good' (Gen. 1: 31). Hesiod introduces Thaumas, bearing 'wonder' in his name, as father of Iris, the rainbow (*Th.* 265). If philosophy arises from *thaumazein*, as Aristotle holds, its roots are present in cosmogonic myth, though less in Hesiod than at Babylon.

There are also combinations of both models, of procreation and creation. This is characteristic of *Enuma elish*, and also of the Orphic cosmogony as known from the Derveni papyrus. In *Enuma elish*, we first get a sequence of generations, with a palace being built above the watery deep in the third generation, and storms arising to disturb the olden Sea with Marduk, the young god of the fourth generation; later, after slaying Tiamat, 'the Sea', Marduk builds our world in all its wonderful details, 'creating marvels'. In the Orphic cosmogony, we learn about Night and Aither first, and the deed of Cronos, castration and separation of Heaven from Earth. Later Zeus, who has become 'the only one', is seen to create everything from himself, to fashion the world with Oceanus, Rivers, Moon, and Stars through powerful 'planning'; *emēsato* ('planned', 'devised') is the interesting term.[44] Thus in both texts *genesis* dominates the first part, and technical construction the second. Evidently this means a kind of progress: the sequence could not be reversed. I would not insist on direct dependence, but rather on the availability of both models, and their essential difference.

The concept of 'creator of the world' is explicitly rejected by Heraclitus: 'This world order . . . no one of gods or men has made'; he evidently presupposes the concept he is rejecting.[45] The statement that Zeus 'created' cosmic arrangements is common in Archaic Greece, usually expressed by the root *the-*: 'He created three seasons'—Alcman (20, 1 *PMG*); he created honey—Xenophanes (B 38 DK). Thus *the-* even becomes the foundation of an etymology of *theos*, as in Herodotus (2. 52. 1). Heraclitus, for one, seems to develop the 'biomorphic' model into a 'phytomorphic' model, the principle of growing according to inner laws, as plants do; this is *phusis*, which likes to hide (*phusis kruptesthai philei*, B 123 DK). And yet hardly any of Heraclitus' successors can do without the concept of creator: Parmenides

---

[44] Pap. Derveni (n. 21 above) col. 19 [new numeration: 23].
[45] Heraclit. B 30 DK.

introduces a female *daimōn* who 'governs everything', and creates divine powers such as Eros;[46] Anaxagoras gives a similar function to *Nous*, 'Mind', the leading power for all differentiation; Empedocles has 'Love' constructing organs and organisms in her workshop; it was only Democritus who, criticizing Anaxagoras,[47] tried to exclude 'mind' from the shaping of macrocosm and microcosm. The reaction came with Plato and Aristotle: Plato's *Timaeus* finally established the term 'creator', *dēmiourgos*.

The rival option, *genesis* in the biomorphic model, leads to a sequence of genealogies. It thus mirrors a form of tradition which is of basic importance in quite different societies for constituting identity and rank through memory, with all the opportunities for continuity and conflict as known from history. There are 'histories' of families and tribes, usually a mixture of name lists and memorable events, which normally concern certain claims in the very real world and preserve continuity by recalling past conflicts.

In cosmogony, the sequence of generations takes a more compact form with the so-called 'succession myth'. This has three or four generations of gods, and ends with the establishment of the lasting power of the ruling god, in contrast to 'ancient gods', who thus become 'fettered gods'. The succession myth is evidenced from *Enuma elish*, from the Hittite text *Kingship in Heaven*, from Phoenician myth as transmitted by Philon of Byblos, and finally by Hesiod and Orpheus.[48] There is no doubt that these versions are related to each other, developing as they do in adjacent cultures with many interconnections; there must have been intermediate versions which are lost to us. Characteristic is the role of 'Heaven' as a predecessor of the ruling god, and a problematic or even mischievous god in between. In the Hittite text Kumarbi swallows the phallus of Anu, 'Heaven', and becomes pregnant with rivers and the Weather-god; in the cosmogony of Orpheus, according to the Derveni text, it is Zeus who swallows a phallus, probably the phallus of Ouranos, 'Heaven', and becomes fertile in consequence, with gods, rivers, and everything else;[49] in the later Orphic version Zeus swallows Phanes, an enigmatic first and

---

[46] Parm. B 12/13 DK.   [47] Democr. A 1 DK = Diog. Laert. 9. 35.
[48] Steiner (1959).
[49] Pap. Derveni col. 9 [13] and 12 [16]; contradicted by West (1983: 85 f.), who combines δαίμονα κυδρόν col. 4 [8], 2 with αἰδοῖον col. 9 [13], 4; this is against the Derveni author's interpretation not only of αἰδοῖον, but also of δαίμονα κυδρόν, which he connects with ἐγ χείρεσσι λαβών twice in his paraphrase, col. 5 [9] 4; 10. See also W.

universal god, and produces 'everything' out of his belly.[50] The interpretation of the Derveni text has been called into question by Martin West and others; the very similarity to the Hittite version may seem suspicious; but it is the Derveni author himself, not the modern interpreter, who understands the mythical events in this way, and I trust he had the integral text before his eyes. If this is accepted, we are dealing with a model case of both continuity and change in the transmission of myth, both across cultural barriers and through long periods of time. There is transmission even of single motifs, but there is also reinterpretation and change, important modifications going on still within the Greek 'Orphic' tradition.

Within the theme of genealogies, a more general, nay a favourite tale type invades cosmogonic myth, beyond the problems of castration: the combat tale.[51] The combat tale needs a champion and an antagonist. The antagonist must be both imposing and disagreeable to provide the foil for the champion's triumph—and the hearer's identification with him. The ideal impersonation of the negative role is the snake, the dragon, feared and hated, devouring and poisoning, to be unfailingly overcome by the hero. Thus the god fighting the dragon gets an important part within cosmogonic myth.

The theme of the dragon fight seems to be present in Sumerian mythology by the middle of the third millennium, with the special image of the seven-headed snake being slain by the champion; but we have only the images, no text from this period.[52] Later there is an Akkadian myth about a gigantic snake threatening humanity, to be overcome by gods; yet the text is still hopelessly fragmentary.[53] The seven-headed snake reappears in Ugaritic myth, with Baal slaying Lotan the serpent of seven heads, a text which has left its trace even in the Old Testament, with Jahwe slaying Leviathan, even if the seven heads have been eliminated there.[54] In Hittite there is the battle of the Storm-god

Burkert, 'Oriental and Greek Mythology: The Meeting of Parallels', in Bremmer (1987), 10–40, at 22 with n. 57.

[50] Kern (1922), fr. 168.   [51] Cf. Burkert (1979), 18–20.

[52] Burkert in Bremmer (1987), 18 with n. 35.

[53] Bottéro and Kramer (1989), no. 27.

[54] *ANET* 138, de Moor (1987), 69; Isaiah 27: 1; Burkert in Bremmer (1987), 18. From the Indo-European side, see Watkins (1995).

with the dragon Illuyankas, in close relation to a special festival called Purulli; this myth in turn seems to have influenced or even created the Greek myth of Zeus fighting Typhon the snake-monster in Cilicia, a myth of which there are several variants, more or less Hittitizing.[55] A comparatively late seal from Mesopotamia offers the most impressive example of a god fighting the cosmic monster—one head only, in this case.[56] Later still is Pherecydes, who has Cronos pressing Ophioneus the Dragon into the ocean, Ogenos.[57]

Yet scholars must beware of the *fable convenue*. It has been common to speak of 'the dragon of chaos', *Chaosdrache*, since Hermann Gunkel's book *Schöpfung und Chaos*.[58] The god slaying the dragon would thus strive to eliminate chaos and to establish the world as a place of order, a 'kosmos'. It is largely correct, of course, to say that the snake represents the 'below', the 'chthonic' aspect as against the heavenly splendour of the god. Snakes are also constantly associated with water. The great event in *Enuma elish* is Marduk slaying Tiamat, 'the Sea', as Ugaritic Baal too fights Yam, 'the Sea'.[59] Yet it is not at all clear that Tiamat, Marduk's antagonist, should be imagined in the form of a snake or 'dragon', although there are monsters with snake characteristics in her retinue. Yet the original water snakes mentioned in the first lines of *Enuma elish*, Lahmu and Lahamu, are not molested at all by Marduk. The Babylonian seal mentioned above most probably depicts a cosmic struggle, since the six dots in the picture seem to allude to constellations; as a matter of curiosity it may be noted that the picture was reused in Greece to depict Perseus and Andromeda fighting the *kētos* (sea monster) with stones.[60] But even Leviathan in Hebrew tradition is not *expressis verbis* a *Chaosdrache*; he may even be an edible fish.[61] The Hittite story of

---

[55] Cf. Burkert (1979), 7–9; *ANET* 125f., Hoffner and Beckman (1991), 10–14; Apollod. *Bibl.* 1. 6. 3; Nonnus 1. 154–2. 29. These texts have elements in common with the Hittite version that are missing in Hesiod; the same situation seems to obtain in relation to the phallus motif, n. 49 above. See also Hansen (1995).

[56] Burkert in Bremmer (1987), fig. 2. 7, with n. 79; reproduced also in West (1971), pl. II a.

[57] Pherecyd. 7 B 4 DK; cf. Schibli (1990).

[58] Gunkel (1895). Note that the very word 'dragon' was established through Revelation 12 f.; 20: 2.

[59] See *Baal* III in de Moor (1987), 29–44; cf. *ANET* 130 f.

[60] Burkert in Bremmer (1987), fig. 2.7/2.8.

[61] Syriac *Apocalypsis of Baruch* 29: 4; Kautzsch (1900), 423.

Illuyankas is not set in a cosmic context, although it presents an interruption and grievous threat to the supreme god's rule, and ends with the god's reinstallation. The same is true of the Greek Typhoeus story—leaving aside the problem of whether it originally belonged to Hesiod's *Theogony*.[62] It is a sequel, not an integral part of the cosmogony proper. In short, not every cosmogony needs a dragon fight, nor does every dragon represent the original chaos. In Egypt, the aboriginal combat tale is the fight of Horus against Seth;[63] Seth may well be said to stand for chaos, but he never becomes a snake. In other words, the speculative energy of cosmogony and the narrative energy of the combat tale are not identical; they may meet but also separate again.

We spoke of two options: creation on the one side, procreation leading to generations in conflict on the other. It must be added that there is a strange meeting of both narrative lines in the idea of creation by killing. To repeat *Enuma elish*: 'The Lord rested and inspected her corpse: he divided the monstrous shape and created marvels . . .'[64] It is from mortification, from the corpse, that the new and stable structure takes its beginning. It is killing that transforms a living and potentially dangerous partner into objective material, to be used for construction. The Vedic myth about Purusha, the 'Man' who is sacrificed and cut up to form the cosmos, and the tale of Ymir in the Snorra Edda, the giant out of whom the universe is made, have long been compared.[65]

Creation by killing is especially prominent, and troubling, in anthropogony. In *Atrahasis*, *Enuma elish*, and other Akkadian texts, in order to create humans from clay a god has to be killed, 'that the god's blood be thoroughly mixed with the clay'.[66] Life comes from killing. Less drastic is Adam's narcosis when Eve is carved from his rib; yet it still means cutting up a living body. Orpheus once more seems to be especially close to the oriental parallels, if the myth about the origin of men out of the Titans,

---

[62] Hes. *Th.* 820–80, still athetized by F. Solmsen (Oxford text, 1970; 3rd edn. 1990); cf. the discussion in West (1966), 379–83.

[63] Griffiths (1960); te Velde (1967).

[64] *Enuma elish* IV 135f. (Dalley (1989), 254f.).

[65] Olerud (1951).

[66] *Atrahasis* I 208–17; Dalley (1989), 15. The interpretation of the passage is controversial; see Chiodi (1994).

killed and burnt by Zeus after they have killed and eaten Dionysus, is accepted as an old tradition; I am still inclined to take it as such, in spite of the recent article by Luc Brisson.[67] Myths of this form remain puzzling; there is no simple tale pattern to account for them, and definitely not the sequence of individual psychological development, but rather uneasiness and feelings of conflict in view of the *condition humaine*, making use of cultural patterns such as magic or sacrificial ritual in order to deal with such uneasiness.

At any rate, the appearance of man must be the final and decisive part of any cosmogony told by humans. It is a strange omission in Hesiod that anthropogony is missing, although it seems to be announced.[68] There were various possibilities to account for the creation of man, even if one was not content with the simple statement 'and god made', or 'Zeus made . . .', as Hesiod was in the myth of the Races. Once more it is impossible to assume one basic form: there is no *single* myth of anthropogony, but a large variety illustrating this or that aspect, problem, or interest in the human situation.[69]

So what finally is the message contained in cosmogonic myth? What is the *raison d'être* of this strange assemblage of motifs and micro-myths along the thread of a comprehensive just-so tale? It is difficult to say what the *Sitz im Leben* of Hesiod's *Theogony* was; the question is no more simple for, say, the book of Anaximander.

The answer is clearer if we keep to the Eastern paradigm, *Enuma elish*. In this poem the *skopos* evidently is the success and the power of Marduk, the supreme god of Babylon. The whole of the last tablet is filled with Marduk's inauguration, with fifty names proclaimed for him on the occasion: this is the creation of a cosmos of meaningful names, the authoritative *Sprachregelung* for a world in which a *zōon logikon* will have to dwell. Practically all

---

[67] Olymp. *in Phd.* I. 3, p. 41 Westerink = Kern (1922), fr. 220, cf. Xenocr. fr. 219 Isnardi Parente = Damasc. *in Phd.* I. 2, p. 29 Westerink; Burkert (1985), 298; Brisson (1992/1995) argues for a late alchemical context for the famous passage in Olympiodorus. But while he cannot explain (484 n. 13) why this text has 'four monarchies', as against six in the Orphic *Rhapsodies*, this very detail agrees with the Derveni theogony. This is an argument in favour of the point that Olympiodorus is preserving an old tradition; note also the reference to Xenocrates in Damascius.

[68] Hes. *Th.* 50; cf. *WD* 108 as another misleading announcement.

[69] See Luginbühl (1992).

the names celebrate power and supremacy. Cosmogony ends in
the installation of religious hierarchy which gives legitimation also
to earthly power. Thus *Enuma elish* is incorporated in the New
Year's festival at Babylon, a complicated ritual[70] during which the
king is deposed and dishonoured to be reinstalled again in all his
splendour, in order to rebuild and to maintain the just and sacred
order, including all the privileges of the god, the temple and the
priests, and the city.

A parallel function of parallel texts is to accompany the re-
building or merely the repair of a temple.[71] Start from the great
'Not Yet', the Flood, tell how fixed soil was produced, and
mountains, and stones, and various gods, and humanity to serve
the gods, and you have the context and the *raison d'être* of the
temple which is to be established with toil, great expense, and
permanent obligations.

There is still a further parallel function and use of cosmogony:
healing magic. Sickness means that something has gone fundamentally wrong with the afflicted person; to recover, one should
get at the 'root' of the evil. The most radical strategy is to begin
with the beginning of everything. Thus in Akkadian we find
cosmogonical texts used against sickness even of a rather banal
sort, a headache or a toothache. But also the creation of mankind
as told in *Atrahasis* can be used as a magical charm to help at
childbirth, and the tale in the same text of how drought was
overcome may become a rain-making charm.[72]

By contrast, we do not know of any ritual context for most
of the other texts, including Hesiod's *Theogony*. As to the
Orphic theogony, a different use comes into view, parallel to the
last Akkadian example: Plato describes the mendicant priests
who are offering 'release' from evil, both in this world and
after death, through ritual, and they do this with reference to
writings of Orpheus and his like.[73] Release from evil requires
a search for the origin of evil; thus it makes sense to start
with the origin of everything. Such tendencies or applications
are not even fully overcome with the books of Presocratics
—look at the promises of Empedocles' *Peri phuseōs* (*On

[70] See *ANET* 331–4.
[71] Bottéro and Kramer (1989), nos. 38 and 34, pp. 497 ff., 488 f.
[72] See Burkert (1992), 124 f.
[73] Pl. *Rep.* 364b–366a = Kern (1922), fr. 3.

Nature).[74] Even Plato plays with the function of Socratic *logoi* as a kind of healing magic, in *Charmides*.[75]

If, on the other hand, *Enuma elish* tends to reinstall the power of god and king, in Hesiod, too, kingship looms large. If Zeus is made king finally, in fact the 'first' king that ever was (*Th.* 881–5), kings have still been mentioned much earlier, real 'kings', apparently, who decide about other people's fate and status, whatever their exact powers and privileges were. In Hesiod's poem these kings are intimately related to Zeus—they are *diotrephees*, 'nourished by Zeus' (82); besides them, there are the Muses, daughters of Zeus. They are the singer's patrons, and it is they who guarantee prosperous relations between kings and singers (*Th.* 80 ff.), thanks to the medium of song, which at this moment manifests itself as theogony. In other words, Hesiod is very much creating his own world, the world of Zeus and Themis, of kings and Muses, and, in displaying his universal knowledge, secures his own position. The message has its aim and social context. The wonderful order of the world is the foil for the distribution of power and knowledge within society.

Through the consciousness of poets, another function seems to evolve: the wise man, the ideal singer, should know 'everything', 'what was, what is, what shall be'—this makes up the Muses' song for Hesiod,[76] including of course the 'beginning of everything'. As the opportunities offered by written records are recognized, a momentous transformation is bound to occur: the 'beginning' of everything, and the continuation through the unfolding of the world and the spreading of men, should follow each other as parts of one comprehensive book. The first example we have of such a written record is precisely Hesiod's *Theogony* plus *Catalogues*, even if the question of the original form of the latter work is unanswerable; the version of the *Catalogues* current in later antiquity cannot come from about 700 BCE, but only from the sixth century, although these may be modernizations of an original Hesiodic scheme.[77] The agglomerate called the Epic Cycle had a *Titanomachia* for its beginning (see note 20); among the early prose writers, Acusilaus had a theogony introducing his

---

[74] Emp. B 111 DK; cf. the beginning of *Katharmoi* B 112.

[75] Pl. *Charm.* 155b–157c.

[76] Hes. *Th.* 38 (cf. 32).   [77] See West (1985).

mythical genealogies.[78] About contemporary, for all we know, is the Book of Genesis, leading from the 'beginning' to the death of Jacob and Joseph. The great difference is that Genesis became a sacred book, whereas the Greeks kept rewriting their 'introduction to everything' incessantly.

We should note yet another function of cosmogonic myth, especially in the form of the succession myth: starting from the great 'Not Yet', myth presents alternatives to the existing order which is confirmed, or rather petrified, by the installation of the ruling god. This need not be so: it was indeed otherwise once upon a time. Cosmogonic myth tends to denigrate the alternatives, introducing a problematic predecessor, primitive, crooked-minded, one among other unsuccessful, vanquished, and fettered gods in the deep below. Still, in the midst of praise of the established power, there remains the message that this has not always been so and hence does not need to remain so for ever; 'fettered gods' may be approached and used for certain goals; and it is imaginable that they could rise again. Even utopian alternatives may take their origin from there: crooked-minded Cronos has been released to rule the 'Islands of the Blest'; excellent men may hope to arrive there, definitively leaving the reign of Zeus.

So much has become clear: there is *logos* in cosmogonic myth from the start,[79] so that no simple change or progress 'from *muthos* to *logos*' is to be observed. The so-called Presocratics were still embedded in the older traditions and were using them, at least as a kind of 'scaffolding';[80] their constructs were helped, though sometimes also somewhat twisted, by this pre-existing scaffolding. And yet there was a unique development that brought about Greek philosophy and science, something which arose nowhere else and at no other time in just this form, but which has been kept alive until the present day by an uninterrupted tradition of books and of 'schools' reading and discussing these very books.

For explanation, it hardly helps to appeal to a very special endowment of the 'Greek Mind'. One might rather recall the

[78] Acus. *FGrHist* 2.
[79] It has been observed recently that Assyrian scholars were themselves progressing on the way to a more rational world picture; see Livingstone (1986); Burkert (1994).
[80] For this metaphor see Burkert (1963), 131 f.

different situation of the intellectual elite in the Near East, where the tradition of 'wisdom' and of literacy was linked to the temples with their 'house of tablets', under the supervision of a great king. In Greece, temples were not economically independent units to feed a priesthood, and monarchy was soon abolished, whereas alphabetic writing is so easy to learn that no class of distinction would emerge from elementary school. If there was to be a new elite of intellectuals, they had to invent new rules of the game.[81]

Let us take a brief look at Parmenides. With him a special form of proof, of conscious argumentation, comes to the fore. His famous paradox—the thesis that Being is, Not-Being is not, and hence there can be neither coming-to-be nor passing-away, neither birth nor death—can be seen to grow directly out of the verbal system of the Greek language. Greek has a marked contrast of aspects: the durative, expressed for instance by es- ('it is'), and the punctual, expressed e.g. by phu- or gen-. Ei gar egent', ouk estin ('if it came into being, it is not'), Parmenides wrote,[82] as if doing an exercise in Greek grammar. But the really strange and surprising fact is that with this formula and its consequences Parmenides was hitting at a principle which even now dominates our physical world view—the laws of conservation, conservation of the duality of mass and energy, as we put it today. Nothing can come from just nothing, and nothing can simply disappear—hence our modern problems with all kinds of refuse which cannot be annihilated. Speaking Greek, Parmenides proved to be right. We find at this crucial point, with Parmenides and his followers, a passion for unequivocal statements, for 'plain truth' in a context of argumentation; and we can state the remarkable success of this style of logos in consequence, both with regard to describing and analysing physical reality, such as phases of the moon and eclipses, and with regard to peithō ('persuasion') within a more and more changeable and competitive society.[83] In a parallel development, mathematics took the decisive step towards its definite 'Greek' form, the axiomatic-deductive system of geometry.[84]

[81] As to the writing system, the western Semites would have had the same opportunities; these were destroyed by the Assyrian, Babylonian, and Persian conquests. If Israel preserved its identity, this could only be done by clinging to a sacred Scripture. This meant literacy without the chances of freedom.

[82] Parm. B 8, 20 DK.   [83] Cf. G. E. R. Lloyd (1979).

[84] See van der Waerden (1961). Qualifications in Waschkies (1989), esp. 302–26.

This may be just one hint at the 'Greek miracle' which was to dominate our tradition. At any rate this style of *logos* was to outgrow just-so stories—which are still dear to our mind. What was lost in the process was the charming simplicity of those earlier essays which had started from wonder, proceeded through tales, and ended with the message that 'everything is very good'. By now we are left to ourselves within a highly complicated cosmos which allows neither tale nor picture for description, but only the most abstract mathematics, with a Big Bang as its first beginning and possibly a Black Hole as its final singularity.

5

Myth, Memory, and the Chorus: 'Tragic Rationality'

JOHN GOULD

DESPITE my title this paper is not a reply to Moses Finley's classic paper of 1965.[1] My concern here is with the deployment of myth in Greek tragedy: that is, with an aspect of the fictionality of tragic theatre. I shall use the deployment of myth in tragedy, and its variable use by both chorus and heroic characters, to try to illuminate the distinction between 'myth' and '*logos*' which is the starting point and focus of all our discussions in this volume.

I shall be using 'myth' here to mean a traditional story, and by 'traditional' I mean (*a*) a story not thought of as the creation of some (potentially) nameable or datable individual; (*b*) the possession not of any individual or (solely) of any family but a collective possession shared by a whole community, where 'community' may cover anything from a single city, town, or village to the entire Greek cultural world, from the Black Sea to the far West. In putting forward this working definition I am, of course, excluding much of what is often (I would say loosely) referred to as 'myth' (let alone 'the mythical'), but the distinction is essential to the argument of the paper, and may moreover be helpful towards formulating more precisely the distinction between 'myth' and '*logos*'.

I shall also make one further assumption, one for which I have argued at length elsewhere,[2] namely, that the tragic chorus does not present a specifically 'rational' critique of traditional stories or values nor does it represent any specifically 'democratic' ideology, and hence that we are not to look to it for the locus of '*logos*' within the dramatic world of the play, as against 'myth' or 'the mythical' as represented by the actions and language of the heroic

[1] Finley (1965).
[2] See my paper 'Tragedy and Collective Experience', in Silk (1996), 217–43, esp. 218–21.

characters. On the other hand, I shall also try to show that the converse is not (simply) true either. Among other things, I shall be interested in the way in which the remembered past becomes 'myth' in the sense that I have suggested, and above all in the 'rationality' of myth, that is, the way in which myth is deployed to reinforce or support reasoned (and yet often conflicting) interpretations of human experience. That will in turn lead me to a consideration of the relationship between myth and *gnōmē* ('general maxim'), in which I shall try to show how closely (and significantly) complementary that relationship is. I shall leave the specific problems presented by the concept of '*logos*' until the end.

My first point is to make a necessary distinction between two different perspectives of 'myth' in Greek tragedy: that of the modern reader or ancient audience, on the one hand, and that of the characters (and here I include the chorus) within the dramatic fiction, on the other. For us, the audience/readers, the Messenger speeches of Euripides' *Bacchae*, for example, are part, an indispensable part, of 'the myth' of Dionysus. But for the characters of the play they are not. Rather they present not remembered but present experience; they are eyewitness accounts of events just now enacted, and hence not 'myth' as I have defined it. So too with Apollo's rape of Creusa in Euripides' *Ion*, which is clearly not 'myth' for Creusa, though for us, the audience, it is. The rape is no less 'exotic' and strange than the myths which define the past of Athens for the characters of the play, but for Creusa it belongs in another register, the 'reality' of personal experience. The shock of the incursion of that reality into the world of the play is a high point in the emotional trajectory of *Ion*.[3]

Both of these perspectives are, of course, within the 'narrative' control of the playwright.[4] So for the audience the mythical perspectives of, say, *Prometheus Bound* (set within the 'Hesiodic'

---

[3] For another example of the distinction between eyewitness account and 'mythical' story within the tragic fiction, see Euripides' *IA* (49–77), where the story of Helen's marriage to Menelaus and her abduction by Paris is reported as 'fact' by the 'eyewitness', Agamemnon, whereas the 'myth' of the Judgement of Paris is cited (pejoratively?) by him as collective report: *hōs ho muthos anthrōpōn echei* ('as the tale told by men holds', 72). By contrast, the chorus (171–84) treat the Judgement of Paris as fact, whereas they refer the report of the fleet assembled to sail for Troy to their husbands, as 'story' (*enepousi*, 'they say', 173–8).

[4] I have discussed (and defended) the concept of 'dramatic narrativity' in Gould (unpublished), Corbett Lecture, Cambridge, May 1991.

time frame of theogonic myth) and *Ion*
discernibly human perspective of compu⎿
very different. Equally, the depth of the past
the fiction, by the characters of the play m⎿
considerably: the remembered past presented ⎿
Euripides' *Phoenissae*, for example, has, as we ⎾
greater depth than that seemingly possessed by ⎿
Sophocles' *Ajax*.

That brings me to another distinction, not so easil⎞ ⎿nade. In
writing elsewhere of Herodotus[5] I have stressed the difference
between familial memories and stories and those of communities,
a difference which is of obvious importance in a historiographical
context (as Rosalind Thomas has shown[6]). That difference also
exists in the world of Greek tragedy, and the difference there too
may be of considerable importance. But because the heroic families of tragic myth are for the most part rulers of communities the
distinction may be blurred or even at times seem to disappear.
The death of Laius in Sophocles' *King Oedipus*, for example, is an
event in the process of becoming community 'myth': it is constantly referred to, by chorus and characters alike, as a *logos* (here,
as often, with the meaning 'story'), as a *phatis* ('something spoken
of'), or as *epē* ('words', 'tales'), something 'told' or 'heard', an
event seemingly 'long past'.[7] It is not, in the early part of the play,
presented as 'family', as distinct and different from 'community',
memory; yet in the course of the play it becomes tragically
'familial', the stuff of eyewitness narrative, told, within the family,
by Jocasta to Oedipus and by Oedipus to Jocasta, narrative which
differs *toto caelo* from what the community remembers. Thus both
'myth' and 'memory' are shifting notions here, with a variable
perspective within the fictionality of the play.

In *Ajax*, on the other hand, a play dominated by a single-
generation perspective and obsessed with 'familial', that is father/
mother/son/daughter, relationships (above all, that between Ajax,
his half-brother Teucer, and their father, Telamon, but also
involving Tecmessa),[8] there is no community memory, no

---

[5] Gould (1989), 19–24, 28–41.
[6] (1989), e.g. 131–54, 235, 252 ff.
[7] 561: *makroi palaioi te chronoi.*
[8] *Ajax* 134, 183, 204, 433–40, 462–6, 470–2, 505–13, 545–51, 567–70, 624–33, 636–7, 641–5, 762–70, 845–51 (Ajax); 1007–18, 1228–31, 1259–63, 1288–9, 1299–1305 (Teucer); 210, 331, 487, 516–17 (Tecmessa).

...tive past as distinct from that of the family. The chorus has no vision of a past which extends in time in any way beyond that of the family of Ajax or has a wider scope: there is no 'myth' within the play to sustain or contextualize present experience.

Even in *King Oedipus* there are no remembered paradigms, no 'mythical' parallels, sought or found for Oedipus' fate. The past beyond Laius exists, but as empty space: Cadmus is remembered and is indeed constantly referred to,[9] as a point of origin, as ancestor, and as the guarantor of Thebes' antiquity, but he has no story. Instead the experience of Oedipus itself becomes paradigmatic. But it is subsumed not into 'myth' but into *gnōmē* (*iō geneai brotōn* . . . : 1186ff.). Indeed the ambiguous relationship between narrated and presented experience and *gnōmē* here (what is the truth status of 1186ff.?) is at the heart of the play's problematic meaning.

King Oedipus and the role of *gnōmē* in it lead to my third general point: as the depth of the remembered past increases, so myth and *gnōmē* progressively converge. At the vanishing point, where past time recedes to something approaching infinity, they become one, become interchangeable: so the gnomic vision of the first stasimon of Sophocles' *Antigone* (332–83: *polla ta deina* . . . , 'many are the wonders . . .') contains no explicit 'myth', no story of the *prōtos heuretēs* (the 'first discoverer') of human culture, but merges and forms one single vision of human experience with the implicit 'myth' of Prometheus (mastery of language; invention of building and clothing; creation of law and communities) and with the Argo myth (the first ship to master the sea), which are its subtext. So too in the second stasimon of *Antigone*: gnomic reflection on human experience and generic metaphor (the violence of the sea and its power to confound earth and water) is juxtaposed with collective memory, that of the history of the Labdacid house and its destruction. There follow an apostrophe to Zeus and evocation of a timeless past (untiring months, powers unaged by time) and an endless future. The song is completed with further *gnōmē* (621: *kleinon epos*, a 'famous saying'; but the phrase could equally be used of a 'mythical' narrative) and further metaphor (man has no inkling of disaster

---

[9] Soph. *OT* 1, 29, 35, 144, 223, 273; in 268 the past goes back to Agenor, but he too has no story.

until he steps on the hot embers). Gnomic reflection and the remembered past dissolve into one another almost without visible break or, more importantly, distinction of status.

I want now to come closer to the theme of this volume by moving on to a consideration of what shapes and holds this particular gnomic sequence in *Antigone* together. The dominant connective particle in this chain of reflections and collective memories is *gar* (not readily translatable, but introducing, as often, an explanation of a statement just made). *Gnōmē* and memory of the past reciprocally reinforce, explain, and illustrate one another: the use of the particle *gar* presents the sequence as a reasoned progression, interpreting experience. This, I want to argue, is one important aspect of the 'rationality' of myth. To take some further examples: for Antigone confronting Creon in Sophocles' play, the timelessness of their past existence (so old that no one knows their *prōtos heuretēs*, *Ant.* 456–7) is what explains and justifies (*gar* again: 456) her assertion that the laws of the gods are *asphalē* ('secure'). Later in the play she cites the story of Niobe (a foreigner but also, as the wife of Amphion, a family member, an ancestress) in reply to the chorus's assertion that she herself will become the subject of 'story' (*kleinē*, 817) because she is without mythical paradigm (*monē de*, 'you alone') in the self-chosen autonomy of her death. But Niobe is already myth (*ēkousa*, 'I have heard', 823; *hōs phatis andrōn*, 'so the talk of men goes', 829) and Niobe's story, for Antigone, offers the reassurance of a heroic precedent remembered by men.

There is less reassurance in the myths referred to by the chorus in the third stasimon of *Antigone* (944–87): the myths of Danae, Lycurgus, and Cleopatra. These evocations of the past are addressed in apostrophe directly to Antigone (*ō pai, pai*, 'child, child', 949; *ō pai*, 987) and they are offered as consoling parallels ('Danae too' (*kai Danaas*, 944) is remembered, for carrying the seed of Zeus; 'Cleopatra also' (*k'ap' ekeinai*, 986) was overtaken by the 'long-living Moirai', despite her glorious (and Athenian) ancestry).

It is, of course, the multivalency of myth, as well as its universal currency, that gives it, here as elsewhere, enduring force: it is important for us to realize that the 'rationality' of myth does not exclude its use to reinforce differing, even opposing, interpretations of experience (and this too is something that it has crucially in common with *gnōmē*).[10] Antigone cites Niobe as a consoling precedent in death; so too she is a precedent, along with Philomela, for Electra in Sophocles' play (*El.* 150–2), but for Electra her story is a precedent for the wished-for eternity of her grief. For Achilles, as Sophocles and his audience will certainly have remembered, she was paradigmatic of a quite different and incompatible gnomic truth, that grief cannot last for ever and that the ordinary necessities of life must be resumed (*Iliad* 24. 602 ff.).

In other plays too we find the same multivalency. In Euripides' *Hippolytus*, the Nurse and the chorus both cite, within the space of a hundred lines (453–4, 554–64), the myth of Semele; both of them to reinforce the same gnomic truth, that Kupris/Eros is a power that no one, human or divine, can resist. But the Nurse, viewing the myth as a story about Zeus, draws the (explicitly reassuring) inference that to be a victim of Kupris is not a cause for shame or for exile: life goes on as before, and acceptance is all. For the chorus, on the other hand, who see it as a story about Semele, the myth carries the terrifying implication that to be a victim of Eros, as Semele and Iole were, is to meet with violence, bloodshed, and, for Semele, instant destruction: smoke, thunderbolt, and flame dominate both images.

A further function of myth within the fictional world of Greek tragedy is visible in these examples: it is to enlarge, often with dramatic suddenness, our vision of human experience, encountered in tragedy often in claustrophobic confines of time and space. I have tried to show elsewhere[11] how the chorus of *Phoenissae* gives anchorage and depth of context to the events of the play by reviewing the mythical tradition of Thebes as inherited memory, while the family of Oedipus is locked into a single-generation perspective. In *Antigone* the events of the play are 'anchored' remorselessly (and much of the power of the play comes from this fact) in the narrow space defined by the royal palace, the buildings and walls of Thebes, with the plain outside and the cave in which Antigone is entombed and dies, just as the play is obsessed with a time-frame which extends only to the events of the past two days and the sufferings of two generations

---

[10] I have argued this point in Gould (1989), 81–2, 105–6.
[11] Silk (1996), 224–5.

of a single family and a single community. So when the chorus's memory brings into view the stories of Danae, Lycurgus, and Cleopatra, this world is suddenly enlarged and illuminated by a vista of other worlds, other experiences, other times. It is thus the less surprising when, in their following song, the final stasimon, invoking Dionysus to come to Thebes, the chorus's image of Dionysus is one that vastly enlarges our sense of the space of the world by including Italy, Eleusis, Parnassus, Euboea, (? Asia), and the stars of the night sky in exuberant celebration of the god's universality and omnipresence, and runs back in time to remember Cadmus and the birth of the god.

In Euripides' *Ion* the citation of the mythical past similarly and recurringly enlarges our sense of space and time; at the same time it creates a parallel world off-stage to match the Delphic world we are witnessing in the theatre. Myth of the Athenian past is not the preserve of the chorus nor of the Athenian Creusa; it is shared by Ion and (less significantly) by the god Hermes, and becomes thereby a universalized narrative of remembered human experience. Nor is the remembered past solely the past of Athens: the chorus in their parodos song recall Heracles' defeat of the Hydra (specifically the Hydra 'of Lerna' and the exploit remembered as a story told by women as they weave: 190, 196–7[12]); Bellerophon, Pegasus, and the Chimaera (201–4); and the struggle between gods and giants, involving not only Athena (note the collective memory implied by *eman theon*, 'my goddess', 211) but also Zeus and Dionysus. The *omphalos* and the ritual procedures of Delphi are also, for the chorus of female slaves who have come from Athens to Delphi, a matter of 'telling' (*houtō kai phatis audai*, 226) and oral tradition. The world is shared and made familiar by such 'telling'.

The specifically Athenian past in this play is shared, remembered, and told by Ion and Creusa; by Creusa and the Paidagogos (both in stichomythia, which serves to reinforce a sense of integrated memory: 265–88, 934–69); it is woven into the hangings described by the Messenger (1163–5) and recognized by him, along with universal images of sky and stars, scenes of naval battles, and hunting scenes. For Ion, the origin of the Athenians is known through what 'men say' (*phasi*, 589); for the Paidagogos,

---

[12] Further references to women talking as they weave at the loom: *Ion* 507–8, 766–7.

the battle of gods and giants is similarly a thing known through 'story' (*ar' houtos esth' ho muthos hon kluō palai*, 'is this the story I have heard long since?', 994). All this is common ground within the fictional world of the play, made so by human talk and collective memory, along with such things as the geography of the Acropolis (*keklēmenos*, 'called', 283, 936–8) and Euboea (*hōs legous*', 'as they say', 295) and Ion's own past (*keklēmetha*; *legousin*, 'so they say', 311, 317), whereas geometry is 'the talk of experts' (*hōs legousin hoi sophoi*, 1139). Memory of the past can be revised (*ho muthos . . . neos*, 'this story . . . is a new one': Ion to the Delphic Prophetess at 1340) but in significant measure the pervasive awareness of a shared past is a factor in our sense of the affirmative tendency of *Ion*.

Here then is another aspect of the 'rationality' of myth: like *gnōmē*, and often interchangeably with it, myth subsumes suffering and loss, the extraordinary, unparalleled, and terrifying event that is the substance of tragic fiction, into shared experience in the form of collective memory and intelligible story. What I have called, speaking of *Phoenissae* and *Antigone*, the 'anchorage' of myth resembles religious explanation as Clifford Geertz has portrayed it: its function is to replace the traumatic inexplicability of events by a structure of reason, 'a system of symbols . . . with . . . an aura of factuality', to quote Geertz.[13] Like *gnōmē*, that collective memory turned into narrative can, of course, serve many different interpretations of the same experience. So too the variable distribution, within the tragic fiction, of that collective memory as between chorus and characters, the differing availability of the past, can in its turn create many variously intelligible worlds. But all are, in the degree that they are narratable, intelligible.

I would suggest then that, in more ways than one, 'myth' in Greek tragedy is properly to be seen as an aspect of the 'rationality' of the tragic fiction, its presentation of human experience as (potentially) arguable and intelligible. But what of '*logos*'? Myth and *gnōmē*, as we have seen, are both used in inferential argument or explanation: the chorus in *Ajax*, for example, explains to itself in the parodos the almost unacceptable fact that appalling stories

---

[13] 'Religion as a Cultural System', in Geertz (1973), 87–125.

of Ajax' behaviour are apparently being listened to and believed in the Greek camp by a sequence of *gnōmai* (general truths not specific to Ajax: 148–66; *gar*, 150, 154, 157, 160); a few lines later (172–85), they explain their assertion that Ajax' behaviour is the product of some god's revenge both by reference to his known character (*oupote gar phrenothen g' ep' aristera . . . ebas tosson*, 'never in your right mind . . . would you have gone so far astray') and by general truth (*hēkoi gar an theia nosos*, 'sickness can after all come from a god'). This is reasoned argument, certainly, and if perhaps at first we are not all inclined to call it '*logos*', that is partly because we have no ready definition of '*logos*' to hand, and partly because we have inherited from Aristophanes a model of the history of tragedy which makes Euripides definitively the play-wright who introduced '*logos*' into the genre. Yet we certainly cannot say that 'logical' argument (logic chopping, as Aris-tophanes presents it) excludes recourse to *gnōmai*: Medea, for example, in Euripides' play, is a consummate pleader and rea-soned explicator of passion, yet also the play's most avid user of gnomic argument, while Haemon in Sophocles' *Antigone*, in a speech which many have felt, under Aristophanes' influence, to be distinctly 'Euripidean' in tone, appeals to no less than seven gnomic truths in the course of his argument (*gar*: 703, 707, 719, 722; *alla* ('but'), progressive/argumentative: 710; rhetorical asyndeton: 712). Nor can we say that appeal to empirical fact is a necessary element in '*logos*' which distinguishes it from (pre-logical?) gnomic 'argument'. I have already tried to show that *gnōmē* and myth are reciprocally connected modes of explanation (a *gnōmē* is 'a very short short story', as Alistair Cooke put it in a recent 'Letter from America' on BBC Radio 4),[14] and neither excludes appeal to empirical fact.

The argument between Teucer and Menelaus in *Ajax* (1052–1158) combines the gnomic and the empirical and ends with a pair of 'rhyming' *ainoi* (moral-like conclusions). No doubt argu-ment of this form is deeply traditional, but I would suggest that neither 'myth' nor *gnōmē* in Greek tragedy implies a way of apprehending human experience that we can simply oppose to

---

[14] Or what Walter Benjamin (1970: 108) called an 'ideogram of a story': '[a] proverb, one might say, is a ruin which stands on the site of an old story and in which a moral twines about a happening like ivy around a wall.'

logos, as some pre-existing and non-logical mode of thought to be replaced by the onward progress of the human mind. The discourse of Greek tragedy is simultaneously a discourse of narrated memory and of reasoned explanation. If the term is useful, I see no reason not to call this '*logos*'.

IV
Polarities Dissolved

6

The Rhetoric of Muthos and Logos: Forms of Figurative Discourse

CLAUDE CALAME

STAUNCHLY clinging to the Alps, the Swiss historian and anthropologist cannot remain unresponsive to the profound transformation undergone by mountain reality at the end of the eighteenth century. Naturally, the change affected the productive basis of societies and cultures whose economy was divided between self-sufficiency and commercial revenues accruing from the crossing of the passes. But it also profoundly affected the *representation* of the mountain landscape from which those communities derived their income, a landscape which was gradually being appropriated by the city-dwellers who came there in search of strong sensations or who made it an object of learned study. Aesthetic aspirations and scholarly interests accordingly combined to produce a wholly new image of the Alps, ranging from the romantic idyll of healthy life on the mountain pasture to the geological upheavals which shape the grandiose and sublime setting. This complex symbolic representation still underlies many of the postcards and brochures published to attract tourists to the Alpine winter- or summer-sports resorts.[1]

The nineteenth century was also the time when, with the first great Alpine ascents, the outlines of the mountains were given names; up till then they were designated only *en bloc*, by generic names: Mont-Blanc, Dent Blanche, Dents Blanches, Cime Bianche, Weisshorn, etc. Traversed for the first time in 1864 by the English gentleman Sir Leslie Stephen, father of Virginia Woolf, the famous and lofty North Ridge of the Zinal-Rothorn

---

[1] Privileging some studies from Lausanne, we may cite Reichler (1994) and Kilani (1984). See also Bozonnet (1992), and the studies collected in the periodical *Histoire des Alpes*, I (1996). I would like to thank my Lausanne colleagues Marie-Jeanne Borel and David Bouvier for their useful critical reading of the present paper. The text has been translated into English by Michael Howarth, and revised by the editor.

was immediately subjected to a process of naming which picked out its salient points: the Arête du Blanc, the Épaule, the Gendarme du Déjeuner, the Rasoir, the Sphinx, the Bourrique, the Bosse, before reaching the summit which looks down on the Kanzel, the promontory of the Chaire. Not confined to indicating the morphology of the mountains by different metaphorical devices, not satisfied with marking the clear linguistic divide between the Val d'Anniviers and the Zermatttal, certain of these names also refer to the stages and procedures of an itinerary. Through their nomenclature the mountains not only become the representation of an area, but they also formulate, through a sequence of names in the form of a scenario, an invitation to climbers. Their 'discursivization' ('mise en discours'), through an ordered sequence which Alpine guides convert into a narrative and 'instructions for use', locates them in a universe of belief which partakes of the ideological, certainly, but, equally, of the pragmatic. As was the case in ancient Greece, the modern mountain landscape is a symbolic construct.[2]

WHAT DO *MUTHOS* AND *LOGOS* MEAN?

In that case, are the Alps just a myth? That is what a recent study peremptorily tends to affirm.[3] But its author has not realized that the only support for his assertion comes from the detached and critical stance which he himself adopts *vis-à-vis* traditional images of the mountain landscape; nor has he seen that, while indeed being largely imaginative constructs, and having scarcely any reality apart from our own self-made representations of them, the Alps nevertheless continue to exert, on the peoples who live in and draw their livelihood from them, an ideological effect both potent and persistent. In so far as they are symbolic constructs and

---

[2] The morphological and practical description of the Zinal-Rothorn is given by Brandt (1986), 307–9. For the symbolic uses of mountains by the Greeks, I naturally refer to Buxton (1994), 81–96.

[3] Crettaz (1993: 151–87), who wonders in particular: 'de même qu'on a parlé à partir du XIXe siècle de 'L'invention des Alpes', devrait-on parler aujourd'hui de 'La fin des Alpes inventées' ainsi que d'un retour à des périphéries mélangées de montagne et d'autres régions économiques avec leur destin propre?' The political success achieved two years ago by the popular initiative labelled 'des Alpes' by itself gave the lie, resoundingly, to this pessimism!

manifestations starting from a given g
cal ecosystem, and also from a prec
situation, the Alps doubtless deserve to b
terminate and fuzzy category of 'myth', o.
category of 'mythical configuration'; but th.
express condition that we recognize myth as a r
Western anthropological thought, and that we gr.
bolic manifestations which we think it legitimate t.
that term in the context of the culture and social pract.
they operate. The (usually narrative and discursive) phe.   .na
which we—from the perspective of detached academic scholarship—understand as myths, for the indigenous population precisely do *not* correspond to the criterion which in our view is
decisive: that of absence of empirical truthfulness!

But how, then, was it possible for a mythical configuration
focused on the Alps, with its representations, narrative accounts,
pictorial manifestations, and itineraries, to emerge at the dawn of
Romanticism and to develop in a booming scientific age, when
the very people who were discovering and re-creating the mountains in order to bring them to our attention were prompted by
their interest in empirical observation and scientific classification?
Were the physicists, geologists, and natural historians of the
Alps—Horace Bénédict de Saussure already in the eighteenth
century, Louis Agassiz and Marc-Théodore Bourrit in the nineteenth—unwitting victims of an accident in the continuous development which is supposed to have led the Greeks and then
their European successors from the obscure gropings of the theological thought of primitive peoples to the enlightenment of
Western reason? Were they casualties of an extraordinary latter-
day overtaking of *logos* by *muthos*?

Without going back over ground already covered and
signposted, we ought here to recall the conventional caveat about
using ancient terms for modern notions. Playing this game, one
runs a double risk: that of conferring, through the sanction of a
Greek word, a historical if not universal value on a recent category; and that of projecting the modern notion backwards on to
the *signifié* appropriate to the ancient term. As far as *muthos* is
concerned, it is now taken for granted that the term in Greek
does not designate what myth has become in our modern encyclopaedic thought—a foundation narrative, albeit fictitious,

superhuman characters in a transcendent age. To the
numerous examples already analysed, it is enough to add that of
the poems of Empedocles. Taking, on occasion, a narrative turn,
the actual exposition of doctrine is presented in the fragments of
this 'Presocratic' poet as a *muthos* 'which does not miss its target
and which does not lack knowledge', a *muthos* which issues from
the deity and which the addressee of the poem is invited to listen
to, a discourse compared to a multiple progression and articulated
in the act of *legein*; inspired, oral discourse, expressly provided
with the pragmatic, if not performative dimension generally
present in utterances designated by the term *muthos* in the Archaic
and Classical periods. These *muthoi*, these words, are the object
both of the speech of the speaker and of the listening of the
person spoken to; they constitute in the same fragment a *logos*,
equally present to the hearing of the pupil; a *logos* whose course
is also clarified with the help of the metaphor of progression, a
logos which corresponds in its form to a *humnos*, that is, to a sung
poem![4]

So, like the *muthōdes* of Thucydides, the *muthos* uttered by
Empedocles is, to be sure, linked to the sung form assumed by
every poem in Greece; but this does not mean that it is set in
opposition to a *logos* which one would have loved to see—
especially in a 'Presocratic' philosopher of the fifth century!—
specifically refer to reasoned discourse expressed in written prose.
From this point of view, the modern hope is vain: if in
Empedocles *muthos* and *logos* correspond to inspired and truthful
discourse, for his contemporary the historiographer Herodotus *all*
reported discourse, as well as the actual discourse of his *Enquiries*,
falls under the head of *logos* and *legein*, whatever its degree of
truthfulness. Clearly, in spite of its Hellenic name, myth is not an
indigenous category.

Passing from the problem of the signifier to that of the signified, we may enquire whether, in the absence of a *muthos* assuming the sense of myth, there exists, at least in Classical Greece, a
notion approximating to the modern category of myth. We are
once again disillusioned. Admittedly we find in Herodotus, and

[4] Emp. frs. 31 B 62, 3 DK = 510, 3 Bollack; B 23, 11 = 64, 11; B 24, 2 = 22, 2; B 17, 14–
15 and 26 = 31, 13–14 and 25; B 35, 1–2 = 201, 1–2. The pragmatic value of discourse
designated by the term *muthos*, in its Archaic and Classical uses, has been studied by
R. P. Martin (1989: 10–26, 37–42), who defines *muthos* as an 'authoritative speech-act
performed in detail'. On the modern notion of myth, see Calame (1991a).

then in Thucydides, the use of terms like *ta archaia* or *ta palaia*: these 'ancient things' are past events such as the thalassocracy of Minos, the reign of Theseus, or the Trojan War. These heroic exploits are ascribed to a *to palai*, an 'ancient time' whose course precedes the *kaina*, recent history, without interruption of continuity. True, one can sometimes cast doubt on the reality of this past, which takes in the age of heroes; but this is less through lack of clues or evidence than by reason of the poetic and consequently imaginative form in which it has been transmitted to us.[5] Here again, there is no myth in the modern meaning of the term. *— Isn't there?*

If it is true that, in spite of the uncertainties now hanging over the indigenous uses of the word *muthos* and its derivatives, it really was the Greeks who showed us the royal road leading from *muthos* to *logos*, this second term would merit the same investigation as the first. Enquiry into the multiple meanings of *logos* is all the more necessary since, in our eyes, the Greek *logos* is reason, reason which, in our encyclopaedic thought, we implicitly identify with *logical* reason. This reason would base every deductive and causal chain on the three principles of identity, non-contradiction, and the excluded middle. Reason is then reduced to the principle of the Aristotelian syllogism which takes the form of the famous schema of inference: 'If every A is B and every C is A, then every C is B'; or else, more strictly, reason is assimilated to the Stoic rule of the *modus ponens* which is at the origin of propositional logic: 'If p then q; but p, therefore q'. No doubt this assimilation will seem something of a caricature in its simplicity. But it is certainly present in, for example, research as well founded as that of Bruno Snell, who devotes a whole chapter of *The Discovery of the Mind* to illustrating the transition in the Classical era from mythical to logical thought. While the former is said to be characterized by thinking in images, utilizing the metaphorical devices of analogy, allegory, and comparison, the latter would satisfy the requirements of repetition, identification, and non-contradiction.[6]

---

[5] I venture to refer here to my investigation (following those of Detienne (1981) and Veyne (1988)) in Calame (1996*a*), 30–46, with extensive bibliography (including Saïd (1993)).

[6] Snell (1953), 191–226. The meanings given to myth considered as a mode of thought are countless; the views of thinkers like E. Cassirer and J. Rudhardt are criticized by Detienne (1981), 190–224.

Within this perspective, Jonathan Barnes has no hesitation in introducing his outstanding study of the earliest Greek philosophers with this brusque assertion: 'The Presocratic philosophers had one common characteristic of supreme importance: they were rational.' Specifically Greek, the reason of the Presocratics is characterized, according to Barnes, not so much by its empirical tendency and its rejection of all superstition as by its devotion to 'argued theory'. This is why it is in opposition, once again, to 'unargued fables', that is to myths, likened to dogma! Barnes concludes: 'The broad and bold theories which [the Presocratics] advanced were presented not as *ex cathedra* pronouncements for the faithful to believe and the godless to ignore, but as the conclusions of arguments, as reasoned propositions for reasonable men to contemplate and debate'.[7]

An analysis as well known as that presented by Plato at the conclusion of the *Theaetetus* undoubtedly shows that *logos*— to return to the indigenous category—is less intimately linked with argument than with description. Even if the conclusion (about the ability of *logos* to turn true opinion into *epistēmē*) proves finally negative, *logos* is successively likened to discourse appropriate to promulgating opinion, to enumeration of the constituent elements of the object of opinion, and to formulation of its distinctive characteristics. Thus, more concretely, the account in the *Republic* of social hierarchy and of its historical establishment in the form of a city is displayed through the mediation of *logos*. After that, *logos* may denote, as in the *Phaedrus*, both the pronouncements of Anaxagoras on the nature of Mind, and the speeches of Pericles, who is said to have found in them the inspiration of his rhetorical art: *logos*, with its persuasive force, obviously corresponds to oratorical discourse. The thorough investigation that the use of *logos* in Plato deserves would certainly show that it is especially through the notion of dialectic that the term can take on its more precise meaning of 'argued discourse' and so of 'reasoned discourse'. In any case, *logos* never corresponds in Plato to the restricted and formal definition given to it by the Aristotle of the *Prior Analytics*: 'The syllogism (*sullogismos*) is a form of reasoning (*logos*) in which, certain things being posited, something other than those

---

[7] (1979), 3–5. See also Mattéi (1990), and Frede and Striker (1996).

premisses necessarily follows, by the mere fact of those premisses'.[8]

The function of *logos* in the Classical period is marked less by argument than by demonstration. In a celebrated passage of the *Protagoras*, when Socrates suggests to the sophist that he 'show' (*epideixai*) whether virtue can be taught, Protagoras offers a choice—the subject of so much commentary—between *muthos* and *logos*. But whereas the idea of exposition (*diexēlthō*) is linked to *logos*, to *muthos* there corresponds precisely the notion of 'demonstration' (*epideixō*), through a narrative which will be the object of *legein*! On reaching the end of his speech, Protagoras declares that *muthos* and *logos* have worked *together* to 'demonstrate' (*epideixamenos*) that value can be taught. No surprise there, since the sophist has presented the narrative of Prometheus as the cause (*aitia*) of the participation of all mankind in justice. In so far as it is a premiss about origins, then, *muthos* contributes to the argument of *logos*. On certain conditions—let us not forget— *muthoi* can also contribute to the education of the citizen of the ideal polis. Moreover, when discourse corresponds, as in the *Phaedo*, to what is being said about the development and function of mystery rites, it is not denoted by the term *muthos*, but is introduced as a *palaios logos*. In the same way, at the beginning of the *Phaedrus*, the *muthologēma* of the abduction of Oreithyia by Boreas is characterized by Socrates as a *logos*—the kind of tale from which only idle *sophoi* have the leisure to withhold their trust by proposing rationalizing interpretations.[9]

RHETORICAL USES OF *MUTHOI*: ISOCRATES

In attempting, even by means of a few very limited examples, to apprehend the meaning of these two key words in their

---

[8] Pl. *Tht.* 206d–f; *Rep.* 369a–c and 376d; *Phdr.* 270a and 271d–272b; Arist. *An. Pr.* 24^{b}18–20; see also *Top.* 100^{a}22–30 and 105^{a}10–13. The relation between argued speech and dialectic is, for example, at the heart of the debate between Socrates and the sophists in *Prt.* 335b–338b.

[9] Pl. *Prt.* 320b–c, 328c–d, and 322d–323a; *Rep.* 376d–378e (see Bouvier (forthcoming)); *Phd.* 70c, with ref. to 63c and 69c; *Phdr.* 222b–e. On these contacts between *muthos* and *logos*, cf. the celebrated passage at *Phd.* 60c–61b, which clearly shows that the notion of *muthos* is associated with poetic form; see Brisson (1994), esp. 139–43, and now (1996), 27–44. But in my view it is not possible to discern in Plato a clear-cut opposition between 'myth'

contextual usage, we certainly seem to have had difficulty in reading the supposed transition from *muthos* to *logos* as the emblem of the birth of Greek reason, and in reducing Greek reason to the logical form of argumentation attributed to the Presocratics and then to Aristotle. To show how the notions understood in the Classical period by these two terms are found not in opposition but in close interaction, we shall take the example of an orator. In fact, the rhetoric of the fifth and fourth centuries BCE not only presents a development of the modes of exposition and argument with which *muthos* and *logos* seem to be intimately linked, but it also offers appeals to those *archaia* or *palaia* which, thanks to our distant perspective in time and space, we apprehend and like to read as 'myths'. If we attempt a reply to the double question of the indigenous understanding of what we call 'myth' and the argumentative function of these 'myths' within the *logos* of rhetorical discourse, the example which inescapably presents itself is that of Isocrates. We shall trace the use he makes of the terms *muthos, ta palaia, ta archaia*, and related expressions (such as *ta tote gegenēmena*) in relation to his use of *logos*. In this contrastive analysis of an extremely limited lexical field, we shall be sensitive to the specificity of the *signifiés* and reference of the selected terms—all this in relation to the modern notions which commentators, from the nineteenth century on, have tried to conceptualize and canonize by the Greek terms *muthos* and *logos*.

Argumentative Functions of Muthoi

In a speech composed by Isocrates expressly for the king of Sparta, probably soon after the battle of Leuctra, Archidamus the Younger attempts a historical justification of the Spartans' claims to control the neighbouring and rival town of Messene. In a procedure of oratorical legitimation still widely used in our own time, he goes back into the *palaion*, the still more remote past; he is in search of *aitiai*, at one and the same time causes, explanations, justifications, and responsibilities.[10] So, reaching back

and 'argumentative discourse', as Detienne (1981: 155–89) also implies. See in this volume the contributions of Lloyd, Murray, and Rowe.

[10] Isoc. *Arch.* 16–25. The complex meaning of *aitios* in the conduct of historiographical discourse is explained especially by Nagy (1990), 234–55.

beyond the settlement of the Dorians in the Peloponnese, one comes to Heracles and his sons the Heraclidae, with the corresponding division of the Peloponnese into three kingdoms. Only when called to the rescue by the sons of Cresphontes, the Heraclid killed by the Messenians, did the Spartans finally take possession of the neighbouring city. In exacting vengeance on the king's murderers, they to some extent re-established Heraclid legitimacy.

Now for Isocrates this process of working backwards in time has a name: *muthologein*; and it has a function: to explain, and thereby to legitimate. Legitimation is twice marked by the use of the expression *dio* or *dioti*, 'that is why'. If the orator forgoes the same mythological gambit as far as the ancestry of the Spartans is concerned, he ends a justificatory narrative, which he undoubtedly considers as historical, with a twofold deductive argument: if the Spartans are inclined to abandon all claims even in respect of their own city, then it is advisable to forget Messene; but if they are keen not to lose their homeland, then they must also keep control of the neighbouring city. The same claims (*dikaiōmata*) are valid for both, but so are the same 'speeches' (*logoi*). So *muthos*, *qua* argument, fits neatly into deductive thinking articulated by *logos*!

As it recounts the ups and downs of the settlement of the Heraclids in the Peloponnese, *muthos* becomes, in the mouth of a sovereign, a historical and political argument to justify his territorial claims 'logically'. When the orator, instead of lending his voice to a statesman, is moved to address directly a son's friend, *muthos* takes on a more allusive form, being offered as an example of moral conduct. In the speech dedicated to Demonicus, the immortality conferred by Zeus upon Heracles on account of his valour, and the perpetual torment to which the god condemns Tantalus for his wickedness, are each presented as the just reward of a father to his sons: examples (*paradeigmata*) from which the addressee is invited to draw inspiration in order to achieve excellence. The narration (*legousi*) of these *muthoi* is that much more pertinent because they enjoy general assent and credence. Moreover, this creation of belief is not achieved exclusively by the statements of orators, such as the speaker himself, but also by those of poets and sages. So ends a speech which presents each group as masters of moral instruction in the service of what is useful (*chrēsimon*).[11]

Also one of paraenesis (exhortation) is the speech addressed by Isocrates to Evagoras' son Nicocles, the young king of Salamis in Cyprus. Concluding his exhortation, the orator again focuses on the modes of communication of the advice given: in addition to written treatises (*suggrammata*) there are poems (*poiēmata*), among which the didactic poetry of a Hesiod, a Theognis, or a Phocylides can be held up as examples. Unfortunately it turns out that human nature, with its propensity for enjoyment, gives its preference among written (*graphein*) or invented (*poiein*) *logoi* not to those which aim at exhortation, instruction, or utility, but to 'the most fictional'; thus one may render *muthōdestatoi*. In fact, after including poems and treatises in the same broad category of *logoi*, whether they aim to please or to educate the public, the orator links the Homeric poems and the earliest tragic poets with the 'fictional' (in the etymological meaning of the word, relating to *fingere*). But far from condemning them, as the Plato of the *Republic* would have done, he expresses admiration for them. In fact Homer emplotted (*emuthologēsen*) in his heroic narratives the struggles and battles which the crowd enjoys seeing, in order to present them to a listening audience, whereas the tragedians made out of these plots (*muthoi*) actions presented to the eyes of the spectators.[12] But, contrary to what one might expect, Isocrates regards this type of seduction as exemplary. He is just careful to distinguish *by their target audience* these seductive genres from the advice given in a paraenesis: whereas Homeric poems and Classical tragedies are addressed to the many, exhortatory speeches are reserved for the man who rules over the many. The former produce their effect through the enjoyment they afford, the latter through the advice they transmit—advice aimed at training not abstract reason, but the capacity for decision (*bouleuesthai*) and the active reflection (*dianoia*) required of a king.

[11] Isoc. *Dem.* 49–51; *Pap. Berl.* 7426 has the reading *muthographoi* in place of the *muthoi* of the MSS.

[12] Isoc. *Nic.* 40–53; cf. Eucken (1983: 231–47) for the connection with Plato. For Plato, at *Rep.* 376e–379a and 392a, the *muthoi* told to children, like the heroic narratives handed down by poets, can present a measure of what is *alēthēs*: hence their educative value, provided one takes care to expurgate them. For relevant comments on this celebrated passage, see Cerri (1996), 39–53 and 67–85. On the meaning of *muthos* as plot in the context of the poetics of tragedy, see Arist. *Poet.* 1450ª15–23, with Fusillo (1986).

Thus, although Isocrates does indeed set up a distinction between exhortatory discourse and fictional poetry with its *muthoi*, while at the same time classifying both genres within the order of *logoi*, and although, like Thucydides, he associates the 'fictional' (this would be an exact translation of *to muthōdes*) with poetry and the enjoyment it provides, still, like Aristotle, he recognizes in the charms of poetry an educative and popular value.[13] In this recognition, in the traditional poems, of the dimension we call pragmatic, the truthfulness of the fictional is not called into doubt. Through enjoyment, the *muthoi* of the Homeric poems and of tragedy offer useful instruction to the very people who seek to elude 'the truth of acts' (*tas alētheias tōn pragmatōn*), especially where their own actions are concerned!

When Isocrates is called on to deliver the funeral oration in praise of Nicocles' father, well after the death of that famous sovereign of Cypriot Salamis, the age of heroes, and more particularly the Trojan War, are invoked to serve as reference points to demonstrate (*epideixeien*) the valour of Evagoras. Set against the *muthoi* which celebrate (*humnein*) the expedition mounted by the whole of Greece against the single city of Troy, is the true account (*tēn alētheian*) of the action of Evagoras who, relying on his own city alone for support, succeeded in waging war against the whole of Asia. Compared to the heroes of epic poetry, Evagoras would deserve even greater praise. Does that mean that truth resides only in the recent past, the time when Evagoras managed to turn his barbarian subjects into true Greek warriors, crowned with glory? The very virtues with which Evagoras successfully inspired his city correspond in fact to the qualities of the Homeric heroes which are praised in the *muthoi* and which the king succeeded in surpassing. There is no question of casting doubt on the epic yardstick of praise, even if the praise itself is extravagant. The orator takes care to point that out at the beginning of his speech: the problem for anyone seeking to praise his contemporaries is twofold. On the one hand, he is held to the truth (*tais alētheiais*) before an audience which has direct knowledge of the exploits of the men deserving praise; on the other

---

[13] Thuc. 1. 21. 1 and 22. 4; see Gentili and Cerri (1983), 5–31. Arist. *Poet.* 1448[b]6–19 derives the pleasure of apprenticeship from that which one naturally takes in *mimēmata*; see also *Rhet.* 1371[b]4–11; on the connection of this pleasure with emplotment, with *muthos*, see Dupont-Roc and Lallot (1980), 164–6.

hand, before a jealous public, he does not have at his disposal, in order to magnify men surpassing in courage the heroes of the Trojan War, the aesthetic effects conveyed by the diction and rhythm of epic poetry.[14] Incidentally, Isocrates squarely envisages the hypothesis of the imaginary character of the Homeric heroes: the public, yielding to enjoyment, 'do not know whether they existed'. The basic point of reference remains none the less the Trojan War, celebrated in 'hymns' and tragedies. Probably for 'imaginary' or 'fictitious' it would be better to substitute, in this case too, the concept of 'fictional'.

All the same, on the basis of the uncertain historicity of heroes who, subjected to the poetry of *muthos*, are quoted as examples without it being possible to certify their existence, should one not, following an often tendentious reading of Plato, draw a distinction between *plastheis muthos* and *alēthinos logos*? This truthful *logos* would consequently be attached less to reason than to the truth of the facts which it reports. The final speech composed by Isocrates seems to compel us in that direction. The orator begins the *Panathenaicus*—virtually his intellectual last will and testament—with a review of his own career and with his considered choice of speeches giving advice on the interests of the city and of the Greeks in general, at the expense of *logoi muthōdeis*; these last are kept for speeches full of miraculous or patently untrue stories (*pseudologia*).[15] By contrast, the deliberative speeches favoured by Isocrates are characterized by a rhetorical style based on antithesis or symmetry, and marked by those 'rhetorical' syllogisms constituted, according to Aristotle and in the context of rhetorical deduction, by *enthumēmata*.[16] However, for an interpreter who would see in this passage a sanction for the divide

---

[14] Isoc. *Evag.* 65–9 and 5–6.

[15] Isoc. *Panath.* 1–5; Pl. *Tim.* 26e, see also *Grg.* 523a and *Prt.* 320c. In this connection the commentary by Detienne (1981: 163–7) is relevant, with the references in Calame (1996a: 25–30): faced with the choice of invented *muthos* or argued *logos*, Plato often opts for the former! In the domain of *doxa*, in particular, the 'fictional' is not necessarily synonymous with the improbable or irrational.

[16] Aristotle (*Rhet.* 1356^{b}5) gives the name *enthumēma* to the rhetorical syllogism which he shows (1402^{b}13–24) can be based on what is probable—on examples, evidence, clues; see also *Top.* 100^{a}25–30 (n. 8 above), where the 'dialectical syllogism' is distinguished from the demonstration (*apodeixis*) in that the former relies on admitted premisses, and not on primary and universally true ones, as well as *An. Pr.* 68^{b}9–14. On the use of different modes of reasoning and rhetorical argumentation in the 'scientific' treatises of the Greeks, see G. E. R. Lloyd (1979), 59–125.

between *muthos* and *logos*, a more attentive reading of this fine exordium holds a double surprise in store. On the one hand, in addition to the fact that untrue speeches are included in the written *logoi*, two other categories are inserted between the miraculous or untrue stories and the exhortatory speeches: namely simple speeches, and speeches recounting past deeds (*tas palaias praxeis*) and the wars fought by the Greeks. On the other hand, it is precisely this last type of speech that Isocrates chooses in order to sum up—through numerous enunciative interventions—his own career and the powers of rhetoric.

So, to defend in the same speech his conception of oratory and of the culture which he feels it his duty to hand on, Isocrates successively evokes for his hearers the battles of Minos to free the Cyclades from the power of the Carians, the control of Sparta over the Peloponnese, and the struggles of the Greeks against Xerxes, returning, apropos the Peloponnesian War, to the decisive contribution made to the Trojan War by the cities of Nestor, Menelaus, and Agamemnon.[17] Furthermore, passing from the history of Greece to the subject of the Athenians' distinctive political regime, he rejects the stories of fratricide, parricide, incest, and cannibalism portrayed in the theatre and goes on to praise the autochthonous kings of Athens, Cecrops and Erichthonius, and their successors up to the institution of democracy by Theseus.[18]

When, by a dialectical mirror-effect, the orator makes an objector intervene in his own speech, this partisan of Sparta and former pupil justifies his evaluation of Isocrates' speech by situating it in terms of the opposition between praise and blame. In the eyes of the pupil, the speech is an artificial one, mixing *muthōdē* with *logoi*. What Isocrates' interlocutor calls into question is not the truth of the facts related, but the unfavourable portrait of the Spartans which is drawn from them. To correct this picture, he cites in his turn the *palaia erga* of the ancestors of the Spartans, harking back to the Dorian invasion and the return of the Heraclids. No doubt the *muthoi* which are incorporated in the

[17] See in particular *Panath.* 42, where Isocrates considers the question of the origin of the *palaioi agōnes* conducted by the Greeks, as well as the protestation of truthfulness in connection with the heroes of the Trojan War in § 89 (cf. § 72).

[18] Isoc. *Panath.* 123–30. Praise of the autochthony of the legendary kings of Athens is a topos found not only at *Paneg.* 24, but above all in funeral orations; see Nouhaud (1982), 60–1; also pp. 172–8 of 1993 French edn. of Loraux (1986).

logoi of the orators sometimes include miraculous and improbable stories, but they mainly consist of those *palaia* which correspond to the ancient history of the Greek communities, celebrated by the poets. That is why Isocrates' pupil does not hesitate to conclude his intervention by comparing his master directly to Homer.[19] So the time has come to define more precisely the profile and function of these *palaia*.

History, Example, and Truth

In the speech composed for him, the king of Sparta, Archidamus, cites Athens as an example of boldness in resisting the enemy. The historical reference is twofold. Under the heading of 'former dangers' (*palaioi kindunoi*) averted by the Athenians, Archidamus begins by mentioning the war against the Amazons, the struggle against the Thracians, and the defence against the Peloponnesians who were led astray by Eurystheus, king of Argos and cousin of Heracles. But from these *archaia*, perhaps too remote from present events (*ta nun paronta*), he moves on to the Persian Wars, with an allusion to the strategy employed at Salamis. Here the *palaia*, or *archaia*, correspond to the heroic period before the Trojan War. Similarly, recounting the history of the conquest of Messenia by his own city, Archidamus characterizes as *archaiotatos*, 'very old', the oracle which, after the murder of Cresphontes, confirmed the attribution of Messene to the Spartans, a perfectly trustworthy (*pistōtatos*) oracle, moreover, which constitutes, together with a later oracle given to the two cities in conflict, resounding evidence (*marturia . . . saphestera*) of the rights of Sparta over Messene.[20] But it is also evidence which the orator uses at once in order to refute the arguments (*tous logous*) of those who deny the legitimacy of the Spartans' claim.

To back up his praise, in the *Panegyricus*, of the virtues of Athens, and to justify, probably on the occasion of the Olympic Games of 380 BCE, his city's rights to hegemony, Isocrates employs the same historical arguments. To the war against the

[19] Isoc. *Panath.* 236–40 and 253–6, with ref. to 177–81; see further 262–3, in connection with the comparison of Isocrates with Homer.
[20] Isoc. *Arch.* 41–4 and 31–3. Isocrates is not the only one to use this 'archaeology', which is a characteristic of the work of the first historiographers; see esp. Hartog (1990) and Jacob (1994).

Persians must be added the struggle against the Thracians, who were supporting Poseidon's son Eumolpus, as well as the engagement with the Amazons, the daughters of Ares. These two legendary wars, also invoked in the *Archidamus*, and presented here as combats against enemies of Greece in their attempts to dominate Europe, prefigure the engagement of the Greeks against Darius and Xerxes. These *palaia*, as such, become evidence (*tekmēria*) no less significant than the Persian Wars in the discussion of ancestral tradition (*ta patria*). In the preceding phase of his demonstration (*saphesteron epideixai*) in relation to the legitimacy of the Athenian dominion over the Greeks, Isocrates took his stand on the support lent by the Athenians to the king of Argos, Adrastus, in giving burial to the Argives who fell beneath the walls of Thebes, as well as on the help given to the Heraclids in overcoming and curbing the insolence of Eurystheus. Located in a dense sequence of *logoi* deployed in support of a thesis (*hupothesis*), these historical arguments are valid as proofs (*pisteis*) in the controversy about tradition. The welcome given to the Heraclids and the punishment of Eurystheus' *hubris*, the granting of burial to the soldiers who died with Polynices at Thebes, the battle against the Amazons, the Trojan War—all these, a century earlier, were the very *palaia erga* which the Athenians (according to Herodotus) added to the recent event (*kainon*) of the battle of Marathon as their justification, against the Tegeans, of their claim to occupy the place of honour in the battle-order of Plataea. In the mouths of the Athenians they amount to a rhetorical and argumentative topos.[21]

In the speech which he addresses to Philip at the very moment of the ratification of the peace between Athens and the king of Macedonia in 346, Isocrates again invokes the time of Heracles and his sons to show the links which, by a common Heraclid ancestry, bind the chief cities of Greece to the sovereign of Macedonia. Being invested with trust, the *palaia* provide yet again a means of legitimation. Further on in the speech, the *archaia* are

[21] Isoc. *Paneg.* 66–70 and 54–60, as well as 63. Hdt. 9. 26–8; see on this passage Zumbrunnen (1996); cf. also Canfora (1995). The same 'historical' references constitute commonplaces of the praise of Athens in funeral orations; cf. pp. 78–97 and 141–3 of 1993 French edn. of Loraux (1986), with the additional references given by Nouhaud (1982), 14–15. It will be recalled that, in the theory of rhetorical argument (*enthumēma*) developed by Aristotle (*Rhet.* 1357ª34 and 1402ᵇ13–24, see n. 16 above), the *tekmērion* is considered as a necessary *sēmeion*.

once more pressed into service to show Philip that what counts for a king is not the power conferred by conquest, but benevolent governance. Against the wealth of Tantalus, the power of Pelops, and the might of Eurystheus, are set, as illustrations, the valour of Heracles, the merit of Theseus, and the courage of those who took part in the expedition against Troy. So, from the age of Tantalus and Heracles to the Trojan War, the temporal arc which covers the entire age of heroes is deftly drawn. Negative or positive, these heroic examples provide both the poet and the deviser of speeches (*logōn heuretēs*) with the reference point for a eulogy, of which the orator perceives the danger in the case of a man as powerful as Philip: that of ranking the demigods below a contemporary. From then on, the example of Athens can be added to the heroic one, in a development which substitutes the civic community for a single protagonist. Set against the city's mastery of the Aegean, for which no praise can be too great, are the proofs of valour furnished by Marathon, Salamis, and, for the Spartans, Thermopylae.[22] Here again, the historical paradigm is twofold, embracing on the one hand the age of heroes, and on the other the exploits of the Persian Wars.

But what happens when the argument, going beyond the Trojan War, beyond the time of Heracles, impels the orator to venture back into the time of the gods? Praise of the most ancient Greek city (*archaiotatē*) and justification of its claim to hegemony require, in the *Panegyricus*, that one go right back to the beginning: the beginning is Reason. The beginning for Athens is the advent of civilization marked by the welcome given to Demeter and the gifts granted by her to the Athenians: agriculture, and hope for prosperity and the kind of happy afterlife which Eleusinian initiation confers. At this point, because one is going

---

[22] Isoc. *Phil.* 32–4 and 142–8. Notice that when the orator is constrained by the subject of his speech to move within the age of heroes, he tries to collect around the *palaia* the agreement of their own protagonists; cf. *Hel.* 22 and 63. This does not prevent him from reorientating the significance of the Trojan War to make out of it, in anticipation of the Persian Wars, a first confrontation between Greeks and barbarians, Europe and Asia (*Hel.* 49–51 and 67–8). The role played by the exemplary battles of Marathon, Salamis, and Thermopylae in the Classical orators has been studied by Nouhaud (1982), 147–61 and 183–6; for Isocrates in particular, convinced as he was of the necessity of the war against Persia, see Mathieu (1966), 51–64. It will be noticed that, where recent events are concerned, the tradition of the funeral oration also requires the orator to confine himself to generalized praise of the heroes who were their protagonists; cf. pp. 129–41 in 1993 French edn. of Loraux (1986).

back so far in time, doubt becomes permissible: is the *logos muthōdēs*, is the account fictional? Isocrates enumerates a series of reasons for placing his trust in it. In addition to the fact that the mysteries are 'still now' (*eti kai nun*) celebrated annually, there is the tradition (*ho logos kai hē phēmē*) which has grown up around these *archaia*, inspiring trust, as well as the signs (*sēmeia*) constituted by the first-fruits sent by the cities of Greece, in token of this ancient (*palaia*) privilege, and the fact that cultivation was granted to the Athenians by the gods. So the congruence between present practices (*ta paronta erga*) and past accounts (*ta palai rhēthenta*) is capable of inspiring confidence (*pisteuein*) in events relating to the age of the gods.[23]

As is the case in Herodotus' *Enquiries*, where only *logoi* are cited, Isocratic argument is based, in its recourse to *muthoi*, on an implicit distinction between an 'age of the gods', an 'age of heroes', and an 'age of men'. These labels, which are modern ones, are only tools for conceptualizing an a posteriori distinction relating to a scheme of periodization whose boundaries are altogether indistinct. In fact, as in Herodotus, and contrary to what may have been asserted in this connection, these different 'eras' are really located along a line of chronological continuity. The events which marked them form part of *ta tote gegenēmena/genomena*, that long past in which the Persian Wars are also included; they lead without interruption to the *neōsti gegenēmena*, the recent past.[24] This continuity establishes the *muthoi* in history; the orator can draw on them for examples and arguments which have their force conferred on them not only by poetic

---

[23] Isoc. *Paneg.* 26–33. Similarly, in the speech placed in the mouth of Nicocles himself (*Nic.* 26), the defence of monarchy relies on the *archaion* constituted by the royal power of Zeus over the gods; if it is not an *alēthēs logos*, the attribution of royalty to a divinity is at least a sign (*sēmeion*) of mankind's predilection for monarchy. Note that there is no difference between *archaion* and *palaion* as far as chronological reference is concerned, since in *Evag.* 81 the genealogical link with Zeus is this time presented as a *palaion*.

[24] The *tote gegenēmena* cover the past in general (*Plat.* 14; *Areop.* 18, etc.) as well as the deeds of the heroic past portrayed by the tragedians (*Paneg.* 122), the protagonists of the Trojan War (*Evag.* 66), and the events of the Persian Wars (*Paneg.* 156; *Plat.* 59); for the recent past, see e.g. *Paneg.* 8 and 37. On the extent of historical space in Herodotus and the artificial nature of the distinction between 'time of the gods' and 'time of men', see Hunter (1982: 86–90, 103–7), who rightly asserts that Thucydides does not distinguish, any more than Herodotus does, between a 'mythical' and a 'historical' period, and Darbo-Peschanski (1987: 25–38), as well as Calame (1998). For the funeral oration, see pp. 160–5 of 1993 French edn. of Loraux (1986), notwithstanding her assertion concerning Plato (ibid. 159).

tradition, but also by their frequent use in the tradition of rhetorical *logos*.

Having legitimated Athens' claim to hegemony, in particular by
reference to *muthoi*, the *Panegyricus* constitutes in its second part a
rousing appeal for reconciliation between Athens and Sparta, with
a view to renewing in a Panhellenic perspective the struggle
against the barbarians, and to gaining control of Asia. The success
enjoyed by the *muthoi* relating to the Trojan War and the Persian
Wars shows that the hostility of Greeks towards Persians was
located in the very make-up of the Athenians. These *muthoi*,
which from now on also included the recent episodes of the
struggle against the Persians, were listened to with the greater
pleasure in that they were the subject of songs (*humnoi*) performed at public festivities. If the poetry of Homer enjoyed such
favour in musical competitions and in the education of the
young, it is because it sang the praises of those who fought against
the barbarians. So, through the medium of poetic songs performed at festivals of the civic community, the *muthoi* of the
Trojan War had the effect of confirming an innate hatred of the
barbarians and of inciting to war against them.[25] There could be
no better way of defining and using as an argument the pragmatic
dimension of both the heroic subject-matter of Homeric poetry
and its mode of performance.

So we come back to the problem of the trust to be placed
in events of the past, in *palaia*. Relating in the *Panathenaicus* to
the actions, first, of the legendary kings of Athens—Cecrops,
Erichthonius, Theseus—and then to those of the Athenian people
up to the time of Solon and Pisistratus, these *palaia* are contrasted
with events which the orator could know accurately (*akribōs*)
through having been present at them. If hearing is nevertheless to
be preferred to sight, this is partly because of the measure of
agreement which obtains among numbers of sensate persons in
respect of what is said and written about *palaia*: but it is equally,

---

[25] Isoc. *Paneg.* 158–60. The inclusion of the Persian Wars among the *muthoi* recalls the
intention stated at the opening of the speech (§ 8) of speaking 'in an antique (*archaios*)
style' about recent events.

in what is presented by the orator as evidence and argument (*elegchos kai logos*), because the actions handed down by oral tradition are greater and finer than those of which chance makes us witnesses. Conclusion: in relying on 'things said' (*legomena*) about *palaia* and on written accounts (*grammata*) handed down from 'that time', the orator is doing nothing *alogon*[26]—he is certainly not giving way to the 'irrational'.

So it falls to Isocrates himself to lead us back to the basic problem. Handed down in the poetic form which destines them to be heard and entrusts them to oral tradition, *muthoi* are put at the service of *logos* and its various procedures of argument. So they do not at all correspond to those 'unargued fables' which some have wanted to contrast with 'argued theory'; nor do they correspond to the assertions and dogma which would separate myths from the arguments and logic developed by the Presocratic philosophers. But neither does their designation as *muthoi* shift in the fifth century—and a fortiori not in the fourth—from the sense of 'narrative account' to that of 'fiction', with a pejorative connotation.[27] And if one readily acknowledges that, in their respective primary senses, *muthos* like *logos* designates speech or discourse; and if one agrees that *muthoi* do not correspond to a precise category of narrative; and if thence one deduces that of course in Greece *muthos* cannot correspond to a specific form of thought; then one cannot at the same time assert, at least as far as Isocrates is concerned, that *muthos* is 'disqualifié du point de vue du vrai dans son contraste avec *logos*'.[28]

---

[26] Isoc. *Panath.* 149–50. Nouhaud (1982: 9–10) is wrong in wanting to break with the 'conception continue des événements' presented by Isocrates. On the nature of the 'Panhellenism' praised by Isocrates, see Cartledge (1993), 42–5.

[27] This is said with reference to the assertions by Barnes (1979: 4–5), and by G. E. R. Lloyd (1990: 23–4, 44–6), who refers to Detienne (1981). While Lloyd does acknowledge that in Plato (*Grg.* 523a–524b and *Tim.* 59c–d) *muthos* and *logos* can designate the same narrative, depending on the point of view adopted in relation to it, when mentioning the 'signature' formula with which the *Genealogies* of Hecataeus opens (*FGrHist* 1 F 1a), he mistakenly translates by 'tales' the *logoi* criticized by a historiographer who designates by the verb *mutheisthai* his own authorial declaration about the writing of what seems to him to be true (*alēthea*).

[28] The assertion is that of J.-P. Vernant in the preface to the 2nd edn. (1992) of *Les Origines de la pensée grecque*, a work whose first edition (1962) overemphasized the development of the 'première forme de rationalité'—as he describes the politically based 'raison grecque'. See also, in the same vein, Vernant (1983), 341–74 (a section called 'From Myth to Reason'), and (1980), 186–207. Responding to Vernant's 1992 modifications, M. Detienne has recently attempted a reformulation of the concept of 'la pensée

Moving from the lexical domain, where we have tried to delimit the contextual meanings of *muthos* in relation to those of *logos*, to the semantic domain, involving an exploration of the scope of the field assigned to *muthos*, we are bound to notice that, in the works of an orator like Isocrates, *muthoi* still do not define a class of narrative with specific content. But we have seen that the accounts often invoked as *muthoi* by the orator relate to *palaia* or *archaia*, that is, to the ancient history of Greece. In the very few cases where the trust which one can place in them is questioned, doubt attaches less to the truthfulness of the facts reported than to their possible amorality, and above all to the poetic form which they take. And in spite of the suspicions which the imaginary character of certain *palaia* may sometimes arouse, Isocrates, unlike Plato, takes these opportunities to express his admiration for the poetic tradition.

So, in the panegyric which he addresses to Evagoras, Isocrates relies once again on the *palaia* handed down by poetic tradition, finding in them examples of triumphant returns from exile. He then proceeds to a clear-cut distinction between the narration of successful returns which have actually taken place and the composition of 'new' and consequently imaginary, fictitious examples. But both kinds turn out to fall within the activity of *muthologein*; this narrative discursivization, this emplotment, goes back to the poets who transform what has or has not happened into examples which compel admiration (*eudokimousin*).[29]

Through the practice of eulogy, poets and orators are pursuing the same goal. This being so, it is out of the question to doubt the reality of the heroic exploits and the ancient events which are cited as examples because they belong to the history of the community. In the pedagogical introduction to his *Progymnasmata*, the rhetorician Theon recognizes in *muthos*, as late as the first century CE, 'an untrue account (*logos pseudēs*) which represents (*eikonizōn*) the truth'; so *muthos*, far from deserving a regular critical examination, can serve *logos*.[30] Moreover,

mythique'; see the introduction to Detienne (1994), 22–8. For the different stages which led from the establishment of the notion of myth to those of mythical thought and then mythology, I refer to Calame (1996a), 12–20.

[29] Isoc. *Evag.* 35–7, where the orator adds the more recent example of Cyrus to show the exceptional character of the exploits of the ruler of Cypriot Salamis.

[30] Theon, *Prog.* 3 (cf. also Nic. Soph. *Prog.* 1), cited by Graf (1993a: 3–5) to show that the transformations undergone by the narratives that we call *myths* are determined by their

practitioners of oratory are not alone in putting *muthoi* at the service of rhetorical argument, since—as is well known—in the works of a philosopher like Plato *muthos* may sometimes be substituted for a demonstration (*apodeixis*) which in itself would not be altogether convincing.[31]

Moving now from ancient notions to recent categories, the question of belief based on truth–status arises at the very emergence of the modern concept of myth. It is because it was conceived from the outset as a fabulous narrative, portraying imaginary beings in a transcendent time, that myth has been ascribed exclusively to 'primitive' cultures; it was as *fabula* that myth could be presented as one of the basic distinctive features of the 'savage mind'; it was as an emblem of the irrational that it became one of the determining criteria of the Grand Dichotomy. In the projection on to antiquity of the characteristics ascribed exclusively to exotic societies so as to locate there the origin of the development of rational thought, myth and mythical thought found a place alongside magic, tradition, faith, and the 'logic of the concrete', to be contrasted respectively with history, scientific knowledge, progress, empirical truth, and the 'science of the abstract'.[32] Posited as a form of thought based on perception, intuition, and imagination, mythology was seen as having been gradually replaced, during the period of Greek civilization, by a kind of scientific thought based on the procedures proper to the deductive and formal logic of Aristotelian and, later, Cartesian reason.

In cultural and social anthropology, as in the study of ancient history, scholars have since become more cautious. In particular, historians of Greek religion seem now to be agreed on a purely

constant adaptation to the circumstances of the moment; see also Buxton (1994), 18–44. The belief accorded to narratives about *palaia* depends precisely on their 'cultural relevance'.

[31] See e.g. Pl. *Phdr.* 245c–246a and 253c, where the demonstration (*apodeixis*) on the immortality of the soul rapidly gives way to the long comparison with the chariot, itself finally designated as a *muthos*; cf. Theon, *Prog.* 3, showing that for *palaioi, mutheisthai* is synonymous with *legein*; see also G. E. R. Lloyd (1987), 8–11, 135–7, 181–2 (also Lloyd in this volume), and Ferrari (1987), 64–7, 125–32.

[32] The distinctive features of the Grand Dichotomy have been summarized, and reinterpreted with the help of the 'oral/written' opposition, by Goody (1977), 146–62. See the celebrated essay by Horton (1967), with his self-critique in Hollis and Lukes (1982: 201–60), where he postulates in a universalist perspective a 'common core of rationality'; cf. also Horton and Finnegan (1973) and Horton (1990); see further n. 36 below.

Claude Calame

instrumental definition of myth. Thus myth becomes 'a traditional tale with secondary, partial reference to something of
collective importance' or, in a simplified formulation, 'a traditional tale relevant to society'.[33] Thanks to its use of the notion of
'tale', that is, 'legend', this definition has the drawback of sustain-
ing an ambiguity about the truthfulness of myth, which is thus replaced within the perspective of our own culture and its criteria
of belief. Considered from the point of view of the canonical
opposition between *muthos* and *logos*, an attempted definition can
remain closer to indigenous categories. So by referring to precise
cases, one shifts from singular to plural, and from the notion of
'tale' to that of 'narrative'. From that point on, the Greek accounts which we understand as myths will turn out to be as
explicit as scientific discourse; they prove to be similarly marked
by causality and motivation as well as by exploration of different
fields, but, like other cultural phenomena, they seem to stand out
because of their 'provocative ambiguity'.[34] Nevertheless, it would
be wrong to infer from that effect of ambiguity that 'myths'
depend on a specific mode of thought, wedded to a 'logic of the
ambiguous', or to a logic of 'the third included' which would
ignore the principle of non-contradiction. To believe that would
mean to refuse the Greek accounts any coherence.

It is essential, then, to emphasize that the stories which the
Greeks often call *muthoi* come under the heading of *logos*, 'discourse': they *are* discourse. As such, they do not seem to be
markedly differentiated from other types of discourse in which
we, by contrast, would perceive the operation of reason. There
remains that stimulating ambiguity, but *this* should be linked with

---

[33] The reference is to the definition formulated by Burkert (1979: 22–6) and simplified
by J. Bremmer, 'What is a Greek Myth?', in Bremmer (1987), 1–9. See also Graf (1993*a*:
1–8), who, relying on the indigenous sense of *muthos*, substitutes for the term 'tale' that
of 'story'; Dowden (1992: 3–7, 169–71), for a comprehensive definition, but restricted to
Greece; and the nuances formulated by W. Burkert himself in 'Mythos—Begriff, Struktur,
Funktionen', in Graf (1993*b*), 9–24.

[34] Buxton (1994: 207–13), in response in particular to the conception of myth developed by G. E. R. Lloyd (1987: 4–6). Refusing to see in Presocratic thought a shift from
muthos to *logos*, Couloubaritsis (1994: 29–36) substitutes for the notion of 'myth' that of a
logic of ambivalence set up in opposition to the Aristotelian type of logic, whereas
Vernant (1980: 239) attributes to myth 'a logic of the ambiguous, the equivocal, a logic
of polarity' in order to contrast it with the logic of non-contradiction of the philosophers.
For his part, Boulogne (1996) sees in Greek science, as contrasted with myth, the
collaboration of an 'assertory' modality of thinking (principle of the included middle) and
an 'apodictic' mode of thought (obeying the principle of non-contradiction).

their operation as metaphors rather than with a specific 'mode of thought'. For what strikes one in the discourse which the Greeks designated as readily by the term *muthos* as by that of *logos*, and which we feel to be 'mythical', is its figurative aspect. Far from referring to 'figurative thought' or to a 'concrete mode of thought', these figures are of the order of *discourse*, discourse whose logic is generally that of an emplotment. This symbolic discourse corresponds, then, to a logic of narrative action and, as such, readily portrays anthropomorphic actors. Each culture seems to have available to it the possibility of recounting and imagining different aspects of its natural and social environment, among which the history of the community has pride of place; by putting them into narrative, each culture locates them in particular in a temporal configuration. But the modes of narrative, as representations, are also means of questioning those aspects of a particular ecological and social system; they allow speculation about them. Among other manifestations of culture understood as an aggregate of practices based on representations, the narratives which we assign to the instrumental category of myth, but which for the indigenous community would fit our own category of history, depend on a symbolic process from which scientific discourse does not escape either.[35]

These narratives find notable application in the argumentation which runs through rhetorical discourse. In that context their logic is dependent on natural logic, which subordinates discursive reasoning less to proof than to persuasion. Indeed, unlike formal logic, natural logic articulates the forms of discourse composed for communication and designed, over and above that, to produce an effect: discourse for the transmission of knowledge, certainly, but also discourse for action. This is why the argumentative procedures which direct them are strongly marked by the presence of the speaker, just as natural logic itself can be defined as a 'logic of subjects'. Postulating the existence of a pre-logical mentality, and making *that* into a 'primitive' mentality, is an epistemological and

[35] In spite of being very critical of the use of metaphor, notably in the domains of formal logic and theoretical demonstration, Aristotle readily resorts to it in his philosophical discourse; cf. G. E. R. Lloyd (1987), 183–7, and Vegetti (1994). On what I mean by symbolic process, I refer to Calame (1996b), 29–54. Regarding the concept of myth and modern theories of myth, Strenski (1987: 2, 199) does not hesitate to see in them mere 'artifacts'. (This work was brought to my attention by C. Grottanelli.)

historiographical *faux pas*:[36] it is a myth! Like other forms of discourse, so-called 'mythical' narrative is no less logical, no less 'rational' than reasoned or theoretical discourse. It is simply less formal, and probably biased more in the direction of practice. Far from opposing myth to reason, the rhetorical use of fictional narratives about *palaia* confronts us with the existence of different regimes of intelligibility, or practices of intelligibility.

The speculative and symbolic aspect as well as the argumentative applications of the discursive and narrative manifestations which we call 'myths' render futile any effort expended in the attempt to define the domain of 'mythology' *vis-à-vis* that of literature. In ancient Greece in particular, these narratives are presented to their public in verse or prose forms which place them in what is for us the domain of literature. Using procedures of figurative narration and different modes of metaphor, they elaborate worlds which are partly fictional and which lend themselves, in the establishment of a tradition, to constant re-orientation and reinterpretation, at the same time appealing to our own interpretative curiosity. But it is also thanks to these forms of communication, entrusted to the voice of a specialist in the rhythmic spoken word or his representatives, that these discursive manifestations of the symbolic process acquire their efficacy. In their pragmatic aspect, they actually establish truth for a specific community of belief. What they require from us is a true anthropology of discursive genres.

That is how, depending on the *poiein* of a man or woman of letters and following the discursive and extra-discursive rules of genres, figurative and metaphorical discourses construct possible worlds capable of impinging on reality. That is how in ancient Greece, thanks to the work of symbolic exploration of the poet or the tragedian, but also of the orator and the Presocratic philosopher, the fictional becomes knowledge. Independently of any exclusion of reason from the domain of figurative narration, we can say that these different specialists of effective utterance

[36] On the distinctive features of natural logic, especially as it works in argument, see M.-J. Borel, 'Argumentation et schématisation', in Borel *et al.* (1983), 1–95, and Grize (1990), 21–3. Developments in the notion of 'pre-logical mentality', starting from Lévy-Bruhl (1922), are well traced and rigorously criticized by G. E. R. Lloyd (1990), 1–7, 135–45; the Grand Dichotomy (n. 32 above) is discussed from the same point of view by Tambiah (1990: 84–110), who nevertheless tries to set against the mode of 'causality' that of 'participation'.

organize their knowledge according to different regimes of intelligibility. Believing in the universal existence of myth, erecting it into a mythology for each culture, seeing in it a specific framework of thought, is to reduce potent symbolic discourses to a series of crudely general plots and themes. Like the Alps, those discourses present themselves to us in all their symbolic potentialities. It is our task to explore them, and to practise them, in a perpetual re-creation.[37]

[37] After its first presentation at the Bristol Colloquium, different parts or versions of this study have been given at Emory University, at the Institute for Advanced Study in Princeton, at the Istituto di Studi sulla Magna Grecia at Taranto, at Johns Hopkins University, at Rutgers University, at Stanford University, at the University of Chicago, at the University of Wisconsin, and at the University of Toulouse. I would like to thank my different *xenoi*, namely P. Bing, G. Bowersock, R. Buxton, M. Detienne, L. Edmunds, Ch. Habicht, I. Morris, P. Payen, P. Rosenmeyer, L. Slatkin, and A. Stazio, for their kind and stimulating hospitality.

7

Mythology: Reflections from a Chinese Perspective

GEOFFREY LLOYD

I SHALL start from two positions, both of which have a certain prima-facie plausibility, but which seem to be in conflict with one another. The first is the idea that every society has its myths. Maybe a particular society will not have myths of a particular kind, say cosmogonic myths or myths to do with technological inventions or myths involving monstrous beasts. Maybe also whatever distinctions we ourselves choose to draw between myths, legends, sacred tales, and folk tales, may, in certain cultures, be eroded or difficult to apply. But will not every society have myths of *some* kind, however used, whether or not closely associated with ritual, whether or not encapsulating the society's view of itself, its past, its values, its ideology?

But the second position questions whether this is not just another typical example of the export of Western, European categories to interpret other societies. *We* make a lot of assumptions about myth, many of which we have inherited from the Greeks. But if we go to other societies, past or present, and start hunting around for their myths, haven't we already begged the key question by assuming there will be some? Why should we expect our search to be rewarded? Isn't that like expecting to find religion, or warfare, or criminality, in every society, just because we find it hard to imagine one without such? Surely that leads to the kind of falsification, or forcing of issues, that happens when we judge every category of unfree labour in terms of one or other of the different concepts of slavery that have been developed, in the main, from the study of the ancient Mediterranean world?

Now a first, immediate, reconciliation between my two starting positions that might look tempting goes like this: maybe every society does have myths, but not every society has

mythology—I mean explicit ideas or theories about myths. Let us
be grateful to Marcel Detienne for arguing so eloquently that
mythology is an invention, indeed one of a particular historical
juncture in Classical Greece.[1] But if that might seem to relieve
some of the difficulty at one point, the problem does not go
away, but resurfaces one stage further back: for why did not every
society have *mythology*? Why was it just the Greeks who invented
mythology? But then why is not this question just as much,
indeed rather more, an example of the export of Western categories than the one to do with myth we started with? We seem to
be faced, in fact, with a recursive problem: whichever framework
for study we choose is a framework *we* have adopted and that we
then impose, with greater or less sense of artificiality, across the
board.

A reaction to that observation in turn—I mean the remark that
seems to undermine *any* general framework for cross-cultural
studies, let alone any concrete generalization within such a framework—a reaction to that that is very common is to insist on an
extreme empiricism (or perhaps I should say *empirisme*). Every
society must be understood in *its own* terms and none in those of
any other. That will leave us speaking Quechua about Quechua
society, Kwakiutl about Kwakiutl, as well as Chinese, Egyptian,
Greek, and ancient Greek for the ancients, modern for the
moderns, of course, let alone South London for South London
and broad Norfolk for the Fens. While I am as keen as anyone to
stress the importance of observing the distinction between actors'
and observers' categories, that means recognizing the distinction,
not (impossibly) trying to ban observers' categories. What we
need is not *no* common framework, but one that, so far as
possible, has, if you will pardon the expression, been
demythologized.

So much by way of an abstract statement of the problems: I'll
return, at the end, to an attempt at some general recommenda-
tions. But that is by way of introduction to the particular case I
want to take as my main theme, namely that of ancient China. I
come to this via a concern with their philosophy, their science—
their astronomy, for instance—their medicine, their mathematics,
where obviously analogous problems, to do with an adequate

---

[1] Detienne (1981).

framework for discussion, arise. But *myth* offers a further interesting study, since on this subject views, both in and outside China, split into two camps, corresponding, very roughly, to the two assumptions that I mentioned at the outset.

First there are those for whom the Chinese lack any recognizable mythology. Indeed many of the classical masterpieces of ancient Chinese literature, in the Confucian tradition especially, present views of the values of Chinese society, of the virtues to be cultivated by humans in their various, distinct, social roles, without any use of mythical material, mythical role models, or whatever. Yet obviously the Confucian tradition is not the whole of the Chinese inheritance, even though the scholarly elite responsible for promulgating what has been called (Girardot) the Confucian-imperial ideology worked hard to that end.

But against such a narrow view there has been plenty of recognition of the richness of Chinese legends, fables, and traditional tales, whether these are thought themselves to date from *very* ancient times—say before the beginning of the Spring and Autumn period (722 BCE) or to have been in some cases the work of historically datable figures. A recent book by Anne Birrell[2] identifies sixteen main types of myths (although with some overlap between categories), for example culture bearers, saviours, destroyers, miraculous births, fabled flora and fauna, and so on. Two even more recent articles by the same author[3] summarize the major contributions to the study of the subject, since 1970, by some thirty-three different authors from across the world. The Chinese even have a word for it, 神話, *shen hua*, literally 'spirit talk'.

But Birrell certainly recognizes, and sees as part of the problem for the interpretation of Chinese myths, that the sources on which she has to draw are scrappy and diffuse. Girardot already identified, in a study of creation myths,[4] what he called the extreme paucity and fragmentation of mythological accounts, and although the situation has been improved, as Birrell notes, by the source books and dictionaries compiled by Yuan Ke and his associates,[5] these are still, of course, *collections* of otherwise

---

[2] Birrell (1993).
[3] Birrell (1993–4) and (1994–5).
[4] Girardot (1975–6).
[5] Yuan Ke and Zhou Ming (1985); Yuan Ke (1986a) and (1986b).

disparate materials. The original provenances of the myths Birrell anthologizes include such works as *Shijing* (Book of Odes), the *Zuo zhuan, Zhuangzi, Chuci, Shanhaijing, Lüshi chunqiu, Huainanzi,* as well as the standard histories (more on them later), the *Shiji, Hanshu, Jinshu,* and such encyclopaedias as the *Taiping yulan.*

This material is itself enormously heterogeneous, and not just in terms of date. If some of the poems in the *Shijing* go back to the sixth century BCE, the *Taiping yulan* was compiled in the tenth century CE. Moreover many of these works are not the literary unities they were once believed to be, but themselves composite works by different hands and from different periods. That has been shown for the *Zhuangzi* by Angus Graham,[6] and although such works as the *Lüshi chunqiu* and *Huainanzi* are both associated with particular—datable—individuals, that is, Lü Buwei (died 235 BCE) and Liu An (died 122 BCE) respectively, neither can be seen (as I shall be explaining for the *Huainanzi* in a minute) as the sole work of a single author.

So, faced with this extreme heterogeneity in the sources, my tactic will be to go back to the actual texts in which the 'myths' appear, to see what they were doing there, and I shall focus, in the main, in the first instance, on one such text (itself a compilation, for sure, from the early Han) namely the *Huainanzi.* This has the advantage, clearly, that we can locate the stories that Birrell anthologized in their—in some sense original—contexts. But if we can avoid, thereby, some of the attendant disadvantages of a scissors-and-paste job, where more or less arbitrary decisions have to be taken as to what precisely to include, there is one massive limitation to my tactic that has to be acknowledged from the start. This is that such suggestions as I have to make (not to call them anything so firm as conclusions) relate to only a tiny proportion of the total material available, and must be accompanied with appropriate disclaimers as to their generalizability.

Understanding of the nature of the *Huainanzi* itself has been transformed, in recent years, first by Ames and by LeBlanc and his team, then by textual studies by Roth and most recently by Major.[7] As already remarked, it is associated with Liu An, king of

[6] Graham (1981).
[7] Ames (1983); LeBlanc (1985); Roth (1992); Major (1993).

Huainan until his death (an enforced suicide) in 122 BCE. One of the earliest commentators, Gao You (writing around 212 CE), has it that the book comes from a colloquium held at Liu An's court, eight of the participants in which he names,[8] though that suggests a more unified picture than the analysis of the text really permits.[9] But it is clear, first, that Liu An himself was not the sole author— even Major's term 'general editor' is optimistic. While, secondly, the core of the work consists of chapters 3–5 (the subject of Major's study, on which I myself shall be concentrating), the whole was built up by a process of accretion that probably lasted several decades.[10] Moreover, thirdly, the work draws heavily throughout on other sources, or in some cases, we should say, it parallels what we find in other writings (since their dates are often uncertain too, and indeed two similar extant texts may both derive from a lost common source). LeBlanc reckons, in total, 269 references to *Zhuangzi*, 190 to the *Lüshi chunqiu*, 99 to *Laozi*, and 72 to *Hanfeizi*. Even in the core chapters, extensive citations, borrowings or parallel passages occur, relating to material in *Shanhaijing* and *Chuci* especially, and in chapter 3, 5b (Major, section VI) we also find material that exactly corresponds to what is said about the five planets in one of the Mawangdui silk scrolls (the *wuxingzhan*) dating to before 168 BCE.

Let me now quote the account of the origin of the cosmos from the opening of chapter 3, 1a, in Major's translations. 'When Heaven and Earth were yet unformed, all was ascending and flying, diving and delving. Thus it was called the Great Inception. The Dao began in the Nebulous Void . . .' Then from primordial *qi* (氣, 'breath') came heaven and earth:

That which was pure and bright spread out to form heaven; the heavy and turbid congealed to form earth. It is easy for that which is pure and subtle to converge, but difficult for the heavy and turbid to congeal. Therefore heaven was completed first, and earth fixed afterwards. The conjoined essences of heaven and earth produced *yin* and *yang* . . . The hot *qi* of accumulated *yang* produced fire; the sun is the essence of fiery *qi*. The cold *qi* of accumulated *yin* produced water; the moon is the essence of watery *qi* . . . To heaven belong the sun, moon, stars and planets; to earth belong waters and floods, dust and soil.

[8] Major (1993), 4.
[9] Roth (1992); Brooks (1993–   ).
[10] Cf. Loewe (1993), 189 ff.

Thus far much of this, though not the *dao* and *qi* and *yin* and *yang* as such, may seem familiar enough to students of Presocratic philosophy, of Anaximander, say, or of Anaxagoras, but then *Huainanzi* 3 goes on:

Anciently Gong Gong and Zhuan Xu fought, each seeking to become *Di* [Major: 'Thearch']. Enraged they crashed against Mount Buzhou; heaven's pillars broke, the cords of earth snapped. Heaven tilted in the northwest, and thus the sun and moon, stars and planets shifted in that direction. Earth became unfull in the south-east, and thus the watery floods and mounding soils subsided in that direction.

There are, clearly, aetiological aspects to this story. The waters subsiding to the south-east, it has been thought, may be related to, seen as an explanation of, the eastward flow of the major rivers of China. The tilting of the heaven is explained by Major as accounting for the obliquity of the ecliptic with regard to the celestial equator (there are problems about why north-*west*, but I shall not enter into these here).[11] But what is responsible for these changes in the cosmic situation at this point in the story is not *qi*, or *yin* and *yang*, or the character or attributes of heaven and earth themselves, but two Titan figures, Gong Gong—often connected elsewhere with stories of a primeval flood—and Zhuan Xu, a Sky-god who figures in a variety of other stories, including one to do with the origin of the Qin people.

So while the beginning of *Huainanzi* chapter 3 may start like Anaximander, the first section ends more like Hesiod. Yet this is a chapter that then goes on to talk about the motions of the five planets (5b–8a, sections VII to XI), giving fairly precise, and in some cases accurate, figures for their periodicities, not just the well-known twelve-year cycle of Jupiter (fundamental in Chinese year reckoning) but also figures for a daily motion of Saturn, the periods of visibility of Venus as a morning and as an evening star, the motions of Mercury through the various lunar lodges, and so on. A later section (27a, section XXXV) gives the twenty-eight

---

[11] The principal difficulty is that, like every point in the northern celestial hemisphere other than the celestial pole itself, the pole of the ecliptic itself rotates, once in every twenty-four hours, round that north celestial pole. The obliquity of the ecliptic is not, then, a matter of its northern pole being either west or east of the celestial pole. It may be that the north-*westerly* tilt of the heavens stems from the requirement that the earth tilts to the *east* (as the flow of the major rivers suggests).

Chinese lunar lodges themselves, and their angular extensions. Thus the last nine read: Turtle Beak, Alignment, Eastern Well, Spirit-Bearer, Willow, (Seven) Stars, Extension, Wings, and Chariot-Platform, with extents, in Chinese *du* or degrees (where a circle is divided into $365\frac{1}{4}$ *du*) of 2d, 9d, 30d, 4d, 15d, 7d, 18d, 18d, 17d respectively. As for the moon's motion itself, that is given at 16a, section XXI. I quote: 'The moon's daily motion is $13\frac{26}{76}$d. A lunar month is $29\frac{499}{940}$ days. Twelve months make a year. The [tropic] year is $10\frac{827}{940}$ days longer [than the lunar year]. Hence in nineteen years there are seven intercalary months.'

That last figure is, of course, what is known as Meton's cycle in Greece, though it is also widely attested elsewhere, notably in Babylonia.[12] There are interesting features, too, to the relationship within these figures: it is clear that whoever is responsible has worked *back* from the figure for the intercalary months (there is nothing inexact about this: Major's suggestion that the figures work out 'almost exactly',[13] is misleading, for they do so exactly— though Major's figures don't because he converts fractions of 940ths to decimal expressions and thereby introduces approximations that are not there in the original).

How much, if any, of the material in these sections is original is unclear. We are evidently not dealing with an author or authors who conducted their own astronomical observations. That *is* the case with the final section, 32a ff., which does refer directly to observations with gnomons to determine the dimensions of the earth and the distance of the heavens (on the basis of the hypothesis of a flat earth). But that, as Christopher Cullen has shown,[14] is not an integral part of the chapter as a whole and is, indeed, inconsistent with it. While some of the earlier sections can be paralleled elsewhere—as we noted, the account of the planets in 5b can with the Mawangdui silk scroll—in many other cases the sources on which *Huainanzi* is drawing cannot be determined. But while these and many other disputed points remain unresolved, that does not matter unduly for my present purposes. The overall impression that the sections of chapter 3 which I have mentioned make is of an extraordinary variety of

---

[12] See Neugebauer (1975), i. 354 ff., ii. 622 ff.
[13] (1993), 96. [14] Cullen (1976).

material handled in a striking diversity of ways. A Hellenist will
think of Hesiod one minute, of Anaximander the next, of Meton
or of Ptolemy the next.

Let me give some other examples from another chapter of the
work before standing back and attempting some comments.
Chapter 4, the 'treatise on topography', deals with the characteristics and inhabitants of different parts of the world, and with
much else besides. For instance, 11b, section xv, relating to the
thirty-six countries beyond the seas, and speaking of the pierced-
breast people, the hog-snouted people, the hairy people, the
people without anuses, the hard-working people, and so on,
mainly derives from, or parallels, the *Shanhaijing*. *Huainanzi* 15b,
section xviii, gives the origins of the different kinds of animals
and plants. Here there are five main groups of animals, 'naked'
(that is, humans), hairy, feathered, scaly, and shelled (Major:
'armoured'). In the last four cases the origin is a creature that
already has, as part of its name, the name of the kind that will
eventually come from it. Hairy animals, for instance, come originally from Hairy Heifer, and Shelled ones from Shelled Abyss. In
each case that first creature gives birth to a particular type of
dragon, and then through various other intermediaries, to the
kind we know. Humans are different: they come not via a
dragon, but from Downyhair, via Oceanman and Ruojun and
sages. But the end of the story, for each of the five groups, is that
the many different kinds of ordinary creatures in the group come
to be. 'The five classes [of animals] in their various manifestations
flourished in the outside world and multiplied after their own
kind.' I may note, in passing, that one of the most popular
creatures in the Chinese mythical bestiary, to judge from the
frequency of its representations in paintings and sculptures,
namely the *qilin*, figures in the 'genealogy' of the hairy animals—
and it also appears in chapter 3, 3b, section ii, as responsible for
eclipses of the sun and moon.

But if section xviii seems reminiscent, in places, of Hesiod's
Theogony, 9a, section x, gives perfectly credible figures for
the periods of gestation of a variety of animals, not just human,
but also horses, dogs, pigs, apes, deer, and tigers, and the following section, 9b, has these correlations and generalizations to
propose:

Shelled and scaly creatures eat during the summer but hibernate in winter. Animals that eat without chewing have eight bodily openings and are oviparous. Animals that chew have nine bodily openings and are viviparous. Quadrupeds do not have feathers or wings. Animals that have horns do not have upper [incisor] teeth. [Some] animals do not have horns and are fat, but do not have incisor teeth. [Other animals] have horns and are fat, but do not have molar teeth . . .

That is as if we had slipped from among the more outlandish verses of the *Theogony* into the *Historia animalium*.

So what are we to make of all of this? I said that *Huainanzi* is a composite work, but it is too easy merely to invoke the undoubted eclecticism and heterogeneity of the treatise and leave it at that. Of course different sources are drawn on, liberally, in different chapters of the treatise, and, as remarked, the final section of chapter 3 is an—anomalous—appendix to that chapter. But the rest of my material all comes from the core chapters, 3–5, and, eclectic though they may be, the question for us remains, *why* they were put together in the way they were.

But then, following up my own earlier, all too facile, references to Hesiod, Meton, and Aristotle, it will not do either to say that what we have here, in *Huainanzi*, is some mythical material incorporated into a rational account. It will not do for us to say that this is *muthos* incorporated into *logos*, or *logos* grafted on to *muthos*, or any other way of expressing the combination of the two, quite simply because in the original there is no sense that there are two ingredients, the *muthoi*, the *logoi*, that are somehow brought into relation with one another. The point is fundamental. While we might be tempted to label one part of this account, *muthos*, the other, *logos*, the original presents itself quite simply as a *seamless whole*. There are no lines drawn to demarcate different types of account, no remarks serving as any kind of guide, or warning, to the reader, as to what kind of account is being offered or what to expect. Those earlier remarks of mine come from a Hellenist's perspective, and betray a typical Hellenist's interest in such demarcations. But then the Greeks themselves were, of course, famous for making such demarcations.

That last remark needs, I know, to be qualified, and plenty of material on which to base such qualifications can be found in other chapters of this book (e.g. Calame and Lenfant especially).

We all appreciate that *muthos* is far from always a matter of some
fictional account, but may be any kind of narrative. We all
know that its regular antonym, *logos*, is itself polyvalent to a
degree and by no means always figures as that antonym. Going
beyond the semantics of the terms, we are all well aware that in
one of the most prominent of all cosmological writings, Plato's
Timaeus, the terms *eikōs muthos* and *eikōs logos* are used interchangeably—for Plato will not have it that anything other than a
'likely' story is possible of the coming-to-be of the perceptible
physical world.

But when all the necessary qualifications have been entered,
we all also recognize that *muthos* is often used in Greece, in
contrast to *logos*, to downgrade the former, especially but by no
means exclusively, in science, in medicine, in philosophy, in
historiography. The sequence of the first three Greek historians
provides a cautionary tale.[15] Hecataeus had begun by ridiculing
the 'many tales of the Greeks' as absurd and, in contrasting his
own accounts, had claimed they are true (*FGrHist* 1 F 1). But
Herodotus castigates early story-tellers, such as Hecataeus indeed,
as just that, for believing and purveying fantastic tales. The story
that the earth is surrounded by Ocean, for instance, is merely
laughable (Hdt. 4. 36, cf. 42). Yet Herodotus receives his come-
uppance (even though he is not named) in the next generation.
Thucydides represents his predecessors—Herodotus by implication included—as offering mere entertainment. Their accounts
are beyond verification and something *anexelegkta*: they have, as
he puts it, 'won their way to the mythical', *epi to muthōdes
eknenikēkota*, 1. 21. While that category of the 'mythical' is not
the only way to put down rivals, whether colleagues in your own
discipline or from other disciplines, it is one of the most frequent
and effective.

Philosophy is even richer in examples, though also, to be sure,
of the creative redrawing of the boundaries and the interplay
between the two, *muthos* and *logos*, as in Plato's *Timaeus*, already
mentioned. Aristotle, to take a prime exhibit, certainly allows
some credit to what had been handed down by tradition from
ages long past—when at least he can reuse the ideas in question
or when he otherwise wishes to accommodate himself to myth.[16]

[15] Cf. Hartog (1988), 276 ff., and in this volume.
[16] Cf. Johansen in this volume.

The belief that the heavenly region is divine, he agrees in *Metaphysics* Λ 1074ᵃ38 ff., is inspired, but the mythical additions, the anthropomorphic or theriomorphic representation of the gods, are nonsense, put in for political expediency and to be persuasive. Again it is not just those whom we might consider the chief proponents of Greek myth-making who get criticized as *muthologoi*: Herodotus is so labelled in *GA* 756ᵇ5 ff.

Aristotle's attack, on a very broad front, in *Metaphysics* B ch. 4, is perhaps especially remarkable. He is tackling the problem of the first principles and in particular the question of whether those of perishable things are the same as those of imperishable things. One might have supposed that he would have treated this as a *new* kind of problem for metaphysics, typically Platonic or Aristotelian. But no: the *aporia* begins at 1000ᵃ9 by referring to what the followers of Hesiod and all the *theologoi* have to say. 'They only considered what is plausible [convincing: *pithanon*] to themselves and gave no thought for us,' says Aristotle (well known himself for the consideration he shows his readers, to be sure). 'For they make the first principles gods or from gods and say that whatever did not taste of ambrosia and nectar became mortal. Evidently they used these terms in a way they were familiar with, and yet as to the application of their causes, they talk above our heads.'

'It is not worth while', he concludes, 'paying serious attention to those who purvey mythical sophistries' (*muthikōs sophizomenōn*). Note the double blow here. The verb *sophizesthai* is often, though of course not exclusively, used of those other foes of Aristotle and of Plato, the so-called sophists. But the likes of Hesiod and his followers too are criticized for playing the sophist, but doing so through myth, *muthikōs*. This reminds us that philosophy, in Aristotle's hands, is locked in combat on several fronts, not just with traditional story-tellers, *muthologoi*, particularly about the gods (when they are often dubbed *theologoi*), but also with new-style claimants to wisdom of all kinds, the sophists themselves and indeed many of those whom Aristotle otherwise labelled *phusikoi*, 'natural philosophers', too, when they did not share his, Aristotle's views, either on substantive questions or on what the aims of the study of nature should be, for example to investigate final causes.

It is not, of course, that there is *one* boundary, in Greece, between *muthos* and *logos*, but rather a coruscating variety of them, in different writers, indeed sometimes within the same writer, and in different contexts. Yet *some such* boundary is repeatedly invoked by Greek savants of one kind or another. Our Chinese text, the *Huainanzi*, has no such boundary and is not concerned with boundary-drawing of any such type at all, but moves with no sense of transition, let alone of strain, from Gong Gong to the number of intercalary months.

But how far does such a point apply elsewhere: how far can the *Huainanzi* be considered in any way typical? How far does my characterization itself ignore other important features of early Chinese texts? Let me concentrate on three main questions: first, are there not plenty of examples of hard-hitting criticisms of other writers to be found in the literature of the Warring States and the Han? How far should that modify my picture of seamless amalgams? Are there not, secondly, instances where different styles of writing themselves are explicitly distinguished? And what, thirdly, about the differences explicitly acknowledged by the ancient Chinese between different genres, the development, for example, of Chinese historiography itself, not a contrast between *muthos* and *logos* maybe, but why not a category-contrast that can be considered equivalent to it?

Let me make some brief comments on the first two of these questions before turning to explore the third in a little more detail. Certainly criticisms of individual thinkers, of groups of them, or of particular ideas, practices, and assumptions, including some relating to deep-seated traditional beliefs, can be found in writers of many different kinds and periods. Sometimes the criticism proceeds by ridicule or mockery (the *Zhuangzi* frequently lampoons Confucius, and pities Hui Shi for wasting his talents) but often also by argument. Wang Chong (first century CE), for instance, argues against those who assume that there is a kind of purposiveness at work generally in things, a belief he associated with the use of turtle shells and milfoil in divination. But it is not that he attacks divination as a whole, only certain applications of it—and he even concedes that a lucky person will find lucky signs in the turtle shells he chances on.[17] Again in the more general

[17] Cf. Loewe (1994), 173 f.

criticisms of groups of philosophers that we find in some texts, the point tends to be not that they have none of the Dao, but rather that they do not have the whole of it. That is the form of the criticism both in the *Tian Xia* chapter (33) in *Zhuangzi*, and in Sima Tan's comments included in the final chapter of Sima Qian's *Shiji* (130). I note, too, that these groups are named after their founder or leader (as Mohists from Mozi) or else from a leading idea or interest, *Yin yang*, the *Dao* itself, or the *Fa Jia* (the 'school of law') or *Ming Jia* (the 'school of names'). The last sometimes figure, in Western secondary sources, as the Chinese 'sophists', but that conjures up all sorts of inappropriate associations. The explosion of creativity, in the Warring States and Han periods, in philosophy and then also in such fields as medicine and mathematics, produced a wealth of new ideas and indeed new styles of enquiry: but it did not give rise to any new category of the rational as opposed to the mythical, nor to the invention of any epithet that stands as the equivalent to the pejorative use of *muthologos*.

That point can be confirmed if we turn to my second question, to do with Chinese reflections on different types of language use. Certainly, there are such reflections, indeed highly sophisticated ones, on, for example, the different modes of poetic writing.[18] The Great Preface to the *Shijing*, for instance, already numbers among the main types of poetry three modes categorized as 賦 (*fu*: descriptive/expository), 比 (*bi*: comparative/analogical), and 興 (*xing*: elevated, evocative), and of these, the middle category, *bi*, has often been hailed as equivalent to metaphorical or as recognizing the role of metaphor in poetry. Yet to that it has to be said that this tripartition is very far from providing an analogue to the dichotomy between literal and metaphorical, or rather between the strict, *kurios*, use of terms and their use *kata metaphoran*, that Aristotle drew, where the latter is a deviation from the norm provided by the former. *Bi*, in the Great Preface, is a virtue of one particular style of poetry, not a universal feature of poetic discourse, let alone a feature in which poetic discourse is contrasted, unfavourably, with the strict use of terms proper to philosophy, indeed essential for the validity of syllogistic.

---

[18] Cf. Jullien (1985).

A second, more general, discussion of language use comes
in one of the 'mixed' chapters of *Zhuangzi*, ch. 27, and again
the comparison and the contrast with the literal/metaphorical
dichotomy yield interesting results. *Zhuangzi* proposes a tri-
chotomy, between *yu yan*, *zhong yan*, and *zhi yan*—in Graham's
translations,[19] 'sayings from a lodging place, weighty sayings, and
spill-over sayings'—and since the first, *yu yan*, can be used,
nowadays, of metaphor, that looks a promising point of comparison. Yet the contrast is far more striking. *Yu yan*, we are told,
works nine times out of ten, and this is explained as where you
borrow a standpoint from outside, while *zhong yan*, 'weighty
saying', works seven times out of ten and is what you say on your
own authority. As for 'spill-over saying', that is 'new every day'
('smooth it out on the whetstone of heaven': 'use it to go by and
let the stream find its own channels, this is the way to last out
your years'). Whatever we make of the glosses, and they are
indeed obscure and disputed, there is no sense, in this passage,
that one of the three kinds is being treated as deviant in relation
to the others. Rather all have their uses and varying effectiveness.
Of course *Zhuangzi* has no cause to insist on one type of language
use purified for the purposes of the formal validity of syllogistic
logic. But that also means that, just as we do not in China have
a category of *muthos* downgraded by comparison with *logos*, so
there is no ambition to set up a category of the metaphorical
opposed to that of the literal.

My third question related to the development of new prose
genres, and especially of historiography itself. Should we not see
Sima Qian, author or compiler of the first of the standard histories, the *Shiji*, as in some sense securing the writing of history
as distinct from what Thucydides or even Herodotus would
have seen as mere story-telling or as entertainment? I cannot, of
course, do justice to all the ramifications of this fascinating question here. But certainly it can be said that the *Shiji* marks a break
from the earlier writing of *Annals* which themselves still owe
much to still earlier divination literature.[20] Whatever we make of

---

[19] (1989), 200ff.
[20] Cf. Vandermeersch (1980). Sima Qian does express doubt or agnosticism about very
early periods (e.g. in ch. 129: 'I know nothing about the times of Shennong and before')
and about stories about ghosts and spirits (e.g. ch. 55 at the end, though that is not an
unequivocal denial) and he certainly corrects other accounts on matters of fact, such as
chronology (as in ch. 97) or geography (e.g. ch. 123 on the Kunlun mountains and the

that hypothesis, we can certainly agree that there is a world of difference between the *Shiji* itself and such a divination manual as the *Yijing*, the Book of Changes, even though (1) the *Shiji* too aims, in a sense, to provide information useful for planning, if not predicting, the future, and (2) it is far from being just a historical account. It contains, for instance, a set of treatises on calendrical and other astronomical matters, and on music, and the office that Sima Tan and Sima Qian held in turn, that of 太史, *Tai Shi*, is one that carried important responsibilities in the fields of astronomy and astrology, even though to translate 'Astronomer Royal' (*vel sim.*) overdoes it.

But we can test the extent to which boundaries of the *muthos/ logos* type preoccupy early Chinese historiography by reviewing how Sima Qian deals with some of the specific material that figures in anthologies of Chinese myths such as that of Birrell. His handling of three stories of origins, in particular, is interesting in this regard, namely those of the Yin (3: 91–2), the Zhou (4: 111– 12), and the Qin (5: 173–4). In all three cases there is something special about the birth of the founder of the line, as Sima Qian relates this. In the Yin and Qin cases, the legendary ancestors Jian Di (often represented as a goddess) and Nu Xiu respectively become pregnant by swallowing an egg, and in the Zhou story, the mother of Qi ('the Abandoned'), Jiang Yuan, does so, it seems, after stepping in the footsteps of a giant she had followed into the fields.

Yet in all three cases the foundation story, in the *Shiji*, is linked to later, or contemporary, institutions. In the Yin case, the child grows up to help Yu in controlling the flood, and is eventually appointed by Emperor Shun to be his officer in charge of the five social relationships. The Qin ancestor is also given a role in flood control and in the domestication of animals, and the Zhou one is appointed by Emperor Yao as master of agriculture.

It is not that any of these stories has been completely sanitized. We are dealing with miraculous births and giants and indeed gods and goddesses. But they are given naturalistic twists, in what has

source of the Yellow River). But as we shall see, he recounts some fabulous stories without undercutting them, including stories about the heroic exploits of founder-figures such as Emperor Yu. Nor does he use a category equivalent to that of the mythical or the merely entertaining in order to downgrade whole classes of writings or beliefs.

been called reverse euhemerism,[21] where the movement of the
interpreter is not to treat myths as forgotten history, but to see
what are represented as historical accounts as overlaying earlier
myths. Thus the founder of the Zhou, Qi the Abandoned, was
also called Hou Ji, Lord Millet, a divinity in charge of grain, who
is celebrated, for example, in one of the poems in the *Shijing*
(Mao 245, Sheng min) as the inaugurator of due sacrifices to
usher in the New Year. While Sima Qian stays close, in certain
respects, to that poem, his Hou Ji not only has a great deal of
success with the hemp and beans he plants as a child, but we
are told that as an adult, as well as being fond of ploughing
and farming, he would also 'study the proper use of land, and
where it was suitable, he would plant and reap'. That conveys the
idea that he was very much the minister in charge of agriculture
even before he received official appointment as such from
Emperor Yao.

The comparisons between Sima Qian's versions of the stories
and some of the sources he draws on show how much, and what,
he has left out. The elements of divine intervention are played
down, though not by any means totally expurgated. That may
seem rather reminiscent of the kind of mixture we get in
Herodotus, say. Yes: but there are still important differences.
Sima Qian does not set out to categorize other people's stories
as ridiculous or incredible. He certainly does not attempt, as
Thucydides did, to downgrade earlier accounts as mere entertainment, let alone deploy for that purpose a vocabulary that distinguished between his true *logoi* and their *muthōdes*.

While we can recognize certain differences, then, between,
say, *Huainanzi* and *Shiji*, there are even greater differences between both of them and many Greek texts that use the *logos*/
muthos dichotomy. I have entered reservations already about the
generalizability of my analysis: but I now want to go further and
raise some even more difficult issues that will take us even further
afield into the speculative. Why, if my generalization holds, up to
a point (at least), do we find (as we appear to) this contrast
between one ancient culture that devotes a very considerable
effort to marking boundaries (and not just between *logos* and
muthos, of course) and another that does not? The importance of

---

[21] Cf. Boltz (1987).

that question, difficult though it is, is that, if we could answer it, the answer should have significant repercussions on how to set about studying what we call myths in different cultures—the comparative study, in other words.

One way forward is to investigate further what both *Huainanzi* and *Shiji* themselves aimed to achieve—for I have been characterizing them, so far, rather negatively, in terms of their non-use of Greek distinctions. The *Shiji*, we said, offers a lot of useful information built round a historical account. The *Huainanzi* does not write history, but it, too, certainly aims to be useful. Like the earlier *Lüshi chunqiu* and the approximately contemporary *Chunqiu fanlu* after it, it is not an encyclopaedia, but an encyclopaedic, by which I mean comprehensive, account of just about everything anyone might need to know. One can be more specific. Its principal target is not just anyone, but the ruler. It is what he needs to know, to rule, that is conveyed, but we have to remember that Chinese rulers had responsibilities far beyond what we might term the political domain. They had to make sure not just that the calendar is right (Metonic cycles included) but that everything 'under heaven' resonated duly *with* heaven. Then it is not just the ruler who is thereby advised: for in indicating how the ruler should rule, any such treatise indicates also how the minister should minister, the servants serve, and all observe their due social role and place. *Huainanzi* chapter 5, following the format of the *Yue Ling* or monthly ordinances, gets down to detail, with instructions not just with regard to what the ruler should do, during each of the twelve months of the year, to ensure that agriculture flourishes, when fishing should begin, and so on, but down to such matters as the colours of the court ladies' dresses and what music they should play, and including dire predictions concerning the disasters that would occur if any of these ordinances was not duly observed.

Both *Huainanzi* and *Shiji* are compilations put together, in the main, after the first Qin unification, in the first hundred years or so of Han rule. Not so long before, the learned elite were still recovering from the multiple traumata of the Qin conquests and of the Qin–Han transition: they included persecutions, executions, and the massive destruction of books. The earliest Han rulers, for their part, had been desperate to consolidate their position. In those circumstances, although one should not exaggerate the extent of the orthodoxy (both cosmological and political) that was actually achieved, there was, as Nathan Sivin has put it, a considerable yearning for one—on the part of rulers as well as on the part of intellectuals. The rulers needed one to confirm their rule, and it suited the intellectuals to provide one, since that secured their own position, in many cases their jobs no less.

Of course a desire for a consensus does not ensure that one will come about. But in China—and not just at the period I am talking of—the modes of operation of intellectuals, and indeed the way they were recruited, both favoured success in that matter. As for the latter, membership of the learned elite was only attained by a long apprenticeship, sometimes marked by rituals of initiation. Memorizing the texts, the canons, *jing*, that were handed to you, came before being expected to understand them, and the prime duty of members of the 'school', *jia* (but the term means 'family'), was indeed the conservation and transmission of those texts.[22] Meanwhile you were expected to show as much loyalty to your teachers as to your own father. You will remark how different all this was from ancient Greece.

As for the former, we have seen that the preferred target for much Chinese intellectual production was the ruler or emperor. He was the one to persuade if you wanted to get anything done, or indeed just wanted a job. Of course differing views, both on matters of public policy and on issues of more theoretical interest, were often expressed to the emperor or to his ministers: recall that it was believed that the *Huainanzi* itself came from a discussion at the court of Liu An. But there was nothing resembling the free-for-all of open public debate before a lay audience that we hear about from our Greek sources.

The pressures favouring consensus were particularly strong, I suggested, in the early Han. But though there were differences between periods, and between different parts of China, during the centuries from the end of the Spring and Autumn 481 BCE to the end of the Han 220 CE, one key factor remained remarkably constant. This is that throughout those centuries, and indeed throughout the whole of Chinese history down to modern times, the political ideal was that of the single rule of the wise and

---

[22] See Sivin (1995*a*); cf. G. E. R. Lloyd (1994) and (1996).

benevolent monarch. Particular rulers, of princedoms or the whole, often fell short: but the ideal itself remained uncontested. While consensus on that issue did not dictate the search for consensus on others, it may well have acted as a stimulus in that direction. As we noted, there was certainly disagreement and criticism among Chinese intellectuals on a wide range of topics. But there is this—I think fundamental—difference from ancient Greece, that Chinese intellectuals did not regularly seek to make their own reputations *by way of* the criticism of their predecessors and contemporaries—let alone (as happened often enough in Classical Greece) by way of the criticism of their immediate teachers.

My—speculative—argument on myth, then, is that the presence or absence of a sharp and explicit *logos*-versus-*muthos* dichotomy is just one feature that, like others, may be correlated with general factors either inhibiting, or favouring, the search for and maintenance of a consensus, in Greece and China.[23] Such factors are, in both Greece and China, enormously complex: political ideologies, and the organization and recruitment of intellectuals, are only part of the story, and diachronic differences, and exceptions, must be allowed for on both sides. Further features, of the impact of social and political institutions and values, on the science produced in Greece and China, and on why the problems themselves were defined in the ways they were, are the subject of the collaborative study on which Nathan Sivin and I have now embarked.

But if there is something to the argument I have presented to you thus far, in this telegraphic form, it is worth spelling out, in conclusion, the lessons that might be drawn from it, so far as the comparative study of mythology goes. It will be apparent to you how far away my own approach here has been from the assumptions that drove the early Lévi-Straussian programme of the structuralist study of myth. There, myths would give one access to universal features of the human mind. What Lévi-Strauss shared with the Saussurean programme of general linguistics was that deep structures would be revealed underlying the apparent diversity of surface phenomena. That in turn has generated, or at least stimulated, massive research efforts, in social anthropology,

[23] See Sivin (1995*b*).

in psychology, in cognitive studies generally, to identify the cross-cultural universals in play, for example in concepts of space, time, number, causation, colour, even natural kinds.

It is not that I object to such programmes in principle, but they are far harder to implement without prejudicing the issues by an uncritical use of essentially Western categories than is often recognized. We cannot, as I said, do without *some* analytical framework. But we need to be more wary of more of our Greek inheritance than we sometimes are. I alluded to the example of the literal and the metaphorical, where the non-applicability of that dichotomy to ancient Chinese materials underlies the need for an alternative framework: my own preference there—for which I have argued elsewhere[24]—is to favour an approach based on the non-dichotomizing concept of semantic stretch. But a similar point applies also to myth. Maybe we all have some sense of the inappropriateness of applying Greek *muthos*-versus-*logos* distinctions to non-Greek materials. But in this case, too, I suggest we need radically to problematize the category of myth itself.

Instead of taking that category as our starting point, as in some sense a given, and then offering some new or refurbished definition or definitions to allow us to apply it to highly diverse materials, it seems to me that we need to begin further back. We have to examine the contexts in which different criteria of truth-telling or of fiction are at work, in which different rules operate, or expectations are entertained, for the use of the imaginative, or the traditional, or the playful, for the purposes of persuasion, or for seeking authority or prestige, or for instruction, or just for entertainment—not that any such rules are likely to be absolute, incapable of transgression. Due attention, in other words, has first to be paid to the contexts of communicative exchange and of interpersonal reaction, to the modes of discourse that the actors explicitly or implicitly recognize, and again to such issues as the perceived need for consensus or the tolerance of competition, for example both between story-tellers themselves and between them and others. That leads, in turn, of course, to an examination of the social and political institutions within which speakers and audiences operated, indeed to the values of the culture within

[24] Cf. G. E. R. Lloyd (1987), ch. 4.

which their exchanges occurred, including the canons of polite-
ness and the expectations entertained in different contexts concerning acceptable public challenge or dissent.

For understanding how 'myths' should be talked about, in
China and in Greece, that seems to me the prior desideratum, not
the comparison of individual motifs, or even ordered sets of
them, but the analysis of what those who used this material used
it *for*, how they thought about it, in particular the use they made
of the various categories they had in which to think about it.
That, at least, is the lesson that this Hellenist brings back from
ancient China.

V
Myth and/or/into History and Ethnography

8

Euenius the Negligent Nightwatchman (Herodotus 9. 92-6)

ALAN GRIFFITHS

No one can properly engage with Herodotus without being forced to take a position, whether openly or by implication, on the essential nature of his marvellous text. It is not a question of aligning oneself behind one or other of the two competing theories which attempt to seize control of the battlefield by launching their campaigns from well-entrenched redoubts on the fringe; for neither the arch-conservatives like A. B. Lloyd or W. K. Pritchett, who would dearly love every word to be true, nor the heretical challengers like Detlev Fehling, who see the historian as a creative inventor not only of the genre but of its material too, have shown any sign of making significant territorial inroads.[1] It is the centre ground where the issue must be fought out; not where favourable terrain provides easy victories for either side, but where matters are complex and delicate. This problem is most intractable in those sections of his book where modes of presentation which strike the modern reader as heterogeneous and incompatible seem to sit amicably side by side. One moment we are travelling smoothly down a Rankean 'wie-es-eigentlich-gewesen' (WEEG) narrative line, the next we are diverted (in more senses than one) into a tale straight from the pages of the Grimm Brothers; but both modes apparently make the same claim on our acceptance. The task must be to make progress towards understanding just how it is possible for what some might be inclined to call *muthos* and *logos*[2] to coexist so easily in the text of the *Historiai*.

---

[1] A. B. Lloyd (1975–88); Pritchett (1993); Fehling (1989).

[2] Let us provisionally define the opposition between these convenient shorthand categories to be that between a discourse whose construction is dominated by traditional components, and whose expression and final shape are thus to a large extent predictable, and another in which elements are individually selected and disposed in a compositional

1

At 9. 92, as the Persian War narrative moves towards its final climax at Mycale, we are (and have been for some time) definitely operating in WEEG mode:

When they had finished, they sailed away . . . for he gave instructions for Hegesistratus to sail with them, regarding his name as a good omen.[3] The Greeks paused for the day, but on the next they set about trying to get a favourable sacrifice; their diviner being Deïphonus the son of Euenius, a man from Apollonia, that is Apollonia in the Ionian Gulf.[4]

At this point, with typically deft and well-practised sleight of hand, Herodotus changes gear. The transition is gradual, at first almost imperceptible:

His father Euenius[5] underwent the following experience. In this town Apollonia they keep sheep[6] which are sacred to the Sun-god. During the day these pasture beside the river Aous,[7] which flows from Mount Lacmon through the territory of Apollonia to reach the sea by the harbour at Oricus; but at night they are guarded—for the Apolloniates attach great importance to these sheep, because of some oracle—by men who are chosen from the richest and most nobly born of the citizens, each serving for a year at a time. The flock is penned up in a cave, some way from the city. So there it was that this Euenius, chosen for the duty, was warden at the time. And one night he fell asleep on his watch, and wolves got past him into the cave and killed about sixty of them. When he woke up to the fact, he kept it quiet and told nobody, planning to buy some more and substitute them. But it didn't work; the citizens somehow got to hear of the incident, brought him before

---

process which is *not* fundamentally predetermined by inherited routines. That is to say: the cusp is the point at which the formula loses its ancient pre-eminence.

[3] Hegesistratus = 'Army-leader'.

[4] The normal way of distinguishing it from the Black Sea Apollonia; cf. 4. 90.

[5] (93.1) Εὐήνιον κατέλαβε] κατέλαβε Εὐήνιον MSS, transp. Stein. Kallenberg deleted Εὐήνιον, but cf. 5. 25. 1 'Οτάνεα . . . τοῦ τὸν πατέρα Σισάμνην . . . , 6. 103. 1 Μιλτιάδης, τοῦ τὸν πατέρα Κίμωνα τὸν Στησαγόρεω κατέλαβε φυγεῖν ἐξ 'Αθηνέων Πεισίστρατον τὸν 'Ιπποκράτεος, 7. 233. 2 Λεοντιάδεω, τοῦ τὸν παῖδα Εὐρύμαχον. . . . A proper name also immediately precedes κατέλαβε at 3. 118. 1, 6. 38. 2, 9. 105.

[6] (93.1) Pace Erbse (1992: 144, 'Kühe'), πρόβατα must here be sheep; sixty cattle would be a tough assignment for even the bloodthirstiest or most ravenous pack of wolves.

[7] (93.1) So Strabo 7. 5. 8; Hecataeus (*FGrHist* 1 F 102bc) called it the 'Aias'. Some go for the more dubious supplement 'Chon'.

a court, and sentenced him, for the crime of falling asleep on guard-duty, to be deprived of his eyesight.

But as soon as they had blinded him, the sheep ceased to bear lambs and the earth to produce crops as usual.[8] Prophecies were delivered to them both at Dodona and at Delphi, when they enquired as to the cause of their current affliction,[9] that they had acted unjustly in depriving Euenius, the guardian of the sacred sheep, of his eyesight—for it was they themselves[10] who had sent the wolves, and they would not stop exacting vengeance on his behalf until they paid whatever recompense he himself should choose and think appropriate for what they had done; and once that was settled, they for their part would grant Euenius such a gift as would make many people think him blest to possess.

So those were the oracles that were given. But the Apolloniates kept them secret, and commissioned ⟨two of the⟩ citizens[11] to handle the matter. And this is how they handled it: they came up to Euenius as he was sitting on a bench,[12] sat down beside him and chatted about various things before eventually coming round to express sympathy for what he had gone through. Leading him on like this, they asked what compensation he would choose, should the Apolloniates be prepared to undertake to make amends for what they had done. Now he hadn't heard the oracle, so he made a choice: if someone were to present him with plots of land, he said (and he named the townsmen whom he knew to own the finest pair of estates in Apollonia), and on top of these the finest mansion he knew in the whole town—well, if he were to get those, then he would drop his angry resentment for ever, and that would constitute sufficient compensation. And hardly were the words out of his mouth when the men sitting either side of him jumped in and said: 'Euenius, the citizens of Apollonia hereby pay you the compensation you have named for your blinding, in accordance with prophecies

---

[8] (93.3) Read perhaps γῆ ἔφερε καρπὸν ὁμοίως ⟨καὶ πρὸ τοῦ⟩; the tradition offers γῆ ἔφερε ὁμοίως καρπόν (a), γῆ ἔφερε ὁμοίως (d). Cf. 5. 82. 3 (where a omits καρπόν) and 6. 139. 1 (whence my supplement; cf. Powell's translation).

[9] (93.4) I follow Hude in accepting Stein's deletion of τοὺς προφήτας and οἱ δὲ αὐτοῖσι ἔφραζον; the whole run ἐπείτε . . . ἔφραζον was damned by Krüger and Powell, but the rest of the first clause is thoroughly Herodotean.

[10] (93.4) Zeus and Apollo, presumably, prophetic father and son working in concert with the aim of initiating a new seer into their mysteries.

[11] (94.1) I suggest ἀνδράσι ⟨δυοῖσι⟩ διαπρῆξαι. If the deputation model exemplified in the final version of *Iliad* 9 (cf. the Achillean ἀμήνιτος, 94. 2) is preferred, Gomperz's ⟨τρισί⟩ may be accepted; but the palaeography is less convincing, and how would they dispose themselves on the park bench? Cf. in general 4. 33. 3 πέμψαι . . . τῶν ἀστῶν ἄνδρας πέντε πομπούς, 8. 135. 2 τῶν ἀστῶν αἱρετοὺς ἄνδρας τρεῖς.

[12] (94.1) Why did de Sélincourt (Penguin) translate '*official* bench'? Was he thinking of Demaratus in state session with the ephors at 6. 63. 2? But E. is in disgrace, ostracized. Marincola's 1996 revision of the Penguin omits the adjective.

received.' Well, he got furious at being tricked, since he then discovered the full story; but they bought up the properties he had chosen from their owners and presented them to him. And immediately after that he got an implanted prophetic gift, which made him famous. It was the son of this Euenius, then, Deïphonus, who was acting as diviner for the Greek forces, having been brought along by the Corinthians. But I have also heard this version: that it was by trading on the name of Euenius that Deïphonus got his work all over Greece, though he wasn't really Euenius' son at all.

And so, our transition eased by this final touch of cynicism, we find ourselves shifted back into WEEG: 'When the Greeks' sacrificing proved favourable, they set sail from Delos towards Samos. And when they reached the part of Samos called Calami . . .'

If the label is worth anything at all, the embedded Euenius pericope is *muthos*—weapons-grade *muthos*. It hums and buzzes with the tones and harmonics of Greek traditional belief. We may start, then, by dismantling it and laying out for inspection some of the more obvious components which identify it as a narrative which blends folk-tale and cultic aetiology. Of course, if I had a simple, monolithic explanation of this story—that it was a reflex of solar symbolism, or of castration anxiety, let us say—it would be easy to deal with it in a few pages. Since however I regard all such material as intrinsically slippery, overdetermined, irreducible to any single formula, all I can do is provide a brief sketch, concentrating on some of the most important allotropes of Herodotus' little story.

The first of these allotropes will no doubt already have been rising insistently into the consciousness of any reader of the tale. Euenius is a relative, at some level, of that other lone shepherd who lives apart from his community, Polyphemus. The cave, the raiders led by Odysseus the grandson of Autolycus ('Verywolf') who evade the guard at the cave mouth, the ill-advised sleep, the blinding—even the prophecy motif finds a dim echo as the Cyclops remembers, too late, the warning he had received.[13] Polyphemus too has a god to exact punishment for the harm done to him. Of course the mytheme-pack has been shuffled and redealt—Odysseus' men pass the guardian in the opposite

---

[13] *Od.* 9. 507 ff.

direction, and the roles of hero and villain are interchanged—but that is exactly how popular tradition goes about generating new narratives, by reversing signs. As to the nature of the relationship between the pair of transforms, I take it that the Cyclops story, widely distributed as a stand-alone narrative, was pressed into service to provide an *aition* for the cult; but I will not attempt to argue the point here.[14]

Behind Euenius' other shoulder hovers the spirit of Epimenides, another holy man associated with sheep. It was midday (not midnight) when the young herdsman, on the way to his father's flock, lay down in a cave for his siesta only to awake fifty-seven years later; and in his purification of Athens he used black and white sheep to find the hot-spots where the pollution was lurking.[15]

Conon's version of the Euenius tale[16] deserves mention if only because his alternative name for the hero, Pithenius, invites us to speculate briefly on the prophet's etymology. Whether he is Euenius ('Goodreins') or Pithenius ('Obeyreins'), we are presented here with an image of the compliant human medium as ridden or steered by the god. If we choose Euenius' aspect as a servant of the Sun-cult, he might be a horse in the god's chariot-team;[17] if we prefer to emphasize his prophetic side, then he is the mouthpiece who writhes and foams under the pressure of Apollo's bit and bridle, imagery well attested at least for the Pythia and other inspired priestesses. And if he has a name so well suited to his job, he ought really to be a hereditary prophet, called after his father's skills, as is usual.[18]

---

[14] Polyphemus: see the thirty-eight variants assembled by Frazer as app. XIII of his Loeb Apollodorus; and the first chapter of Page (1955). The Cattle of the Sun episode in book 12 provides a further Odyssean overlap; there as here, as Nagler (1980–1: 102) observes, the slaughter of the Sun's beasts takes place when the hero drops off to sleep. See now Cook (1995), 84 f.

[15] Epimenides: Diog. Laert. 1. 109 ff. Missing sheep and western prophecy are linked again in the story of Mardylas at Dodona, told by Proxenus, Pyrrhus' court historian; see *FGrHist* 703 F 7.

[16] Conon: *FGrHist* 26 F 1. 30.

[17] Cf. *RE* vi, s.v. 'Euenia' (Tümpel), another name for the Argonautic Chalciope, daughter of Aietes, and thus a member of the Sun family.

[18] Sons named after their father's expertise: e.g. *Telemachus* son of the archer Odysseus; *Eurysaces* son of Ajax who carried the great shield; *Hippolochus* born to Bellerophon who ambushed the Chimaera on horseback. Democedes ('Care in the community') and Stesichorus ('Choirmaster') will have followed their fathers' professions in medicine and music respectively.

Next, a sample of some relevant items which may be loosely assembled under the 'folk-tale' heading. Our tale shows the standard diptych structure, with disaster and dissension succeeded by the restoration of a new order; and the familiar structural formula by which elements occurring in the opening passage are recycled in the second section. In this case, Euenius' failed attempt to keep his *hamartia* secret from the citizens is matched by the citizens' successful concealment of the oracle from the prophet-to-be. The loss of two eyes finds its counterpart, perhaps, in the acquisition of two estates.[19]

What of Herodotus' vague and evasive mention of the oracle, 'some oracle or other', which was supposed to underpin the cult? It is easy enough to see (even if Herodotus, eager as usual to play down the element of 'superstition', is reluctant to admit it) that the sheep were, in folklore terms, the town's external soul, its talisman.[20] Any damage to the flock imperilled the fortune of the city itself; hence the savage punishment, worthy of Moses or Zaleucus. Euenius had kept blind watch, *alaoskopiē*, and had to suffer accordingly. Eyes closed temporarily in sleep were to be closed permanently. But merely human justice lacks the broader vision of Olympus. How galling to exact condign punishment, to think that you've got it right (for what could be fairer?),[21] and then to be told that the offence was all part of some mysterious divine strategy! The citizens of Paros received an identical rap over the knuckles from Delphi when they wished to execute the priestess Timo, who had tried to betray the island's talismanic objects to Miltiades. These too were kept in a sacred precinct outside the town.[22]

There are many other treatments of the ever-fascinating question of what constitutes appropriate compensation, and how the

---

[19] Or cf. perhaps Di-poinos (n. 23 below)? Doubled penalties are regular in Greek law. As for the town house, no doubt it was pointed out to visitors as the building in which the prophet first exercised his new-found gift. Compare Pausanias' mention of the 'mantic' house in Phlious where Amphiaraus once slept and prophesied for the first time; it had been kept locked up (as *hieros*?) ever since (2. 13. 7).

[20] Communal talismans: Troy (Palladion), Paros ('objects'), Megara (Nisus' hair), London (ravens), Gibraltar (apes). For a recent analysis, see Faraone (1992).

[21] Blinding: is this a credible *state* punishment, even for those Draconian times? Zaleucus supposedly passed a law prescribing blinding for adultery; when his son was caught *in flagrante*, Zaleucus offered one of his own eyes (Aelian, *VH* 13. 24).

[22] Miltiades also ends up in court after his Parian adventure: 6. 135.

rules can be stretched, skirted, or evaded;[23] I draw particular attention only to another *mantis*, Tisamenus, who appears in Herodotus as Euenius' shrewder counterpart: he does realize what a high value the community (in this case the Spartans) has set on his co-operation, and is accordingly able to extract maximum benefit from signing his contract.[24]

If we shift our attention now from story to cult and ritual, we find resonances just as rich. The Apollonia sheep-fetish has the ring of authenticity. It is entirely appropriate that Helios should have been worshipped at this site in the extreme west, for the sun seems to have attracted cult not only on acropoleis and mountain-tops, straining up towards the god at his zenith, but also at marginal promontories, where Greeks could reach out to trace the southern- and easternmost points of his annual progress.[25] And this is after all Apollonia, Apollo-ville; the god was probably already identified with the sun in Aeschylus' *Bassarai*, and conflation of the two is definitely established in Euripides' *Phaethon* (l. 225).

Those who see ephebic coming-of-age ritual everywhere may well sniff its presence here too. Euenius must have (or should have) slept most of the day in order to keep proper watch at

---

[23] A word about some compensation stories. In this context, one thinks first of other prophets: Tiresias' receipt of inner vision to replace his ordinary sight, Cassandra's blighted gift. There are many other examples of the 'blank cheque' motif: the Delphic oracle told the Lemnian Pelasgians, suffering from famine and sterility after the murder of their Attic wives and children, to 'pay the Athenians whatever they ask for' (Hdt. 6. 139); Apollodorus (3. 15. 8) reports that the Athenians, in their turn, were instructed by the same source to pay to Minos the same restitution for the lifting of the same punishment, after their killing of Androgeos. Compare too Pliny's story about the Cretan sculptors Dipoinos ('Double-punishment'?) and Scyllis, who were able to renegotiate 'magnis mercedibus' their contract which the Sicyonians had broken, after famine had ensued; once more Apollo was the enforcer (*HN* 39. 9). Further examples of open-ended promises are found at Hdt. 4. 154 (Themison and Etearchus in Crete) and 6. 62 (the Spartan Ariston's trickery of his friend). In the 'real world', meanwhile (the famous Cretan inscription BM 1969. 4-2.1, published by Jeffery and Morpurgo-Davies (1970)), the *poinikastas* Spensitheos was to receive fifty jugs of new wine 'from whichever plot he chooses to take it'; a clearly practical method to ensure that the beneficiary was not to be fobbed off with substandard vinegar. When it comes to trickery in grant-gift, it is usually the *recipient* who pulls a fast one: compare the story of the oxhide at Carthage. Contrast Pittacus' modest request at Plu. *Malice of Herodotus* 858b: offered huge rewards by the Mytileneans, he asks for 'only as much land as I can throw a spear over'.

[24] Tisamenus the prophet: 9. 33.

[25] Helios-cult on the heights (Taygetus, Paus. 3. 20. 4; Acrocorinth), in the south (Taenarum, *HHApollo* 410–13), and east (Rhodes).

night. As such he is a classic reversed initiate, a 'Contrary' like the Indian in *Little Big Man* who sits backwards on his horse and says 'Goodbye' for 'Hello'. Euenius saw the moon not the sun—he was already in some sense 'blind'. Like the young Spartans away from their community on the *krupteia*, he came to life at night. Indeed the light/dark, day/night, waking/sleeping, vision/blindness oppositions run through the story as a leitmotiv; no doubt cutting the cake at a different angle would bring out the way in which the sheep hidden in the cave at night-time correspond to the dark days of winter when the sun withdraws from the Greeks and, as Hesiod says, retreats south to shine on the black men. If he is to return in spring, it is vital that nobody should do anything to disturb the magic, in the way that poor Euenius did.

Perhaps the most interesting account to set beside that of Euenius is Herodotus' description of the annual rite associated with the ancestral emblems of Scythian kingship:[26]

This sacred gold is guarded with special care by the kings, and they show their reverence towards it in a great sacrificial ritual every year: whoever should fall asleep under the open sky during this festival, while he is in possession of the gold, is said by the Scythians not to survive the year. And because of this he is granted as much land as he can ride around in a single day (4. 7).

Here, from beyond the borders of the Greek world, Herodotus reports a ritual which displays suspiciously similar lineaments to the complex we have been examining. Once more a guard succumbs to Morpheus and receives both reward and punishment. 'Under the open sky' recalls Euenius' sentry-post at the mouth of the cave; and perhaps the Apollonian sheep were originally golden, as is often the case with talismans which embody the authority of the state.[27] The treatment handed out to

---

[26] On this tantalizing fragment, see Glaser (1937), who is, however, in my view too willing to recognize genuine (if refracted) Scythian tradition here, and underplays elements which are inconsistent with what we know of Scythian culture and seem to be more economically explicable in terms of Greek traditions; see n. 29 below.

[27] For the nexus between golden talismans (especially golden flocks) and political power, see L. Gernet, ' "Value" in Greek Myth', in Gordon (1981), 111–46, at 131–7 (cf. von Reden in this volume): there is the golden fleece which secures Jason's kingship, and the golden lamb which does the same for the Pelopids (the latter to be recognized, I think, on the Apulian bell-krater in New York published by Trendall (1994), 129). The multiplicity of sheep here suits Apollonia's aristocratic oligarchy better than the single talisman of kingship.

the unfortunate Scythian king identifies him as, in Greek terms, a kind of *pharmakos* ('scapegoat')-figure.[28] Strabo (11. 4. 7) provides a further variant, again set among the Scythians—this time those of Albania, near the Caucasus:

As for any [of the *hierodouloi* (temple slaves)] who becomes excessively possessed, and wanders through the woods all on his own, the priest seizes him, binds him in sacred fetters, and maintains him sumptuously during that year. Afterwards he is [sacrificed].

Here the *pharmakos* echoes ring still clearer. Surely both are cases of Greeks imaginatively transposing their own practices, in appropriately wilder form, on to neighbouring, or more distant, peoples.[29]

2

But enough of this irresponsible Frazerian comparativism.[30] Enough scuttling haphazardly along a few threads of the intricate network which constitutes Herodotus' worldwide web. We have seen enough to make it clear that in the case of this Apollonian prophet, as Joseph Fontenrose put it, 'The historical person steps into the shoes of a traditional hero and either his actual deeds are reshaped on legendary models or he is credited with wholly imaginary deeds of the sort that occur in traditional tales'.[31] Euenius, the father of the seer in the Mycale campaign,

---

[28] For *pharmakoi*, typified by the period of luxury followed by expulsion or death, the basic texts relate to Colophon (Hippon. frs. 4–9 Bergk = 5–10 West), Abdera (Callim. *Aet.* 4, fr. 90 Pfeiffer), and Massilia (Petron. fr.1 Müller); the fundamental treatment is that of Bremmer (1983).

[29] What use was a gift of land to a nomadic Scythian? The 'dying within the year' motif is certainly at home in Greece: it is the fate which Pausanias records as afflicting anyone who entered the sanctuary of Zeus Lycaeus in Arcadia (8. 38). See Carpenter (1946), 20.

[30] I allow myself one last, shamelessly random note on the subject of the staying-awake ordeal. Besides Gilgamesh's abject failure (Tablet XI), compare Turnbull (1961), 78: 'Apparently one of the greatest crimes that a pygmy male can commit, if not the greatest, is to be found asleep when the *molimo* [a festival figure] is singing.' The anal-retentive Fafner sleeps on his gold ('Ich sitze, und besitze') but the griffins are permanently alert in guarding theirs.

[31] Fontenrose (1968), 87 n. 21. Of the heroized figures there discussed, the one who comes closest to matching the Euenius template is Euthycles the Locrian athlete (Callim. *Aet.* 4, fr. 84 f.): wrongly convicted by his fellow citizens on a charge concerning animals (mules, this time; acquired, not lost), his unjust punishment triggers the usual sequelae of plague and famine, intervention from Apollo, and eventual honours.

arrives in Herodotus' text trailing clouds of mythological glory.

But what's the upshot? What lessons can we draw from Euenius that relate to the theme of this book, the tension between two complementary or opposed forms of discourse? What is a gobbet of what we may unhesitatingly categorize as *muthos* doing in the middle of this long stretch of *logos*? For what is striking about this story is its splendid isolation—there has been nothing quite similar, so far, in book 9.[32] We are quite used to paradigmatic moral digressions (compare perhaps Glaucus the Spartan at 6. 86, narrated by a character)—but this one sticks out like a sore thumb. Worse, its inclusion seems arbitrary, and quite unmotivated by the action.[33]

So what is going on? Let me make a couple of preliminary points.

First: Euenius' story seems to have a general function as a retardatory element, building up expectation before the climactic battle of Mycale which ensues. It is, partly, a tease-pause, like the famous flashback of the scar of Odysseus.[34] Secondly, and more importantly: Archaio-Classical Greeks were of course perfectly used to encountering texts which regularly 'changed gear'. Greek literature had developed a familiar strategy for narrating a past, and then from time to time reaching back beyond that narrative baseline to a still more remote plane of action: Pindar's myths back-projected behind the victory celebrations, or Nestor's anecdotes in the *Iliad*, will do as gestural examples. Present is to past as past is to further past. And the audience were used to that secondary level being 'stranger', and conforming to different rules.

So the mundane and the mythical may coexist without conflict. But a recognition of this fact does not mean the Greeks were somehow unable to distinguish between reality and fiction,

---

[32] Anecdotes about the soothsayers present on either side at the battle of Plataea are also introduced at the corresponding point, on the eve of battle (9. 33-7); but these are less expansive, and concern the prophets themselves, not their fathers. The Melampus digression (ch. 34) is, however, broadly analogous.

[33] Macan (1908) ad loc.: 'The passage here looks like an addition, perhaps of later date.'

[34] Anyone still impressed by Erich Auerbach's claim (1953: ch. 1) that the scar-digression in *Od.* 19 occupies so much precious foreground space at a crucial moment of the plot because that is the only way Homer could mention it at all should compare another notorious 'long moment'—the outrageous digression on gun-types in Nicholas Freeling's *What Are the Bugles Blowing For?* (Harmondsworth, 1975), 106 f.

actuality and literary convention; any more than we are unable to tell the difference between the status of statements like 'There are fairies at the bottom of my garden' and others like 'There are fir-trees at the bottom of my garden'. For that reason I am not altogether happy with the way John Herington expressed himself in an article in 1991. Commenting on F. A. Wolf's cameo description of Herodotus as a writer 'as devoted to truth as he was a passionate narrator of fiction', Herington wrote: 'In that phrase he neatly caged for display the literary centaur that is H. . . . [it has a] human forepart . . . [but] the body indissolubly joined to it is something out of the faraway mountains, out of an older, freer and wilder realm where our conventions have no force.'[35]

I'm not sure I'd put it in quite those Nietzschean terms. When Herodotus 'changes gear' in the way I have suggested, he knows perfectly well what he is up to, and the audience too knows what to expect; there are regular verbal cues to signal such transitions from the plane of the main narrative to areas where less strict standards of verisimilitude apply. A couple of these markers are a genealogical reference, and some such phrase as 'an incident of the following kind';[36] a full analysis would be welcome.

Furthermore—to leave Herodotus for a moment—there are other data which seem to me to make it clear that his contemporaries could tell the difference between a centaur, on the one hand, and a man on a horse, on the other. I am thinking of the way in which institutions like the Delphic oracle, exposure, stoning, and Bacchism are represented in Greek texts. In all these cases the literary picture is painted in more lurid colours than the real events to which it corresponds. In reality, the Delphic oracle provided little more than a Yes/No answering service; its textual counterpart routinely utters hexameters.[37] Exposure and stoning

---

[35] (1991: 8), enlarging on Wolf's pithy paradox, 'veri amantissimus pariter et fictorum cupidus narrator' (*Prolegomena ad Homerum*, ch. 14).
[36] Genealogy: cf. e.g. 8. 137. 1 τοῦ δὲ Ἀλεξάνδρου τούτου ἕβδομος γενέτωρ Περδίκκης . . . (leading into the *Märchen* of the magic loaf and the sunbeam), then 139 ἀπὸ τούτου δὴ τοῦ Περδίκκεω Ἀλέξανδρος ὧδε ἐγένετο. . . . Even pushing the narrative back one generation may be enough to transpose it into mythical time: cf. 6. 127, where one of Agariste's 7th-cent. suitors is 'Laphanes son of Euphorion, who entertained the Dioscuri'. For 'the following incident', cf. e.g. 3. 139. 1 f. . . .τῶν ἦν καὶ Συλοσῶν ὁ Αἰάκεος, Πολυκράτεός τε ἐὼν ἀδελφεὸς καὶ φεύγων ἐκ Σάμου. τοῦτον τὸν Συλοσῶντα κατέλαβε εὐτυχίη τις τοιήδε· . . . (and there follows the story of the cloak, perhaps thus implicitly signalled as improbable).
[37] See Fontenrose (1978), ch. 7, 'The Mantic Session'.

happened, but not with the exciting frequency that drama and historiography present. Aspasia may have worshipped Dionysus, but I doubt whether she wrenched the still-pulsating hearts out of young lions. When served up by authors, descriptions of these phenomena expected, and received, different standards of response.

To sum up so far: Herodotus not only rides the two Phaedrian horses *muthos* and *logos* with ease, but he knows it, delights in it, and consciously exploits it. And the listeners collude in the enterprise.

3

All these considerations provide sufficient but not necessary conditions for the inclusion of such a folk-tale. Still the question remains: why here? Why has he chosen to give it houseroom precisely at this point? After all, in spite of all the reasons I have so far given he seems a little apologetic. I have not so far laid much emphasis on the little coda to the story in chapter 95: 'I have also heard this version,' writes Herodotus, 'that it was by trading on the name of Euenius that Deïphonus got his work all over Greece, though he wasn't really Euenius' son at all.' If this acerbic touch has a literary ancestor, it is surely the unusual and exceptional authorial remark with which the *Iliad* poet rounds off the Glaucus and Diomedes passage in book 6: 'Zeus must have taken Glaucus' wits away, for he exchanged gold armour for bronze.' That is another case of 're-entry' into the main narrative after a fanciful digression, and its function seems to me to be similar: to distance the author from responsibility for the improbable material he has just been narrating, to cut the oil with a dash of lemon and signal a return to the groundline.

If then the tale of Euenius is apparently pointless, breaks into an otherwise homogeneous account of the Plataea and Mycale campaigns, and appears to cause the author himself some slight wriggle of embarrassment, what is its function? I will suggest, with extreme brevity, a possible answer.

Herodotus has designed his *Historiai* as a coherent unity structured by ring-composition. On the first page, the Phoenicians move to a new country; on the last, the wise Cyrus advises the

Persians not to do the same. Within this outer ring, we find allusions to the Trojan War at both beginning and end. The first extended story we come to is that of Gyges and the wife of Candaules; the last is a horrific reprise, sharing the theme of the first and much of its detailed verbal expression, the story of Xerxes and the wife and daughter of his brother Masistes. And the next ring comprises a similar matching pair of two extended stories which are Greek, which seem superficially to be unmotivated, and which examine the theme of suffering and redemption. The second member of the pair is the story we have been considering. The first, its twin, is the tale of Arion and the Dolphin at 1. 24.

Consider first their position: Arion's story is inserted between the first two historical attacks on Greek cities by oriental monarchs, those by Alyattes on Miletus and Croesus on Ephesus. The tale of Euenius is similarly sandwiched between the culminating Greek victories of Plataea and Mycale.

Then the characters: as poet and prophet, both are protected by their patron Apollo and are associated with his sacred animals (though, true to form, Herodotus has of course rationalized the intervention of Apollo Delphinius, the Dolphin-god, out of his version of the Arion story). The Euenius tale is indeed carefully timed to make its appearance while the Greeks are temporarily anchored off, precisely, Apollo's island of Delos.

Both stories concern the west of Greece, and in particular Corinth (Euenius has been brought to Mycale in the Corinthian contingent), even though the focus of the main narrative, on each occasion, is concentrated on the East. Each hero experiences brutal treatment, but is ultimately restored to honour and respect.

And the moral? The two Queen stories which are placed 'outside' this pair in the frame were negative and apotreptic, enforcing the thought that oriental monarchy is doomed to repeat its mistakes, the second time in more sadistic form. These two offer a more optimistic thought: that the Greek gods (not only Apollo, but Zeus himself: Arion was a traveller, a stranger, and a suppliant, and so triply under Zeus' protection; Euenius found support at Dodona, Zeus' sanctuary) will ultimately support their faithful worshippers and assert Greek Justice, in spite of sufferings and setbacks that will have to be endured *en route* to that final point.

I conclude that Herodotus knows very well what he is about. He would have no problems with our differentiation of material between the categories of mythical and historical. As a chronicler of past events, he understands that his primary duty is to feed his audience with WEEG material—or what can plausibly be presented as such. But as a literary artist—the article of Herington to which I have referred is properly entitled 'The Poem of Herodotus'—he is aware how much suggestive depth can be added to a narrative by the selective inclusion of stories with an aura of the irrational. His only problems were how to choose the right stuff from the wealth of popular tradition which was available to him, and how to manipulate and arrange it to best effect.

9

'Myth into Logos*': The Case of Croesus, or the Historian at Work*

FRANÇOIS HARTOG

I SHALL begin with some preliminary remarks concerning Herodotus and the divisions or the interplays between *muthos* and *logos*.

As we all know, the word *muthos* is very seldom used by Herodotus (twice only). To characterize a *logos* (narrative) as *muthos* is for him a clear way of rejecting it as unreliable and unconvincing. When the term *muthos* does appear, it is surrounded by a very specific vocabulary: what the Greeks claim concerning the coming of Heracles to Egypt (2. 45) is said *anepiskeptōs* ('without due consideration') and is *euēthēs* ('foolish'). On what grounds? Because what they say contradicts the Egyptian *phusis* ('nature') and *nomoi* ('customs'). The second occurrence of *muthos*, still more famous, deals with the vexed problem of the Ocean. Herodotus is quick to dismiss Hecataeus' statement, because 'it is grounded in obscurity and needs no disproof' (*es aphanes ton muthon aneneikas ouk echei elegchon*, 2. 23). Located somewhere beyond what is visible, a *muthos* cannot be proved. With *muthos* one enters the realm of poetry ('Homer, I think, or one of the preceding poets has found [*heurein*] this name: Ocean'). The very choice of the word is intended to be a signal to the listener or the reader.[1] How does one recognize and set something apart as *muthos*? By using the notion of *eikos* ('plausible, probable') as a critical tool; more broadly, the term *eikos* helps to make a choice among different versions proposed, and provides a way of organizing the logic of the narrative.

But, as we also know, Hecataeus opens his *Genealogies* with 'Hecataeus *mutheitai* . . .', followed by *tade graphō*: 'Hecataeus narrates . . . I write'.[2] Then, the same Herodotus who was using

---

[1] Hartog (1988), 295–6; Detienne (1981), 99–104.
[2] Hecat.: *FGrHist* 1 F 1; Hartog (1990), 177–8; Jacob (1994), 171–3.

muthos to undermine the validity of Hecataeus' considerations about the Ocean calls both Aesop and Hecataeus *logopoios* ('maker of *logos*'), not a very positive epithet (2. 143, 2. 134). Yet Herodotus always speaks of his own narrative as *logos* or *logoi*. That is already enough to indicate that the division between the two terms is unstable and that, depending on the contexts, their meanings can overlap. Part of a *logos* can be circumscribed and rejected as *muthos* and, at the same time, an author can be designated as *logopoios*, that is to say, as one presenting a form of knowledge which has no proper grounds of its own, or is beyond verification.

That first point having been noticed and acknowledged by the commentators, those same commentators often immediately add that Herodotus himself is definitely a great story-teller (Aristotle once called him *muthologos* (about Egypt, *GA* 756^{b}6))—as if he couldn't restrain himself from telling stories, fragments of novels, myths, tedious anecdotes, especially about the barbarians or the most exotic peoples; as if he was unable to resist the pleasure of the ear (to phrase it with Thucydides). There is also a somewhat different and more general line of interpretation. As a man located between two periods, Herodotus is already 'enlightened', an *Aufklärer*, but not yet a complete one:[3] he represents precisely one who cuts the road from Mythos to Logos, but in his work the previous religious *Hintergrund* is still pretty much active. Man's destiny is in the hands of the gods. In their own manner the *Histories* are still the presentation or the verification of the 'ways of gods to man'.

After those brief opening remarks, which sketch out a framework for the discussion, I shall come now, after so many commentators, to a specific and famous episode (but is there an episode or even a word not by now famous in Herodotus?): the story of Croesus, the strategic importance of which was clearly marked by Herodotus himself, since Croesus is the man designated in the prologue as *aitios* ('responsible'): the first to commit *adika* ('unjust deeds') toward Greeks. So it is not really astonishing if a scholar has recently suggested that the whole episode was actually composed and written at the very end of the work.[4]

---

[3] Nestle (1940).
[4] Lateiner (1989), 122–3; see also Erbse (1992), 10–30.

Concerning those chapters, one cannot avoid an initial hesitation. What do you call them, as soon as you regard them as forming a whole? 'Croesus' Tragedy', or, with Dumézil, 'Croesus' Novel', or 'Short Stories', that is to say a story which combines oriental and mythical elements with pieces of Greek wisdom, as expressed by Solon and formulated by the oracle of Delphi? Perhaps even something like 'Croesus' Story, or "Myth into *logos*"'! But which *myth* and what *logos*? For whom and why?

CROESUS, THE ORACLE, AND THE HISTORIAN

Reviewing trends in mythical studies ten or fifteen years after Marcel Detienne's *L'Invention de la mythologie*, Claude Calame calls for a re-evaluation of literary genre, paying particular attention to context of enunciation, to how the native peoples behave or react in regard to these discursive objects. Revisiting myth in the light of enunciation and reception theory, he goes one step further and proposes the notion of 'mises en discours symboliques'.[5]

What Do We Do with Croesus?

As far as Croesus' story is concerned, several strategies have been used. Dumézil, for example, read the Croesus episode as an 'apologue' or illustrative fable, the meaning of which is for him obviously inscribed in the context of the three Dumézilian functions.[6] It is because the king obstinately repeats the same mistake that he receives such a lesson in three sequences (with the functional quality of the three successive punishments). His 'sin' is *hubris*, pride. So Croesus appears as 'the Western companion of the legendary sinners of Iran and India'. Where does the story come from, asked Dumézil? Does it have a Lydian, Phrygian, or Ionian origin?[7] In any case there is, noted Dumézil, a reworking, leading to a historization, a process not fundamentally different, I imagine, from what Dumézil had first recognized at work in the case of the Roman annals.

[5] (1996a), 46–55. [6] Dumézil (1985), 67. [7] Ibid. 67.

Without commenting specifically on their oriental flavour, another scholar, Timothy Long, refers to the same chapters as 'short stories', as 'finished novellas', but he adds that he is not concerned with distinctions between tales, fables, and legends. He develops his analysis by focusing on Herodotus' style, more precisely on the use of repetitions. In his final chapter he draws a comparison with Greek tragedy, emphasizing the differences.[8]

Focusing not extensively, but occasionally, on Croesus, Gregory Nagy recently proposed what comes close to a general interpretation of the whole Herodotean enterprise.[9] What first interests me when Nagy deals with Herodotus is that here we have a scholar moving, so to speak, from epic to history, or from myth to history. Usually poetry is not the main field of expertise of scholars who deal with historiography, and with Herodotus in particular. So whenever they do take poetry into account, they go the other way: from history to epic, or from history to myth. In his *Pindar's Homer*, with its explicit subtitle *The Lyric Possession of an Epic Past*, Nagy puts at the forefront the notion of *ainos* ('authoritative speech'). And he advocates, at length and eloquently, a parallelism in the appropriation of epic through, respectively, *ainos*, with Pindar, and *historia*, with Herodotus. *Ainos* is the essence of Pindar's lyric poetry, and '[e]ven if the medium of Herodotus cannot be called *ainos* in form, it is parallel to the *ainos* of a poet like Pindar in both *function* and *content*'.[10]

The word *apodeixis* ('public presentation')—as it is used by Herodotus—is also common ground for both *aoidos* ('master of song') and *logios* ('master of speech'). According to Nagy, if for the *aoidos* the code of his message is *ainos*, for the *logios*, who expresses himself in prose, the implicit part of his message, the *ainos* (with its derivatives *ainigma*, 'riddle', and *ainissomai*, 'I utter riddles') has to be sought in the poetical register—that is, in poetic citations and Delphic oracles, in particular. '[T]he prose of Herodotus', says Nagy, 'can combine with the poetry of oracles to convey the same sort of message that is conveyed by the uninterrupted lyric poetry of Pindar.'[11] I'm not quite sure I'm fully convinced by his demonstration, but that is not an issue I want to argue about now.

---

[8] Long (1987), 7.   [9] Nagy (1990).
[10] Ibid. 329; my italics.   [11] Ibid. 326.

Another approach may be mentioned here which also pays attention to literary genre, but in a different way. I mean, first, the oriental tradition of Biographies, especially Kings' *Vitae*, from Sargon to Cyrus, and secondly, within the Greek tradition, the literary figures of the Seven Sages. Of course the *Histories* do not directly borrow from or copy such genres or literary patterns, but the work does represent different possible intrigues, narrative threads, or styles. What is new with Herodotus' *Histories*, however, is that they are not written in praise of kings, who are neither the heroes nor the implied readers of his *logos*.[12] The Croesus episode is built according to the rhythm of a circular composition. His story is one of conquest and command (*archē*: 1. 6, 1. 92). As soon as he becomes king, Croesus' only aim is to go to war and to conquer. The traditional pattern of the *Vita* (the oriental one) seems to change to fit this exclusive objective. The impetus to conquer is what makes the narrative move forward. Being the first to build an empire, Croesus opens up, in the *Histories*, the time of the conquerors. And even after his failure, he remains a counsellor in conquests, repeating for Cyrus the same (bad) reasoning with the same bad results (since Cyrus met his fate while subjugating the Massagetae).

Before closing this brief survey I shall mention, even if it does not concern Croesus, the analysis proposed by Claude Calame of another and in a way more complex episode: the founding of Cyrene. How does Herodotus tell that story? Why, asks Calame, does Herodotus 'mythicize' the narrative, not mentioning at all either the legendary stories reported by Pindar or the historizing story which takes as its starting point actual political unrest? Leaving aside here the answers proposed by Calame, I shall concentrate on what the two episodes have in common: the role of the oracles. Concerning these, says Calame, one has the impression that they play an essentially *narrative* role: they tend 'to reinsert into the tradition of great epic poetry prose description of events and actions which have no other motive than human will or material circumstances'.[13] 'By conferring meaning on the narrative action, the oracles thus have for the audience of the *Histories* a cognitive function. We are entitled to ask whether

---

[12] Payen (1997), 60–2, and, on Croesus specifically in association with Cyrus, as the first conquerors, 219–28.
[13] Calame (1996a), 151.

their often poetical form does not, from a narrative point of view, aim at making up for the deficiencies of prose in a history which aspires to be epic.'[14] So as far as an appreciation of the role of poetic or epic reference is concerned, Nagy's and Calame's analyses, different as they are, converge.

Enargeia *and Oracular Utterances*

The material collected, treated, and reworked by Herodotus in those chapters is obviously so abundant and so rich that the question is how to find an orientation among these multiple bits of narrative following various patterns and belonging to different literary genres. To these multiplicities there correspond, on the side of the modern commentators, various analyses, no less multiple and heterogeneous. By focusing on the way Herodotus frames the Croesus sequence and treats his material, might we find a hint of how he actually works as an historian?

First, the omnipresent oracle: why does it intervene as a privileged instrument of divine revelation? Perhaps it acts as an intermediary between men and gods, a role more 'likely' and hence more credible than the direct, visible, and constant interventions of the 'earlier' Homeric gods. Without their interventions (but within the limits fixed by Destiny), the epic narrative, as we know, could not proceed: no reversal could happen in a situation, no battle could be decisively won, no final end could occur. But the time of epic and heroes has now passed away.

What, in that time, was the mode of epiphany of the gods? 'The gods are terrible in their appearing in their forms' (*enargeis*, *Il.* 20. 131), Hera says, fearing that Apollo may come against Achilles and that consequently the hero may become frightened. When Ino gives Odysseus the magic veil, she immediately orders him to 'look the other way'; when safely ashore he returns the talisman (*Od.* 5. 350). In the *Iliad*, the gods manifest their presence first of all through their voices. In the *Odyssey*, on the other hand, divinity reveals itself physically, but in disguise: Athena appears frequently, but in different disguises (3. 421, 7. 201, 13. 225).[15]

---

[14] Calame (1996a), 153.   [15] Pucci (1987), 110–23.

In any case, to express such divine manifestations Homer makes use of the word *enargēs* (composed of *en + argos*): 'in full light, truly'.[16] That is a way to express epiphany. Either the god or goddess makes him/herself visible to one person only, with the others present not seeing anything, as Athena did with Odysseus, or else the brightness of the divine presence is so glaring—at least, far too bright for human eyes—that the divinity cannot even be seen. *Enargēs* designates the mode of visibility of what one cannot see, what mortals can no longer see or look at (still, the gods, in the *Odyssey*, visit 'visible in person' (*enargeis*) the banquets of the Phaeacians and the Ethiopians, where Poseidon attends as a regular guest). But in the world of humans, 'bread-eating men', the distance separating mortals and immortals has *already* greatly increased, even if the gods are still willing to manifest themselves to the heroes for whom they care. Of course that is also a world where diviners, as mediators, are present and active.

With the 'epoch' of the Delphic oracle—in Herodotus, at least—the divine seems no longer so visible, or less available to be seen, so words have become or tend to become the principal and most effective medium. Later, following the path opened by the sophists and in rhetoric, *enargeia* was to become an attribute and a product of *logos* itself.[17] But, for the moment, the divine seems to manifest itself more and more through words: apparitions and dreams need interpreters and explanations, that is to say, words. If not the exclusive way to communicate with the upper and invisible world, oracular consultation appears to be the regular or 'civilized' one. It proceeds through the established protocol of questions and answers. But like omens, oracular words are signs which demand interpretation.

Like the 'old' gods of epic, 'modern' oracles cannot bypass the limits fixed by Destiny. 'None may escape his destined lot, not even a god' (*tēn peprōmenēn moiran adunata esti apophugein kai theōi*), answers the Pythia to Croesus' claims and protestations (1. 91). They leave a margin, a space opened for discussion and action— that is, for blindness, pride, stubbornness, refusal of any discussion, failure, and tragedy. In the Greek context, to interpret is not

---

[16] Chantraine (1968–80), s.v. A dream can also be presented as *enarges: Od.* 4. 841, *enarges oneiron*, about the phantom sent by Athena to Penelope with the features of her sister. Hdt. 8. 77: the oracle of Bacis is said by Herodotus to speak clearly (*enargeōs*).

[17] Zanker (1981); Calame (1991*b*).

to read or decipher something that has been written by the gods. The Greek gods do not write, and the exegetes are in no way skilful readers. It is rather a matter of calculating and assigning the meanings of the words first pronounced by the oracles (and *then* written down), producing what seems to be the 'best' interpretation (which will not necessarily turn out to be the 'right' one).

Sēmainein

After having briefly mapped the ways in which the gods have to manifest themselves, the distance which separates the 'time of gods' and 'the time of men', between the time of epiphanies (*enargeia*) and the time of oracles, let us come back to Croesus. When Odysseus sails to the gates of Hades to consult Tiresias, the diviner predicts all that will happen to him: his return, the new departure, and finally his death. Tiresias knows or sees 'in one glance' the end (*teleutē*), and the whole way leading to it. Proteus is likewise able to tell Menelaus what his final destination will be (the Islands of the Blest). They see what has been and what will be.

Confronted by Croesus' questioning, Solon is not in a position to know the end (*teleutē*) or the way leading to it, but he does know that one has to wait until the end before risking a general statement about a human destiny. Knowing that he does not know, Solon occupies none the less a quasi-oracular position *vis-à-vis* Croesus, who understands too late, on the pyre, the rightness of Solon's answer: 'No living man was blest' (Hdt. 1. 86). And he persuades Cyrus that in human affairs stability can never be achieved (*ouden . . . asphaleōs echon*).

Exactly like Solon, Herodotus knows how fundamentally unstable are the cities of men (*astea anthrōpōn*). The whole history of Croesus, punctuated by the utterances of the Pythia, proceeds as if it was, we might say, the projection of the point of view of Apollo. But the god or the diviner sees all, at once and synoptically, starting from the original mistake committed by Gyges, the ancestor, down to Croesus himself, the fifth descendant presently confronted by King Cyrus. Whereas the historian (who in that case happens also to know the end, as does the reader) has no choice but to convert the *sunopsis* into a *diēgēsis*, a continuous narrative, where the repeated interventions of the Pythia are the leading threads of the plot, or, to use a different image, play the role of a periodizing principle (the oracles succeeding one another). So the oracle functions as an organizing pattern of the narrative, as a reservoir of meaning and as a principle of intelligibility, with the familiar phrase: 'Since it was necessary that misfortune befell him.'

Croesus is always consulting, either too much or, in one critical case, not enough, but anyhow with excess: as a barbarian, he seems not to know exactly how to use oracles properly. He, so to speak, 'buys' the oracle (and the Delphians) and, after testing the different sanctuaries, he takes what is said by Apollo for granted, as being immediately clear, at the first level, without double or hidden meaning. A 'normal' Greek consultant would ask the god to indicate which one of the two possible ways might be the best, reasoning in the context of a binary logic.[18]

Once we recognize the oracle as constituting a guiding (and misleading) line of the narrative, we see the different *logoi*, so to speak, taking their respective positions along this axis, from the first sin of Candaules to the final accomplishment of the original oracle. The deeper and slower oscillation between *adikia* ('injustice') and *tisis* ('reparation, vengeance') is punctuated and dramatized by the oracles. History can then be understood as the interval of time between these two poles and as something like the delay of divine wrath. The oracles point to the path and the historian inscribes his work within this movement, taking the measure of that distance, making it visible and intelligible through his narrative. Therefore the whole history of Croesus can be understood as a long exemplum or, as we might describe it, a great historical oracle.

What are the meanings of *sēmainein* in the *Histories*? 'To signify', in all senses of the word, that is to say 'to express, transmit, interpret' what you have seen or what someone else has seen (in a dream). *Sēmainein* means also to be able to indicate, for example, the distances of the royal road from the sea up to Susa, as Tiresias and Proteus are said to know the roads and the distances on the sea.[19] More precisely, *sēmainein* belongs to the vocabulary

---

[18] Vernant et al. (1974), 17–19.
[19] Hdt. 8. 8, 21, 79, 4. 99, 5. 54.

of divination.[20] Homer and Hesiod have, says Herodotus, 'taught the Greeks of the descent of the gods . . . and drawn their figures' (*eidea . . . sēmēnantes*, 2. 53). Last but not least, Herodotus points (*sēmēnas*) to the man who was the first to act aggressively toward the Greeks. As Nagy puts it: 'When Herodotus indicates (*sēmainei*), he is indirectly narrating the actions of the gods by directly narrating the actions of men', but at the same time he is relying on his own knowledge.[21]

Then comes the end of the *Histories* with the death of the Persian Artayctes. Why Artayctes? Partly because he is indeed not a nice fellow, a man *deinos kai atasthalos* ('terrible, clever, and wicked')! But first and foremost because he offended the hero Protesilaus, by confiscating for his personal profit Protesilaus' sacred property (*temenos*). And who was Protesilaus? Listed in the Iliadic *Catalogue of Ships*, he is remembered as the first Achaean (Greek) to be killed, when he jumped on to the Trojan shore. Captured by the Athenians who were besieging Sestos, and under arrest, Artayctes receives a sign from Protesilaus: '*Teras . . . emoi sēmainei*', says Artayctes, 'it is to me that Protesilaus of Elaeus would signify that though he be dead and dry he has power given to him by heaven to take vengeance on me that wronged him' (9. 120). Finally Artayctes and his son are put to death (crucified and stoned) exactly where Xerxes had bridged the strait, but on the European shore. His expiatory death is also clearly an answer, a long-delayed one, to Protesilaus'. The long cycle which opened with the Trojan War (and the killing of Protesilaus) has ended with Artayctes' punishment. By recalling Protesilaus' fate and the last *teras*, Herodotus is, for the last time in the *Histories*, the one who *sēmainei*, making visible the 'longue durée' of the divine wrath.

The last *sēmainein* clearly echoes the first, pointing to Croesus as the first offender against the Greeks. What are the relations between the two: the opening one, the Herodotean one, the 'historical' or 'professional' one, and the last one, the heroic one, the Protesilaan one? They seem to reduplicate each other, or better, to produce an effect of reverberation: Croesus opens, Artayctes closes, Protesilaus *sēmainei*, Herodotus *sēmainei* too. And of course, the latter is the architect of the *Histories*.

[20] Hdt. 1. 34, 78, 4. 179, 8. 37; on *sēmainein* in relation to Apollo, see Detienne (1998), 138 ff.
[21] (1990), 273.

So the multiplicity of narrative forms or genres, the plurality of explanatory levels or causal relations, is what the Croesus episode shows, or rather: it is *made* of such multiplicity and plurality, its texture and, eventually, its meaning derive from that. Not a monodic but a polyphonic episode, with interplays, echoes, but also incongruences and even discrepancies between the different lines, threads or levels, the only common denominator being the inescapable instability of everything.

SĒMAINEIN/HISTOREIN

Sēmainein introduces, I suggest, the point of view of the god, and leads to the problem of who is *aitios* ('responsible'). So we are clearly treading on Apollo's territory. The oracle *sēmainei*, and the first historian presents himself as the one who *sēmainei*, who 'signifies' the past. That is exactly how Aristotle retrospectively defined Epimenides' craft: he was the one 'who did not apply his divination to what was about to happen, but to what had already happened and remained none the less obscure' (*Rhet.* 1418ª21–26). But, in the case of Herodotus—and that is not a small difference—what fundamentally authorizes him to *sēmainein* is what he personally knows: his own knowledge. Regarding Croesus, Herodotus attributes to himself the same position as Solon, but a Solon who not only knows that one has to wait until the end, but who actually *knows* the end, and the beginning as well. Like the modern historiographer who, commissioned by a prince, tries to see events with the eyes of his patron, occupying, at least for a while, and narratively speaking, 'his position',[22] Herodotus intends to see *as* Apollo, to adopt his point of view; but to do so he has to express it or convert it into words and sentences, that is to say into a narrative. Positioned *post eventum*, the historian goes backwards from the accomplishment to the first oracular utterance. But he organizes his *logos* as if he took the oracular phrases as his real starting-point, with the wrong inter-pretations and the bifurcations, from which result the suspense and the dramatic movement of the narrative: he makes visible for the reader (who also knows the end) the blindness of the actor

---

[22] Marin (1981), 90–1.

who makes the wrong choices, one after the other, unable to escape from the deep and slow historical process which leads in the long run from *adikia* to *tisis*. In a way he proceeds like the modern historian who organizes his narrative as if he were really starting from the past to meet the present, using with more or less care or sophistication the convenient *post hoc propter hoc* explanation.

A 'modern' Epimenides, perhaps, but Herodotus was never seen as and does not at all present himself as a diviner. If he retains something of that craft or knowledge, he makes use of it in a different manner, with an agenda of his own. To speak a different language, he maintains the formal aspect of such a practice (intellectual with a social dimension too), but he employs it differently.[23] For the action of *sēmainein* appears to be based upon his own knowledge.

After noticing the weakly operative character of the *muthos/ logos* division in the *Histories*, we have concentrated, in the wake of many commentators, on the Croesus episode. The importance of the episode is undeniable: its length (ninety-one chapters) and its location (at the very beginning of the whole work) offer ample clues of this. Nevertheless, the episode disconcerts because it seems to mark a 'regression' in regard to the historical ambitions of the prologue. There the historian, relying on his own knowledge, located the beginning of his narrative with Croesus, who was designated as the one responsible for the hostilities between the Greeks and the barbarians. It is as if *muthos*, pushed aside for a while, made a comeback, blurring the border just drawn by the narrator, and almost reoccupied the brand new *spatium historicum*.

But, as we have seen, such an approach prevents us from understanding the intellectual context of the Herodotean moment. The repeated consultation of the Pythian oracle plays at least a triple role. It allows for 'a historical possession of an Epic Past', to phrase it in the manner of Nagy. More precisely, following Calame's emphasis on their narrative and cognitive functions, the oracles are a means 'to reinsert prose description into the tradition of great epic poetry'. Moreover, and from an

---

[23] From a very different context, I borrow freely this notion of the 'formalité' of a practice from M. de Certeau (1975), 165–7.

epistemological point of view, how could the intellectual project of Herodotus be formulated? To which question did he seek an answer? How can one produce an epic when it is no longer possible to do so? What might replace the poetical devices of the epic? What could replace the vision of the Muse? In a world where narrative action is no longer punctuated, as in the *Iliad*, by divine epiphanies, the oracle offers a more 'verisimilitudinous' mode of divine intervention. Not insignificantly, it also gives an opportunity to confer meaning on a long period of time: between the fault and the punishment, history becomes the progressive manifestation of the delays of divine wrath. And, by endowing himself with the capacity to *sēmainein*, the first historian retains something (not the content, but rather the form) of the ancient knowledge of the diviner. Therefore to claim to be in a position to designate Croesus as the one 'responsible' means at the same time to be able to journey far away back to the original sin of Gyges and, putting aside the rationalizing explanations proposed by the *logioi* Persians, to declare that 'my history starts precisely with Croesus'.

Sēmainein ('to signify') is one way to deal with the invisible, to work on the border between what one has and hasn't seen, what one can and can't see. The other way is *historein*, which is also, but in a different register, an intellectual process for dealing with the invisible.[24] With *sēmainein* it is the figure of the diviner who comes to the forefront, by pointing to the gods, by recalling the signs of their interventions in human affairs, by making visible and readable through narrative the invisible and, ultimately, divine structure of what happened (*ta genomena*).

---

[24] F. Hartog, 'Hérodote', in Brunschwig and Lloyd (1996), 702–8.

10

Monsters in Greek Ethnography and Society in the Fifth and Fourth Centuries BCE

DOMINIQUE LENFANT

THAT *muthos* and *logos* should not be seen as opposed to one another, as if the one succeeded the other in a progression of Greek thought towards increasing rationality, may be exemplified by Greek views of monstrous beings. Such views may be observed in three areas, namely mythology, ethnography, and society. The present study will not deal with properly 'mythological' representations, but will survey (1) what Greeks wrote on monsters observed in their own society, and (2) ethnographic descriptions which claim to report foreign and distant things, and which give much space to monstrous peoples.

Ethnographic accounts of monsters are in certain respects analogous to myths—indeed, they were called *muthoi* by those who wanted to stress their unreliability.[1] If the ethnography of the ends of the world is not strictly speaking mythology, its imagery looks in many ways like that of myth, and the spatial distance involved in it allows the same type of representation as the chronological remoteness typical of myth.[2] Accordingly, ethnography, like myth, must be understood in connection with the society which produced it.[3]

In the present article, the ethnographical counterpoint, which was developed in Classical times, is preferred to the mythical one. (Mythological monsters had appeared already in the Archaic period.) Since ethnography claims to report on the contemporary world, it has to be considered in relation to contemporary Greek societies and their self-representation. My aim will be to try to

---

[1] e.g. Strab. 1. 2. 35, on Herodotus, Ctesias, Hellanicus, and the authors of *Indica*.

[2] The images of Ctesias' India or Herodotus' Hyperboreans and Long-Lived Ethiopians have obvious affinities with that of the Hesiodic Golden Race. Cf. Lenfant (1991), 117–18.

[3] See, for myth, Buxton (1994).

connect what was written by the Greeks about near and real
monsters with their view of remote, foreign, and imaginary
monsters, in order to understand better the attitudes and feelings
of the Greeks towards monsters in their own society, the meaning
of some of their ethnographic representations, and the relevance
of these issues to the connection between *muthos* and *logos*.

MONSTERS IN GREEK SOCIETY

The word 'monster' is derived from Latin *monstrum*, which originally referred to an unnatural phenomenon through which gods
warn ('monent') men. The corresponding Greek term is *teras*,
which originally had, just like *monstrum*, the special meaning of a
divine sign, a 'portent', with different sorts of referents. It also
more specifically designated mythological monsters (like Cerberus
or the Sphinx) and actual monstrous births.[4] It does not precisely
tally with the modern and more limited notion, which the
present study addresses: 'monster' will be understood here as a
'human being with abnormal formation', which can be denoted
or described without this term.[5] So, our scope will not be confined to a word or a concept, but will also include concrete cases
of human beings with abnormal formation.

However, *teras* is also used as a general term in the sense with
which we are concerned, and this use helps us to see how a
monster was perceived. Monsters in Greek society are defined in
a negative way, as beings who do not resemble their parents, in
that they deviate from the characteristics of their species.[6] Such a
definition is found in literary texts such as those of Plato and
Aristotle,[7] and also in curses within official oaths. Thus in the
oath sworn by the Amphictyons, according to Aeschines, an
imprecation against perpetrators of sacrilege on sacred land was

---

[4] Cf. Chantraine (1968–80), s.v. τέρας; Stein (1909).

[5] For instance, the Hippocratic treatises never use *teras* to designate a monstrous being;
the only occurrence where it could do so refers to the world of dreams: 'Crossing rivers,
hoplites, enemies, monsters with strange forms [*terata allomorpha*] indicate disease or
madness' (*Regimen* 4 (=*Dreams*) 93. 5 (Littré, vi. 662)). The fact is sufficiently explained
by the excessive looseness of the term in a medical context.

[6] On the diverse degrees of unlikeness to the parents (as individuals, as male or female,
or as human beings), see Arist. *GA* 767ª35–769ᵇ10.

[7] Pl. *Cra.* 394a; Arist. *GA* 769ᵇ8 and 770ᵇ5.

expressed as follows: 'That the women bear no children who resemble their parents, but monsters.'[8]

Concrete cases of monsters are rarely described, explained, or even mentioned in our sources, except in the writings of the Hippocratic physicians and the biology of Aristotle. The *Corpus Hippocraticum* reports a few cases of deformed stillborn children or invalid viable newborns, but the physician confines himself to a brief description of the anomaly or an explanation of it by an accident or a disease during the pregnancy. The interest of the physician differs according to the type of case. For deformed stillborn children, he only briefly describes their anomaly without explaining its origin,[9] and his first concern is to remove these foetuses.[10] By contrast, regarding invalid viable newborns, he always strives to explain their case by an accident or a disease during the pregnancy.[11] But the vast *Corpus Hippocraticum* mentions only a few instances of congenital malformation, and Hippocratic physicians did not construct a teratology.

---

[8] μήτε γυναῖκας τέκνα τίκτειν γονεῦσιν ἐοικότα, ἀλλὰ τέρατα (Aeschin., *In Ctes.* 111). This oath would be subsequent to the First Sacred War and date from the early 6th cent. BCE. Similar words are found in the apocryphal oath of the Athenians before the battle of Plataea, in a curse against would-be perjurers: καὶ εἰ μὲν ἐμπεδορκοίην τὰ ἐν τῷ ὅρκῳ γεγραμμένα . . . γυναῖκες τίκτοιεν ἐοικότα γονεῦσιν, εἰ δὲ μή, τέρατα. The inscription was published by L. Robert (1938: 307–16), who suggested dating the forgery to the last third of the 4th cent. BCE. In his edition, P. Siewert (1972: 98–9) argues that the inscription is genuine and dates from the Second Persian War. But all scholars agree that the curse is copied from the Amphictyonic oath. Similar curses occur in other inscriptions dating from Hellenistic and Roman times (references in Siewert (1972), 98 n. 197), but they do not include the expressions τέρατα and ἐοικότα γονεῦσιν.

[9] As in the case of the child born with an arm adherent to the side (*Epid.* 5. 13 (Littré, v. 212)) or the 'little plump child, whose most important parts were separate, four-fingers long, without bones' (*Epid.* 2. 19 (Littré, v. 92)).

[10] *Mul.* 1. 47, 70 (Littré, viii. 106, 146–8); *Superf.* 7 (Littré, viii. 480).

[11] The maimed foetus which is born 'lame, blind, or affected with another disability' has certainly been ill *in utero* during the eighth month of the pregnancy (*Septim.* 5 (Littré, vii. 444)). Those born with a short arm must owe that infirmity to a dislocation suffered in their mother's womb (*Art.* 12 (Littré, iv. 114)). Finally, the treatise *On Generation* assigns two possible mechanical causes to the state of the maimed child: either external violence (blow, fall, . . .) suffered by the mother or the extreme narrowness of the womb which has impeded, at some point, the normal development of the foetus. For a much more slight anomaly, which one should not call monstrous, such as a mark on the head of the child, the physician even puts forward, exceptionally, the influence of the so-called longings of the pregnant woman, and their satisfaction: 'If a pregnant woman longs to eat some mould or coal and does it, the child who is born has on his head a sign which results from those things' (*Superf.* 18 (Littré, viii. 486)). Lastly, the physician sometimes indicates a way of correcting a congenital malformation, as in the case of club foot (*Art.* 62 (Littré, iv. 262–8)).

Aristotle's biology, by contrast, dwells at greater length and more systematically on monsters, and does outline a teratology,[12] of which the essential is to be read in the fourth book of the *Generation of Animals*.[13] In Aristotle, *teras* clearly designates a monster, without implying any religious interpretation.[14] The philosopher deals with monsters rather methodically, and is the first to do so. He strives to define the monster, to distinguish between degrees of malformation, and to discriminate between several types of monsters; he does not hesitate to describe some examples, and to try to explain their causes.

He defines the monster, in commonplace enough fashion, as a human being who does not resemble his parents,[15] or as a being who does not even resemble a man, but rather an animal.[16] He distinguishes between slight anomalies, which do not threaten life, and others, which affect vital organs.[17] Lastly, he presents different sorts of monsters: those which have a part of their body resembling a different species (for instance, a being with an ox-head),[18] those which have supernumerary limbs or organs (for instance, several heads),[19] and those which lack limbs[20] or have an orifice closed (for instance, that of the uterus).[21]

In all these cases, Aristotle refers to nature.[22] Furthermore, he is keen to emphasize that speaking of a being with an ox-head is a simple metaphor to underline a resemblance to the bovine species, and that to admit the mixing of two species is out of the question.[23] Finally, for several of the monstrosities he describes, he propounds purely biological explanations.[24]

Such a survey of monsters is particularly noteworthy, for it

---

[12] Cf. P. Louis, 'Monstres et monstruosités dans la biologie d'Aristote', in Bingen, Cambier, and Nachtergael (1975), 277–84.

[13] *GA* 769^{b}3–773^{a}32.

[14] The term was already so used before Aristotle, as appears from his own words (cf. e.g. ἃ δὴ καὶ λέγεται τέρατα, *GA* 769^{b}10). Cf. Stein (1909: 11) for other instances.

[15] Cf. n. 7 above.

[16] 769^{b}8–10.   [17] 771^{a}11–14.

[18] 769^{b}13–14.   [19] 769^{b}26–7.

[20] 770^{b}30–3.   [21] 773^{a}14–20.

[22] The monster is παρὰ φύσιν, contrary *to the ordinary process* of nature, but not contrary to nature in an absolute sense, since 'nothing occurs against nature' (770^{b}9–17).

[23] 769^{b}13–17.

[24] The cause derives generally from the matter (ὕλη), which is supplied by the female: if not sufficiently mastered by the movements, which come from the male, the animal aspect dominates and produces a monster partially resembling another species (769^{b}11–13); if the matter is superfluous, it causes the hypertrophy of a limb or its splitting in two (772^{b}14–19).

stands out against the general silence of the sources on the matter. In fact, it is striking how Greeks kept silent about monstrous births in their society—a silence which concerns at the same time the existence of monsters, the nature of their monstrosity, and the fate of such creatures, in relation to Greek attitudes towards them.

It is generally assumed that monsters and deformed newborns were eliminated. But even on this subject the texts remain for the most part silent or allusive.[25] It is well known that in Sparta the civic community used to decide to dispose of deformed newborns by throwing them into the chasm of the Apothetae.[26] But the exposure of deformed babies seems to have been a more widespread practice. For Athens, the most conclusive allusion is in Plato's *Theaetetus*, which mentions, in a metaphor, the baby who is stolen from his mother and exposed as being 'unworthy of being brought up'; but the text does not specify what makes him unworthy.[27] All in all, the evidence is very scanty and inconclusive.

Such a silence cannot be explained only by the scarceness of monstrous births: nowadays, in Europe, 2.5 to 3 per cent of newborns are deformed or monstrous,[28] and there is no reason to think that there were fewer in Classical Greece. Furthermore, palaeopathologists have observed ancient skeletons which attest a number of congenital malformations.[29] Lastly, the account which Aristotle gives of monsters implies that there were indeed some to be seen.

If the scarceness of monstrous births cannot sufficiently explain

---

[25] The allusions in Plutarch, Plato, and Aristotle are (differently) analysed by Delcourt (1938), 36–44, and by Dasen (1993), 206–10.

[26] Plu. *Lyc.* 16.

[27] 160e, cf. 151c and 160e–161a. Delcourt (1938: 42–4) quotes also Plato and Aristotle, who prescribe the exposure of malformed newborns. Cf. Pl. *Rep.* 460c ('As for the children of worthless men and those who may be born crippled, they will be hidden in a secret and invisible place, as is fitting.—Indeed so, if the race of the guardians is to be pure'), and Arist. *Pol.* 1335[b] ('As to exposing and rearing the newborns, let there be a law forbidding the rearing of any maimed child'). As is well known, both philosophers set forth a fictive, ideal legislation. Delcourt assumes that this reflects Athenian practice, but for the questions under consideration the model seems rather to have been Sparta (e.g. the community of wives and children both in Sparta and Plato's *Republic*). Moreover, if the elimination of deformed newborns was a general custom, Aristotle's wish to impose it by law would be surprising. It is most probable that the practice was imposed by law in Sparta, whereas it devolved upon the family in Athens (cf. Dasen (1993), 205–6).

[28] Fischer (1991), 14, 114.

[29] Cf. Grmek (1983: 109–18), who describes several of them.

the silence of the Greeks about monsters, two other explanations may be considered: either monstrosity gave rise to a religious interpretation, which made it a matter of outstanding importance, or, on the contrary, a monstrous birth had no particular significance.

The first view was particularly developed by Marie Delcourt: according to her, the birth of a monster was considered by Greeks as a manifestation of divine anger and as a bad omen that inspired religious fear in the whole community: this would explain its removal, in so far as Greeks hoped to suppress in this way the calamity which it revealed or foretold.[30] Furthermore, the silence of the sources would itself be explained by a religious dread.[31] But this view includes many assumptions which have no support in the ancient evidence or rely on questionable interpretations of the sources.[32] It leads to a coherent picture, but it is no more than a hypothetical construction.[33]

In what respect, then, did Greeks connect monsters with the divine?

First, the two meanings of *teras* suggest a link between the malformed being and the divine sign which indicates the (generally dark) future.[34] But such a link can hardly be perceived in Classical Greece, and the monstrous births which are seen as portents either affect animals,[35] or seem to be impossible,[36] or are

[30] Delcourt (1938), 9–21, 29–49, 67–9. This view has become widespread. See e.g. den Boer (1979): 'To have given birth to deformed children was generally looked upon as a punishment, and it is understandable that the community took measures against these unfortunates whenever possible' (p. 133). 'All that was considered was the interest of the community, which might be threatened by the "abnormal" child' (136). Den Boer here makes no reference to sources.

[31] Delcourt (1938), 47, 93.

[32] e.g. Hes. *WD* 244 οὐδὲ γυναῖκες τίκτουσιν is understood by Delcourt (1938: 11) as 'les femmes n'enfantent plus *normalement*', whereas the Greek wording only suggests sterility. The abandoned newborns which manifest, in Sophocles' *OT* (180–1), the curse which strikes the Thebans, are interpreted as being monstrous newborns (Delcourt (1938), 31–5)—which can be no more than a hypothesis. Delcourt argues that in the 4th cent. BCE the exposure of malformed newborns received a rationalistic explanation which replaced the ancient religious motivation; but such motivation is not attested . . .

[33] Delcourt's religious interpretation was rejected especially by Roussel (1943) (concerning exposure) and, more recently, by Dasen (1993), 209 (concerning monsters as evil omens which inspired religious dread).

[34] Cf. Stein (1909), 7–31, for the first meaning (something unusual, especially a malformed being), and 32–62 for the second (portent).

[35] e.g. Plu. *Per.* 6. 2 (often quoted, although a quite isolated instance).

[36] e.g. Hdt. 7. 57 (a mare gives birth to a hare).

supposed to occur in the East, where teratomancy was far more developed than in Greece.[37]

If we compare the Greek situation with that in Babylonia, where treatises on divination obligingly enumerate various monstrosities either possible or impossible,[38] or with that in Rome under the Kings and the Republic, where monsters were ominous and abundantly described,[39] the scarcity of Greek mentions or descriptions would rather tell against their religious significance, and certainly not in favour of the dread put forward by Delcourt.[40] Nothing provides support for the idea that, faced with a bad omen, the Greek reaction would have been silence: on the contrary.

Secondly, the interpretation of a monstrous human birth as a divine punishment is suggested by two facts. First, we have seen that the monster was defined as a creature which does not look like its parents, and Hesiod presents the birth of such beings as a punishment which gods inflict upon unjust societies.[41] Secondly, when monsters occur in curses, as in the Amphictyonic oath, they appear as a divine punishment threatening those who would violate this oath.[42] However, these sources should not lead us to overestimate the importance of the Greek interpretation of monstrous births as divine punishments. In Hesiod as in the

[37] e.g. Hdt. 7. 57, Ctesias, *FGrHist* 688 F 13 § 14, and Ps.-Callisth. *Alex.* 3. 30 (on the link between the last two and their Babylonian context, cf. Lenfant (1996), 372–3). It is striking how Herodotus, who is perhaps the most fond of divine signs among Classical writers, so rarely mentions monstrous births; the only one which concerns humans is both impossible and located in the East (1. 84: a woman who bears a lion—which is not in itself a monster . . .).

[38] Cf. Bottéro (1985), 1–28; (1987), 166. The majority of the preserved omens derived from unusual births (more than two thousand) are published by Leichty (1970) (transcription and English translation).

[39] Cf. Delcourt (1938), 49–59. See, above all, Pliny, Livy, and Julius Obsequens (this last compiled, in the 4th cent. CE, a list of unusual births).

[40] (1938), 93.

[41] Hes. *WD* 182 οὐδὲ πατὴρ παίδεσσιν ὁμοίιος οὐδέ τι παῖδες, a condition Zeus will inflict upon the Fifth Race, by contrast with the one he will offer to just societies: τίκτουσιν δὲ γυναῖκες ἐοικότα τέκνα γονεῦσι (l. 235).

[42] As a matter of fact, monstrous human births rarely occur in curses (in addition to the Amphictyonic oath and the oath of Plataea which copies it on that point, Siewert (1972: 98 n. 197) refers to six later inscriptions which present similar formulas, such as μὴ γυναῖκες εὐτεκνοῖεν (*SIG*³ 360) or μὴ γυναῖκας τίκτειν κατὰ φύσιν (*SIG*³ 527; *Inscr. Cret.* iii. 5, p. 50; Pouilloux (1960), no. 52)). But what is exceptional is the detailed formula in which they appear: in Classical times, a short, abstract formula is generally used: εὐορκοῦντι μὲν πόλλ᾽ ἀγαθὰ εἶναι, ἐπιορκοῦντι δὲ κακά (cf. Siewert (1972), 26–7).

curses—which reveal more about Archaic than Classical beliefs—
monstrous births are mentioned as a threat, as a potentiality,
but they do not account for real, historical monsters. Furthermore, the connection between monstrous births and divine anger
should not be understood as a symmetrical one. In other words,
divine punishment may consist, according to curses, in monstrous
births, barrenness of land, disease,[43] 'defeat in war and in legal
cases and in the market-place',[44] and so on. But this is not to say
that all these evils were always felt as a divine punishment. What
R. Parker says about disease probably applies to monstrous births
also. Divine interference in human life is not considered in the
same way by different persons, or even by the same person in
different circumstances: gods may be sometimes credited with
punishing the bad, sometimes with giving way to chance or to
fate, and these religious explanations of disease coexist at all
periods. But, on the whole, disease was only exceptionally interpreted as a punishment, being more usually regarded as a random
event.[45] In the same way, it seems likely that monsters in general
lacked religious significance.

This view is not invalidated by the scientific writings of the
Hippocratics and Aristotle. Although it is usually assumed that
their rational approach to monsters contrasted with general superstition on the matter,[46] nothing allows us to be so categorical.
True, they do not consider monsters as portents or as divine
punishments, and they both refer to nature.[47] But nor do they
attack a religious interpretation of monstrosities. Hippocratic
medicine refuses, as a general rule, to consider any disease as
having a divine origin, or at least as expressing a divine intention
towards the affected person or his community. It considers every
disease as having a natural cause.[48] Its specific attacks concern

---

[43] Cf. the oath of Plataea (n. 8 above).

[44] Cf. the Amphictyonic oath quoted by Aeschines, *In Ctes.* 111.

[45] Parker (1983), 255–6.

[46] See e.g. Neumann (1995), at 47–8 (on Hippocrates), and Louis in Bingen, Cambier,
and Nachtergael (1975), 282 (on Aristotle).

[47] For Aristotle, cf. n. 22 above.

[48] Cf. *Aer.* 22: 'no one [disease] is more divine or more human than any other; all are
alike, and all divine. Each of them has a nature of its own, and none arises without its
natural cause' (trans. W. H. S. Jones, Loeb edn.). See above all *Morb. sacr.* 1–2 (Littré, vi.
352–64). On these questions, cf. Jouanna (1992), 259–97.

epilepsy (or 'the sacred disease'), usually interpreted as having a divine origin,[49] or the disease of Scythians who become impotent, a condition understood *by themselves* as a divine punishment.[50] The Hippocratics never criticize a religious interpretation of monstrous births. This fact is not surprising, given that Hippocratic concern with monsters was limited; in any case, it does not support the idea that medical views on monsters stood in opposition to a generally held religious interpretation.

There is thus no reason why the elimination of monsters should be seen as a religious act.[51] The ancient sources justify it, rather, on eugenic grounds: the aim was to preserve a healthy and strong community.[52] That could be no more than philosophical idealism (Plato, Aristotle) or late rationalization (Plutarch).[53] But it is awkward to replace ancient explanations with modern ones which are not attested and might simply be anachronistic.[54] All in all, Greek silence on the fate of the deformed is no more note-worthy than the scanty evidence on exposure in general.[55]

So we come back to the silence of the sources. If this was on the whole not due to religious dread, it may rather be connected with a fear which is probably unavoidable at all times, but which was increased by the sensibilities of Greeks, who valued so highly physical harmony and integrity and were particularly horrified by

---

[49] *Morb. sacr.* 1 (Littré, vi. 352).   [50] *Aer.* 22.

[51] *Contra* Delcourt (1938), 41–9. Parker (1983: 221) argues that an abnormal birth was sometimes seen by Greeks as a source of pollution which required purification by being burnt, although this is 'a kind of concern that, in contrast to the conspicuous Roman obsession, scarcely penetrates our sources'. We may add that the sources quoted by Parker (his n. 75) are either unclear or late.

[52] Cf. Pl. *Rep.* 460c (n. 27 above) and Plu. *Lyc.* 16. 2: 'it was better for himself and for the city that the newborn who from the outset was not disposed for health and strength did not live.'

[53] Delcourt (1938: 41–6) argues that these authors assign a rational justification to practices that originally had a superstitious motive. Dasen (1993: 209) stresses that 'these views must be taken cautiously because they come from philosophers' and 'they cannot be regarded as revealing the popular opinion'.

[54] Generally speaking, understanding of Greek practices and beliefs in relation to monsters seems to have been distorted by knowledge of Roman ones. It is striking how often modern statements on prodigies 'in antiquity' rest in fact on Latin sources and Roman instances.

[55] The evidence on exposure is especially scanty for Classical Greece. Cf. Germain (1995), who stresses that we do not know of a single instance of exposure in Classical Greece (pp. 235–41). The extent of the practice is also controversial. Some references are given in e.g. Eyben (1980/1), 14 n. 31, and Dasen (1993), 206 n. 3.

a deformed or mutilated body (see below). However, such silence about monstrosity close to home is in striking contrast to the Greeks' extensive descriptions of monsters which belong to another world, either to the mythical past or to the contemporary, distant space of ethnography. I will now deal with that second sort of representation, the ethnographical one.

MONSTERS IN ETHNOGRAPHY

Greek ethnography describes all sorts of monsters, sometimes in a very detailed manner, especially in depicting the confines of the world, those regions which are only known from hearsay and to whose distance corresponds a deterioration of human attributes.

Herodotus and Ctesias mention a number of monstrous peoples. The former locates some of them at the edge of Scythia, that is to say in the northern confines of the inhabited world: here dwell the Argippeans, who 'are said to be all bald from their birth, male and female alike',[56] the one-eyed men,[57] the 'men with goats' feet' or those 'who sleep for six months of the twelve';[58] others he locates in the western part of Libya, that is to say in its most distant part: for example 'the Dog-heads and the Headless that have their eyes in their breasts'—one cannot say whether Herodotus considers them as human beings or not—and also 'the wild men and women'.[59]

Ctesias, for his part, mentions in his description of India, at the eastern confines of the world, peoples whom he describes in greater detail than does Herodotus, such as Pygmies, flat-nosed, ugly, very small men, whose bodies are covered by long hair and who have a thick penis which stretches down to their ankles;[60] or the men with a dog-head, 'black like other Indians', but like dogs for the rest of their body, borrowing from them head, teeth, claws, tail, cry, and way of copulating;[61] also the men without anuses who can only consume milk and evacuate through

[56] 4. 23.   [57] 3. 116, 4. 13, 27.
[58] 4. 25.   [59] 4. 191.
[60] *FGrHist* 688 F 45 §§ 21–3 and F 45f α.
[61] F 45 §§ 36–43, F 45p α, β, γ; Psellos (in Maas (1924)).

vomiting;[62] the people whose women can give birth once only in their life,[63] whose babies already have teeth, but also white hair which darkens when they get older and becomes black when they are old;[64] those who have eight digits on each hand and foot,[65] whose ears are so big that they cover their back and arms;[66] those who have only one leg,[67] who have no neck, and whose eyes are in their shoulders;[68] or the Sciapodes, whose feet are so big that they overshadow them when they lie down with their legs up.[69]

Such monsters can be divided into two types: one group seem to be hybrids (men with goat-feet or with a dog-head), the others have an anatomical anomaly, which is generally an absence (of hair, of an eye, of the head, the neck, the anus, or a leg) or an excess (limbs with eight digits, ears or feet out of proportion). These two types of anomalies might have been inspired by actual monstrosities: as we have seen, Aristotle distinguished among the monsters the ones who looked like hybrids, such as beings with an ox-head, even if he indicated that the expression aimed only at suggesting a likeness. As for the type of monster characterized by a lack or an excess, this can be connected with anomalies or monstrosities actually known, such as those exhibited by dwarfs, monopods, or polydactyls.[70]

But naturally, even if ethnographers could have been inspired by actual monstrosities and were also sometimes influenced by oriental iconography and legends,[71] these were no more than a starting point for the construction of an imaginary world.

Ethnographical 'alchemy' presents the following features. First, it chooses to locate monsters in those countries which are the most distant from the Greek world. Then it changes an individual anomaly into an ethnic feature. That anomaly is thus hereditary, contrary to the usual definition of *teras*, according to which

---

[62] F 45 § 44.
[63] F 45 § 50 and F 45t.
[64] F 45 § 50, F 45t, F 52.
[65] F 45 § 50.
[66] Ibid.
[67] F 51a.
[68] F 51.
[69] F 51a, F 51b, F 60.

[70] Polydactyly is common, but generally affects one single hand or foot. Imperforate anus is also attested. See Saint-Hilaire (1837), i. 230–7 (polydactyly), 177 (imperforate anus), and *Stedman's Medical Dictionary*, 26th edn. (Baltimore, 1995), s.vv. 'polydactyly', 'atresia'.

[71] See, for Ctesias' Indian monsters, Lenfant (1995), 319–20 (on the influence of the hybrids of Mesopotamian and Achaemenid iconography) and 323 (on their likeness to the strange creatures of Indian epics).

monstrous children do not resemble their parents.[72] Furthermore, the anomaly is, of course, not inconsistent with life. More paradoxical is the fact that it involves no disadvantage, for physiology and habits adapt themselves (thus, men without anuses evacuate in another way); it can even constitute an advantage (thus, Pygmies use their hair as clothes and Sciapodes guard against sun thanks to their feet). Lastly, another paradox contributes to situate ethnographical monsters far from those evoked as a threat in the Greek world by Hesiod and the curses. Ethnographical monsters do not come into the world to punish the unjust; on the contrary, they live, at least in Ctesias' India, in the most just society.[73] How can we explain these diverse paradoxes, and what is the meaning of an imagining process which follows such well-defined rules? To understand it, we must first consider the Greek mental universe, since ethnography does not form—any more than mythology does[74]—a world apart.

Monstrosity deviates not only from the species, but also from an aesthetic canon. One of the most striking features of Greek Classical culture is a concern with physical harmony and the perfection of the human body. This is to be seen in the practice of athleticism, which strives to model the human body, as in art. Not only do painters and sculptors choose man as their chief subject: they also strive to give him a perfect body. Even if caricature and the grotesque are not unknown, 'iconography reflects the sensitivity of the Greeks to the human body, its proportions, its integrity':[75] V. Dasen points out that 'Greek artists had little interest in showing human physical anomalies', and most mythological monsters are usually composed of normal human and animal elements, whereas the rare physical anomalies are never emphasized.[76] For the same reason, they were reluctant to depict mutilated bodies.[77]

In contrast to such a cultural background, the foreign countries

---

[72] But biologists admit that malformations may sometimes be transmitted (Hippoc. *Genit.* 11 (Littré, vii. 485); Arist. *GA* 721^{b}17–20 and 724^{a}3–4, *HA* 585^{b}29–33). Hippocrates applies that principle on an ethnic scale in the case of the Macrocephals (*Aer.* 14).

[73] The great justice of Indians is a leitmotiv of the *Indica*. Cf. F 45 § 16, etc.

[74] Cf. Buxton (1994), 4 and *passim*.

[75] Dasen (1993), 165.

[76] Because dwarfs are an exception to that rule since they were often depicted, Dasen infers that their anomaly was seen as acceptable.   [77] Dasen (1993), 166.

evoked by ethnography are the place *par excellence* of the deterioration, indeed the dislocation, of the human body—in other words, the reverse of the exhibited ideal. This is obvious for monstrous peoples placed at the edges of the world: Ctesias' Pygmies, with their smallness, flat nose, and disproportionate hair and genitals, may be considered as a Greek pattern of ugliness.[78] But it is also true, to a lesser degree, among peoples living nearer the Greeks, like those of the Persian empire. There, the human body is also affected, although not on an ethnic scale, but individually, through mutilations and tortures. Herodotus' account of Persia includes many examples of mutilation, castration, impaling, beheading, or flaying;[79] and Ctesias' *Persica* accumulates severed heads, pulled-out eyes, stonings, impalings, flayings, as well as more original tortures like cutting out the tongue, pulverizing the head between two stones, or pouring molten lead into the ears.[80] We may add that Ctesias, especially attentive to the body as a physician, gives clinical and very detailed descriptions of several tortures or pains caused by the taking of a poison.[81]

Such practices could only horrify the Greeks,[82] even if torture was not unknown in their own society.[83] Why, then, did they play down tortures[84] and monstrous births, changing them into oriental attributes? They undoubtedly strove to suppress what

---

[78] Ibid. 176.

[79] See the examples quoted by Lévy (1992), 214–15.

[80] Severed heads: F 9 § 5, F 13 § 19, F 14 § 39; pulled-out eyes: F 9 § 6, F 26 § 14, 10; stonings: F 15 §§ 49 and 52; impalings: F 9 § 6, F 14 §§ 39 and 45, F 16 § 66, F 26 § 17, 7; flayings: F 9 § 6, F 15 § 56, F 16 § 66, F 26 § 17, 7; cutting out the tongue: F 16 § 58; pulverizing the head between two stones: F 29b § 19, 9; pouring molten lead into the ears: F 26 § 14, 10.

[81] For instance, the trough torture (F 26 § 16): the condemned person is laid down in a trough on which one puts, as a cover, a second trough, letting only the head and the limbs protrude; the face of the condemned is painted with honey and soon after becomes covered in flies; he is compelled to eat, and his excrement feeds a profusion of worms which devour his entrails; or the results of the taking of a poison derived from the Indian purple snake (F 45l): 'he will be seized with convulsions of the utmost violence; next, his eyes squint and his brain, being compressed, drips through his nostrils, and he dies a most pitiable, but fast death.'

[82] Cf. Lévy (1992), 214.

[83] But it is true that, in Classical Athens, the law prohibited the torturing of a citizen, and that only slaves, and sometimes free foreigners, could be subjected to it (MacDowell (1978), 245–7). As for the death penalty, the three methods we hear of (precipitation, *tumpanon* (the victim being clamped to a pole and left to die), and poisoning) do not imply any mutilation, and it is noteworthy that beheading is never mentioned (ibid. 254–5).

[84] See, especially, the unclear allusions to the *apotumpanismos* (Gernet (1924)).

could sully the image of the Greek world, and it is not surprising that ethnography, like myth,[85] exhibited aspects of social life that were otherwise concealed. Imaginary rejection of the malformed to the edges of the world could symbolically express the rejection such persons actually suffered in Greek societies[86] and, in this respect, the study of ethnographic representations simply confirms some impressions given by the scanty evidence on Greek monsters. As the picture of the Greek world was affected, so was that of the barbarian world, as being inhabited by a physically and morally degraded humanity. In that field as in others, Greeks strove to deepen artificially the difference between themselves and others.

Yet, that difference could take on divergent meanings, as appears from a comparison between Herodotus' view of monsters and that of his successor Ctesias. Two divergences are especially noteworthy.

First, Herodotean ethnography makes physical and moral perfection converge: Long-Lived Ethiopians not only surpass other men in height, strength, beauty, and longevity, but they are at the same time just, refusing to attack other peoples and rejecting Cambyses' presents.[87] By contrast, Ctesias makes a paradoxical association, for, in the Indian world as he describes it, one can be at the same time just *and* ugly, monstrous or hybrid, like the Pygmies or the Dog-heads. Moral qualities are thus independent of physical beauty.

But the gap between Herodotus and Ctesias is still wider, and we should not be misled by the examples of monsters quoted above. First, there are many more monsters in the *Indica* than in the *Histories*. That disproportion is all the more pronounced as the people described by Ctesias live in the heart of India, the subject of his book, whereas Herodotus mentions monsters only in connection with marginal regions, the confines of Libya and Scythia, which he describes briefly. And if the peoples depicted by Herodotus are in many respects aberrant and can be understood as expressing an increasing negation of the Greek norm, their anomalies are above all moral, and not anatomical.[88] Furthermore, the two authors have diametrically opposed attitudes towards the

---

[85] Cf. Buxton (1994), 210.
[86] Cf. Dasen (1993: 188) on pygmies and dwarfs.
[87] 3. 20–3.   [88] Cf. Rossellini and Saïd (1978).

monsters they describe. Whereas nothing attests any reservation from Ctesias about monsters,[89] Herodotus insistently rejects what he considers as incredible legends. He is sometimes content with ascribing what he reports to intermediaries: for instance, he says that he heard about one-eyed men through Scythians who were informed by Issedones . . .[90] But he generally expresses his scepticism more clearly: he indicates twice that he does not believe in the existence of men with goats' feet or of those who sleep for six months of the twelve,[91] and declares also: 'I regard it as incredible that there can be men in all else like other men, yet having but one eye.'[92]

These two attitudes correspond to two degrees of critical sense and two distinct manners of understanding the ethnographer's duty.[93] But they also express, more basically, two views of human identity. Herodotus is intent on clearly distinguishing man from animal. He does not describe animals by a partial assimilation with man, whereas Ctesias depicts the *bittacos*, a bird which can speak like a man, or the *martichoras*, which has features of the lion and the scorpion, but whose face has human attributes.[94] The legend of the Dodonean doves speaking with a human voice is rationalized by Herodotus, who interprets the term 'dove' as a

---

[89] On the contrary, Ctesias stated (*FGrHist* 688 F 45 § 51) that his account was most truthful, that he relied on what he had either seen or heard from eyewitnesses, and that he preferred not to mention many other things still more marvellous for fear of being suspected of telling 'incredible things' (ἄπιστα).

[90] 4. 27.

[91] He reduces their existence to an assertion of the Argippeans, the bald men, and twice expresses his scepticism (4. 25).

[92] 3. 116. We may add that his enumeration of the strange creatures inhabiting the edges of Libya is undercut by a few words expressing his reservations (ὡς δὴ λέγονταί γε ὑπὸ Λιβύων, 'at least according to the Libyans') and ends with καὶ ἄλλα πλήθεϊ πολλὰ θηρία κατάψευστα, 'and a lot of other *incredible* beasts'. The MSS read ἀκατάψευστα, 'not incredible'; but the meaning 'incredible' is not in doubt, considering the scepticism expressed before. Thus modern editors generally choose either to amend the manuscript (with Reiz's correction, adopted by Legrand in his Budé edn.) or to keep the manuscript reading, either by contrasting the last-mentioned beasts with the former, or by giving the term an ironical sense (so Medaglia and Corcella (1993), 204, 381).

[93] One should certainly not underrate the context in which Herodotus' statements appear and their effect on the reader. In 4. 25, Herodotus' expression of scepticism about what lies beyond the bald men implies that the existence of a population of bald men is above suspicion (cf. Buxton (1994), 157). Nevertheless, the contrast between Herodotus and Ctesias remains intact: bald men are very different from men with goats' feet or from people whose eyes are in their shoulders, for baldness has nothing monstrous about it and is perfectly human.

[94] *Bittacos*: F 45 § 8; *martichoras*: F 45 § 15, F 45d α, β, δ.

metaphor designating barbarian women whose language sounded like the song of birds until they seemed to acquire a human voice when they spoke in Greek:[95] 'For', he says, 'how could a dove speak with a human voice?'[96] That is precisely what Ctesias admits with the *bittacos*, which 'has a human language and a human voice'.[97] Conversely, the peoples depicted by Herodotus are not described through comparisons with animals, at least regarding physical features: the only assimilations with animals concern behaviour, that of peoples who, unlike Greeks and Egyptians, are not reluctant to copulate in sanctuaries 'and hold a man to be like any other animal',[98] or the behaviour of those who, like peoples of Caucasus and southern Indians, do it 'openly, like beasts'.[99]

Thus, for Herodotus, man answers to a well-defined model. The historian does not admit monstrosity on an ethnic scale. He distinguishes sharply between the anatomy of man and animal, and considers that the dignity of man implies giving up the behaviour of the beast. Ctesias, by contrast, through his representation of monstrous peoples, questions the human model known to the Greeks. The men and beasts of the *Indica* easily exchange their physical attributes and also some of their behaviour: the *martichoras* shoots like a Saca bowman,[100] and the Dog-heads, although having a number of canine features and copulating on all fours like dogs, are the most just of men.[101]

Such an ethnography perfectly plays the role that R. Buxton assigns to myths: 'myths often fulfil the role of pathfinders, testing out boundaries, imagining the consequences of interferences between categories.'[102] The point here is to define the limits of the human and its attributes, but also to question certain moral norms (for instance, does the manner of copulating imply anything about the practice of justice?) or certain common opinions (for

---

[95] 2. 55–7.
[96] ἐπεὶ τέῳ τρόπῳ ἂν πελειάς γε ἀνθρωπηίῃ φωνῇ φθέγξαιτο;
[97] γλῶσσαν ἀνθρωπίνην ἔχει καὶ φωνήν.
[98] 2. 64.
[99] 1. 203, 3. 101. This fact might seem to be refuted by the case of the Garamantes, whose language resembles the shrill cries of a bat (4. 183). But such a comparison obviously reflects the feeling of a foreign hearer and recalls the case, quoted above, of the Dodonean doves.
[100] F 45d β.   [101] F 45 § 43.   [102] (1994), 204.

instance, is it necessary to be beautiful to be just?). Ethnography, like myth, reflects the society that produced it and expresses a questioning of its norms.[103]

CONCLUSION

In Greece, there was no general evolution either from a religious to a rational rejection of monsters, or from a belief in mythical monsters to a rational disbelief on the matter: quite the contrary. Greeks generally agreed in removing, physically and symbolically, from daily life and from their writings, the monsters which were born in their society. But monsters reappeared all the more vividly elsewhere, in myth and ethnography, which thus expressed what Greeks wanted to exclude from their society. They appeared as a figure of the stranger[104] and even Aristotle, the only one who outlined a teratology dealing with monsters from a biological viewpoint, believed that foreigners more readily bore monsters.[105] Nevertheless, the monstrous picture of foreigners was not confined to giving a negative idea of them: it also allowed the Greeks to embody paradoxical situations and to question implicitly the norms of *doxa*, 'common opinion', such as the anatomical or moral definition of man, the boundaries between species, the advantages and disadvantages of civilization, the relations between beauty and justice or nature and morals . . . More

---

[103] I do not wish to suggest that Ctesias' main *object* was to challenge norms and to re-educate his readers: he obviously practised paradox in order to surprise. But I think that his representations had such an *effect*. Not only did they entertain, but they also produced unusual associations which might prompt reflection.

[104] In the same way, the mythological monsters of Archaic literature have been interpreted as a metaphor of the resistance of indigenous tribes to Greek colonizers (cf. Hall (1989), 49–50). An extreme example of such a tendency to identify monsters with foreigners is given in the Middle Ages (12th cent.) by Gui de Bazoches, who wrote in his *Apologia contra maledicos*: 'France alone has no monsters, but abounds in able, strong, and most eloquent men'; quoted by Friedman (1981), 53 and n. 56.

[105] Thus, since he considers that being multiparous promotes confusion between embryos and explains in this way the fact that monsters are more frequent among beasts, he compares to the latter the Egyptians, whose women are multiparous and give birth to more monsters (GA 770^a34–6); besides, in that same country, 'children survive even if they are born monstrous' (HA 584^b9). In a word, more human monsters live in Egypt than anywhere else, and this feature makes its inhabitants resemble beasts.

214 Dominique Lenfant

than the dishonesty or the ingenuousness of Classical and medieval authors,[106] more than the simplicity of their readers, the implications of such pictures[107] seem to explain the great success of an entire tradition.

[106] Ctesias' picture of the Far East and its monsters was handed down from antiquity to the Middle Ages and beyond, especially through Pliny, whose enormous influence is attested by fantastic humanity pictured in cartography, literature, and art. Apart from Pliny and Solinus, the basic texts on monstrous races are Augustine, *City of God* 16. 8, and Isidore of Seville, *Libri etymologiarum* 11. 3. On monstrous peoples in medieval thought and Christian attitudes towards them, see Friedman (1981). On fabulous creatures in medieval art, see Wittkower (1942).

[107] After Augustine, medieval texts often raise the question of the humanity of monstrous races, which render uncertain the notion of man and lead to reflection on his definition (reason, morality, social organization . . .). Cf. Céard (1977), 46–50, and Friedman (1981), 178–96. They make explicit a question which often remained implicit in Classical times.

11

Rationalizing Myth: Methods and Motives in Palaephatus

JACOB STERN

> The crude commercialism of America, its materialising spirit, its indifference to the poetical side of things, and its lack of imagination . . . are entirely due to that country having adopted for its national hero a man who, according to his own confession, was incapable of telling a lie.
>
> Oscar Wilde, The Decay of Lying[1]

A RATIONALIZER of myths, a student of Aristotle who debunks the implausible tales of an earlier age by providing *logoi* for *muthoi*—surely such a figure must be thought to cooperate with the familiar thesis under examination in this book: that the Greek world witnessed a development from *muthos* to *logos*. But the truth is not so simple. For the writings of Palaephatus will illustrate a variation on the theme: that although Greek society may have advanced in the direction of *logos* it did not simultaneously lose its obsession with its own *muthoi*. Though Palaephatus may debunk myth, he argues ultimately that myths are not to be discarded, but that rather, stripped of their most fantastical elements, they are all the more to be accepted and believed. Palaephatus finally is a corrector not a rejecter of the myths he inherits. His writings demonstrate that the application of reason to myth may have as its primary purpose the strengthening rather than the weakening of belief in those very myths and that the appearance of *logos* does not of necessity require the disappearance of *muthos*.

About Palaephatus himself there is hardly a non-problematic statement that can be made. Even his name—an adjective familiar

---

[1] I owe the citation to my colleague Professor Felicia Bonaparte.

from Homer and tragedy—has been thought pseudonymous.[2]
The following, however, can be offered as more likely than
not to be true: that Palaephatus was born in Egypt, or on the
Hellespont at Parium or Abydos; that he moved to Athens where
he became an associate of Aristotle (according to sources cited in
the *Suda* he was no less than Aristotle's *paidika* (beloved)); that in
Athens he wrote *inter alia* a work called *Peri apistōn* ('On Unbelievable Tales') which the *Suda* describes as 'solutions of things
said in myth'; and that this work, originally of five books, was
epitomized to a single book, presumably in the ninth or tenth
century CE, about the time that Bishop Photius was epitomizing
a similar collection of myths by Conon.

The text of Palaephatus which survives to the present day is
comprised of fifty-three items in what Wilamowitz called a
nondescript 'Allerweltsgriechisch':[3] the first of these items is a
general statement of the rationalistic principles which Palaephatus
employs. The next forty-five items are instances of rationalized
myths. The format is fairly consistent: Palaephatus first offers
a brief summary of the familiar myth; he then asserts that this
traditional version is 'false', 'laughable', 'silly', or 'impossible'; and
then he presents a rationalistic version in which the impossible is
explained away. So Palaephatus will briefly tell the familiar stories
of Medea (43) or of Cerberus (39), after which he will tell us
what he calls 'the truth': that Medea did not rejuvenate old men
by boiling them piecemeal in a caldron, but that she invented
hair-dye and the steam bath; that Cerberus was not three-headed,
but that he was called 'Tricranite' because he came from the city
of Tricarenia. And so it goes for forty-five items.

About the last seven items in the corpus we may say with
assurance that they are spurious. This was the judgement of
Nicolaus Festa, the Teubner editor, and it is clearly shown to be
true by the fact that in these seven items we find only the
straightforward telling of traditional tales without any mythological rationalization. That these last seven items are not part of the
genuine Palaephatean corpus is a significant point to which I shall
return in a moment.

Let me now turn to a few comments about Palaephatus'

[2] Stern (1996), 1. To orient the reader of this essay I have recapitulated here a certain
amount of basic material from the introduction to Stern (1996), which was published a
few weeks before the Bristol Colloquium. For Palaephatus' biography, see especially
FGrHist 44 T 1–4.   [3] Wilamowitz-Moellendorff (1895), 101.

introductory statement. Here are discovered the author's two fundamental principles. First, that the natural world is immutable: that what is not now—a centaur, for instance—cannot have existed in the past either. And secondly, that heroic myths would not have been created nor transmitted if there were not in them some kernel of historical reality—misunderstood and distorted as it may be.

For the first of these principles Palaephatus quotes with approval the statement of Melissus and Lamiscus:[4] 'What came into being is now and will for ever be.' The Hesiodic representation is thus rejected: as Herodotus (1. 68) had demonstrated in the story of Orestes' bones buried beneath the shop of an iron-worker; as Plutarch (*Theseus* 36. 2) had illustrated in the story of Theseus' coffin unearthed on Scyros together with a bronze spear, the *familiar* mythological tradition had accepted the principle of the Ages of Humanity and in particular the separation between the Age of Heroes and our own fallen Age of Iron. But Palaephatus supposes a continuum from the present to the past, and nothing which does not exist now is to be imagined as having existed at any time then. On this last point Palaephatus is, of course, wrong, although for our purposes the mistake is unimportant. For all, I suppose, will agree that there is no classical myth which is to be explained or interpreted in light of natural evolution.

The second principle, however, is more insidious, and in some sense it lasts to the present day. For Palaephatus is not alone in believing that myth is twisted history and in supposing that the interpreter's proper task is to discover the kernel of 'historical' truth and to expose the fantasies which have over time obscured it. It is, as Plato saw in *Phaedrus* 229c–d, a fundamentally absurd undertaking: it cannot be, the rationalist thinks, that mythological narrative is the product of the human imagination or of deliberate fabrication; it must rather be that some ordinary past event—misunderstood over the course of time—is the basis on which myth is formed.

In Palaephatean thought these primal 'historical' events tend to be of a few recognizable types. A *prōtos heuretēs*—an imagined inventor who acts as culture hero from the early days of human history—is misunderstood:[5] Lynceus (9) cannot have seen beneath

---

[4] Listed as spurious in [20] B 11 DK.
[5] See Henrichs (1975*b*), esp. 111.

the earth—rather he must have been a miner for metals who
invented the lamp which miners use for their subterranean work;
Pandora (34) can hardly have been fashioned from earth—she
must rather have been the inventor of the earth-based cosmetic
which Greek women applied to their faces.

A second type of primal 'historical' event imagined by
Palaephatus involves an ambiguous metaphorical use of language
or a pun which was at some point misunderstood: the single eye
of the Graeae, we learn (31), was a human adviser who travelled
between islands ruled by three sisters and who was known as
'The Eye', like Amphiaraus in Pindar, *Olympian* 6. 16, or the
familiar Persian spies (Hdt. 1. 114. 2). Elsewhere, Palaephatus
employs simple onomastic puns which depend on the confusion
of a man who has an animal-name with the animal itself: Krios
('Ram'), Drakon ('Snake'), or Tauros ('Bull'). So too Palaephatus
will frequently claim that a casual remark uttered far in the past
came to be misinterpreted by some innocent naïf and that from
the misunderstanding arose the myths we know: Diomedes (7)
spent so much money raising his horses and Actaeon (6) his dogs
that their friends said they were being 'eaten alive'. In short,
Palaephatus at all costs will save the letter of the myth, even if not
its spirit.

It is only the myths of heroes, heroines, and the monstrous
creatures that they encounter that Palaephatus rationalizes; at no
point does he rationalize myths of the gods. In the genuine
corpus of Palaephatus—the first forty-five tales in the extant
text—the Olympians, in fact, are mentioned only eight times.
Five of these—in items 3, 31, 33, and 42—are utterly trivial
allusions; and the remaining three cases are almost as insignificant:
so, for example, on one occasion Palaephatus will remark in an
offhand way that Zeus, had he wanted Europa to go to Crete,
would no doubt have found a better method than transportation
on the back of a bull (15); elsewhere, while rationalizing
the myth of the Hecatoncheires ('Hundred-Handers'), he will
incidentally refer to the battle of the Olympians and the Titans
(19).

But, in fact, Palaephatus not only avoids rationalizing myths of
the gods, he even avoids mentioning the gods in his brief
accounts of the *traditional* versions which he intends to reject.
Callisto, we learn (14), was turned into a bear and Atalanta (13)

into a lioness, but no divine agency is indicated: it is not an angry Artemis or Hera who transforms Callisto; nor an angry Cybele, as in the usual myth, who transforms Atalanta and her husband. Rather, Palaephatus says simply that Callisto and Atalanta 'turned into animals (*egeneto*).' The reason is clear: if Palaephatus, in his rendition of the traditional tale, had specified a divine agency, he would have been required to offer rationalistic explanations of divine myths—and this he never does.

This point is of major importance: in the genuine tales of Palaephatus it is *only* the heroes and heroines whose myths are rationalized. Those who have asserted otherwise—among them most recently Paul Veyne[6]—have been misled by their failure to distinguish the genuine from the spurious items in the text: it is only in the latter—the last seven items in the corpus—that we find the gods as important actors: here are told, among others, the stories of Apollo and Marsyas; Apollo and Daphne; Aphrodite and Phaon; and the birth of Orion from Zeus, Poseidon, and Hermes. But this merely confirms what was argued earlier: that these last seven items, which have neither the structure nor the rationalizations of the genuine items, are in fact spurious.

Palaephatus himself, on the other hand, is essentially silent about the gods—a remarkable statement to make about a mythographer. He is neither Xenophanes nor Pindar nor Plato: he does not censure the behaviour of the Olympian gods. Nor, most importantly, is he Euhemerus, and the Euhemeristic tradition must be carefully distinguished from the Palaephatean.[7] For although Palaephatus and Euhemerus begin from the same basic assumption, that myth originates in misunderstood human history, yet their motives are fundamentally different. The Euhemeristic tradition is essentially atheistic and aims to create disbelief. Palaephatus, on the other hand, ignores the gods and concentrates instead on reinforcing belief—belief, however, not in the existence of the gods, but rather in the historicity of the heroes of old. We may continue to accept the reality of these legendary heroes because the rationalizer has eliminated from their myths anything which might tend to produce incredulity. It is for this reason that rationalism of the Palaephatean type—as

[6] (1988), 67–8.
[7] Geffcken (1912), 573; Osmun (1956), 136.

Wipprecht, Nestle, and others have demonstrated[8]—is found almost exclusively in the ancient historians and geographers. From Hecataeus and Pherecydes to Diodorus Siculus, Plutarch, and Pausanias, it is the historians who alone offer clear parallels to the Palaephatean model. In the poetic tradition the instances are quite rare: one thinks, for example, of Tiresias' rationalization of Dionysus' birth from the thigh of Zeus (Eur. *Ba.* 286–97). But otherwise it is among the truth-tellers, not the poets, that Palaephatean rationalism will be found.

For it is noteworthy that Palaephatus understands *pseudos* and its cognates only in the sense of 'false', never in the sense of 'intentional lie'. In this, the model for Palaephatus is Herodotus' portrayal of the early Persians, who, when confronted with the story of a matricide or a parricide—that is, when confronted with the myth of Orestes or Oedipus—simply assert that it must be an error (1. 137. 2). Such a story cannot be 'true'—that would run counter to the Persian view of nature; nor can it be a 'lie', since then it would violate a fundamental Persian *nomos*. And so it must be a mistake: the child must have been fraudulently substituted or illegitimately conceived. For it is not until Darius in Herodotus' account (3. 72. 4) that the unpoetical Persians learn the value of the conscious lie.

But Palaephatus in the Greek setting illustrates the opposite development. For the Greeks and the Greek literary tradition knew the lie from the very beginning—from Odysseus' false tale to Athena and the Muses' first speech to Hesiod on Mount Helicon (*Th.* 27–8). It is rather Palaephatus—the later author, the harbinger of the age of *logos*—who seems to have forgotten what his ancestors knew: the essential value of the lie. To Hesiod and Homer, who understood deception, belief was never in question, but to the literal-minded Palaephatus myth must be stripped of its errors so belief can be comfortable. It is, we might say, an application of *logos* to *muthos*, but the result is not that the mythic disappears, but rather that it is made prosaically credible.

So to Palaephatus myth is always shown to be the result of mistake, never of intention. Briefly in his introduction, and in passing at one other point (6), Palaephatus hints at a more

---

[8] Wipprecht (1902), 20–7, 38–43; W. Nestle (1940), 133–48.

imaginative, Critias-like presumption (88 [81] B 25 DK): that myth may have been formed intentionally to frighten humanity away from depravity. Yet at no point does Palaephatus actually rationalize or explain any myth or mythological detail by assuming such an intentional lie. Myth with Palaephatus is always the result of misunderstanding, never of design. It is the emblem of his ordinary mind.

An additional difficulty is found in Palaephatus' thought. On the one hand, in nature at large Palaephatus demands an unchanging universe—a universe which will not allow for a past different from the present and in which we can easily discredit past events simply because they are impossible in the present. But in his anthropology Palaephatus' modes of rationalization are typically evolutionary. He speaks frequently of a distant rustic past—the time of *hoi tote anthrōpoi* ('the men who lived then')— a time of simple virtue, before humanity was corrupted by familiar amenities. Money and coinage had not yet been invented and people used chattel or barter instead. So in the tale of the musicians Amphion and Zethus (41) we are told that people worked on the town walls instead of compensating the heroes with money for the pleasure of hearing them play their music: it was thus that the story arose that the walls had been built 'by a lyre'. So too we learn that servants and slaves did not yet exist to do one's work in this simple, past time; self-sufficiency was the rule: Actaeon and Diomedes, however, lacked this industriousness and allowed themselves and their livelihood to be 'devoured' by their passion for hunting-dogs and horses. Various cultural innovations and luxuries typical of today's world had not yet been made in this early time: horseback-riding was as yet unknown (1); as were hair-dyeing and cosmetics. And the sculptor's art—not yet refined by Daedalus' 'striding statues' (21)—was as yet at a crude stage of development.

So the modes of Palaephatean analysis assume in language, in social institutions, and in technology a significant development from the past to the present. Within this evolution implausible myths are imagined to be created when one generation misunderstands the customs, the metaphoric language, the inventions of its forebears. Between the imagined historical event which is the kernel from which myth arose and our own day there must have been, it appears, a generation of utter fools.

It is a mode of explanation which dies hard. To the rationalist's mind the Trojan Horse must be a misunderstood siege instrument designed to breach the Trojan walls,[9] rather than an imaginative representation of the belly of the beast into which heroes from Jonah to Pinocchio have been swallowed as they cross the threshold of the *skaiai pulai*[10]—though we never find identified the generation so foolish as to have misinterpreted the siege device in the first place. The mythographer's presumption is that *he* represents the triumph of *logos* over *muthos*—that anything 'real' is a better explanation of myth than the human capacity to fabricate. But the truth is that Palaephatus' even more fundamental presumption is this: that a primal age of *logos* must have been followed by one of moronic *muthos*.

[9] Paus. 1. 23. 8.
[10] 'Western' or 'ill-omened' gates. *The* 'Skaian Gates' were at Homer's Troy.

12

Demythologizing the Past, Mythicizing the Present: Myth, History, and the Supernatural at the Dawn of the Hellenistic Period

ALBERT HENRICHS

'MYTH' AND 'HISTORY' may derive from Greek words, but they are thoroughly modern concepts that together comprise but one aspect of the myth/*logos* relationship. For more than 125 years, these terms have been perceived as virtual opposites, as contradictory ways of looking at the world. We consider 'history' to represent objective truth, and myth to signify the collective product of a culture's imagination distilled into paradigmatic narrative scenarios. Historians of ancient Greece have tended to keep myth at arm's length, and students of Greek mythology have often treated myth as though the Greeks had lived in a historical vacuum. Fortunately, perceptions are changing, albeit gradually. Over the past quarter century, awareness has grown that 'myth' and 'history' are inseparably interwoven and must be seen as complementary and interdependent aspects of Greek culture. It is generally recognized that, at least for the Archaic period, self-proclaimed myths are to a large extent synonymous with history. If I were to produce examples for this revalidation of myth and, indeed, of religion as fundamental vehicles for historical enquiry, I would not only mention the names of Jean-Pierre Vernant, Pierre Vidal-Naquet, and Nicole Loraux, but I would also emphasize the renewed interest in oral traditions, in foundation myths, and in Herodotus as a cultural historian, as well as the recent appointment of Robert Parker—a historian of Greek religion—as the Wykeham Professor of Ancient History at the University of Oxford.[1] To my mind at least, these names and trends share a common direction and represent landmarks along

---

[1] Cf. Vernant (1980); Vidal-Naquet (1986); Loraux (1986) and (1993); Thomas (1989); Prinz (1979); Malkin (1987); Calame (1996a); Boedeker (1987); Nenci (1990); Parker (1996).

the road to burying the ghosts of historicism and rethinking what Greek history is all about.

Far from being total opposites, *muthos* and *logos* were for the Greeks complementary cognitive tools for articulating their understanding of the world around them. But the relationship between *muthos* and *logos* was complex, and the boundaries between the two were constantly shifting. The same holds true for myth and history. Not only is myth an integral part of Greek history, but it is also an important expression of cultural identity. In many cultures, myth performs the function of history and serves as a sort of collective memory that articulates the distant past chronologically as well as conceptually.[2] For the Greeks in particular, myth was a continuing process of interpreting the past in terms of the present and in the light of the individual and collective self.[3] In fact, the boundary between myth and history was never firmly drawn in antiquity—least of all in the fifth century BCE. Herodotus begins his *Historiai* with a series of mythical abductions that he treats as actual events. This mythical opening serves as a prelude to further adaptations of mythical material in the course of his work. Yet Herodotus' willingness to take myth seriously does not turn him into a mythographer or a mythologist. Thucydides took a different approach: as a historian, he sought to separate mythical fiction, *to muthōdes*, from historical fact, although he, too, believed in the historicity of the Trojan War and regarded the legendary King Minos as a genuinely important historical figure. Does that make Thucydides any less a historian? On an even larger scale, Attic tragedy and epideictic oratory derive their distinctive character in part from the way these genres create mythical paradigms that fold the heroic past into the political and social realities of the present.[4] Throughout the Classical period, poets and prose writers alike fashion memorable analogies between myth and history, past and present, that share an important feature—they

---

[2] Cf. Eliade (1968), 123–5, 134–8; Toulmin and Goodfield (1965), 23–32 ('Memories and Myths').

[3] C. Brillante, 'History and the Historical Interpretation of Myth', in Edmunds (1990), 93–138; Graf (1993), esp. 121–41 ('Myth as History'). A splendid example of myth functioning as a foil for history is Simonides' poem on the battle of Plataea, in which the Trojan War and the death of Achilles function as a prelude to the poet's encomiastic account of a historical battle (Boedeker and Sider (1996)).

[4] Vernant and Vidal-Naquet (1988); Loraux (1986).

reflect the aspirations of the polis rather than those of the individual.

This attitude would change in the Hellenistic period. Between the death of Euripides and the emergence of Callimachus, in the course of just over a century, Greek culture would undergo a drastic transformation. Literature and visual art, the two principal repositories for myth, would be deeply affected. How would Greek myth emerge from the Classical period, and what would be its role in the more cosmopolitan and more individualistic new era? It is well known that myth became the playground of the erudite elite, who did their best to bring the old tales back to life, and added more than a few of their own. I will not talk about the intellectualization of myth in the Hellenistic period, nor about the enormous efforts made by generations of Hellenistic scholars to preserve, classify, and reshape their mythical heritage, a process that turned myth into mythology. Instead, I will focus on some connections between myth and history, and will argue that the boundaries between them remained fluid, facilitating a curiously successful symbiosis of the two realms in the Hellenistic period.

The complementarity of myth and history is captured paradigmatically in a Hellenistic work of art.[5] On a highly symbolic relief sculpted by Archelaus of Priene, a majestic, Zeus-like Homer sits on a throne surrounded by personifications of the *Iliad* and *Odyssey*. Standing behind him are representations of Chronos and Oikoumene, who crowns the poet with a wreath. The heroized Homer is presiding over a sacrificial scene which comprises Myth and History flanking an altar behind which a bull waits to be sacrificed. Mythos is represented as a boy carrying ritual vessels, and Historia as a young woman sprinkling incense. The procession that approaches the altar from the right includes three female figures identified as Poetry, Tragedy, and Comedy. On a higher register, Zeus occupies the summit of Helicon or Parnassus, and hovers over Mnemosyne and the chorus of the nine Muses, who file down the mountain to join Apollo playing the kithara in a cave. On a pedestal outside the cave an unknown poet stands next to a tripod, a symbol of victory in a musical competition.

---

[5] London, BM 2191. Pinkwart (1965); Pollitt (1986), 15 f., with pl. 4; Stewart (1990), i. 217 f., with pls. 761–3; cf. Fraser (1972), ii. 862 n. 423.

Several scholars have suggested that the relief commemorates the foundation of the Alexandrian Homereion by Ptolemy IV and that the personifications of Chronos and Oikoumene bear the features of the king and his sister-wife Arsinoe III. If this interpretation is embraced, the pairing of Mythos and Historia becomes even more poignant. Homer then emerges as the prototype of the divinely inspired poet whose song encompasses myth as well as history. This description fits not only poets like Pindar and Simonides, but also the vast majority of the Alexandrian court poets, who praised their royal patrons by comparing them with the heroes of the mythical past.

By providing a mythico-historical repertoire for articulating the individual, myth acquires a new lease on life as creative horizons broaden in the wake of Alexander's conquests. In patterns that never cease to astonish, history takes myth under its wing, while the mythical imagination encroaches upon the domain of history and shapes the Hellenistic perception of actual events, both past and contemporary. The various ways in which myth and history interact help determine the status and stature of gods (Apollo, Dionysus, and Isis, among others) and of privileged mortals (especially heroes and kings), and range from the silly (ostentatious imitations of gods or heroes[6]) to the sublime (mythical utopias and divine kingship, for example).

Anybody who can say with conviction that 'Pausanias is the equal of any of the great nineteenth-century German philologists or philosophers' is either a fool or a genius.[7] It is this latter characterization, I trust, that defines Paul Veyne, who made this statement in an important book that appeared in 1983. In *Les Grecs ont-ils cru à leurs mythes?*, he anticipates some of the concerns raised in the present volume. For instance, he makes short shrift of the dichotomy implicit in the title: 'Despite Nestle, myth and *logos* are not opposites, like truth and error. Myth was a subject of serious reflection, and the Greeks still had not tired of it six hundred years after the movement of the Sophists.'[8] With wit and insight, Veyne analyses Greek attitudes towards myth from the

---

[6] This trend began as early as the mid-4th cent. BCE with the Argive general Nicostratus, who dressed up as Heracles, club, lion skin, and all (Diod. Sic. 16. 44. 3; Athen. 289a–c; cf. Ephippus, fr. 17 *PCG*; von Staden (1992), 135, 137).

[7] Veyne (1988), 3.

[8] Ibid. 1.

fifth century BCE to the fourth century CE. One of his most revealing observations on the Hellenistic period is that 'myth must pass as history' to be acceptable in the sceptical and ambiguous climate of that era.[9] The result, he adds, is a paradoxical blend of rationalism and mystification, which indulges the supernatural and the marvellous while pretending to transcend it. To drive home his point, he refers to the historian Timaeus, whose work Polybius criticizes as 'full of dreams, prodigies, incredible tales (*muthōn apithanōn*), and, to put it shortly, craven superstition and womanish love of the marvellous'.[10] Not only does myth pass into history, but in some cases, history turns into myth. I will explore two areas in which myth and history are particularly tolerant of each other.

Before I begin in earnest, I feel I should warn the squeamish that much of my paper revolves around the problem of human sacrifice, which is an especially rewarding vehicle for studying the interplay of myth and history. Human sacrifice is among the grimmest themes explored by the Greek mythopoeic imagination. From the sacrifice of Iphigenia at Aulis and the slaying of Polyxena on the tomb of Achilles to the dismemberment of Pentheus by his mother, the myths of epic and tragedy abound with stories of human victims slaughtered to please a divinity or to appease the ghosts of the dead. Compared to their frequency in myth, reports of ritual killings in historical settings are rare. Fewer than half a dozen cases are attested. Their very existence invites a question that is more easily raised than answered: did the Greeks at any time in their history kill humans for ritual purposes? The answer is made more perplexing by virtue of the Greek tendency to situate human sacrifice precariously in the intersection of myth and history.

The modern debate has been long and partisan. With few exceptions, scholars of Greek religion have been constitutionally curious about human sacrifice. After all, human blood is infinitely more fascinating and more suggestive than the blood of animals. By contrast, ancient historians are on the whole more sceptical; they either reject the ancient accounts of ritual killings as untrustworthy or they withhold judgement altogether. Both

---

[9] Ibid. 46.
[10] Polyb. 12. 24. 5 = *FGrHist* 566 T 19, p. 585 (in the translation of Veyne's translator).

camps, it must be said, have missed the point. Stories of human sacrifice never tell us what the Greeks actually did; their relevance lies in telling us what the Greeks thought. Throughout antiquity, the reality of human sacrifice and its powerful hold on the imagination did not lie in its actual occurrence, but in the pretence—or even possibility—that it once occurred.

Like few other acts of violence, human sacrifice blurs the boundaries between imagination and reality, between myth and history. Liminal by definition, human sacrifice provokes extreme and anxious reactions in most people. Outwardly disparaged, it is secretly relished and vicariously performed. The Greeks, too, were caught in this conundrum that even modern scholars have been unable to escape. This is particularly true of archaeologists who claim to have discovered evidence for the practice of human sacrifice in the Bronze Age. More than once in recent decades archaeologists have unearthed physical remains that continue to stir our imagination: a skeleton found in apparently ritual surroundings near Arkhanes on Crete; hundreds of human bones with knife marks discovered at Knossos; and the warrior buried at Lefkandi on Euboea with several horses and, even more ominously, the body of a woman.[11] The ritual scenarios reconstructed from these physical findings are remarkably similar to the mythical scenarios of human sacrifice found in literature, namely, human victims sacrificed in times of crisis, children murdered as a prelude to cannibalism, and a princess killed to grace the afterlife of a chieftain.[12]

In all three cases the convergence of the ancient myths and the modern interpretation of the archaeological data is surprisingly close. One wonders whether the new evidence might indeed reveal a historical dimension behind the principal myths of human sacrifice, or whether the excavators have rather imposed the familiar mythical patterns on their discoveries. Indeed, archaeologists must be careful lest they find only what they are looking for. The mythical sacrifices would appear in a different light if we could be absolutely certain that they preserved the distant memory of an actual ritual

[11] For a critical assessment of the Bronze Age 'evidence' see Bonnechere (1993); Hughes (1991), 13–17 (Arkhanes), 18–24 (Knossos), and 46f. (Lefkandi).

[12] Mythical paradigms that come to mind include Iphigenia, the children of Thyestes, and Polyxena. Cf. Hughes (1991), 60–5, 189f.

practice.[13] If this were the case, myth would mirror history, and archaeology would serve chiefly to confirm the presence of the historical roots that nourished the imagination of the earliest myth-makers. Such a factual, almost rectilinear, explanation for the prominence of human sacrifice in Greek myth would be an evolutionist's dream come true. But there is considerable room for doubt. So far, archaeology has been less than successful in establishing a pattern of human sacrifice for the Bronze Age.[14] One day, perhaps, the ancient ghost of a human victim will rise from the Greek soil, display his wounds like the ghost of Clytemnestra, and demand punishment for the modern sceptics.

Two recent books on the subject of human sacrifice, one by Dennis Hughes and the other by Pierre Bonnechere, have done much to clarify the issue.[15] Although their approaches differ substantially, both authors come to the conclusion that human sacrifice in Greek culture was essentially an imaginary construct, 'a mythical exaggeration' as Bonnechere puts it, with no secure base in fact or history.[16] Not surprisingly, they find the so-called historical cases the hardest to deal with and disagree on the most notorious of them all, the alleged sacrifice of three Persian princes by the Athenians before the battle of Salamis. According to Hughes, the story has too many holes in it to be true, and he concludes that it is a total fabrication.[17] His scepticism is only partially shared by Bonnechere, who tries to have it both ways. While acknowledging that the story 'suffers from some embarrassing imprecisions', as he puts it, he nevertheless finds its basic pattern and intrinsic dynamic compelling.[18] In a bold move, he folds myth into history and interprets the reported incident as a deliberate anachronism. The Athenians, he argues, perceived their

---

[13] Myths of human sacrifice have often been taken as 'survivals' of an earlier practice, most recently by Lloyd-Jones (1983), 88f. (= Lloyd-Jones (1990), 309f.). Cf. Hughes (1991), 71f.

[14] Hughes (1991), 13–48, 194–8; Bonnechere (1993).

[15] Hughes (1991); Bonnechere (1994). Cf. Bonnechere (1995).

[16] Bonnechere (1994: 311–18) speaks repeatedly of the 'concept' rather than the practice of human sacrifice, which he characterizes as 'une exagération mythique' (314). Similarly, Hughes (1991: 185–93) concludes that the Greek dossier on human sacrifice 'is more a testament to the capacity and breadth of the imagination of the Greeks than a documentary record of their practices' (193).

[17] (1991), 111–15. Hughes adopts the conclusions I had reached in 1981 (n. 20 below). [18] (1994), 288–91.

myths to be genuine history and, in a moment of extreme crisis, performed this human sacrifice as a historical re-enactment of an ancient mythical remedy. On this reading, the Athenians would have used the three Persian victims to re-enact the fate of Iphigenia at Aulis in the hope of achieving a similarly successful outcome.

Before we turn Salamis into another Aulis and allow myth to pass as history, however, I propose we take a closer look. Although the year is 480 BCE, the alleged human sacrifice is not mentioned in any extant source until some 150 years later, at the threshold of the Hellenistic period. The principal account is embedded in Plutarch's *Life of Themistocles*, the acknowledged source of which was Phaenias of Eresus, one of the earliest pupils of Aristotle and a writer of wide interests ranging from science to cultural history and biography. Phaenias flourished during the reign of Alexander the Great, and his cast of mind can be described as proto-Hellenistic, rather than pre-Hellenistic. In a series of anecdotes about Themistocles, Phaenias tells a remarkable story.[19] While Themistocles was performing the animal sacrifice (*sphagia*) customary before a military engagement, three noble prisoners, nephews of the Persian king, were brought into his presence. Prompted by favourable omens, the seer Euphrantides instructed Themistocles at once to sacrifice the three youths to Dionysus the Raw-Eater (Omestes). Shocked by the enormity of the request, Themistocles hesitated, but he was overruled by *hoi polloi*, who cast reason aside, seeing their best hope of salvation in this irrational exercise. Despite Themistocles' reluctance, the crowd invoked the god with one voice and led the prisoners to the altar to see that the sacrifice would be carried out.

This is the earliest instance of a human sacrifice allegedly performed by Greeks in the glaring light of history. No paraphrase can do justice to the wealth of ritual detail and the calculated psychological touches that lend a semblance of credibility to Phaenias' account. His beguiling blend of mythical and

---

[19] Plu. *Them.* 13. 2–5 = Phaenias, fr. 25 Wehrli (in Wehrli (1969), 16, 35); cf. Plu. *Arist.* 9. 2, *Pel.* 21. 3 (n. 28 below). Wehrli's brief comments are inadequate; I have been able to consult the full and up-to-date commentary on Phaenias by Dr Johannes Engels, which will appear in part IV of the *Fragments of the Greek Historians* (the continuation of F. Jacoby's *FGrHist*).

historical elements has divided scholars for over a hundred years. There is no need to repeat the numerous arguments that have been marshalled for and against its authenticity.[20] What really gives the game away is the name of the divine recipient of the human sacrifice, Dionysus Omestes. Although unheard of in Athens, he is well attested as a cult deity for Phaenias' native island of Lesbos.[21] But Phaenias is not the only Hellenistic author who connected the Raw-Eater with human sacrifice. According to his fellow Lesbian, Myrsilus of Methymna, who composed *Lesbiaca* in the first quarter of the third century BCE, Dionysus was called Omestes because in the distant past a man named Omestes had sacrificed a human victim of royal blood to the god.[22]

In this bizarre *aition*, which was discovered twelve years ago in an Oxyrhynchus papyrus, homonymy and human sacrifice make for strange bedfellows as they are pressed into service jointly to make sense of Dionysus' perhaps most savage epithet. Divine epithets are often explained with the help of etymologies or aetiological myths. One of Athena's epithets, Pallas, attracted the attention of Apollodorus of Athens (*c.*150 BCE), the greatest Hellenistic authority on divine names. The comic poet Epicharmus provided Apollodorus with the explanation that Athena was called Pallas because the goddess had killed a giant of the same name and had then used the giant's skin as a garment.[23] By slaying the previous owner of that name, the goddess comes by her epithet honestly. According to Myrsilus, however, Dionysus the Raw-Eater has done nothing to deserve his epithet. Instead, Omestes has earned it for him. In this Euhemerizing explanation, one of Dionysus' most revealing cult names becomes essentially a transferred epithet, and the god's own claim to savagery is

[20] Cf. Henrichs (1981: 208–24), where I argue that Phaenias created the story out of whole cloth. In a discussion appended to my article, Robert Turcan attempts to separate fiction from fact by differentiating between non-ritual execution and human sacrifice: three Persians may indeed have been executed by the Athenians, but the suggestion of human sacrifice would be secondary elaboration on the part of Phaenias or his source (op. cit. 242). This cannot be ruled out (n. 37 below), but the fact that Phaenias is the only author who mentions the killings inspires caution.

[21] Alcaeus, fr. 129, 9 *PLF*. A Chian myth connects human sacrifice with Dionysus Omadius (Euelpis of Carystus *apud* Porph. *De abst.* 2. 55. 3). On Dionysus Omestes and Omadius see Graf (1985), 74–80. Like Henrichs (n. 20 above) and Hughes (1991), Graf, too, rejects the historicity of Phaenias' account (p. 76).

[22] *P. Oxy.* 3711, col. 2, 17 ff., ed. M. W. Haslam, *The Oxyrhynchus Papyri*, 53 (London, 1986), 112–25. The new fragments of Myrsilus are ignored by Jackson (1995).

[23] *P. Köln* iii. 126, 8–16 = Austin (1973), fr. 85a; cf. Henrichs (1975*a*) 23 f., 29 ff.

eclipsed by the mortal performer of human sacrifice. The peculiar inner logic of Myrsilus' explanation amounts to a reductionism that manipulates the god's mythical image.

Taken at face value, the name Omestes conjures up the image of a god who consumes raw flesh and whose mouth is dripping with blood. The inscrutable wildness of the 'Raw-Eater' stirred the imaginations of Friedrich Nietzsche and Walter F. Otto, who found in him a confirmation of their conception of Dionysus as a god of polarities.[24] If these two founding fathers of the modern Dionysus had been familiar with Myrsilus' explanation, its banality would have stunned them. Myrsilus' *aition* is indeed a stark reminder of the enormous distance that separates the modern understanding of Dionysus from that of the Hellenistic period. At the same time, the *aition* underscores some of the prevailing Hellenistic attitudes towards myth and cult. By turning the god's epithet into the name of a sacrificing mortal, Myrsilus effectively demythologizes the god, whose wildness is transferred to a human surrogate and to the realm of ritual. Conversely, by aetiologically linking the epithet to human sacrifice, he mythicizes the violence of the perverted sacrifice. Either way, Dionysus is perceived as a destructive power, who destabilizes the world of mortals, even though this power loses some of its steam with the creation of the mortal Omestes. The *aition* is symptomatic of one of the Hellenistic tendencies with which we are concerned: the relaxation of boundaries between myth and ritual, as well as between human and divine.

In Phaenias' story, too, we encounter an almost inseparable blend of mythical and historical elements, with Dionysus playing a similarly destructive role. However, the emphasis on historical accuracy and ritual performance is so pronounced that the mythical substratum has been virtually obliterated. Previous attempts to determine the status of the human sacrifice at Salamis have concentrated on its historical background and ritual procedure as criteria for authenticity.[25] But such criteria can be very deceptive, especially when we are dealing with a tradition throughout which myth tends to be presented as a ritual event. I propose to adopt

---

[24] Henrichs (1984*a*), 236f. n. 88; Otto (1965), 110f., 113f. (= 103, 105f. in Ger. orig.).

[25] Phaenias is more plausible on the ritual scenario than on the historical setting—ritual details are easier to fabricate convincingly than are historical facts. Cf. Henrichs (1981), 210–18.

a different approach, one that ignores the historical setting and that takes narrative myth rather than ritual as a clue.

When we compare Phaenias' dramatic representation with mythical versions of human sacrifice, we see that his account duplicates the basic mythical pattern with astonishing accuracy. Broadly speaking, mythical accounts of human sacrifice follow a narrative pattern that incorporates all or most of the following five features: (1) the device of divine intervention, in which a god or seer prescribes the sacrifice; (2) a specific *Sitz im Leben* that situates the event in a crisis situation and relates it to a cultic setting; (3) an emphasis on the ritualization of violence that often takes the form of an elaborate description of the ritual process; (4) a comparison with, or veiled reference to, animal sacrifice; and finally (5), some form of geographic, social, or moral displacement by which the narrator distances himself and his audience from the horror of human sacrifice.[26] Two of these motifs—the simulation of a crisis situation and the elaboration of the ritual process—are designed to authenticate the mythical event by enveloping it with an illusion of factuality; human sacrifice becomes more believable when described in painstaking detail. This lesson was not lost on mythographers eager to historicize a mythical scenario, nor was it neglected by historiographers looking for an opportunity to superimpose the concept of human sacrifice on a given historical situation. A notorious example of the latter type is Livy's novellistic account of the Roman Bacchanalia of 186 BCE, which draws on Republican sources.[27] Like Phaenias on the sacrifice at Salamis, Livy's account has divided scholars into two distinct camps: ancient historians searching for the 'facts' of the event, and religious historians searching for ritual patterns of human behaviour *in extremis*.

Hellenistic stories of human sacrifice adopt one form or another of the fivefold pattern I have just outlined.[28] In book 4 of

---

[26] The description of Iphigenia's sacrificial slaughter as told by the chorus in Aesch. *Ag.* 104–248 exhibits all five features. Narrative patterns of human sacrifice or ritualized murder in the plays of Euripides (esp. *Hcld.*, *Hec.*, *El.*, *Phoen.*, and *Ba.*) vary considerably, but to a degree they all follow the pattern outlined above. Cf. Henrichs (forthcoming).

[27] Livy 39. 8–19. Cf. Pailler (1988).

[28] Before the battle of Leuctra in 371 BCE, the Boeotian commander Pelopidas had a dream vision in which he was instructed to sacrifice a virgin if he wanted to achieve victory (Plu. *Pel.* 21–2, whereas Xen. *Hell.* 6. 4. 7, Diod. Sic. 15. 54, and Paus. 9. 13. 5–6 merely mention a propitiatory animal sacrifice performed in response to an oracle). In the debate that ensued, proponents of the sacrifice supported their position with a series

Callimachus' *Aetia*, the *pharmakos* ritual at Abdera precedes two consecutive *aitia* involving human sacrifice, both of which take place in an imaginary temporal interstice that functions as a buffer zone between the heroic past and recorded history.[29] The first *aition* explains how the Lelegians of Tenedos commemorated the drowning of Melicertes by his mother, Ino, with a public ritual during which a mother sacrificed her child on an altar and was instantly blinded. The ritual was only performed in dire emergencies, and the custom was abolished when the descendants of Orestes colonized Lesbos. In this astonishing scenario, a one-time mythical killing generates a pattern of ritual infanticide which is repeated at irregular intervals until ritual normalcy is restored in due course. The evolution of sacrificial ritual from extreme to more mitigated forms is a pattern typical of foundation myths.[30] Untypical, and therefore noteworthy, is the double projection of child murder into a multi-layered distant past that becomes increasingly historicized as the aetiology proceeds from Ino to the Lelegians and finally to the first colonizers of Lesbos. Myth creates its own time references, which are at least as complex as actual historical chronologies. The total recollection of the past is a goal common to the collective memory of myth and history alike. But they are distinguished not only by the distance in time from the recollected events, but also by the nature of the events they represent.[31]

Where Callimachus observes the mythical pattern, Phaenias exhausts it completely. In his account, Phaenias incorporates not merely three or four of the narrative elements, as is usually the case, but all five. His employment of the fourth element—the relationship between human sacrifice and animal sacrifice—is most revealing. In the earliest versions of the Iphigenia myth as well as in other myths of this type, the human victim is replaced

of mythical and pseudo-historical examples of human sacrifice, including the alleged sacrifice to Dionysus Omestes at Salamis. In the end, a filly would be sacrificed instead of the maiden. True or not, the story illustrates the paradigmatic importance of mythical exempla in the post-Classical discussion of human sacrifice.

[29] Callim. *Aet.* fr. 90 (Abdera), frs. 91–2 (Melicertes), and fr. 93 (Theodotus). The narrative content of the three *aitia* is preserved in the paraphrase of the Milan *Diegeseis*; only a few lines of the actual poetry remain.

[30] The pattern is reversed in Greek reconstructions of the origin of culture. Cf. Obbink (1988).

[31] Cf. Eliade (1968), 138.

with an animal victim.[32] But in Phaenias the pattern of substitution is reversed, and a sacrifice that begins with an animal victim ends with a human one. This worst-case scenario has its closest analogues in the tragedies of Sophocles and Euripides.[33] In Sophocles, Lichas and Sidero are murdered in the course of a regular animal sacrifice.[34] The list of tragic victims who suffer this same fate is even longer for Euripides, and includes Neoptolemus, Aegisthus, Polyphontes, and the children of Heracles.[35]

It is hard to imagine that, at Salamis, history deliberately imitated myth—as Bonnechere would have it[36]—and still harder to imagine that Athenian copycats should have outperformed their mythical model. The Athenians did not make myth into history by re-enacting a mythical human sacrifice. On the contrary, Phaenias turns history into fiction by foisting a tragic scenario of human sacrifice and sacrificial crisis on to a concretely historical crisis situation.[37] In one stroke, Phaenias dislodges human sacrifice from its traditional home in myth and tragedy only to relocate the practice—or, rather, concept—in a rising genre, namely prose fiction. In so doing, he turns myth into pseudo-history.

By incorporating several cases into the ethnographical parts of his *Histories*, Herodotus had taken the first steps towards demythologizing and fictionalizing human sacrifice. His approach became the model for Hellenistic ethnographers, geographers, and historians like Posidonius, Strabo, and Julius Caesar, who miss no opportunity to describe the broad spectrum of ritual murders actually or allegedly performed by barbarian tribes.[38] In

---

[32] Cf. Henrichs (1981), 198–204; Brulé (1987), 179 ff.; Dowden (1989), 9–47; Bonnechere (1994), 26–48.

[33] Henrichs (forthcoming).

[34] Soph. *Trach.* 756 ff.; fr. 669a Radt.

[35] Eur. *Andr.* 1112 ff.; *El.* 838 ff.; *Cresph. apud* Hygin. *Fab.* 137, cf. Harder (1985), 16, 28, 56; *Heracles* 922 ff.

[36] See n. 18 above.

[37] According to Green (1970: 185) and Hughes (1991: 115), Phaenias used an anti-Themistoclean source—'an anonymous Athenian propagandist' (Green)—in which Themistocles was blamed for the killing of the three Persian prisoners. If so, Phaenias changed the inherited story in at least two important respects: he transferred responsibility for the ritual murder from Themistocles to *hoi polloi*, and he introduced Dionysus Omestes as the divine agent; the prominent role Phaenias assigns to this Dionysus also suggests that he invented the sacrificial setting and added the ritual details.

[38] Strab. 3. 3. 6, p. 154 (Lusitanians), 4. 4. 5, p. 198 (Celts), 4. 4. 6, p. 198 = Posidon. fr. 276 Edelstein–Kidd = *FGrHist* 87 F 56 (Namnites, cf. Detienne (1989), 42 ff. (= 67 ff. in

236   *Albert Henrichs*

the early Hellenistic period, clever mythographers like Dionysius Scytobrachion and Palaephatus would take up well-known and not so well-known myths and 'transmute them into a kind of prose romance' by suppressing or de-emphasizing the supernatural elements.[39] Phaenias displays more subtlety, but also more flippancy: he takes a mythical concept—human sacrifice—and renders it a literary cliché. He thus inaugurates a long tradition of secularizing human sacrifice as prose fiction, and sets the stage for the gruesome scenes of ritual murder in the later novels of Lollianus and Achilles Tatius.[40]

In Herodotus, supernatural forces, oracles, omens, and even the occasional divine epiphany shape the course of history.[41] Thucydides, on the other hand, goes out of his way to minimize the role of divine intervention in his *History* while setting events against the backdrop of traditional Greek cult.[42] Each had his supporters and detractors in the fourth century and in the Hellenistic period.[43] In Phaenias' account, the supernatural returns with a vengeance that exploits the relationship between *muthos* and *logos*. As Phaenias tells it, the assembled Athenian host in the heat of the moment abandoned rationality (*ta euloga*) in favour of the irrational (*ta paraloga*).[44] With this remark, Phaenias constructs a mass psychology of this historical moment, and, in so doing,

Fr. orig.), 7. 2. 3, p. 294 = Posidon. *FGrHist* 87 F 31 (Cimbri), 11. 4. 7, p. 503 (Albanians); Caes. *BG* 6. 16 (Celts).

[39] I borrow the phrase from Peter Parsons ('Identities in Diversity', in Bulloch *et al.* (1994), 152–70, at 166, on Dion. Scytobr.). Cf. Rusten (1982); and Jacob Stern, in this volume, on Palaephatus.

[40] Ach. Tat. 3. 15; see Stephens and Winkler (1995: 314–57) on Lollianus' *Phoenicica*; cf. Xen. Eph. 2. 13. 1 ff.

[41] Nilsson (1967), 759–67; Lateiner (1989), 196–205. Herodotus reports epiphanies of gods or heroes (2. 91. 3, 3. 27. 1–3, 4. 179. 2, 6. 106. 1, 8. 65), but remains sceptical; cf. W. Burkert, 'Herodot als Historiker fremder Religionen', in Nenci (1990), 21 f.

[42] Marinatos (1981), with the comments of Dover (1988), 65–73; Hornblower (1992) (emphasizing 'Thucydides' neglect of the religious factor in his narrative', 169); Crane (1996), 163–208 ('Thucydides may have little interest in religious practice, but he does give to religious scruples great weight as indices for civilized behavior', 193).

[43] Momigliano (1990); Hornblower (1995) ('Thucydides kept the gods out, and the hellenistic world was not happy with this exclusion', 64); Murray (1972); Wardman (1960).

[44] Phaenias, fr. 25 (n. 19 above): ἐκπλαγέντος δὲ τοῦ Θεμιστοκλέους ὡς μέγα τὸ μάντευμα καὶ δεινόν, οἷον εἴωθεν ἐν μεγάλοις ἀγῶσι καὶ πράγμασι χαλεποῖς, μᾶλλον ἐκ τῶν παραλόγων ἢ τῶν εὐλόγων τὴν σωτηρίαν ἐλπίζοντες οἱ πολλοὶ τὸν θεὸν ἅμα κοινῇ κατεκαλοῦντο φωνῇ καὶ τοὺς αἰχμαλώτους τῷ βωμῷ προσαγαγόντες ἠνάγκασαν ὡς ὁ μάντις ἐκέλευσε τὴν θυσίαν συντελεσθῆναι.

temporarily derationalizes the Athenians and specifically inverts the evolutionist perspective questioned by the very title of this volume, *From Myth to Reason?* Phaenias leads his Athenians from *logos* to *muthos* by means of a myth that emerges as human sacrifice. In mythicizing history, he amplifies another truth, namely that, far from being an acquired virtue, rationality is vulnerable, and that for the Greeks myth was the preferred vehicle for articulating the fragility of the rational and the lure of the irrational.

The success of Phaenias' construct explains why human sacrifice is likely to remain controversial so long as scholars attempt to separate myth from history. This approach has not worked to date, and indeed it never will. We are in no position to separate human sacrifice's history from its myth because, in the Greek context, the two are culturally and conceptually synonymous. Indeed, I submit that the Greek version of this myth is still in the making. The mythology of human sacrifice includes not only the sacrificial scenarios embedded in ancient sources, but also interpretations and transformations of them in modern scholarship. But this is the stuff of another story, or perhaps another myth.

Dionysus' dark side is integral to many of his earliest myths, and is dramatized to great effect in the Pentheus and Lycurgus plays of Attic tragedy. In Hellenistic literature, however, Dionysiac violence is commonly suppressed or mitigated; only exceptionally does it flare up to become the focus of direct attention. Where it is confronted, as in Myrsilus' *aition*, the emphasis tends to shift from the god to his worshippers, and from myth to sacrificial ritual. This sort of conflation of myth and cult has ancient roots, especially in connection with Dionysus,[45] and would be pushed to new extremes in the Hellenistic period, when ritual and, by extension, cult were routinely superimposed on myth in order to make myth more authentic, immediate, and relevant.

Theocritus' *Idyll* 26 stands as a perfect example of the sort of conflation of myth and cult that continues to confound interpreters.[46] The poem relates how Agaue and her two sisters build

---

[45] Cf. D. Obbink, 'Dionysus Poured Out: Ancient and Modern Theories of Sacrifice and Cultural Formation', in Carpenter and Faraone (1993), 65–86, at 71 f.

[46] Cf. Cairns (1992), who maximizes the ritual connotations of the poem and, more precariously, postulates 'a common ritual source' that inspired both Eur. *Ba.* and Theoc.

twelve altars—three for Semele and nine for Dionysus—before they tear Pentheus apart. The king makes the terrible mistake of watching their secret rites, during which the maenads take sacred objects from the *cista mystica* and place them on the new altars. The narrative culminates in a graphic description of Pentheus' dismemberment (20–4): Agaue decapitated her son, Ino tore off one of his shoulders, Autonoe the other, and 'the other women distributed amongst themselves the remaining flesh' of Pentheus (24 *hai d'allai ta perissa kreanomeonto gunaikes*). The narrator's preoccupation with ritual violence and body parts recalls and amplifies the second messenger speech in Euripides' *Bacchae*, which served as Theocritus' model. As commentators point out, the poignant verb *kreanomeō* normally refers to the distribution of meat that follows animal sacrifice.[47] The use of this term indicates that a sacrificial meal is about to occur. According to some interpreters, Theocritus' maenadic ritual culminates, literally, in the 'eating of Pentheus'.[48] But the poet is more oblique. The ambiguity created by his use of cultic language teases the audience's imagination by pushing the myth to its conceptual limits. Like Euripides, Theocritus explores the tension between animal sacrifice (the cultic norm) and human sacrifice (its perversion in myth) and raises the spectre of cannibalism without confirming our worst anxieties.[49] 'Covered with blood' (*pephurmenai haimati*, 25), the maenads carry the mangled remains of Pentheus back to Thebes, 'bringing from the mountain not Pentheus but a *penthēma*' (26), that is 'grief and lamentation'.

Id. 26: 'Seen in these terms, *Idyll* 26 *qua* hymn consists not only of the god's exploit in bringing about the sacrifice of his enemy Pentheus to himself but also, like certain parts of the *Bacchae*, of allusions to initiation ceremonies in which the myth was re-enacted and to the official ἱερὸς λόγος of the μυσταγωγός which related the myth' (21).

[47] Gow (1952), ii. 480 ad loc.; Cairns (1992), 7 with n. 42. Cf. Puttkammer (1912); Berthiaume (1982), 50; Baudy (1983); Seaford (1984), 152f.; van Straten (1995), 145f. If the sacrificial meat was usually distributed by males, Theocritus' collocation of κρεανομέοντο and γυναῖκες would add a new dimension to the perverted sacrifice. But see Osborne (1993).

[48] Cairns (1992), 4, 'Then Pentheus appears, is killed, and is eaten', and again, the 'killing and eating of Pentheus'. Similarly, Seaford (1996: 244) on *Ba.* 1184 (see n. 49 below) compares Theoc. *Id.* 26. 24 and 'the mythical theme of maenads eating their own children (Plu. *Mor.* 299e, Apollod. *Libr.* 3. 5. 2)'.

[49] In her madness Agaue wants to share her prey—Pentheus, whom she mistakes for an animal—with the rest of Thebes in a communal feast (*Ba.* 1184, 1242), but she is restored to sanity before she can make good on her promise. In Aeschylus, the ritual killing of Iphigenia is described as 'a sacrifice without a meal' (*Ag.* 150f. θυσίαν . . . ἄδαιτον).

With this wordplay, the poetic voice changes abruptly from the third person of the narrator to an unidentified first person. This refocalization marks a shift from past to present and from maenadic myth and ritual to the more properly Alexandrian preoccupation with esoteric Dionysiac cult.

The lines that follow are among the most mysterious in all of Theocritus, and their intrinsic allusiveness is compounded by serious textual problems (27–9): 'I don't care [about Pentheus]. Nor should anybody hated by Dionysus be of concern to me, not even if he should suffer a more grievous fate than Pentheus and be nine years old or even approaching his tenth.'[50] The speaker— a chorus of boys according to one recent critic[51]—clearly distances himself from Pentheus and wants to be in more respectable ritual company: 'As for myself, I aspire to be holy and pleasing to the holy ones (30 *autos euageoimi kai euageessin hadoimi*).' Εὐαγής (*euagēs*) belongs to the language of esoteric cult.[52] Given the Dionysiac emphasis of the poem as a whole, the paragons of ritual propriety whom the speaker wishes to please were presumably members of one of the numerous Dionysiac mystery cults that flourished under the first Ptolemies.[53] A similar allusion to contemporary esoteric cult occurs in a subsequent line: 'The better lot belongs to the children of the pious, not of the impious' (32 *eusebeōn paidessi ta lōia, dussebeōn d'ou*). The 'better lot' suggests a veiled reference to the blessings of a privileged afterlife, such as the mystery cults promised their initiates.[54] Thus the confrontation between believers and non-believers, between pious and impious in the mythical past functions as a paradigm

[50] On the discrepancies between the text of the MSS and that of the Antinoe papyrus codex, see Gow (1952), ii. 480 f.; di Benedetto (1957); Cairns (1992), 12. In lines 27–8, I follow the readings of the papyrus, with E. Lobel's restoration of the beginning of line 28.

[51] Cairns (1992: 13) classifies the poem as 'a choric hymn with a boy-chorus speaker' and tentatively identifies these boys as Dionysiac initiands. But the poem's hymnic credentials are doubtful, and there is no reference to choral performance or performers in the text.

[52] *HHDem.* 274 and 369; Eur. *Ba.* 1005 ff.; Callim. *Hymn to Delos* 98 (the closest parallel); Orph. fr. 32d7 = 32e7 (gold tablets from Thurioi) and fr. 222 Kern. Cf. Gow (1952), ii. 483 ('ritual formula'); di Benedetto (1957), 273 f.

[53] See Tondriau (1946); Zuntz (1963); Fraser (1972), i. 202–5; Dunand (1986), esp. 97 f.; W. Burkert, 'Bacchic *Teletai* in the Hellenistic Age', in Carpenter and Faraone (1993), 259–75, esp. 261–4.

[54] Cf. Richardson (1974), 310–12; Burkert (1987), 21–4; Merkelbach (1988), 128–32; Riu (1989), esp. 45 ff.; S. G. Cole, 'Voices from beyond the Grave: Dionysus and the Dead', in Carpenter and Faraone (1993), 276–95.

for resolving similar tensions in an unspecified here and now, the temporal boundaries of which the poet leaves vague and elusive. Despite the poem's idiosyncrasies—or perhaps because of them—*Idyll* 26 exemplifies the Hellenistic tendency to concretize and historicize myth by grounding it in contemporary human experience.

The Dionysus of Theocritus' poem, much like Euripides' Dionysus, remains an inscrutable god whose contradictory qualities are reflected in the actions of his maenads. At one moment, they are engaged in the orderly performance of an arcane but innocent ritual, doing 'as Dionysus himself had instructed them and as was his pleasure' (9 *hōs edidax'*, *hōs autos ethumarei Dionusos*), a moment later they tear Pentheus apart and soil themselves with his blood. This is hardly the Dionysus that the Hellenistic period liked to remember and emulate. According to the prevailing Hellenistic image of Dionysus, the god was seen as the divine inventor of wine, patron of the theatre and the arts, role model for the rich and famous, and cultural activist who traversed the earth in a never-ending succession of impromptu appearances—or 'epiphanies'—and who brought the blessings of civilization and a refined lifestyle to Greeks and non-Greeks alike.

Such an image of the god owes its existence and much of its success to Socrates' contemporary Prodicus of Ceos as well as to Alexander the Great. This construction of the god is the result of two developments which, at first glance, would seem to lead into opposite directions but which turn out to be complementary, with one reinforcing the other. Both developments changed the way the Greeks looked at the relationship between gods and mortals. At one extreme—the view propagated by Prodicus— gods like Dionysus, Demeter, and Zeus were deprived of their original divinity, removed from Olympus and relocated as mortals in the earliest stages of human history and civilization.[55] At the other, mortals of eminent status like Alexander the Great and his successors were recast in the image of the gods and moved closer to Olympus.[56] The deification of Ptolemy I, for instance, is envisaged by Theocritus as the king's taking up residence on Olympus. Rendered equal in honour to the immortal gods, Ptolemy sits on a golden throne in the house of

---

[55] Henrichs (1975*b*), 107 ff.   [56] Badian (1981) and (1996).

Zeus, with Alexander the Great and Heracles by his side. Heracles' reinforced chair is made of solid steel so that it can sustain the hero's bulk.[57] Dionysus is conspicuous by his absence.[58] As gods became more human and mortals more divine, the traditional distinctions were blurred, and movement from one realm to the other, whether from mortal to divine or from history to myth, was now facilitated and the transitions proved far easier than they once had been for Heracles or for the Dioscuri.

Prodicus was almost universally considered an atheist in antiquity.[59] Paradoxically, his historical explanation of the origin of the gods was enormously influential and contributed significantly to shaping the Hellenistic perception of divinity. According to Prodicus' cultural theory, gods like Demeter and Dionysus had been mortals before they became gods. They were deified by their fellow men for their inventions of viticulture, agriculture, and other essentials necessary for the survival of the human race.[60] As benefactors-turned-gods, they were remembered and worshipped through the ages. Prodicus' remaking of the gods set new standards for divine performance. He reduced the gods to human proportions, but at the same time had them work hard for their special status and perform on a superhuman level. His reconceptualization of the gods' place in history gave them a cultural role and promoted the activist divine image that prevailed throughout the Hellenistic period. Not only were the gods expected to be performers of miracles, a role which they had performed for a long time, but they were also expected to touch the lives of men in more tangible ways by acting as cultural forces. The conceptualization of gods as culture heroes, benefactors, and deified supermen is the theological core of Prodicus' message, which enjoyed extraordinary success. Its origins and repercussions may be traced from Tiresias' speech in Euripides'

---

[57] Theoc. *Id.* 17. 16ff. On the dynastic claim that underlies the genealogical connection with Heracles and Alexander, see G. Weber (1993), 214f., 247f., 350 n. 1. Ceremonial thrones for the deified Alexander the Great and Ptolemy Soter were carried in the Dionysiac procession staged by Ptolemy Philadelphus in Alexandria (Athen. 202a–b = Callixeinus of Rhodes, *FGrHist* 627 F 2, p. 175; cf. Rice (1983), 116f.).

[58] G. Weber (1993), 344 n. 1.

[59] Epicurus *apud* Philodemus, *On Piety* 524f. ed. Obbink (1996); Sext. Emp. *Adv. math.* 9. 51; cf. Henrichs (1976).

[60] Henrichs (1975*b*), 111f.; Obbink, in Carpenter and Faraone (1993), 83–5.

Bacchae via Euhemerus to the Isis aretalogies and the 'history' of Dionysus in book 3 of Diodorus.[61]

Prodicus redefined the nature and role of divinity in such a way that the gods themselves were effectively demythologized and historicized. But the logic of his approach could easily be reversed. If the traditional gods were former mortals who were deified as benefactors of mankind, then any mortal who had a significantly beneficial impact on the lives of his fellow men could register his claim to divinity and be made into a god. After Alexander the Great, Demetrius Poliorcetes ('Besieger of Cities') was the first in a long succession of Hellenistic rulers and potentates to model his own public image on that of Dionysus. Again, the Athenians were instrumental in setting the stage for this *imitatio dei*. They associated Demetrius' name with that of Dionysus by renaming the City Dionysia after Demetrius and calling the festival 'Dionysia and Demetrieia'. At least temporarily, the Macedonian king, now formally deified, could assume some of the trappings and honours of Dionysus. A decree from this period stipulates that each time Demetrius came to Athens, he was to be entertained as a guest of the city and receive the same treatment as Demeter and Dionysus during their visits.[62]

Again life imitates myth. Various myths were told of the arrival of Demeter and Dionysus in Attica.[63] The two gods did not come with empty hands; they brought their gifts and taught the Athenians how to grow grain and grapevines. Patriotic and paradigmatic, these myths had been popularized in the fourth century BCE by the Atthidographers and remained extremely popular throughout the Hellenistic period. The Marmor Parium, an inscription from the early Hellenistic period, tabulates major historical events in chronological order from the reign of Cecrops to the archonship of Diognetus (264/3 BCE). The first historical figure mentioned is Hesiod; he is preceded by twenty-seven mythical entries that record the deeds of gods and heroes.

[61] Henrichs (1984*b*).

[62] On the Athenian honours for Demetrius and his entourage (Plu. *Demetr.* 10–13; Athen. 253a = Demochares of Athens, *FGrHist* 75 F 1), see Habicht (1970), 50–5, and (1995), 94–103; Parker (1996), 258–63.

[63] Flückiger-Guggenheim (1984), 81–119; Kerényi (1976), 129–88; C. Sourvinou-Inwood, 'Something to do with Athens: Tragedy and Ritual', in Osborne and Hornblower (1994), 269–90, at 274–8 and 284f.

A particularly relevant example reads: '1146 years since Demeter arrived in Athens and invented the cereal fruit, and since the first pre-ploughing festival was held under the guidance of Triptolemus, son of Celeus and Metanira, while Erechtheus was king in Athens.'[64] As in Herodotus and Thucydides, myth is treated as the earliest part of history, and mythical events are given exact dates as if they were recorded history.

The Athenians saw to it that the sacred history embedded in these myths of arrival would repeat itself. Each year they commemorated the arrivals of Demeter and Dionysus with lavish ceremonies, and Demetrius did not hesitate to fill the shoes of both divinities. When he returned to Athens from Corcyra and Leucas in Boedromion of 290 or 289 BCE, his arrival coincided with the celebration of the Eleusinian Mysteries.[65] In a demonstration of extreme flattery that aroused the displeasure of Demochares, the nephew of Demosthenes, the Athenians danced in the streets and welcomed Demetrius with incense, crowns, and libations.[66] In his honour, the pro-Macedonian party in Athens commissioned a hymn that effectively praised Demetrius as the only true god, whose presence was so much more real and beneficial than that of the conventional gods. This anonymous song, preserved by the historian Duris of Samos, is one of the most remarkable examples of the convergence of myth and cult in a historical figure.[67] It is worth quoting in full.

In its transmitted form, the hymn lacks a proper beginning and

[64] Marmor Parium, *FGrHist* 239 A 12.

[65] The controversy over the exact year hinges on a number of imponderabilia, about which see Wilamowitz-Moellendorff (1881), 241–3 ('die Eleusinien 290'); Beloch (1927), 249 (Boedromion 292 or 291); Flacelière (1937), 65 and 73–5 ('aux Grandes Éleusinies de 291'); Habicht (1995), 98 (Great Mysteries of 291 or 290). In an unpublished paper, John D. Morgan argues for a date of 289. The festival in question is that of the Great Mysteries, not the Eleusinia.

[66] Athen. 253c = Demochares of Athens, *FGrHist* 75 F 2.

[67] Athen. 253d–f = *Carmina Popularia* 46 in T. Bergk, *Poetae Lyrici Graeci*, iii, 4th edn. (Leipzig, 1882), 674–6 = Hermocles (cf. Athen. 697a = Philochorus *FGrHist* 328 F 165) in J. U. Powell, *Collectanea Alexandrina* (Oxford, 1925), 173–5 = Duris of Samos, *FGrHist* 76 F 13. The metre is, appropriately, a combination of iambic trimeters and ithyphallics (West (1982), 148). A prose paraphrase of part of the song can be found at Athen. 253b–c = Demochares of Athens, *FGrHist* 75 F 2. Major studies of the hymn in praise of Demetrius include Weinreich (1926), 646ff. (= 190–2 in *Ausgewählte Schriften*, ii); Scott (1928); Ehrenberg (1931) as well as (1965), 503–19; M. Marcovich, 'Hermocles' Ithyphallus for Demetrius', in Marcovich (1988), 8–19 (with ample bibliography); Habicht (1970), 232f. and (1995), 98–100.

end. The structure of the preserved part is tripartite.[68] The first part (lines 1–14) establishes the occasion and introduces the two *laudandi*, Demeter and Demetrius:

> Look, the greatest and most beloved of the gods are present in this city [*tēi polei pareisin*].
> For a lucky coincidence [*ho kairos*] has brought here Demeter and Demetrius both at the same time.
> She has come in order to celebrate the sacred mysteries of Kore,
> And he is present, joyous as befits the god, beautiful and smiling [*kai kalos kai gelōn paresti*].
> He is august to look at, and his friends encircle him: he is in their midst.
> His friends are like stars, and he is like the sun [*hēlios d'ekeinos*].
> Hail, son of the mighty god Poseidon and of Aphrodite.

These lines re-create the mythical arrival of Demeter and Dionysus and relocate the event in the Athenian here and now. Without being explicitly identified with Dionysus, Demetrius is clearly cast in the god's image. The qualities ascribed to Demetrius—his conspicuous presence, relaxed mood, good looks, and radiant smile—are all associated with Dionysus in the *Bacchae*.[69]

The second part (lines 15–20) comprises a peculiar piece of theological reasoning in which Demetrius' tangible presence and easy accessibility are sharply contrasted with the aloofness and indifference of the conventional gods, who are found wanting:

> The other gods are either far away, or have no ears [*ē ouk echousin ōta*],
> Or don't exist, or pay no attention to us, but you we see present among us [*se de paronth' horōmen*],

[68] Marcovich (1988: 8) recognizes 'a bipartite structure' consisting of an '*aretalogy* of the God-King' (lines 1–19) followed by the '*prayer* to the new Savior' (lines 20–34). In support of a tripartite structure, I would argue that the contrived comparison of Demetrius with the conventional gods (lines 15–19), with its emphasis on the king's physical presence in the Athenian here and now, serves as the poem's centrepiece and as an ideological link between the hymn and the prayer.

[69] Eur. *Ba.* 47ff., 380, 434ff., 453ff., 622, 636, 1021; cf. Accius, *Ba.* fr.11, l. 15 Warmington (of Bacchus), '*praesens praesto irridens*'.

Not made of wood or stone, but real. So we pray to you
[*euchomestha dē soi*].

The categories of inaccessible gods of no help to mortals function
as a negative priamel and draw attention to the one 'god' who
can deliver because he is 'real' (*alēthinos*), namely Demetrius,
a quasi-divine presence for all to see.[70] Paul Veyne, if I may
quote him again, said of the Greek belief in divinity: 'Not
everyone was disposed to believe in the reality of the gods, for
no one could see them with his own eyes.'[71] Nevertheless,
many Greeks—some modern observers would say too many—
claimed to have seen their gods. Pan 'appeared' (*phanēnai*) to
Phidippides before the battle of Marathon in 490 BCE; around
300 BCE, an Athenian woman named Meneia commemorated
an epiphany of Athena with a dedication on the Acropolis; and
a surprising number of Hellenistic inscriptions record epiphanies
of such diverse gods as Apollo, Athena, and Isis.[72] Visible
presence manifested in frequent epiphanies is one of the divine
qualities most frequently ascribed to the gods who enjoyed
the greatest popularity during the Hellenistic period. Ascribing
such a powerful presence to Demetrius was tantamount to
elevating him to the most conspicuous rank of divinity, that of
a *deus praesentissimus*. Still, he remained very much a 'mortal
god'.[73] As one contemporary critic put it, the Athenian
champions of Demetrius 'turned the honours owed to the gods
over to mortals' (*tas tōn theōn timas poiount' anthrōpinas*).[74] In so
doing, they also narrowed the distinction between myth and
history.

The third and last section of the hymn contains the actual
prayer (lines 21–34). But it also juxtaposes myth with contemporary history, which is the reason why I draw attention to this text
in the first place.

---

[70] The various types of divine non-performance mentioned in this passage can be
paralleled from Plato (*Laws* 10) and especially Epicurus. See Marcovich (1988: 13–17) for
details.

[71] (1988), 42.

[72] On Phidippides/Philippides see Hdt. 6. 105f. and Paus. 1. 28. 4; also Borgeaud
(1988), 243 n. 3 (= 195f. n. 3 in Fr. orig.). Meneia's dedication: *IG* ii² 4326 = *SIG*³ 3.
1151. Hellenistic epiphanies: Nilsson (1961), 225–9; Totti (1985); Lane Fox (1986), 102–
67 ('Seeing the Gods').

[73] Parker (1996), 262.

[74] Philippides, fr. 25, 6 *PCG*, from an unknown comedy.

Above all, restore peace, most beloved one. For you have the
    power [*kurios gar ei su*].
Punish the Sphinx that holds in its grip not Thebes but all
    Greece[75]—
The Aetolian who sits on a rock [*epi petras kathēmenos*] just like
    the Sphinx of old [*hōsper hē palaia*],
And who kidnaps all our men, and I am in no position to fight
    back.
For it is the Aetolians' way of life to rob their neighbours of
    their possessions, and now even those more distant.
Best of all, punish them yourself. Failing that, find some
    Oedipus [*Oidipoun tin' heure*]
Who shall either overthrow [*katakrēmniei*] this Sphinx or turn
    her into stone.

The hymn thus ends with a mythical exemplum, which employs
myth as an analogy for history. At the time of the composition of
the poem, the Aetolians had seized Delphi, were raiding Attica,
and apparently continued to pose a threat to Thebes. The Theban
connection triggers the mythical exemplum in which the
Aetolians sitting on the proverbial 'rock of Delphi' and controlling the oracle are compared to the man-snatching Sphinx
perched high on her Theban rock; Demetrius, as the would-be
saviour of Athens, is compared to Oedipus who kills the Sphinx
in some versions of the myth, although in other versions she
throws herself from a cliff.[76] Whatever one makes of this extraordinary comparison, it is surely designed to underline the divinity
ascribed to Demetrius and to enhance the aura of supernatural
performance surrounding him. Just as in the distant past the gods
had sent Oedipus to liberate Thebes from the Sphinx, Demetrius
is expected to send a saviour who will rescue Athens from
Aetolian aggression.

In his book *Imaginary Greece*, Richard Buxton adopts a rather

---

[75] The text and interpretation of lines 23 f. are doubtful (περικρατοῦσαν Isaac
Casaubon, περιπατοῦσαν MSS). Marcovich (1988: 18) defends the transmitted reading.

[76] Palaephatus 4; Diod. Sic. 4. 64. 4 (ἑαυτὴν κατακρημνίσαι, the same verb which
occurs in the last line of the hymn to Demetrius; Gantz (1993), 497f. The Theban
Sphinx/Phix 'was sitting (ἐκαθέζετο) on Mt. Phikion' (Apollod. *Libr.* 3. 5. 8); in art, she
perches on a rock or a column (C. Robert (1915), i. 48–58; Demisch (1977), 96–100; N.
Kourou *et al.*, 'Oidipous', *LIMC* viii/2. 794ff., figs. 31, 55, and 184; Hoffmann (1997),
figs. 41 and 48). The 'rock' occupied by the Aetolians is the proverbial 'Delphic rock'
(Δελφὶς πέτρα in Soph. *OT* 464, Eur. *Andr.* 998, Anth. Pal. 6. 336. 4 = Theoc. *Epigr.* 5
Gow and Page); cf. Wilamowitz-Moellendorff (1881), 242.

striking metaphor: 'In all these instances', he says, 'myths function like shoes: you step into them if they fit.'[77] The shoes, as it turns out, are the mythical images of Greek heroes like Achilles, one of the role models for Alexander the Great, and of divinities such as Dionysus, and the would-be wearers eager to step into these shoes are prominent political figures, Greek as well as Roman. These leaders enhanced their own images by emulating Dionysus and assuming his identity, at least externally, thus superimposing an adopted mythical persona on to their historical selves.[78] In some cases, these shoes fit comfortably. Demetrius, Plutarch informs us, 'especially emulated Dionysus, as most terrible in his pursuit of war, but again most skilful in turning from war to make peace into joy and pleasure'. By casting himself in the role of Dionysus, Demetrius the Sacker of Cities becomes a happy warrior whose two-sided dynamism reflects the polarity of the god.

But not every aspiring Dionysus would be so lucky. Sometimes the mythical shoes would pinch and the strategy of re-enacting Dionysus would backfire. Mark Antony exemplifies the problem. He, too, dreamt of being another Dionysus, but his dream was shattered, and he came to a bad end. During the night before Octavian's capture of Alexandria, the inhabitants of that myth-ridden city heard the noise of a revelling thiasos leaving the city and heading in the direction of Octavian's camp. Plutarch provides this comment: 'Those who tried to interpret this sign believed that the god [Dionysus] now abandoned Antony, that god after whom he had modelled himself and whom he had always imitated.'[79] When myth is thus treated by mortals as a personal commodity, to be lovingly worn or quickly discarded like a pair of old shoes, the gods appear to part company with those who have emulated them.

In the course of the Hellenistic period, myth becomes demonstrative as well as performative, and turns into a powerful instrument of individual self-presentation and political propaganda. The later impact of Greek mythology on the Roman self-image in the

---

[77] (1994), 196.

[78] On the Hellenistic potentates and their Roman successors who modelled themselves on Dionysus, see Nock (1972), i. 144–52; Henrichs (1982), 157f. with nn. 135 and 190.

[79] Plu. *Ant.* 75. 6. On Antony's emulation of Dionysus see Fraser (1972), i. 205, ii. 349 n. 124; Pelling (1988), 179f., 303f.; P. Zanker (1988), 44–7.

age of Augustus illustrates how profoundly the mythical reconstruction of Rome's distant past shaped the historical conscience
of a nation that esteemed deeds more highly than words, and
history more highly than myth.[80]

[80] Cf. Graf (1993*b*); Bremmer and Horsfall (1987). I am grateful to Prof. John D.
Morgan for discussing the date of the hymn to Demetrius Poliorcetes with me (n. 65
above), and to Maura Giles for improving the successive versions of this paper.

VI
Philosophers' Myths

VI

Philosophen-Motto

13

What Is a Muthos *for* Plato?

PENELOPE MURRAY

'WE cannot tell (nor could Plato himself have told) where the figure or myth ends and the philosophical truth begins.'[1] This comment of Benjamin Jowett's on the *Timaeus* encapsulates the problem which I shall be considering in this paper: what constitutes *muthos* for Plato, and how far can we speak of Platonic myth as something separable from Platonic philosophy?

I shall begin by summarizing the discussion of myth in *Republic* book 2, where the question is raised as to what kind of education the young guardians should receive in the ideal state. The educators begin with *mousikē*, and *mousikē* includes *logoi*—stories (or discourse perhaps). There are two kinds of *logoi*, says Socrates at 377a1, one true, the other false (*to men alēthes, pseudos d' heteron*).

'Should children be educated in both, or only in the false ones?'
'I don't know what you mean.' [Adeimantus' comment is a sure sign that what follows is not going to be totally familiar to Socrates' audience, or, by implication, to his readers.]
'Don't you know that we tell *muthoi* to children first of all? And myth is in general false, but also contains some truth' [*hōs to holon eipein pseudos, eni de kai alēthē*].[2]

Problematic truth status is here presented as a defining characteristic of myth. And myth is by implication contrasted with a form of discourse that is true. But *muthos*, we should note, is nevertheless a kind of *logos*. I should say here that I am not going to focus on problems associated with the difficult question of how we should translate *pseudos*, which of course has a wide semantic range covering lies, falsehood, deceit, and fiction. The question of how far Plato (and the Greeks in general) distinguished

---

[1] Jowett (1953), iii. 698, quoted by Guthrie (1962–81), v. 253.
[2] All translations are my own unless otherwise stated.

between these different modern categories is highly debatable, as
several recent studies have shown. Christopher Gill in particular
has written extensively on this subject,[3] and I am inclined to
agree with him that the distinction between lies and fiction was
not a primary concern of Plato's, even though the concept
of fiction is clearly discernible to us in Plato's writing. So I shall
stick with 'lies' or 'falsehood' as a translation of *pseudos* and its
cognates.

Myth, Socrates continues, has a vital part to play in the education of the young, since it is through myth that the values of
society are handed down. Children must not listen to myths
made up by anyone that they happen to come across, because, if
they do, they run the risk of absorbing beliefs which are the
opposite of those that they should have when they grow up.
Hence the first task of the founders of the state must be to
supervise the production of stories (377b11) by laying down *tupoi*
(patterns or guidelines) which mothers and nurses must follow in
order that they may mould the souls of children by means of
muthoi. Poets too are to be constrained by these same *tupoi*, and
indeed poets in particular need to be controlled since it is they
who have been responsible for the perpetration of myths which
are false (377d5–6). When Adeimantus asks for clarification on
this point, Socrates replies that Hesiod, Homer, and the other
poets are guilty of the greatest wrong, namely that which occurs
'if someone doesn't lie well or finely' (*ean tis mē kalōs pseudētai*),
that is 'when someone makes a bad likeness in words about the
nature of gods and heroes, like a painter whose portrait bears no
resemblance to the things he wants to portray' (377d9–e3). For
example, the story of Cronos and what Zeus did to him is an ugly
lie and should not be repeated, *even if it were true* (378a2), because
it would encourage young men to commit horrible crimes against
their fathers. So the objection to a myth such as this is not that
it is untrue in terms of factual accuracy, but that it would set the
wrong ethical example. The question of whether the story happened or not is irrelevant to Plato's purpose: he is not concerned
with the factual veracity of history here, but with the ethical truth
that should be expressed through myth. If they are going to
persuade prospective guardians that no citizen has ever quarrelled

---

[3] See his essay 'Plato on Falsehood—Not Fiction', in Gill and Wiseman (1993), 38–87.

with any other, all stories of gods and heroes quarrelling must be suppressed, and story-tellers and poets must be compelled to make up stories which foster excellence of character and the cohesion of society.

Plato does not object to myth as such; on the contrary myth, defined as a form of discourse which is 'in general false, but also contains some truth', is seen as an essential instrument of persuasion.[4] But myth has traditionally been the province of poets, and the problem with poetic myth in Plato's eyes is that it is wholly false. 'What sort of *muthoi* should we tell, then?', asks Adeimantus at 378e5, to which Socrates replies: 'You and I are not poets at the moment, but founders of a city. And founders need to know the patterns according to which poets are to compose their stories, but they don't need to compose the stories themselves.' 'We are not poets *at the moment*'. At this point in the dialogue Socrates is more interested in controlling poets than in appropriating their function for himself, but that will change later on. The *tupoi* or patterns which Socrates proceeds to lay down concerning gods and heroes are all designed to promote the values which the founders of the state require in their society. And once again the discussion focuses on the problematic truth status of myth: no one wants to be deceived about the real nature of the most important things, we are told (382a–b), but spoken falsehood (382c6) can be useful as a kind of medicine (a *pharmakon*) provided it is used by experts, that is, by the rulers of the state (389b). In the case of stories about the gods such as they have been discussing—and Plato uses the term *muthologia* here— human beings, unlike the gods, *cannot* know the truth about the past; all we can do is to make our falsehood as like the truth as possible (382d2) so as to make it useful.[5] As before, 'truth' here clearly means something other than factual knowledge of events: the truth of myth has to be distinguished from the truth of history.

The myths of the poets are severely criticized by Plato, but it is not long before we are provided with an example of the kind of myth that should be promulgated in the ideal state. The

---

[4] On this topic see Brisson (1994), 144–51; Detienne (1981), 160, 173–82; Cerri (1996), 53–74.

[5] Adam (1963) ad loc. rather tartly remarks that 'Plato seems to have supposed that ancient history and mythology could be manufactured to order'.

so-called 'noble lie' is introduced at 414b8 with an explicit reference back to the earlier discussion:

Can we devise one of those lies—the kind which arise as the occasion demands, which we were talking about just now—so that with a single noble lie [*gennaion ti hen pseudomenous*] we can persuade the rulers themselves, if possible, but at least the rest of the community? [It would be nothing new], but a Phoenician sort of tale like those the poets tell and have persuaded people to believe about the sort of thing that often happened 'once upon a time', but doesn't happen now and is not likely to: indeed it would take a lot of persuasion to get people to believe it.

The noble lie, that the citizens of the ideal state sprang up from mother earth, and that god put gold, silver, iron, and bronze into the different categories of people when they were made—this *pseudos* is explicitly introduced as a fantastic tale, and one which has much in common with the myths of the poets. Plato takes care to assimilate his myth as far as possible to traditional tales by skilfully combining the motif of autochthony with the familiar association of different metals with different degrees of worth. As Adam points out, the reference to a 'Phoenician' sort of tale recalls Cadmus, the Phoenician, who sowed the dragon's teeth from which the Spartoi or earth-born men sprang, a myth to which Plato refers in the *Laws* (663e) as an example of the incredible stories that people will believe. But the difference between Plato's noble lie and the false myths of the poets rests in the fact that the former is specifically designed to foster noble ends: patriotism, brotherly love, and social cohesion. As a charter myth it also legitimizes the practice of promoting or demoting citizens to their appropriate class. The story with all its circumstantial detail is avowedly false; what matters is the moral and social purpose which the myth is designed to achieve, and it is this which makes the difference between a *pseudos* which is good or fine and one which is not.

The noble lie is constructed in accordance with the principles laid down in the earlier discussion; but what of Plato's other myths? The narratives which we commonly designate as Plato's myths characteristically deal with non-verifiable aspects of experience that are beyond ordinary mortal knowledge: the distant past, the life of the soul after death, the divine creation of the

universe, and so on.[6] When a myth is introduced there is generally some kind of break in the dramatic dialogue, signalling that
we are moving into a different register, and some reference is
usually made to the truth status of the myth that is to follow. For
example, in the *Protagoras* (320c) the sophist prefaces his myth
with words that highlight the mythical nature of his narrative:

'Would you rather that I showed you [that virtue is teachable] by telling
a story (as an older man speaking to his juniors) or by going through a
systematic exposition [*muthon legōn epideixō ē logōi diexelthōn*]?' Several of
those who were sitting around asked him to proceed in whichever way
he preferred. 'Well,' he said, 'I think that it will be more enjoyable
to tell you a story,' [which he then proceeds to do]. 'Once upon a time
[*ēn gar pote chronos*] . . .'.[7]

This is a typical way of beginning a myth, the *pote* setting the
story in some distant and timeless past.[8] When he has finished his
story Protagoras once again explicitly draws attention to the
distinction between *muthos* and *logos* which he had made at the
beginning: on the question of why good men cannot make their
sons better he says, 'I shan't tell you any more stories, but rather
give a literal exposition' (*ouketi muthon soi erō alla logon*, 324d6).
The Atlantis myth which Critias tells at the beginning of the
Timaeus, discussed by Christopher Rowe (in this volume), is
given a very elaborate introduction, beginning with the words
(20e):

Listen then [a very typical opening] . . . the story [and this time it is a
logos] is a strange one, yet wholly true, as Solon, the wisest of the Seven
Wise Men declared. He was a relation and close friend of my great-
grandfather . . . and he told the story to my grandfather . . . who in turn
repeated it to us when he was an old man.

In the *Gorgias*, before the myth of the judgement of the dead,
Socrates signals that he is about to launch into a story with some

---

⁶ See e.g. Brisson (1994), 109–38.
⁷ Trans. Taylor (1991). It makes no difference for my purposes whether this myth is
based on Protagoras' own work or not (on which see Taylor, 78–9), since what interests
me is the way in which *Plato* incorporates the myth into his dialogue. Nevertheless Plato's
portrayal of Protagoras suggests that he chooses to use myth for the wrong reason—purely
for entertainment value (Taylor, 76). This impression is confirmed by Socrates' reaction to
the sophist's display—he is spellbound, but remains unconvinced by the message that the
myth is designed to convey. Could it be that this is an example of how *not* to use myth?
⁸ For timelessness in myth see Brisson (1994), 30, and Rowe in this volume.

highly teasing words: 'Listen, then . . . to a very fine story [*kalou logou*], which will, I suppose, seem to be myth [*muthon*] to you, but is fact [*logon*] to me; what I'm going to tell you I tell you as the truth' (523a). He then tells his story about the judgement that awaits us after death, which he says he has heard from some unnamed source, and believes to be true (524a8–b1). Similarly in the *Phaedo* Socrates, who is in any case filled with prophetic powers like a dying swan (84e ff.), says that he has heard about what happens to the soul after death, again from some unnamed source (108c7–8). In this case Socrates does not insist on the truth of his account, indeed he explicitly refuses to commit himself, saying at 114d:

> To insist that these things are exactly as I have described them would not befit a man of intelligence. But to think that this or something like it is true . . . is fitting and worth risking . . . one should repeat such things to oneself like a spell, which is why I myself have been spinning out my story [*muthon*] for so long.[9]

The effect of this kind of strategy, and particularly the practice of attributing the myth to a source other than the narrator,[10] is to distance the protagonist (Socrates, Critias, or whoever) from the story he is telling and to mark off the myths from the dialogues in which they are embedded in such a way as to draw attention to their problematic status, particularly through the playing around with the notions of *muthos* and *logos*. What, after all, is the difference between the *logos* of the *Gorgias* and the *muthos* of the *Phaedo*? It is as if Plato sets up a distinction between *muthos* and *logos* only to confound it. There is, to be sure, a reason why Socrates' *logos* will seem to be *muthos* to Callicles, since Callicles has insisted throughout the dialogue that philosophy is merely child's play.[11] But the fact that an eschatological myth can be labelled as *logos* in one dialogue and *muthos* in another suggests

---

[9] Cf. *Phdr.* 265b–c; *Tim.* 29d1, 72d4–8. This is one respect in which the noble lie differs from Plato's other myths. For the recipients of the noble lie are apparently expected to believe the story just as it is given, and there is nothing tentative about the 'truth' which the lie is designed to promote. See further Gill in Gill and Wiseman (1993), 56–7.

[10] Cf. e.g. Diotima at *Smp.* 201d. Also relevant here is Burkert's observation (1979: 3) that myth is 'non-factual story telling—the telling of a tale while disclaiming responsibility'.

[11] See especially *Grg.* 485a4–e2. For the notion of philosophy as play in Plato, see Guthrie (1962–81), iv. 56–65.

that the meanings attached to these words depend to a large extent on context. What we have here is an example of the polemical use of the *muthos/logos* distinction to which Geoffrey Lloyd has drawn attention.[12]

Plato's concern is not so much to free the mind from myth, but rather to appropriate myth from the hands of the poets and construct new myths that will serve the interests of philosophy. This is nowhere more apparent than in the myth of Er, which is introduced (at 614b2) with words which implicitly contrast it with traditional poetic myth: 'What I am going to tell you won't be like Odysseus' tale to Alcinous, but the story of a brave man, Er, son of Armenius, a native of Pamphylia, who once upon a time died in battle [*hos pote en polemōi*] . . .' Odysseus' tale to Alcinous in books 9–12 of the *Odyssey* includes, of course, the visit to Hades, with which Plato's vision of the afterlife will be starkly contrasted. But at a deeper level Plato is highlighting the difference between his own philosophical myth and the false myths of the poets which he had so vehemently criticized earlier on in book 10.[13] The myth with which the dialogue closes, takes on a poignant urgency if we look back to the words of the aged Cephalus in book 1 (330d):

You know, Socrates, when a man faces the thought that he will die, fear and anxiety about things that did not trouble him before come upon him. The stories [*muthoi*] about Hades, and about the punishment to be suffered there for wrongs done here, at which he once used to laugh, torment his soul with the fear that they may be true. And . . . he becomes full of doubts and fears.

The *Republic* is very far from being an abstract discussion of the nature of *dikaiosunē*, framed as it is between the realistic setting of book 1, and the mythical narrative at the end of book 10, itself surely the prime example of the kind of *muthos* an old man on the threshold of death should be contemplating. I cannot agree with the view that the myth of Er is merely an appendage to the argument, or that Plato uses myth either here or elsewhere as a last resort, as if *logos*, rational discourse, were his primary concern,

---

[12] See the papers by Lloyd and Johansen in this volume. On the differences between the eschatological myths in the *Gorgias*, *Phaedo*, and *Republic* in terms of their philosophical content, see Annas (1982).

[13] See Halliwell (1988) on 614b2.

and *muthos* somehow second best. Plato recognizes that myths are necessary for human beings, even for philosophers; hence the importance of appropriating myth from the domination of the poets.

I have spoken about Plato's myths as if they were easily separable from their contexts, and indeed the famous myths are signposted and set apart as mythical narratives in ways which I have indicated. But the notion of myth in Plato's dialogues is rather more pervasive than my analysis so far has suggested. This is certainly the case in the *Republic*, where Plato repeatedly draws attention to the quasi-mythical status of his own text. He even prefaces the discussion of myth in book 2 with words which liken his own activity to that of a myth-maker: 'Come now, let us educate our guardians as if we were at leisure and telling a story' (*hōsper en muthōi muthologountes . . . logōi paideuōmen . . .* , 376d). Again, at 501e he uses the term *muthologein* of his own activity (*hē politeia hēn muthologoumen logōi*) and at 536c he apologizes for getting carried away and speaking too seriously: 'I was forgetting that we are amusing ourselves [*epaizomen*].'[14] When he is asked to explain how the ideal state will degenerate, Socrates invokes the Muses:

How will Auxiliaries and Rulers begin to quarrel with each other or among themselves? Shall we, like Homer, invoke the Muses to tell us 'how the quarrel first began'? Let us suppose that they address us in a tragic and lofty style as if they were speaking seriously, though they are really only playing with us and teasing us as if we were children. (545d5–e3)

There then follows an account of how the breeding arrangements in the state go wrong, which includes some obscure mathematics[15] and makes reference to the metals of the noble lie. This explanation must be right, says Socrates, because it comes from the Muses (547b). The myth of the noble lie is thus balanced by an equally mythical account of the degeneration of society. It is precisely

---

[14] For other such comments see e.g. 369c, 378e, and 588b–c, where Socrates suggests that they mould (*plattein*) an image of the soul in words, like the traditional mythological images of Chimaera, or Scylla, or Cerberus. The language here recalls Socrates' earlier words at 377b–c (quoted above) about the necessity of moulding children's souls by means of myths. It is also significant that the process of constructing the ideal state is frequently described in terms of artistic metaphors. See e.g. 472d–e, 488a, 540c and, for further references, Rutherford (1995), 224.

[15] On this see Ehrhardt (1986), and Annas (1982: 296) on the problem with the argument here.

because Socrates has no rational explanation to offer that he draws
attention to the poetic nature of his discourse at this point.

I would argue therefore that the mythical element in Plato's
writing is evident not only in the so-called Platonic myths, but
also in his general mode of narration. Imagery of one sort or
another pervades the *Republic*: the ship of state, the sun, the line,
the cave, the tyranny of desire, the soul as a many-headed beast
and so on. Socrates is teased for his habitual use of images (*eikones*,
487e), and the provisional nature of his explanations is repeatedly
made explicit.[16] So how much of the dialogue should we regard
as *muthos* and how much as *logos*? The closer we look the more
difficult it becomes to maintain a clear-cut distinction between
the two, for the 'philosophy' of the *Republic* cannot be separated
from the mode in which it is expressed.[17]

Socrates' highlighting of his own activity as narrator relates to
one of the central questions of the *Republic*, the question of
whether the ideal state can ever be realized. When he is chided
for not tackling this issue, he replies (472d–e): 'Would you think
a painter any the less good if he were to paint a picture of the
most beautiful man . . . but be unable to show that such a man
could exist . . . Haven't we been making a word-picture of an
ideal state [*paradeigma . . . logōi*]?' What is a *paradeigma logōi* if it is
not a myth?[18] Even when Socrates suggests that the ideal state *is*
realizable he does so in language which emphasizes the impossibility of what he is saying:

If those who are pre-eminent in philosophy are compelled to take
charge of the city, whether it has happened in the infinity of past time,
or is happening now in some foreign place far away from our sight,[19] or
whether it will happen in the future, we are ready to insist that the
society we have described has existed, does exist, or will exist, whenever
the Muse of philosophy herself gains control of the city. (499c–d)[20]

---

[16] See e.g. 472c–d, 504b–c, 506d–e, 517b, 533a, and Rutherford (1995), 235–6.
[17] On the integral relationship between the arguments of the dialogues and their literary
frame, see M. Frede, 'Plato's Arguments and the Dialogue Form', in Klagge and Smith
(1992), 201–19; and, on the whole question of what constitutes philosophic discourse, see
Nightingale (1995), 148, 163–71.
[18] Christopher Rowe has pointed out to me that strictly speaking it is an analogy, like
that between statesmanship and weaving in the *Politicus* (279b), which is referred to as a
paradeigma. But I would describe the ideal state as a mythical kind of analogy.
[19] ἔν τινι βαρβαρικῷ τόπῳ, πόρρω που ἐκτὸς ὄντι τῆς ἡμετέρας ἐπόψεως. The alliteration
in the Greek reinforces the point.
[20] Cf. 471c–473b, 540d, 592b.

As Charles Segal has put it, 'The critical ambiguity of the *Republic* is ultimately a question about the status of myth: is the ideal state capable of realisation or is it only a metaphor for the soul's self discovery in truth and justice?' As he sees it the *Republic* has 'two planes of organisation, one philosophical and analogical (the relation between microcosm and macrocosm, soul and state), the other mythical (descent, journey, vision). It is surely no accident that "I descended" (*katebēn*) is the first word of the dialogue.'[21]

But I wonder how easy it is to make the distinction between the philosophical and the mythical. At the beginning of the *Timaeus* the *Republic* itself is referred to as a city which was described as it were in myth (*hōs en muthōi*, 26c9) and contrasted with the true story (*alēthinon logon*, 26e5) of Atlantis and its inhabitants which forms the subject of the present dialogue. But this distinction between *muthos* and *logos* appears to have little validity. If the *Republic* is a *muthos*, so is the *Timaeus*, which takes me back to the quotation of Benjamin Jowett's with which I began: 'We cannot tell (nor could Plato himself have told) where the figure or myth ends and the philosophical truth begins.' Myth is essential to Plato's conception of philosophy.

But what is a *muthos* for Plato? A falsehood containing some truth, a story which aims at truth but which is not in itself true. Myth can have different functions.[22] It can, as in the case of the noble lie, be used as a *pharmakon*, a medicine or drug, to promote very specific social and political ends. Or it can be a 'likely story', an approximation to the truth. Human beings, not being gods, can never know the truth,[23] hence myth-making is an essential human activity. But for Plato the difference between poetic and philosophical myths is that the philosopher is aware of the approximate status of his myths, whereas the poet is not. Plato tells stories, and not only in those parts of his work which we commonly call his myths. The dialogues themselves are stories, stories which, of course, contain rational argument, but which also share some of the characteristics of his mythical narratives. I am thinking, for example, of the elaborate settings of many of the

---

[21] Segal (1978), 329 and 323. On the significance of *katebēn*, see also Clay (1992).

[22] See J. E. Smith (1985), with bibliography of previous treatments of the subject.

[23] See e.g. *Rep.* 517b–c, cf. 382d; *Phdr.* 246a3–6, 278d; *Tim.* 27c–29d, 68d3–4, 72d4–8. On myths as 'likely accounts' see J. E. Smith (1985), and Lloyd and Rowe in this volume.

dialogues, so full of authenticating detail, but which often serve to distance the teller from his tale (I heard it from X who heard it from Y, etc.). The most perfect example of this is the *Phaedo*, where the usually invisible author, Plato himself, is mentioned. 'Plato, I think, was ill' (*Platōn de oimai ēsthenei*), says Phaedo at 59b10. By distancing himself from the narrative being reported, Plato can have it both ways: the account can appear to be utterly realistic, but there is no guarantee of its veracity. So the *Phaedo* is not presented as an exact report, but becomes, rather, a message about Socrates' true nature, an invitation to engage in the kind of philosophy that Socrates himself practised.[24] Story-telling, imagery, myth are fundamental to Plato's meaning.

If we look in Plato's work for a consistent distinction between *muthos* (myth) and *logos* (reason), let alone a development from one to the other, we look in vain.[25] Even if we were to restrict the meaning of *logos* to rational argument or dialectic, dialectic is always embedded in dialogue. And though it operates in a different way from myth (whether in the narrower sense of the set-piece narratives like the myth of Er, or in the broader sense of story-telling), dialectic is never enough: it supplements rather than replaces myth. Dialectic and myth may be viewed as different modes of explanation, but Plato does not present the one as being superior to the other, and neither mode is self sufficient. Myth is not simply the expression of a primitive form of mentality; it is, in Claude Calame's words, 'a mode of discourse rather than a way of thinking'. Hence *muthos* and *logos* exist side by side, and indeed are often indistinguishable, since both are in essence types of discourse.

To think about the place of myth in Plato's work is ultimately to think about how we should read his texts. I was struck by the

---

[24] See L. Kosman, 'Silence and Imitation in the Platonic Dialogues', in Klagge and Smith (1992), 73–92. The difficulty that Phaedo's remark has generated amongst commentators can be exemplified by Burnet's note: 'Of course it is an advantage from a dramatic point of view for Plato to keep himself out of his dialogues . . . At the same time it is hardly credible that he should represent himself as absent on this occasion unless he had actually been so. It has been said that, had Plato really been ill, he would have had no occasion to make the reservation implied by οἶμαι [I think]. He must have known whether he was ill or not. That is so; but it does not follow that Phaedo was equally well informed, and he is the speaker, not Plato' (Burnet (1911) on 59b10).

[25] See e.g. Annas (1982), 119–22; Brisson (1994), 109–43; Detienne (1981), 91 ff.; and above all, the works of J.-P. Vernant. The *muthos/logos* issue is addressed most recently in Vernant (1996), 237–64, 352–6.

comments of Julia Annas on the account of the decline of state
and individual through the four stages of timocracy, oligarchy,
democracy, and tyranny (*Rep.* 543–80). 'The resulting eight
vignettes of state and individual', she says, 'have been admired
for their literary power, but they leave a reader who is intent on
the argument unsatisfied and irritated.'[26] If the passages which
demonstrate Plato's literary powers merely get in the way
of the argument, what are they there for? I shall end with a
quotation from Martha Nussbaum:

The tendency to regard arguments as expressing the content of a
philosophy, image, story, and conversation as giving it a pleasing,
decorative surface goes very deep in our entire philosophical tradition.
Philosophy has developed a style for itself that powerfully expresses its
claim to have separated out the rational from the irrational, to have
purified itself of the confusions of emotion and sense, which are the
stuff of poetic discourse. The deductive argument keeps these messy
irrational elements at bay, protecting reason's structures against them. It
is evident that the question of philosophical style is connected at a very
deep level with a conception of the rational and the relation between
'rational' and 'irrational'. Plato's writing tells us, in its multifaceted
progress, that these questions need to be reopened, these polarities reexamined.[27]

---

[26] (1981), 294.
[27] The quotation is taken from p. 91 of ' "This Story Isn't True": Poetry, Goodness
and Understanding in Plato's *Phaedrus*', in Moravcsik and Temko (1982).

14

Myth, History, and Dialectic in Plato's Republic and Timaeus-Critias

CHRISTOPHER ROWE

THE purpose of this paper is to explore, with the help of one central example, some aspects of the interplay between the notions of *muthos*, centred on the sense of the 'fictional', and *logos*, or whatever term might be used to denote the opposed category of the non-fictional, in Plato.[1] My example is one that Penelope Murray also refers to in her contribution to the present volume: the construction of the ideal city of the *Republic*, and what seems[2] to be represented as the same city (exemplified, according to Critias, by a primitive Athens), in the *Timaeus-Critias*. In inviting us to make this identification, or in so far as it does so, the

---

[1] The contrast here is that between what is, or is represented as being (to a greater or lesser extent), invented, constructed, or imagined, and what is not, or is not represented as being, so invented, constructed, or imagined. While I accept many of Christopher Gill's strictures (Gill (1993)) against too easy an attribution to Plato of modern concepts of fiction, it still appears to me that such a contrast is fundamental to Plato's complex deployment of the notion of *muthos*.

[2] 'Seems' is a necessary qualification, because the characters assembled for *Tim.-Criti.*, apart from Socrates, are different from those in *Rep.* However, the coincidences between the city Socrates describes in *Rep.* and the one whose features he summarizes at the beginning of *Tim.* are sufficiently large to make it unreasonable to suppose that we are not meant to make the connection. Quite why the notion of philosopher-rulers, apparently fundamental to *Rep.*, is omitted in the *Tim.* summary is a difficult, but separate, question: see e.g. McCabe (1994), 186, and Rowe (1997). But it is worth noticing that 'the *politeia* whose story we are telling in words' at *Rep.* 501e4 in fact strictly refers to a *politeia* without philosopher-rulers; philosopher-rulers are introduced as the means by which that *politeia* might be established. (True, it was agreed at an earlier stage—i.e. at 375a–376c; cf. *Tim.* 18a, 19e—that the 'guards' must possess a 'philosophical nature'. But this 'philosophical nature' will not in itself make them philosophers, unless dogs too can reason philosophically.) Primitive Athens has Hephaestus and Athena as founders, and gets its institutions from them, so that the need for philosophers—as opposed to 'philosophical natures'—is bypassed. According to *Rep.* 497c–d, the maintenance of the appropriate laws will depend on the presence of people who understand the principles on which they are laid down (cf. also 412a); among the primitive Athenians, their institutions and educational system seem to be self-sustaining. But then they are an ideal race, brought into existence by the gods themselves.

Timaeus-Critias treats what is at least in part the result of a series of dialectical arguments simply as a fiction, i.e. a *plastheis muthos*,[3] while presenting its own fiction as true history (more strictly, as a *palaios logos*, *Tim.* 21a7, which is also true: 26d1, e4–5). What I propose to do is firstly to investigate the details of this particular instance of the jumbling of otherwise seemingly recognizable classifications of discourse; and secondly to ask to what extent those classifications remain as useful points of reference in the Platonic context. The ultimate issue is about the distinction between 'myth' and '*logos*', or more generally, between the 'mythical' and the 'non-mythical'. Plato is both a writer who uses—or plays with—such a distinction more than any other in the Greek context, and one who seems to offer particularly beguiling accounts of it, in terms of the difference between non-rational and rational discourse, and/or the (wholly or partly) false and the true. The question I mean to raise is whether 'myth' is a term—a 'name', as Plato would put it—which successfully picks out any real and permanent category in the Platonic universe. I shall suggest that it does not, or, alternatively, that if it does, it does so only uncertainly and fitfully; if so, then our main ways of understanding the nature of 'the mythical' will be undermined and destabilized by what seemed to be one of the exemplary sources for it.

Part of the task I am proposing has already been carried out by Penelope Murray.[4] She points out that while 'myths' are sometimes separable from, and marked off from, other, more 'philosophical', elements in the dialogues, Plato—or his Socrates—also frequently blurs the distinction, by interweaving '[s]tory-telling, imagery, myth' (p. 261 above) into the very texture of his argument, and by recognizing the similarities between his position as narrator and those of the story-teller. 'Myth is essential to Plato's conception of philosophy'; again, '[h]uman beings, not being gods, can never know the truth, hence myth-making is an

---

[3] Socrates at 26e4, picking up Critias' *polin hēn chthes hēmin hōs en muthōi diēieistha su* at 26c8. The same idea is of course present in *Rep.* itself (see the passage at 501e4 referred to in the preceding note), but the perspective in *Rep.*, and the sense of *muthos/mutholegein* there, is more complex: see below.

[4] In the original version of the present paper, as presented at the Colloquium, I responded briefly to some points in Dr Murray's; in this more considered version I take the opportunity of extending our conversation (continued by correspondence), which has enabled me to establish more precisely what my own position is.

essential human activity', in so far as it can provide 'an approximation to the truth' (p. 260).

So far so good. But there seem to me to be two possible readings of this perspective on Plato, one more radical than the other. On the less radical version, the idea will be that the telling of stories is a necessary adjunct to, or extension of,[5] philosophical argument, one which recognizes our human limitations, and— perhaps[6]—the fact that our natures combine irrational elements with the rational. Rational argument can only take us, and the philosopher himself or herself, so far; from then on, it must necessarily cooperate with myth, just as the speakers in the dialogues may adopt a story-telling or imaginative mode. But on a more radical interpretation of Murray's position, the distinction between 'the philosophical' and 'the mythical' will—at one level—virtually disappear. On this interpretation, the use of a fictional narrative form (the dialogue) will mean that any conclusions reached, by whatever method (including 'rational argument'), may themselves be treated as having the status of a kind of 'myth'. The reader is perpetually invited to reflect on, and to move beyond, the text—as, on Murray's view, the narrative structure of the *Phaedo* seems designed to make us question its veracity, and so to invite us 'to engage in the kind of philosophy that Socrates himself practised' (p. 261).

It is a version of this second reading that I should myself, in the final analysis, wish to advocate. In this case, a sense of the 'fictionality' of human utterance, as provisional, inadequate, and at best approximating to the truth, will infect Platonic writing at its deepest level, below other and more ordinary applications of the distinction between mythical and non-mythical forms of discourse. The point about the limitations of human nature will work, as it were, from further back than in the other case: it is not that 'myth' will fill in the gaps that reason leaves (though it might do that too, as well as serving special purposes for particular audiences), but that human reason itself ineradicably displays some of the features we characteristically associate with

---

[5] Better the second, in that Dr Murray insists that *muthos* (as e.g. at the end of *Rep.*) is not a second best to 'rational discourse' (pp. 257–8 above). Cf. n. 37 below.

[6] This I derive from the passage from Martha Nussbaum quoted by Dr Murray at the end of her paper; the passage rests on epistemological conceptions that Dr Murray herself does not explicitly endorse.

story-telling. That is one important reason why Plato, self-effacingly, writes dialogues which—at least on the surface—exclude himself (that is, because he is aware of the provisionality of his own written offspring); and that is why he can have Socrates, in the *Phaedrus*, treat all writing as *paidias charin* ('by way of pastime', 276d2), or as containing *paidian . . . pollēn* ('much that is fanciful', 277e5–7). At its best, it will act as a treasure-house, not of wisdom acquired, but of 'reminders [*hupomnēmata*] . . . for everyone who follows in the same track' (276d3–4), that is, perhaps, reminders of the direction or directions in which the path has led so far.

The point is never explicitly expressed in terms of the notion of *muthos*, and could not, of course, be expressed directly at all (unless in one of the *Letters*, if any of these are genuine). But it is, I think, reflected in one or more of several passages, in different works, in which *muthologein* and related verbs appear either paired with, or apparently as a substitute for, other less colourful words for 'examining' or 'conversing (about)'. I list four such passages: *Phd.* 61e1–2, which couples *muthologein* with *diaskopein* (*peri tēs apodēmias tēs ekeî*); *Phd.* 70b6, where *diamuthologein* seems to be treated as equivalent to *diaskopeisthai* (70c3); *Ap.* 39e5, in which *diamuthologēsai*, according to Burnet, 'means little more than *dialechthēnai*'; and *Phdr.* 276e3 ('A very fine form of amusement,' says Phaedrus, '. . . that of the man who is able to amuse himself with words, telling stories—*muthologounta*—about justice . . .'). In the first, third, and fourth cases the use of (*dia*)*muthologein* might be explained without reference to any theory about the nature of philosophical discourse.[7] But the second case is more difficult to explain away, because it introduces the first of a series of arguments; if the argument begins from a *palaios logos* (70c5 ff.), there is no clear sense of a reference in *diamuthologein* to that. My own view is that the word is rather carefully chosen to indicate in advance the kind of attitude Socrates' listeners, and we, should adopt towards

---

[7] 'Socrates regards all definite statements with regard to the next life as *muthoi*', Burnet on *Phd.* 61e2; 'the Ionic sense of *muthos* (=Att. *logos*) has survived in the compound', *id.* on *Ap.* 39e2; and how better to 'amuse oneself' than by telling stories (*Phdr.* 276e)? LSJ simply gives *muthologein* a special sense in the first *Phd.* passage, and in the *Phdr.* ('tell tales', 'converse'); but there seems little to justify such a reductivist approach (similarly with Burnet's treatment of *diamuthologein* in *Ap.*), given the apparent self-consciousness of Plato's use of the notion of *muthos* elsewhere.

what follows: that is, that we should receive it, perhaps, with a certain reserve, as we would the products of the story-teller.[8] There is (I take Plato to be saying) the same sort of issue about the seriousness with which an argument should be taken—in the light of the truth of its premisses and/or its validity—as there is about how we should take stories. 'This is the kind of story', as we might say, 'which we shall tell for now, and it may or may not be true, or true only in part';[9] and as it turns out, Simmias and Cebes are distinctly unimpressed by the argument that Socrates offers.[10]

In the end, of course, such passages will count for little by themselves. The main evidence for attributing to Plato the kind of attitude towards his 'gardens of letters' that I have proposed will lie in the signs of his awareness of his position as narrator, in combination with the repeated, and characteristic, stress that is laid on the provisionality of any results reached.[11] So in the case of the account given of justice and the just individual in *Republic* book 4: it was undertaken 'for the sake of a *paradeigma*' (472c4), but was no more than a sketch (*hupographē*, 504d6), which will need to be superseded by a more accurate investigation. Given the continuing interdependence of the arguments about the city and those about the individual, and especially the initial claim that the essence of justice will be the same in both, the same qualification may reasonably be taken to apply equally to the treatment of the just city; and indeed the ideal 'artist of *politeiai*', i.e. the ideal legislator who would actually found the best city, is himself described as beginning by 'sketching in the outline of the constitution' (*hupograpsasthai to schēma tēs politeias*), and then finishing his picture partly by reference to 'the just by nature and beautiful and self-controlled and all such things' (i.e., presumably, the forms, ? which one would guess to be the basis—whatever procedure that

---

[8] It is then tempting—though perhaps no more than that—to read the other passages in a similar way.

[9] Cf. Rowe (1993*a*), n. on *Phd.* 70b6.

[10] See Rowe (1993*b*). Here I am conscious of making a large claim, which cuts across whole traditions of Platonic interpretation; but the chief weight of my argument on the present occasion will ultimately be elsewhere, and it will do no harm to have given an indication of my general position, without the larger argument that would be needed to support it.

[11] Not all conclusions agreed to by characters in the dialogues are explicitly hedged with qualifications, or to the same degree; but they are certainly far more often qualified than not.

might involve—of any 'more accurate' investigation of justice).[12]
But I take it that the provocative way in which Socrates presents
his proposals (as e.g. in the case of the discussion of the proper
treatment of women), and the—surely?—obviously ironic tone of
some of the proposals themselves (e.g. that the legislator might
start by sending away everyone over the age of ten),[13] makes it
hardly necessary to say that they should not be regarded as
constituting the definitive paradigm.

Immediately after the passage about the legislator as 'artist of
politeiai', Socrates changes the metaphor. He has been arguing
that people may be persuaded to accept philosophical rule: 'Then
will they still respond savagely when we say that before the
philosophon genos takes control of a city, there will be no respite
from evils either for city or for citizens, nor will the *politeia* whose
story we are telling in words [*hēn muthologoumen logōi*] achieve its
fulfilment in practice [*ergōi*]?' (501e2–5). It is this reference to the
construction of the *politeia* as *muthologein* which is—so we might
reasonably suppose—being picked up by Critias in the *Timaeus*
(and possibly by Phaedrus at *Phdr.* 276e);[14] and the context seems
to show us how to interpret it: 'our story-telling' is the equivalent
of the sketching of the legislator-artist, which will be 'finished' by
the more complete insights of the ideal philosopher. (What else
has been going on in the previous books if it is not a 'sketch' of
a *schēma politeias*; and why, apart from a comparison with that
process, would this 'sketching' be singled out as the first step[15] in
the artist's creation?)[16] Just as the painter will rub things out and
draw/paint them afresh (501b9), so too, perhaps, the ideal legislator will modify and improve on the outline of the story so far
told by Socrates and his interlocutors, in order to achieve the full
realization of their goals.

In this context, then, Socrates' account of the best city seems

---

[12] 501c4–5, a9–10, b1–3.

[13] 540e–541a, with 501a. If it is the case that the legislator needs a fresh canvas, mass
expulsions are not the only method available, as the *Laws* shows; and, however low an
opinion of Plato we may hold, we can scarcely suppose him to be deaf to the irony of the
suggestion that the 'quickest and easiest' way of achieving a 'happy' (*eudaimōn*) city is to
get rid of the majority of the original inhabitants (504a1–7).

[14] Luther (1961).

[15] NB *epeita* at 501b1. Admittedly, any painter might start with an outline sketch; but
504d surely demonstrates that this is not a merely accidental feature of the metaphor.

[16] Cf. 543d1–544a1 '(you described the good city and the good man) although—as it
seems [i.e. after the account of the philosopher and his/her training?]—you would be able
to describe a still finer city and man'.

to be a kind of 'myth' in so far as it is a merely provisional
description which may need to be amended in the light of better
knowledge. But there is also another, and more obvious, way in
which it will count as a 'myth' (and one which is also closer to
the sense of *muthos* in *Tim.* 26c–e): that is, in so far as it describes
an *imaginary* city,[17] one that is not presently realized in practice,
and one that—at least, in all its details—might never be. This is
in fact the dominant sense of the idea of the 'city in words' in the
Republic as a whole; it is also certainly present here in 501e, since
the context represents the culmination of Socrates' extended
justification of the proposal for philosophical rule, as a way of
converting a merely theoretical ideal into actuality. The original
question, raised in book 5 (471cff.), was whether the best city
could ever be realized. Well, Socrates said, it is always easier to
describe something in theory (*logōi*) than to achieve it in practice
(*ergōi*: 473a5–6); if we can't show that our city is realizable in all
its details, we should not be blamed—and here again he uses the
analogy of the painter, but (in a way) to reverse effect: we should
not be blamed, any more than a painter would be blamed for not
being able to show that the ideal human being he had painted
could actually exist. But something like our city could come
into existence, *if* political power were put in the hands of
philosophers . . .

Thus, looked at from the point of view of ordinary experience,
the 'best city' as described is a theoretical paradigm, an imaginative 'story' of what ought to be.[18] At the same time, looked at

[17] Cf. Burnyeat (1992), who emphasizes that 'the non-existence of the ideal city is a fact
of history, not of metaphysics . . . If the description of the ideal city is an exercise in
imaginative story-telling, it must be wrong to think, with Cornford and Popper, that the
ideal city belongs to the ideal world in the sense of the world of Forms' (176). My
proposal that the description of the ideal city is *also* a 'myth' in that it falls short of the
ideal description is consistent with Burnyeat's position. On the other hand, I suspect that
Burnyeat is going too far in ruling out the possibility of a Form of the city: at any rate
the philosopher will be able to say what a city should be like, and it is not clear to me
what difference there would be, in principle, between this kind of exercise and the one
which would be involved in specifying what justice (or, if we prefer, Justice) really is. See
below. However Burnyeat's main aim is to show that the difficulties in the way of
realizing the best city have 'nothing to do with the metaphysical difference between
Forms and their exemplifications' (ibid.), and in that he is surely right.

[18] From this perspective too, as from the other, it can be, or become, a kind of 'play'.
See 536c1, where Socrates corrects himself for beginning to treat his construction as if it
were a reality: 'I forgot that we were amusing ourselves [*epaizomen*] . . .' The connection
between imaginary constructions, *logōi*, and 'story-telling' is made as early as 376d9–10:
'Well then, let us educate the men *logōi*, as if we were telling it in a story, at our leisure'
(when in fact it will be in earnest, no *mere* story-telling: see below).

from the point of view of the perfect philosopher, it is also a
provisional 'story' of what both ought to be and could be. The
shift between the two perspectives, or the overlaying of the first
by the second, is explained by the way in which the argument
develops. In 471–3, the question is whether the radical changes
suggested would be possible at all. Yes, says Socrates, if we give
power to philosophers. The immediate objection to that is that
philosophers look rather unlikely candidates for political power,
and in 521 he is winding up his answer to the objection: the true
philosopher can in fact be shown, on rational grounds (which
everyone might be brought to accept), to be the only person who
is capable of seeing what needs to be done, in so far as he or she
will possess the relevant knowledge. Reference to that (perfect)
knowledge takes us on to a level beyond anything that has been
achieved in the present conversation, which is thereby reduced to
a 'sketch'. The philosopher, through his or her insight, would be
able to achieve in practice (*ergōi*) what we have outlined in words
(*logōi*).[19] The sketch is still itself an approximation to the truth, a
sketch *of* the truth, and one which will be no less so simply
because it cannot be demonstrated to be practicable just as we
have drawn it: so, at 473a1–3, even while he is emphasizing the
difference between paradigms created *logōi* and what is possible
ergōi, Socrates claims that it is nevertheless the nature of *praxis* to
'have less of a grasp of truth' (*hētton alētheias ephaptesthai*) than
lexis, 'even if someone denies it'.[20] But it will be part of the task
of the philosopher–legislator himself, or herself, to negotiate the
difference between *lexis* and *praxis*, to transform theory into
practice.[21] Meanwhile 'our city', the one described, will remain a

---

[19] The claim that people generally will listen to the argument and be persuaded to
accept philosophers as rulers is itself a part of the case for the possibility of the 'good city'
(though how important a part is not clear—if philosophical rule is supposed to be by
consent of the governed (book 4), still the absence of consent would surely not be
sufficient grounds for abandoning it: so, at any rate, according to the argument of the
Politicus).

[20] In that case 'myth' will be truer than 'reality'; but of course it will more nearly
represent true reality. Socrates' insistence that the story about the judgement of the dead
in the *Gorgias* is a *logos* for him, even if it is *muthos* for Callicles, has similar implications—
from the ordinary perspective, the story *is* a story, and yet it contains truths that take us
beyond ordinary conceptions.

[21] Unfortunately the text appears to be corrupt, at a crucial point (501b3–4). But NB
c1, *eis hoson endechetai*; and presumably the 'rubbing out and redrawing/painting' will be
in reference both to the forms and to what human nature allows. To an extent, this means

muthos (*hēn muthologoumen logōi*, 501e4) because it is not based on perfect knowledge, and—partly in virtue of that—is purely at the level of *lexis*.

I now turn to the *Timaeus-Critias*. Whatever we may finally decide about the specific meaning of *muthologein* in its own context at *Rep.* 501, Critias at *Tim.* 26c8 must surely be talking about Callipolis *qua* imaginary, in so far as he opposes it, as something described *hōs en muthōi*, to what is true, i.e. something that actually happened; and it is this aspect of *muthologein*, the creation of imaginary constructs (Socrates' *plastheis muthos*), in the intersection between *Republic* and *Timaeus-Critias*, that will concern me in the rest of the paper. (But the final moral, about the shifting nature of the 'mythical' in Plato, will be the same.)

I begin from the form of words at *Tim.* 26c8: Critias' *polin hēn chthes hēmin hōs en muthōi diēieistha su*. Penelope Murray follows Taylor in supposing that *hōs en muthōi* introduces a qualification ('*as it were* in myth'; Taylor, 'as in a fable'), while Shorey is content to translate 'in fiction'. The story of the good city in the *Republic* is in any case an unusual 'myth'. This is not because it has 'some grasp of truth', which any myth or fiction may do. Rather it is because of the way the pieces of this 'myth' are, mostly, put in place on the basis of hard argument, as those of other (Platonic) myths are not. Platonic mythical narratives frequently contain arguments of a kind, but these are usually only hypothetical, in the sense of working within the framework of the fiction: if we imagine this to be the case, then that too must follow.[22] This kind of hypothetical necessity is hardly operative in the political argument of the *Republic*.[23] The reasons advanced, for example, in *Republic* 5 for parity of treatment between the genders, or for the 'community of children' and the abolition of the nuclear family, are not dependent on any prior fictional

that Socrates' answer to the question 'is it possible?' is 'yes, if people are put in place who can work out how to implement it'—which hardly seems to take us forward. However, the real point is that the good city will be possible if power is given to those who have the same (rational, philosophical) conception of society and the way it should be run as Socrates and his partners in the conversation (cf. 497c–d).

[22] The argument for immortality contained within Socrates' second speech in *Phdr.* might be one exception; but it is not wholly clear that the *muthikos tis humnos* of 265c1 is meant to include it (see Calame, this volume, p. 139 above).

[23] The reason for this is, I think, that Socrates is (explicitly) not working with a purely *fantastic* city. See below.

assumptions (even though they are advanced in a fictional framework, of a kind), but would retain whatever validity they have in any conceivable political context. Indeed it is a feature of the description of the 'beautiful city' in general that it continually invites the reader to reflect on *his or her own* assumptions. (That may also be true, in a way, of those stretches of the dialogues we traditionally mark off as counting among 'Plato's myths', like the story of Er in *Republic* 10, or Socrates' story of the soul's travels in the *Phaedrus*; but it will rarely be true of the individual elements out of which the story is woven.)

A further peculiarity of the *Republic*'s 'story' is that it might, conceivably, turn out, at some point in the future, to be a description of a real city, for, as Socrates (mostly) insists, it or something like it is not an impossible dream. This is a crucial element in his account, and one that is closely connected with the previous point. As he says at 457e–458a, he means not to be indulging in mere day-dreaming, talking to himself like someone on a solitary walk. There is nothing merely *fabulous*, or fantastic, about what he is putting forward. And yet, for the moment, it is no more than a *paradeigma* created in words (472d9–e1), one which is neither presently realized nor, perhaps, realizable as it stands, in all its details; and as such it will retain its quasi-mythical status.

I say 'quasi-mythical': yet by a complicated manœuvre, the *Timaeus-Critias* transforms the city of the *Republic* into a genuine myth, of a recognizable type (Penelope Murray's 'charter myth'). This is through its identification, by Critias, with the primitive Athens that once defeated Atlantis. Critias represents his account as historical: it is a well-documented account of what actually happened in the datable past. But we know that it is nevertheless a fiction; it is like those other founding myths on which Athens prided itself, and which it colluded with itself in treating as history, simultaneously erasing the differences between past, present, and future.[24] What Athenians once were, by implication

---

[24] Cf. Loraux (1986). The degree, if any, to which any actual Athenian might have understood such myths as fictions is irrelevant to my argument; at any rate we as readers not only know that Critias' 'history' is fiction, but are meant to know it. If Critias and his audience are represented as believing it authentic, that is itself a necessary part of Plato's fiction (for the purposes of which it is equally irrelevant whether such people would *really* have believed the story).

they are now, and may be again. In Critias' 'history', fictional past becomes identical with possible future; all that is missing is the link with the present—because, after all, ancient Athens was utterly destroyed, and any future re-creation of it will require a complete restructuring of society. Instead of serving to reinforce present aims and values, myth becomes a means of reconsidering and replacing them.

One might object that such a reading misses out an essential part of Critias' version of the story: the overlap between the picture he paints of an earlier Athens and the real achievements of the genuine article. The parallel between his Athens' defeat of the massive power of Atlantis and historical Athens' actual role in the defeat of the massively superior forces of Persia is so obvious that it may be tempting to read the *Timaeus-Critias* story just as an imaginative rewriting of real history—one which in fact *validates* a past Athens, by picturing her as having approximated to the good city of the *Republic*. In this case, Plato's appropriation of the charter or foundation myth would be less complete: he would be talking as if what enabled Athens to achieve what she did was because of her *Republic*-type institutions, just as the funeral speech tended to ground her achievement in the natural, autochthonic, virtue of the citizens. The moral would be the same as in the other case, that virtue is something that has to be *worked for*, on the basis of a total reform of state institutions, and of education; only the moral would be accompanied by a (partly) positive evaluation of what Athens once was, and did—perhaps when the original Solonian constitution obtained, before it was wrecked by the disease of extreme democracy as excoriated in the *Republic*.[25]

The contrast between these two possible interpretations of the *Timaeus-Critias* is mirrored in two different kinds of interpretation of the *Menexenus*. The *Menexenus* is either written in praise of

[25] After all, it was Solon who recovered the account of early Athens from Egypt; might we not then infer that he applied his knowledge of this model in his role as legislator? However, *Tim.* 21c–d suggests rather that his preoccupation with immediate political problems led him to neglect his newly acquired knowledge; at any rate he neglected his poetry, and never 'completed the *logos* he brought back here with him from Egypt'. As it is, apart from the memory of the time Solon told it in person, it has been obliterated by the lapse of time and the death of the original protagonists, the early Athenians themselves (20e, 21d). Here and elsewhere, it is the discontinuity, not the continuity, between history and prehistory which is emphasized.

Athens as she once was (i.e. at the time of Marathon), but is no longer; or it is a parody of a funeral oration, in which Marathon itself is as much a part of the parody as the self-deluding consciousness of greatness that is built upon it. The first type of interpretation is represented by Charles Kahn:

> This [i.e. in the *Menexenus*] is the only time we know of that Plato spoke out publicly on a matter of Athenian policy. And as usual he chose to speak anonymously and indirectly, in the guise of a dialogue where Socrates pretends to deliver a funeral oration composed by Aspasia 'from the scraps left over from the funeral oration she composed for Pericles' (236b). The criticism of Athenian policy is itself indirect, conveyed by ironical praise of the Athenians for the courage and loyalty they no longer displayed in 386 BCE. But the message must have been unmistakable for Plato's contemporaries.[26]

On the other hand, the *Menexenus* can be read as illustrating Plato's view of the funeral oration as what Nicole Loraux terms a 'narcissistic ecstasy':

> A journey outside time, a loss of self: the ecstasy induced by the funeral oration is very like that experience of the timeless that Plato calls *anamnesis*. But this—caricatured—resemblance conceals a profound opposition: it is not enough to escape time, for one must also know how to unite one's soul with the divine and not with some such deified simulacrum as the Athenian ideal. Far from being identified with salvation-bringing *anamnesis*, the narcissistic ecstasy is, in Plato's view, a drug for which there is no remedy except a return to reality, the most primary form of reminiscence. Moreover, this return is not easy, for the funeral oration possesses a formidable capacity to induce oblivion, that is, for the philosopher, death. Although the oration says a great deal about immortality, the eternal glory promised by the city is merely a parody of the 'fine risk' of the *Phaedo*.[27] Every *epitaphios* misleads the Athenians by concealing from them their condition as living beings . . .[28]

The *Menexenus*, on this reading, is a subtle and dismissive treatment of the way in which the orators/politicians construct the Athenians' view of themselves; and by implication the parody will include the use such constructions make of Marathon itself.

---

[26] Kahn (1996), 54; cf. Kahn's earlier essay (1963).
[27] In a footnote, Loraux suggests that *Menex.* 234c1 is a 'sarcastic echo' of *Phd.* 114d6.
[28] Loraux (1986), 266.

Which of these two interpretations should we prefer? Should we suppose Plato to be accepting, or rejecting, that part of the Athenian self-image which rejoices in the solid achievement of its single-handed defeat of the Persians? Loraux's marshalling of the arguments for treating the *Menexenus*—from beginning to end— as a parody or pastiche[29] seems to me to be conclusive. But, given the impossibility of certainty on such issues, I shall for the moment content myself with working on the basis that her reading of the dialogue is at least possible (and the one that I think more likely). It is in general hard to find unqualified praise of Athens' past, or any aspect of it, in the dialogues. The closest that we come to it is perhaps in the narrative of Athenian history in book 3 of the *Laws*. His city reached her high point, so the Athenian says, with Marathon and Plataea; and what allowed her to do so was a combination between two kinds of fear—fear of the enemy, combined with 'fear' of the established laws. The second kind of fear seems, initially, to be given pride of place; but in the end (though the text in the crucial passage at 699c is difficult and perhaps uncertain[30]) the outcome seems to be rather less than a full endorsement of the Athenian character. They had established laws, to which every citizen must be subject, and which enjoined the right response to the situation; yet if it had not been for their fear for themselves, they would never have come together to fight for the city. The Athenians of the early fifth century serve here to illustrate the kind of social cohesiveness under law that a city needs. But the ultimate diagnosis seems to be, in effect, that they were terrorized into fraternity. The passage recalls something that the Visitor from Elea says in the *Politicus*: that even cities which govern themselves in an orderly way, sticking to established law, are liable in the end to be ruined. He remarks on the extraordinary natural strength of the institution of what we call a city, which allows it sometimes to survive despite the weakness of its foundations in traditional law; 'however, we see many instances of cities going down like sinking ships to their destruction. There have been such wrecks in the past and there surely

---

[29] Ibid. 304–27.

[30] With Burnet's text, the sense of 699c6–7 must apparently be that there were at any rate significantly large numbers of cowards among the citizens, who would not have joined in defence of the city had it not been for the size of the external threat (*hon* [sc. *ho deilos*] *ei tote mē deos elaben, ouk an pote sunelthōn ēmunato*).

will be others in the future . . .' (302a). The continuation of the narrative in *Laws* 3 pictures Athens herself sinking, as the laws increasingly lost their hold.

It is, I suggest, the *difference* between Critias' Athens and the real Athens of Marathon, and Plataea, that matters more than the similarities. Most importantly, the primitive Athens of the *Timaeus-Critias* was able to achieve what it did because of the excellence of its citizens, *instilled systematically by a divinely inspired educational system.*[31] If we suppose that Athens' defeat of Atlantis was an achievement on roughly the same scale as the defeat of Persia, still it was (as Critias emphasizes) only one—if the greatest—of her achievements;[32] she did many great things, and it was only the misfortune of natural disaster which interrupted her proud course. By contrast, the victory of the real, historical Athens was a high point, followed by eventual decline. There is a delightful passage in the *Laws*, which refers to a saying that 'when an Athenian is a good man, he is exceptionally good. It is only at Athens that goodness is an unconstrained, spontaneous growth, a genuine "gift of God" in the full sense of the word.'[33] When Athenians *did* get things right, they did so spectacularly; the trouble is that because they fail to give systematic attention to the thing that really matters, the production of 'goodness' or virtue in the citizens, they could not, and cannot, be counted on to get it right in any consistent way.

Critias' Athens, then, is a city of virtuous people. That, of course, is what the real Athens claims to be—a claim that the *Menexenus*, parodying Pericles, treats (I propose) with sardonic wit. Socrates/Aspasia describes Athenian democracy like this: 'Then as now, and indeed always, from that time to this, speaking generally, our government was an aristocracy—a form of government which receives various names, according to the fancies of men, but is really an aristocracy or government of the best which has the approval of the many.'[34] Something like the same idea, about the *quality* of the citizens under Athenian democracy, appears in Protagoras' Great Speech in the *Protagoras*, where Socrates gives it equally short shrift. What the *Timaeus-Critias* offers is a story of what Athens would have to be in order for its citizens actually to acquire the kind of excellence on which its

---

[31] *Tim.* 24d–e.   [32] *Tim.* 23c–e; *Criti.* 112e.   [33] 642c–d, trans. Taylor.
[34] *Menex.* 238c5–d2, trans. Jowett.

present-day citizens already, complacently, imagine themselves to possess. It replaces one story with another, truer one, transposing future possibility into quasi-history, or quasi-prehistory.[35]

But the implications of the *muthos* of Athens and Atlantis are not restricted to Athens herself. What Athens fictionally was is at least in outline how every city ought to be, or the model to which every city ought to approximate. In Plato's terms, it represents what a city has to be in order to be called a city at all— just as, according to the *Politicus*, only the true 'constitution', or *politeia*, really counts as a constitution at all, and only the true, knowledgeable, *politikos* counts as a *politikos*. Any other so-called *politeia*, or *politikos*, past, present, or future, will (strictly speaking) be no better than an impostor. Similarly, I suggest, in the case of the polis. So far as I know, Plato nowhere explicitly draws such a conclusion, but it would be quite consistent with what seems to be a general pattern in his thinking not only in the political but in the ethical and aesthetic spheres. In short, what is being described, however provisionally and sketchily, in the Athens of the *Timaeus-Critias*—and in the 'beautiful city' of the *Republic*— is just what a city *is*.[36] In this way, both myths (those of the *Timaeus-Critias* and of the *Republic*) become timeless, mimicking the timelessness of the city's own story of itself. It is a matter of complete indifference to Plato whether he locates his *muthoi* in the past, the future, or indeed (as in the case of his eschatological myths) the present. The sole connection with time will be to the extent that we may be judged to have failed, or to be failing, to adapt ourselves to the ideal, and might succeed in doing so in the future. 'Myth', in this sense, appears peculiarly adapted to a Platonic context—that is, in so far as, or if, myth typically describes or refers to things at a distance from ordinary experience, whether things in the remote past (perhaps), and/or things

---

[35] Even the 'history'—the account of *ta genomena*—in *Laws* 3 appears to count, until it is analysed and its lessons learned, as a kind of *muthologia*: see 699d8. Loraux herself seems to see the resemblance between *Tim.-Criti.* and *Menex.* as problematic, and as evidence that Plato himself was (perhaps) unable to 'resist the temptation of "the eulogy of an unreal past" . . . Perhaps the only way of ridding oneself of the funeral oration would be to *put it at a distance*, by showing [as *Menex.* does] behind its fine words the inanity of certain grandiloquent propositions . . .' (Loraux (1986), 303–4). Rather, I think, *Tim.-Criti.* deliberately appropriates the form of the charter myth; but this is in the end not much more than a difference of emphasis from Loraux's account.

[36] It is the microcosmic counterpart of Timaeus' treatment of the cosmos as a whole, with the difference that at the (macro)cosmic level the necessary compromise between reason and unreason is an established fact, not something awaiting negotiation.

imagined; but always with the qualification that, for Plato, things that are said (*lexis*) may have a greater 'grasp on the truth' than the more familiar (*praxis*).

We may ask, finally, what remains of the distinction between the mythical and the non-mythical in Plato. If he continually plays with that distinction, blurring, obscuring, and transgressing it, must it not nevertheless somehow survive, battered but intact, if we are to be able to attach any sense to the play? The answer, I think, is that what survives is a broad contrast between story-telling, or (more or less) imaginative discourse, and those sorts of discourse which are—comparatively at least—lacking in an imaginative dimension. To the extent that Plato envisages the use of *muthoi* as an alternative to rational argument, in order to inculcate beliefs and attitudes in the non-philosophical, there is also a clear sense in which the contrast between mythical and non-mythical corresponds to that between rational and irrational. But that does not mean that 'the mythical' is simply defined by irrationality; it is simply that story-telling, by virtue of the simplicity and direct-ness of its appeal, may be used as a means of control in the context of people for whom other means are inappropriate by virtue of their own inadequate degree of rationality. In a different context, myth can actually be a tool of dialectic, as it is in the case of the *Politicus* story about the reversal of the world, which is introduced in order to illustrate mistakes made in the preceding process of division. Just as, then, the rational may—in a way—be transformed into the mythical through its presentation as a narrative, so the mythical may itself become an element in the philosopher's progress towards the truth. Story, imagery, meta-phor, simile: all may serve, if perhaps only for the moment,[37] to indicate something that is true of 'the things that are'.

---

[37] 'Only for the moment', in the sense that the philosopher's progress will always continue (so he hopes), in the direction of truth, and the things themselves. In some particular contexts, as e.g. in the case of the similes of *Rep.* 6–7 (see esp. 506c–e), images and likenesses may appear as a kind of second-best; but they remain in general as a useful, even perhaps necessary, part of philosophical discourse itself. As the Visitor from Elea says to the younger Socrates at *Plt.* 277d1–2, 'it is a hard thing to demonstrate any of the greater subjects without using models [*paradeigmata*]': if 'myths' are not quite *paradeigmata* as the *Politicus* understands these, nevertheless they may, and do, serve the same purpose, of helping to 'demonstrate the greater subjects'.

15

Myth and Logos *in Aristotle*

THOMAS K. JOHANSEN

LET me start with a familiar picture of Aristotle. Aristotle invented logic, the art of valid reasoning. He also invented the notion of empirical science, being the first to insist that theories of nature should be based on systematic observation. Aristotle brought together his two inventions, empirical science and logic, in his theory of demonstrative understanding (*epistēmē*). According to this theory, we have understanding when, through a process of induction from sense-perception, we come to grasp definitions that are intelligible, necessarily true, explanatory, and unambiguous, and when we are able to use these definitions as premises in syllogisms that demonstrate their conclusions. In this way Aristotelian science combines observation with logic so as to represent a paradigm of empirical and rational knowledge.

If this is the only picture you have of Aristotelian science you will not expect to find room in it for *muthoi*. How could *muthoi*, understood as fictional, imaginary, ambiguous, and set in distant time or space, contribute to a model of scientific reasoning that only accepts *logoi* that are necessarily true, unambiguous, and derived from observation of facts?

This picture of Aristotelian science comes naturally with a certain view of how Aristotle and other Greek philosophers at the time used the *logos/muthos* distinction. According to this view, expressed by Geoffrey Lloyd in his *Demystifying Mentalities* and in his contribution to this volume, the distinction between *logos* and *muthos* arises in the polemic between different styles of enquiry. Calling somebody's account '*muthos*' is a way of dismissing it as *mere* fiction. By contrast, calling one's own account '*logos*' is to make a claim for it as factual, reliable, and truthful. As Lloyd puts it: '[I]n origin, the distinction between the literal and the metaphorical—like that between myth (as fiction) and rational account—was not just an innocent, neutral piece of logical analysis, but a weapon forged to defend a territory, repel boarders, put down rivals.'[1] However, because the distinction is used polemically it tends also to disguise the continuity between the account of the self-styled rationalist and the account of his allegedly 'mythical' rival. One tends not to acknowledge debts at the same time as one is trying to establish one's own independence. This polemical use of the distinction is well attested in Thucydides and other Greek historians. But it is also found amongst the philosophers. Penelope Murray argues in this volume that Plato tends to regard the traditional myths of the poets as wholly false, whereas the status of the myths that Plato himself uses is much more complex. In this paper I shall first show that Aristotle too uses the distinction polemically in the manner suggested by Lloyd. But I shall then go on to show that Aristotle also uses *muthoi* as *positive* evidence in developing his own theories. Finally, I shall argue that this constructive use of *muthoi* can be seen as compatible with the polemical use of the *muthos/logos* distinction if we consider Aristotle's philosophical method and his view of history. I hope therefore to show in this paper that the picture of Aristotle that excludes myths is far too restrictive.

I shall base my discussion of Aristotle's views on myth on his uses of the term '*muthos*', in order to avoid prejudging any questions about what he might or might not have recognized as 'mythical'. Under '*muthos*', H. Bonitz in his *Index Aristotelicus* lists two groups of entries: (1) *fabula*, 'fable', as opposed to *alētheia* ('truth') and *logos*; and (2) specific senses of *muthos* in the *Poetics*, such as 'a subject of poetry' or 'plot'. In what follows I shall disregard the *Poetics* and focus on the first group of passages, since it is this group that promises to give us the examples of the polemical use of the *muthos/logos* distinction that we are looking for in the first instance. As we shall see, however, Bonitz was wrong to see *muthos* as opposed to truth and *logos* in some of the passages he uses as examples of *muthos* as fable.

I begin with some passages from Aristotle's biological works. At *HA* 597[a]7 ff. Aristotle writes concerning cranes that:

they migrate from the steppes of Scythia to the marshlands south of Egypt where the Nile has its source. And it is in this region that the

---

[1] G. E. R. Lloyd (1990), 23.

Pygmies live. For this is not a myth, but there is truly a race of small men,[2] and the horses are little in proportion and the men live in caves underground.

Here Aristotle clearly draws a contrast between a *muthos* and a true account.

However, when we consider the source of Aristotle's account of the Pygmies his use of the contrast appears problematic. The story of the Pygmies is of course common. In *Iliad* 3. 6, for example, we are told that the cranes migrate every winter to a land near the Ocean where they bring bloodshed and destruction to the Pygmies who live there. However, the fact that Aristotle, at the same time as he tells the story, also identifies the source of the Nile as the marshes south of Egypt suggests that he is drawing, in particular, on Herodotus 2. 32. 6. If so, this is significant, since we would not normally expect Aristotle to rely on Herodotus for scientific evidence. Thus Herodotus in *GA* 756[b]4–14 is denounced as a *muthologos*, a fable-teller, who subscribes to the simple-minded and much repeated claim that fish conceive by swallowing the milt, that is the seminal fluid of the male fish. Aristotle points out two reasons why this claim is wrong. First, what passes into the stomach can only contribute to nutrition and not to conception. Secondly, the uterus of the female fish is full of fertilized eggs; but how did they get there if conception took place through the mouth? Herodotus seems here to be dismissed as a *muthologos* because he simply repeats an old story without checking it sufficiently against observation. Aristotle's own account, by contrast, is presented as based on close observation and rational inference.[3]

However, three points might seem to undermine Aristotle's

---

[2] οὐ γάρ ἐστι τοῦτο μῦθος ἀλλ᾽ ἔστι κατὰ τὴν ἀλήθειαν γένος μικρὸν μὲν ὥσπερ λέγεται.

[3] *GA* 756[b]4–14: 'The fishermen do not notice this [sc. that fish copulate by placing themselves alongside each other] but they do notice the swallowing of the milt and eggs by the female, and so they join the chorus and repeat the same old stupid tale [*ton euēthē legousi logon kai tethrulēmenon*] that also Herodotus the fable-teller [*ho muthologos*] tells, to the effect that fish conceive by swallowing the milt. It never strikes them that this is impossible, but of course it is, because the passage whose entrance is through the mouth passes down into the stomach, not into the uterus, and whatever goes down into the stomach must of necessity be turned into nourishment, because it undergoes concoction. The uterus, however, as we can see is full of eggs: so we ask, how did they find their way there?'

attack on Herodotus here. First, Herodotus is in good company when he says that fish conceive by swallowing the milt. As Aristotle says, it is a belief held also by fishermen, and fishermen are elsewhere, because of their firsthand experience, an authority for Aristotle on fish.[4] Secondly, if Aristotle can use the presence of eggs in the uterus as evidence for his claim that conception takes place there, then Herodotus and the fishermen, by the same token, might use as evidence for their claim that the female fish conceive by swallowing the milt the observation that many fish carry the fertilized eggs in their mouths. Finally, Aristotle finds the account of how fish conceive in Herodotus 2. 93, the same book which he seems to be quite happy to draw on for his account of the Pygmies.

The passages show that Aristotle uses the words '*muthos*' and '*muthologos*' to denounce competing accounts as fictional and false. They also bring out perfectly the other point which Lloyd makes, namely, that the polemical use of the distinction between *muthos* and *logos* hides considerable continuity between Herodotus and Aristotle. Aristotle seems to borrow, without acknowledgement, from Herodotus with one hand and repel him with the other. However, it is also significant that what decides which account Aristotle picks out as *muthos* seems to be not so much the degree of empirical evidence available for the account as whether or not the account fits with Aristotle's theoretical presuppositions. In the case of the Pygmies and their diminutive horses it is unlikely that either Aristotle or Herodotus had more than hearsay as evidence for their existence. What makes both Aristotle and Herodotus accept the story is surely rather their agreement on the theoretical presupposition that the extremes of the world, such as Scythia and Africa, tend to be inhabited by people and animals that represent extremes in relation to the Greek mean.[5] In the case of the parturition of fish, however, it is

---

[4] Cf. *HA* 533^{b}10 ff.: fishermen know that fish have hearing for they use noise to hunt them down.

[5] Cf. Hdt. 3. 106–16 and Arist. *Pol.* 1327^{b}19–37. Notice also the close parallels between *HA* 8. 28, where Aristotle discusses the impact of the locality on animals' physiognomy, and Herodotus 4. 28–30 on the animals of Scythia: 'Horses stand the winter well, but mules and donkeys cannot stand it at all . . . I think the cold may explain the fact that the cattle in this part of the world have no horns: a verse in Homer's *Odyssey* [4. 85] supports this view, where the poet speaks of Libya, *where horns grow quickly on the foreheads of lambs*; a sensible remark indicating that a hot climate favours the rapid growth of horns; whereas

clear that Herodotus' account runs counter to the Aristotelian view expressed in *GA* 3. 5–6 that digestion and conception are discrete functions that are served by discrete organs. In sum, Aristotle, like Herodotus, is willing to accept an account from 'what is said' without any empirical evidence if it is consistent with his theoretical presuppositions. On the other hand, he is also willing to discount firsthand empirical evidence such as that of the fishermen if it disagrees with his theory. On this point, at least, not much seems to separate Aristotle, 'the scientist', from Herodotus, 'the fable-teller', despite Aristotle's rhetoric.

I turn now to two passages in which Aristotle mentions *muthoi* not simply to dismiss them but to highlight a puzzling observation. The *muthos* here represents an attempt to explain a puzzling fact which Aristotle too believes stands in need of explanation. In *HA* 579ᵇ2–8 Aristotle dismisses as 'silly' the *muthos* told about the lioness discharging her womb in the act of parturition. However, he also says that the *muthos*

was invented to account for the rarity of lions, because the person who invented the *muthos* was at a loss as to its explanation [*aitia*]; for the animal is rare, and is not found in many places—in the whole of Europe it is found [and only found, cf. 606ᵇ16] in between the rivers Achelous and Nessus.

Notice again that Aristotle's source of information on the habitat of the European lion may well be Herodotus (7. 126. 4).[6] However, what is new is that the passage shows that Aristotle

in severe cold cattle do not grow them at all, or hardly at all' (trans. A. de Sélincourt). Arist. *HA* 606ᵃ18–606ᵇ6: 'in Libya the horned rams have horns at birth—not only the males [ἄρρενες] as Homer says [some editors therefore emend to ἄρνες] but the others too. And in the Pontus near Scythia the opposite: they occur hornless. . . . In many places the climate too is a cause, for example in Illyria and Thrace and Epirus the donkeys are small, while in Scythia and the Celtic country [i.e. Gaul] they do not occur at all; for these animals winter badly' (trans. D. Balme). J. Gould's description (1989) of Herodotus' symmetrical model of a world in which 'Scythia is the antithesis of Egypt' (p. 100) and 'things become progressively more strange as one moves outward from (Greek) normality at the centre' (98) could also be applied to Aristotle. (See also Lenfant in this volume.)

[6] Hdt. 7. 126: 'The boundary of the lions' country is the river Nestus [*sic*] which flows through the territory of Abdera and the river Achelous which flows through Acarnania'. It has been argued that there were no lions in northern Greece in Classical times; cf. Brown (1960), 166–7. (I am grateful to Lin Foxhall for drawing my attention to this.) If so, and if Herodotus is one of Aristotle's sources on the European lion, then we would have the interesting case of Aristotle, 'the scientist', being misled by Herodotus, 'the fable-teller'.

recognizes that the intention of a *muthos* may be *to explain* a
puzzling observation. Similarly, at *HA* 580ᵃ17 the myth about
Leto's assuming the form of a she-wolf is said to have been
introduced to explain the parturition period of the wolf.[7] Aristotle recognizes that the myth may be rooted in the same world of
experience as science and may attempt to explain the same
puzzling facts as science.

Now the aetiological intention of some myth-telling goes
some way towards explaining why Aristotle sometimes mentions
muthoi in his scientific works. For Aristotle the aim of science is
to provide explanations or causes (*aitiai*): 'We say that we know
something when we know its *aitiai*' (*Metaph.* 983ᵃ24–26). So a
myth, if it is trying to explain a puzzling observation, has the
same objective as science. In *Metaph.* 982ᵇ11–22, having said that
men began to philosophize out of wonder, he adds that 'even
the lover of myth in a sense is a lover of wisdom, for myth is
composed of wonders'. Myth like philosophy and science is an
expression of the wonder generated in us by the natural world.
Myth can therefore be seen as an attempt to answer the same
questions as science. Myths are our predecessors' answers to the
same puzzles that we scientifically or philosophically are now
trying to solve. It should come as no surprise therefore that
Aristotle makes use of myth-tellers and poets such as Homer,
Hesiod, and Musaeus in his scientific works as well as recognized
natural philosophers such as Empedocles, Anaximander, and
Democritus.[8] That is of course not to say that Aristotle always
agrees with the myth-tellers any more than he always agrees with
the natural philosophers. The point is rather that Aristotle sees
the myth-tellers as sufficiently involved with the explanation of
natural phenomena for their opinions to be relevant.

The aetiological intention behind some myths does not of

---

[7] *HA* 580ᵃ14–23: 'There is an account [*logos*] given of the parturition of the she-wolf
that borders on a myth. For it is said that all wolves give birth within twelve days of the
year. And they give the reason for this in the form of a *muthos*, namely that whilst they
transported Leto in so many days from the land of the Hyperboreans to the island of
Delos, she assumed the form of a she-wolf because she was afraid of Hera. Whether the
period of parturition is this or not has not yet been established by observation, I give it
merely as it is told. The common claim that the she-wolf bears only once in her lifetime
is clearly untrue.' (On this passage see R. Buxton, 'Wolves and Werewolves in Greek
Thought', in Bremmer (1987), 60–79, at 66–7.)

[8] For Homer, cf. e.g. *Mete.* 351ᵇ35; *De an.* 427ᵃ24; *HA* 513ᵇ27, 578ᵇ1, 615ᵇ9, 618ᵇ25,
629ᵇ22; for Hesiod, cf. *Ph.* 208ᵇ29; *Cael.* 298ᵇ28; *HA* 601ᵇ2; for Musaeus, cf. *HA* 563ᵃ18.

course in itself ensure that those myths are ever successful in explaining puzzling data. We can see a myth as an early expression of the same explanatory instinct as science without thinking that we can learn anything today from myth. Myths may be proto-science, but as long as the emphasis remains firmly on '*proto*' there may be no need to take them seriously. However, I turn now to two texts, the first of which shows Aristotle drawing on myth to develop his own theory, and the second of which explains why this is so. At *MA* 699ᵃ27–32 Aristotle discusses the question whether what moves the entire universe must itself be immovable or movable. His own answer is that it must be immovable. But before drawing this conclusion he introduces a myth:

Now those who mythically [*muthikōs*] make Atlas stand with his feet on the earth would seem to have a rational basis [*apo dianoias*] for presenting the myth in so far as he is like a diameter [*hōsper diametron onta*],⁹ whirling the heavens round the poles. This would happen in accordance with reason [*kata logon*] since the earth remains still. But if they give such an account they must concede that the earth is no part of the universe.

To understand Aristotle's use of the myth of Atlas in this passage we need to keep in mind Aristotle's distinctive philosophical method. Since G. E. L. Owen's paper '*Tithenai ta phainomena*'¹⁰ it has been widely accepted that Aristotle uses *endoxa*, that is, 'reputable or received opinions', or more generally *phainomena*, 'appearances', to establish his own philosophical and scientific principles. Aristotle's method prescribes that we should first lay down the *endoxa* on a given topic; then discuss the difficulties (*aporiai*) involved in the *endoxa*, trying, if possible, to defend them against objections; and finally, if it is impossible to preserve all the *endoxa*, we should preserve as many as possible or

---

⁹ To make sense of the example it may be that by "διάμετρος" we have to understand the radius rather than the diameter; cf. Nussbaum (1978), 304 n. 29: "διάμετρος here means 'radius'. Farquharson notes that Greek has no separate word for this, other than ἡ ἡμίσεια διάμετρος." This ignores the fact that Aristotle could have referred to the radius without mentioning the διάμετρος, as is shown by his use of "ἡ ἀπὸ τοῦ μέσου ἐκβαλλομένη [sc. γραμμή]" at *Cael.* 271ᵇ29. Aristotle's choice of διάμετρος, if he specifically wants us to understand the radius rather than the diameter, therefore remains puzzling. (I am grateful to Walter Burkert on this point.)

¹⁰ First published in Mansion (1961), 83–103 = Owen (1986), 239–51.

the most authoritative.[11] Developing Owen's argument, Martha Nussbaum observed that 'it has often been noted with alarm that the *History of Animals*, Aristotle's data book, mentions beliefs and stories side by side with the records of the field work. Properly understood, this should not alarm us.'[12] The stories and general beliefs are *endoxa* that Aristotle, alongside more direct observation, uses to derive his theories.[13]

Now our passage from *Movement of Animals* provides a perfect example of how a *muthos* can be processed by the endoxic method. First of all the opinions are summoned, one of which is the myth of Atlas. Aristotle then goes on to defend the myth by saying that it is spoken on the basis of reason (*dianoia*) and *kata logon*. The reason why it is *kata logon* is that it follows from saying that it is Atlas who moves the universe that Atlas, or rather the diameter of the earth along the poles, must remain still. And Aristotle agrees with this view, for he himself insists that the earth is unmoved. However, the myth also involves a difficulty, for just as a man cannot push a boat while standing inside it, so what moves the universe cannot itself be inside the universe. So the diameter of the earth and hence the earth itself must be outside the universe, a conclusion which Aristotle finds unacceptable. We see then in this passage how Aristotle's endoxic method allows an account explicitly referred to as *muthos* to contribute positively to his enquiry. However, the passage also shows that before the *muthos* can be used as an *endoxon* it must be translated into the terms appropriate to the enquiry, in this case the language of geometry which Aristotle uses to analyse motion. Thus redescribed, the myth constitutes a theoretical position that can take part in the critical interchange with other views through which Aristotle arrives at his own theory. In this critical interchange part of the theory is saved (that the earth remains still),

---

[11] *EN* 1145[b]2–7; cf. Barnes (1980).   [12] (1986), 479 n. 13.

[13] Compare R. L. Fowler's description of Herodotus' methodology (1996: 80): 'One first obtains whatever λόγοι [*logoí*] are available, and then tests them by various means: by gauging their inherent probability; by detecting their bias, if any; by comparing them to similar stories; by appealing to everyday experience; by comparing the evidence of surviving monuments or practices; by applying elementary logic, for example by finding contradictions.' The similarity between Herodotus' and Aristotle's methods lies both in the wide range of *phainomena* and *legomena* they consider and in the way their enquiries process those data. We should not be surprised, therefore, if their *historiai* sometimes, as in the case of the Pygmies and the horned lambs, deliver the same results.

part is rejected. In this respect the treatment of the *muthos* is exactly parallel to that of earlier philosophical theories.[14] The *muthos* is part of the endoxic material out of which Aristotle builds his own theories.

This conclusion, however, raises two questions. First, how is it possible for Aristotle to accept that an element of the *muthos* is *kata logon* when he normally uses '*muthos*' to contrast with '*logos*'? Secondly, why does Aristotle think himself entitled to attribute to his predecessors an insight expressed in his own terms (such as 'diameter') rather than in the terms of the *muthos* (such as 'Atlas')? Is Aristotle naïvely ignorant of the distinction between actors' and observers' categories or does he deliberately flout it?[15]

My next text provides answers to both of these questions. In *Metaph.* 1074^{b}1–14, Aristotle wants to argue that the heavenly bodies are eternal and divine. For this purpose he calls on the *endoxa*:

Our forefathers in the most remote ages have handed down to us, their posterity, a tradition, in the form of a myth, that these [i.e. the heavenly bodies] are gods and that the divine contains the whole of nature. The rest of the tradition has been added later in mythical form with a view to the persuasion of the multitude and to its legal and utilitarian expedience. They say that these gods are in the form of men or like some of the other animals, and they say other things consequent on and similar to these which we have mentioned. If we were to separate the first point from these additions, however, and take it alone—that they thought the first substances to be gods—we must regard this as an inspired utterance, and reflect that, while probably each art and science has often been developed as far as possible and has again perished, these opinions have been preserved like relics until the present. Only thus far, then, is the opinion of our ancestors and our earliest predecessors clear to us.

There are hints of earlier 'rationalist' critiques of myth in this passage.[16] But it is exactly in the presence of such critiques that

---

[14] Another example is *Metaph.* 1071^{b}22–72^{a}4, where the mythologists are aligned to the natural philosophers and in the end shown to be half-right.

[15] Cf. G. E. R. Lloyd, p. 146 in this volume, and (1990), 7.

[16] In particular, Xenophanes' and Plato's critique of anthropomorphic gods; cf. Xenoph. frs. 11, 14, 15, 16, 23 DK; Pl. *Rep.* 377d–383c. The idea that the mythical elements have been added to persuade the masses recollects the noble lie in *Rep.* 414b–415d (referred to as a *muthos*, 415a2, c7), invented to persuade the entire citizen body *or at least the non-ruling masses* (414b8–c2).

Aristotle's positive use of the myth stands out. The myth has been constructed around the insight that the first substances are gods. The rest of the tradition has been added to this insight to persuade the many or for other utilitarian reasons. Aristotle justifies his belief that there is such an insight through the doctrine of periodic cataclysms. The myth is a relic from the period before the last cataclysm when science and arts were as perfect as possible.[17] As Myles Burnyeat has stressed, Aristotle's endoxic method must be seen in the context of his cyclical view of history.[18] According to this view, each art and each science is rediscovered innumerable times after periodic cataclysms with 'the same opinions recurring in rotation amongst men not once or twice but infinitely often'.[19] The reason why Aristotle thinks that man can repeatedly come up with the right theories is that he believes that man by nature is a potential knower and that natural potentialities generally are realized. The truths grasped by our predecessors have been preserved for us in the form of *endoxa*. That is why we can grasp the truth adequately if we attend correctly to the *endoxa*.[20] As Aristotle says in the *Politics*, 'we should make the best use of what has been already discovered and try to supply the defects' (1329^{b}34–5).

Here the need to attend *correctly* to ('make the best use of') the *endoxa* should be emphasized. The endoxic method does not prescribe a passive reception of the *endoxa* whereby we automatically assimilate the insights of our predecessors. We need to put in the sort of critical questioning and conceptual analysis shown by Aristotle in so many of his introductory chapters before the *endoxa* will yield their insights.

The correct methodology is perhaps particularly important when dealing with mythical material because of its obscurity. Aristotle thus objects to those who sophistically use *muthoi* to generate spurious explanations:

---

[17] Cf. Pl. *Tim.* 22b–24d, where astronomy has been preserved for the Athenians since the last catastrophe in the form of a myth (*touto muthou men schēma echon legetai*, 22c7).

[18] Burnyeat (1986).

[19] *Cael.* 270^{b}19–20.

[20] Cf. *Rhet.* 1355^{a}15–18: 'To see the truth and what is similar to it belongs to the same faculty. At the same time, people are by nature sufficient in relation to the truth, and in most cases they reach it; that is why someone who is likely to hit on the reputable opinions [*endoxa*] is also likely to hit on the truth'.

One puzzle [*aporia*] which is as great as any and which has been
neglected both by the present and the previous thinkers is the question
whether there are the same principles [*archai*] for things that are perishable as for things that are unperishable or whether they are different. For
if they are the same, how are some things perishable and others not, and
what is the reason [*aitia*]? Hesiod and his followers and all those who
wrote about the gods [*theologoi*] concerned themselves only with what
was plausible to themselves and had little regard for us. For making the
principles gods or from gods, they say that those that did not taste nectar
and ambrosia became mortals. It is clear that they are using these words
in a way familiar to themselves and yet they have spoken above our
heads concerning the application of these causes. For if the gods taste
the nectar and the ambrosia for the sake of their pleasure, then the
nectar and ambrosia are not the cause of their being, but if it is the cause
of their being how could gods be immortal when they need nourishment? But it is not worth while paying serious attention to those who
purvey mythical sophistries [*muthikōs sophizomenōn*].[21]

The people Aristotle has in mind are the sort of clever people
(*sophoi*) criticized by Socrates at *Phaedrus* 229c–e, who try to
correct (*epanorthousthai*) mythical sayings (*muthologēmata*, 229c5)
by finding natural explanations for them. For example, they
explain the story of the rape of Oreithyia by Boreas by saying that
the north wind blew the girl off a rock. Like Aristotle, Socrates
describes this sort of person as *sophizomenos*, 'purveying sophistries', and the term (in conjunction with *sophoi*) is surely meant
to remind us of the practice of allegorical interpretation of myth
associated with sophists such as Protagoras. The key words in
Aristotle's attack on 'those who purvey mythical sophistries' are,
'they have spoken above our heads in the application of these
causes'. What goes over our heads in the myth is clearly not the
point that the gods are immortal (Aristotle would agree with that)
but the attempt to use another feature of myth, that gods consume ambrosia and nectar, *to explain* their immortality. There is a
superficial plausibility to this account of divine immortality in so
far as we think that humans continue to live because they eat and
drink. So one might think that the reason why gods can continue
living for ever is that they consume a special sort of food and

[21] *Metaph.* 1000ª5–18. I borrow Lloyd's translation of the last sentence, cf. p. 155 in this
volume.

drink. However, the plausibility is only superficial, as Aristotle shows: for if you need food and drink of any sort to continue living it means that you are not *necessarily* immortal as required of the gods. The target of both Socrates' and Aristotle's attacks is the practice of manipulating *muthoi* to generate apparently plausible, but in reality spurious, *explanations* rather than myth-telling itself.[22] That is why Socrates can proceed in the *Phaedrus* to make positive use of *muthos* by presenting his own palinode as a *muthos* (253c7)[23] and that is why Aristotle thinks that, despite the abuses of others, he can salvage something from the *muthoi* by using the correct endoxic method.

Aristotle's cyclical view of history explains why the *muthos* can be useful in science, for on this view the *muthos* itself is a relic of an earlier scientific understanding. However, seeing the *muthos* as a relic of past *logos* also explains the negative aspect of *muthos* as fictional, obscure, and unreliable, the aspect that is picked out by the polemical use of the *muthos/logos* distinction. For what is properly speaking 'mythic' (*muthikos*) about the *muthos* is the way it has been altered since the last cataclysm. The *logos* has become *muthos* by being used as a propaganda tool to deceive the masses. The gods, for example, were originally understood correctly as Aristotelian 'first substances'. But out of this *logos* came *muthos* when the gods were given human or animal shape by politicians who wanted to use them as guarantors of their own preferred social order. As we saw in the case of Atlas, we now have to restore the *muthos* to its original form before we can get to the insight of the original *logos*. The term '*muthos*' carries a pejorative meaning since it is associated with what has to be discarded in order to gain access to that insight. That is why, even when we accept the contribution that *muthoi* can make to scientific understanding, the term '*muthos*' will still tend to be contrasted with '*logos*'.

Finally, we can see how Aristotle might defend himself against the charge of confusing actors' and observers' categories. Aristotle sees his own philosophy as near perfect. So his terminology and

---

[22] Note in both cases the damning reference to what is plausible (*tou pithanou*, *Metaph.* 1000ᵃ10; *to eikos*, *Phdr.* 229e2), the standard of argument expected of rhetoric but considered substandard in relation to philosophy, of which we expect proof (cf. *apodeixeōs*, *Metaph.* 1000ᵃ20; *apodeikteon*, *apodeixis*, *apodeixeōs*, *Phdr.* 245b7, c2, c4).

[23] Cf. Murray, p. 253 in this volume.

conceptual apparatus are those that any near perfect philosophy would employ. But since Aristotle's philosophy is also the recurrence of a near perfect philosophy of an earlier cosmic cycle, he can be confident that they too must have employed his concepts: for example they too will have talked about 'first substances' and 'the diameters of circles' in those terms. Since the *muthos* is a relic of this earlier near perfect philosophy, we can conclude that the original theory before it was invested with mythical language must have been expressed in Aristotelian terminology. Aristotle thus has a justification for thinking that his categories must have also been those of his antediluvian predecessors.[24]

We began with a picture of Aristotelian science that excluded *muthos*, a picture that was supported by the polemical use of the *muthos/logos* distinction. However, we saw that Aristotle was a good deal more accommodating towards *muthoi* than this picture suggested. The reason for this was twofold: first, Aristotle recognized the same explanatory intention in *muthos* as in science; secondly, his endoxic method allowed for a wide range of beliefs, theories, and stories, including some labelled as '*muthoi*', to count as data and not just direct empirical observation, as suggested by our original picture. The justification for allowing *muthoi* back into the rational fold in this way rested ultimately on the doctrine of periodic cataclysms, which explained why *muthoi* could contain rational insights. It is perhaps ironic if this doctrine today seems to us, in the pejorative sense, a mere *muthos*.

[24] It is no doubt correct, as Jonathan Barnes has argued (1980: 501), that amongst Aristotle's *endoxa* are beliefs that have not been explicitly expressed by his predecessors, beliefs which he nevertheless ascribes to them because they are similar to others expressed by them or because they act in a certain way that one would explain in terms of holding those beliefs or because they use language in which those beliefs are latent. However, my point here is that Aristotle has reason to believe that the insights of Aristotle's predecessors *from before the last cataclysm* which were concealed and preserved as *muthoi* were originally expressed in the way Aristotle would express them. This is compatible with saying that Aristotle also redescribes many of the views of his predecessors since the last cataclysm. Indeed, both points emphasize the teleological manner in which Aristotle conceives of epistemic progress within each cosmic cycle: throughout each cycle thinkers are grappling with the same problems, and they eventually arrive at the same correct views at the end of each cycle because of their inborn potentiality to grasp the truth. This is *both* the reason why Aristotle might think that he is entitled to rephrase the views of his predecessors within this cycle in his terms (which they are obviously, as Aristotle sees it, on the way towards formulating) *and* the reason why he might think that his predecessors in the previous cycle actually developed their thinking to a point where they solved the problems using the correct Aristotelian terms.

VII

Myth, Reason, and Techniques

16

The Use of Purple in Cooking, Medicine, and Magic: An Example of Interference by the Imaginary in Rational Discourse

MIREILLE BÉLIS

IN antiquity, purple was the only luxury product which could be used to adorn clothing and yet be eaten like any other foodstuff. It occupied a position at the top of the hierarchy of dyes: ancient sources unanimously acclaimed its splendour, brilliance, and fastness. It fell naturally into the category of social markers, expressing distinction in all fields of public life as well as in the situations of private life. It was worn by deities, heroes, priests, and potentates; it was flaunted by parvenus.

Pliny the Elder quite reasonably queried the coexistence of the double practice which led his contemporaries to subvert the natural order:

What connection is there [he asked] between the sea and our clothing, between the waves and waters and woollen fabric? We only enter that element in a proper manner when we are naked! Granted that there is so close an alliance between it and our stomach, but what has it to do with our backs?[1]

These questions point up the paradox well enough. In fact purple comes from the liquid exuded on death by the murex and the whelk, molluscs found along almost all the Mediterranean coastline and harvested by fishermen and divers to supply the coastal workshops. The purple industry made the fortune of Tyre, before spreading to Crete, to the coast of Asia Minor, and the Greek seaboard, arousing the same passion, and still functioning as a social marker, in all the civilizations acquainted with its use.[2]

I would like to dedicate this paper to Pierre Vidal-Naquet.

[1] Plin. HN 9. 105, trans. (here and subsequently) H. Rackham (Loeb edn.).

[2] Meyer Reinhold (1970) devoted a complete treatise to the use of purple as a sign of social prestige. His work does not concern itself with the gastronomic, therapeutic, or

So it is on the shores of Phoenicia that mythological accounts locate its discovery, and Achilles Tatius is the writer who gives the most interesting version of it:

Once upon a time the elegance of purple was a secret kept from all mankind: a small mollusc kept it hidden in the inmost chamber of his spiral shell. A fisherman casting his net caught this shellfish; he hoped for fish, and when he saw its spiny shell, he cursed his catch and tossed it aside as sea trash. A dog, coming upon this lucky find, began gnawing on it, and as the juice trickled through his mouth, it made his jaws seem to run with blood. The blood stained the dog's jaws and dyed its mouth purple. The shepherd, seeing the dog's jowls stained with blood, thought he was injured. So he tried to wash it with sea water, but the blood only glowed a deeper crimson, and when he touched it, his hand too was stained. The shepherd realized that it was something in the nature of the shell, some powerful ingredient of natural beauty. He took a handful of wool and pushed it into the winding interior, seeking to reveal the mysteries of the mollusc, and like the dog's jaw it turned blood-red. He had discovered the source of the colour purple. Using stones to break through the wall enclosing the elixir, he opened the sacred shrine of the purple and exposed a treasure chamber of dye.[3]

Depending on the author, it was either an unnamed fisher-man, as here, or even Heracles himself, who was credited with

magical powers of purple and the shells which produce it. He distinguishes the Near East from the world of the Greek cities influenced by Ionian fashions arriving from the Far East, and then shows that Alexander and the Hellenistic states developed the use of purple as a symbol of political power. This use reached Rome via Magna Graecia, where purple denoted both power and wealth, during the Republic. In spite of a 'nationalist' and moralizing reaction which attempted to limit its abuse, the empire extended its use, reserving a monopoly for itself, but without succeeding in keeping exclusive control of it. The later empire marked the high point of imperial purple, before the Fathers of the Church condemned purple in general as a culpable luxury.

Reinhold's study confines itself strictly to a chronologically and geographically articulated description of fashions in clothing. My perspective here will be less chronological, since I shall attempt to distinguish the reasons why, from Greece to Rome, from one literary genre to another, and in all sectors of society, certain constants ran through all periods; why the same vocabulary persisted; and how the myth operated even in medical texts, which precisely tend to dissociate themselves from the irrational and from magical modes of thought. I shall not attempt to give a historical survey of a phenomenon represented by the continuing gastronomic and therapeutic uses of purple, but rather to identify the characteristics of this persistence, its apparent variations, and the thought structures which underlie this particular conception of the properties attributed to purple-shells. Hence my approach is more like that adopted by M. Detienne and J.-P. Vernant (1978) in their study of *mētis* (see n. 60 below) than that of M. Reinhold.

[3] Ach. Tat. *Leucippe and Clitophon* 2. 11. 4–8, trans. adapted from John J. Winkler in Reardon (1989), 194.

the discovery. Whatever the version, each master notices that his dog, seeking to allay its hunger with a murex, appears to have been wounded: the purpurogenous juice 'bloodies' its chops, and when the wound is washed, contact with sea water serves only to enhance the brilliance of the fluid. By revealing the secret of purple to her, the hero wins the favour of the nymph he sought to seduce. In this episode of the *prōtos heuretēs* ('first finder'), the two themes, the foodstuff and the dyestuff, are set in a relation of cause and effect; already in the foundation myth, in the original representation intended to explain the twofold system in which shell and dye would, albeit independently of each other, take their place, our sources are using the terminology which was to persist both in workshops and in naturalists' texts, and which enduringly inspired the richest metaphors in poets and dramatists when they came to exploit the symbolic force of purple. Achilles Tatius uses all the key terms found elsewhere: from the chops of the hungry dog runs 'the blood of the flower', that is, the red fluid secreted from the mollusc's vein; the intrigued fisherman-shepherd breaks the 'rampart' which protects the 'drug' (*pharmakon*) and 'open(s) the shrine of the purple', to discover 'the treasure chamber of the dye', concealed at first beneath the rough exterior of the shell.

What happens to this mythological background when purple-shells become straightforward seafood, or are used in dietetics or medicine? Does it become blurred? Is it transformed? What path does medical rationalization follow? Does it bring about the disappearance of the foundation images contained in the only vocabulary in which murexes and whelks can be described, a vocabulary common to dyers, naturalists, and writers?

EDIBLE PURPLE

All the peoples living around the Mediterranean coast ate murexes and whelks, with the sole exception of the Jews, whose dietary laws forbade the eating of marine creatures without fins or scales. Yet the Jews used purple to dye fringed prayer-shawls, a practice which recalled not only a divine commandment (Num. 15: 37–41) but also the colouring of the curtains of the Taber-nacle and of the veil before the Holy of Holies (Exod. 26: 1, 31;

cf. 28: 6). Evidently they were anxious to make a strong distinction between the sacred and the profane, between the symbolic
and the dietary: while the dyeing of the fringes came under the
heading of obligation, the eating of the shellfish which produces
the dye came under that of prohibition.[4] As for the southern
Mediterranean, we know from Greek sources of the existence of
a taboo on fish and salt for Egyptian priests. Herodotus does not
dwell on it, but Plutarch devotes a passage to it in *Isis and Osiris*:[5]
these priests have such an aversion to the marine world that they
will neither speak to pilots nor eat any seafood, whereas other
Egyptians are allowed to eat certain kinds of fish. Modern
criticism may see in this practice the effect of the religious
particularism and resulting xenophobia of the Egyptians; however
that may be, 'the image of a fish was used as an ideogram or
determinative in several words expressing hate and disgust'.[6]

Greeks and Romans, by contrast, were very keen on seafood,
and used their ingenuity to find suitable ways of preparing it to
bring out its flavours.[7] Purple-shells were easily harvested along
the seashore, and provided ready-made sustenance for folk who
made their living from the sea. Sailors and fishermen ate them
raw, a practice which disgusted urban gourmets. For seafood to
become an authentic dish, it had to enter the economic chain and
be transformed to acquire added value. When raw, the murex
was no more than the product of an almost primitive harvest.
Eating the mollusc alive, moreover, and drinking its 'blood',
assimilated the man who sated himself on it to a cannibal. This

[4] On fringes, see the entries 'Tallit', 'Tekhelet', and 'Tsitsit' in *The Oxford Dictionary of
the Jewish Religion* (= Werblowsky and Wigoder (1997)). The prohibition is formulated
twice: Lev. 11: 9–11, and Deut. 14: 9. See Mary Douglas, 'The Abominations of
Leviticus', in Douglas (1966), 41–57, repr. in Lang (1985), 100–16: 'Holiness requires that
individuals shall conform to the class to which they belong. And holiness requires that
different classes of things shall not be confused . . . The dietary rules merely develop the
metaphor of holiness on the same lines' (Douglas (1966), 53, 54 = Lang (1985), 112, 113).
In Lang (1985), 117–26 ('One More Time: Leviticus Revisited') Michael P. Carroll gives
a different analysis of these dietary prohibitions. He shows that the unclean animals which
it is forbidden to eat are those which come from the wild world and improperly invade
man's space, illustrating the intrusion of the natural into the cultural.
[5] Hdt. 2. 37; Plu. *De Is. et Os.* 353c and 363e.
[6] Plu. *De Is. et Os.* = *Œuvres morales*, v. 2, p. 284, n. 9 to p. 205, by Christian
Froidefond (Paris, 1988).
[7] The Pythagoreans refrained from eating it. According to Diogenes Laertius (8. 1. 5),
Pythagoras could remember having been Pyrrhus, a fisherman from Delos, an island
whose coasts abound in murexes.

theme underlies an epigram in which Martial gives the power of speech to personified murex shells, and which likens them to the person who eats them alive: '*Murexes*: "Ungrateful one, you put on cloaks dyed in our blood, and even that is not enough for you: you eat us as well."'[8]

But as soon as shells had been passed on or sold, they could be considered acceptable foodstuffs and negotiable commodities: for a pair of oars, a certain sailor exchanged a brill, a sole, a mullet, and thirty-five whelks.[9] The excessive price of seafood constituted an inexhaustible pretext for sarcasm against fishmongers. True, in Athens, an official called the *opsonomos* regulated the price of foodstuffs, and in particular that of fish. None the less, observed Plutarch, 'what is certain is that seafood is sold *para logon* ('*against all reason*') at a higher price than all other food'.[10] We shall come back later to the expression *para logon*.

A high price which offended against reason became all the more offensive as it coexisted with the repulsive vulgarity of the vendors. Fishmongers enjoyed a dreadful reputation: dishonest, uncouth, bad-tempered, unscrupulous cheats,[11] they were arrogant in their speech, palmed off rotten produce, and fleeced their customers. Enveloped as they were in the pestilential stench of their fish, in particular that of murex shells, which always smelled of rotten eggs,[12] they were 'the foulest breed of all' and 'all murderers'.[13] But, as soon as the basic material was transformed into a dish through the expertise of a chef, purple-shells moved up the hierarchy of flavours. When raw, they were no good at all; once cooked, seasoned, spiced, and combined with other flavours, they became worthy of a place on sophisticated menus. Thus we leave behind the category of mere subsistence food, and move into the realm of superfluity, not to say luxurious profusion. 'Oiling his skin with yellow unguents, flaunting soft

---

[8] Mart. 13. 87.

[9] Alciphron, *Letters of Fishermen* 1. 7.

[10] Plu. *Mor.* 668b; my italics.

[11] Aristotle reports in the *Mechanics* (849^b34–850^a2) various ruses employed by purple-sellers to rig the scales in order to defraud their customers.

[12] See Radwin and D'Attilio (1976), 12.

[13] Athenaeus (224b–227a) cites thirteen texts of some length which, taken together, make up a satirical indictment of fishmongers. Roman ones were apparently every bit as bad as their Greek counterparts. See 224d, quoting Amphis' *Planos* (= PCG fr. 30) for the term 'murderers', and 226e, quoting Antiphanes' *Misoponēros* (= PCG fr. 157), for what precedes. I use C. B. Gulick's Loeb translation here and below.

cloaks, shuffling fine slippers, munching bulbs, bolting pieces of cheese, pecking at eggs, *eating periwinkles*, drinking Chian . . .'[14]— these are habits which mark, if not a dissolute lifestyle, then at least a predilection for a life of leisure. The art of the cook lies in the ability to metamorphose the molluscs' raw 'blood' into a skilfully prepared food. Totally absorbed in their *logodeipnon* ('feast of words'),[15] Athenaeus' Deipnosophists ('sophists at dinner') celebrate with multiple quotations cooks distinguished by their inventiveness, while slaves serve them 'oysters in abundance and other ostracoderms'.[16] Such cooks know how to wash shellfish carefully; they balance the salinity of the mollusc by correcting excess or deficiency; they choose whether to boil or grill it, adding appropriate herbs and spices to bring out the flavour. As connoisseurs of the seafood which they are handling, they adapt their recipes to its provenance. The chef's expertise makes him more like a physician than a dyer: he doesn't just follow his intuition, or use empirical knowledge, or content himself with reproducing a lucky 'workshop defect', like the one which led to the chance invention of amethyst purple.[17] Whereas the diver, the purple-shell fisherman, and the dyer who buys their wares, are looked down on, the chef is an artist who wins general acclaim.

Purple and the Gourmet

The first task is to wash the shells. They must be rinsed clean of sand, silt and, sometimes, fine gravel which comes from where they lay on the sea floor. This needs finesse, or else '[it] spoils the flavour'.[18] When they are ungarnished, moreover, there is general agreement in finding murex and whelk on the mediocre side as far as taste is concerned. The flavour of murexes places them, according to the physician Diphilus, above whelks, but below pinnas, themselves considered fairly indigestible.[19] From

---

[14] Athen. 548c (Anaxilas, *Luropoios* = PCG fr. 18).

[15] Athen. 1b. Gulick goes further, translating 'feast of reason'.

[16] Athen. 85c. 'Ostracoderms', and not 'other testaceous foods', as Gulick writes, in order to distinguish between malacodermatous crustaceans and hard-shelled testaceans.

[17] Plin. *HN* 9. 140.   [18] Ibid. 32. 58.   [19] Athen. 91 f.

Hippocrates to Oribasius, physicians distinguished the mediocre qualities of the *flesh* of murexes and whelks, which they found indigestible and unnutritious, from those of the *stock* made from it: in its liquid form, this preparation is laxative. Only Galen seems more guarded, and condemns the secretion of mollusc flesh in general, because it is thick; molluscs are not very nutritious and they generate black blood, so that they are not suitable for old men.[20]

But the ingenuity of Greek chefs would have been unremarkable if it had not occurred to them to treat the parts of one and the same mollusc as two distinct dishes. In fact natural historians had distinguished three principal organs within the murex: the *trachēlos*, 'neck', the *anthos*, 'flower', which secretes the dyeing agent, and the *mēkōn*, literally 'poppy', a term which is usually rendered by 'liver', to designate the creature's bladder.[21] Hicesius, a physician of Smyrna cited by Athenaeus, distinguishes not only murexes from whelks, but also the *trachēloi* and *mēkōnes* of each species, as if there were in fact four different shellfish, each with its own flavours and attributes. He compares their medicinal virtues and adds: 'But even when the "necks" of purple-shells are cooked by themselves, they are good for stomach affections.'[22] Here, where medicine meets gastronomy, there is every probability that chefs prepared the 'necks' and the 'poppies' of purple-shells separately, a refinement whose equivalent is found only in a traditional American recipe handed down from the time of the Pilgrim Fathers: New England clam chowder, in which the hard and soft parts of the clams are cooked separately.

In the case of edible purple, the 'poppy' remains, but the 'flower' disappears. The reason is that it dies at the same time as the mollusc, and, while human beings can *eat* the 'poppy', only textile fibres can '*drink*' the 'flower' which is the vehicle of purple-shells' 'blood'. As Pliny puts it: 'This produces that much admired paleness, avoiding deep coloration, and the more diluted *the more the fleeces are stinted.*'[23] In a brief epigram, Martial amusingly turns this to account, playing on etymology: '*Amethystine wool*: "Since I am drunk with the blood of a Sidonian shellfish, I

[20] Gal. vi, p. 339 Kühn.   [21] Arist. *HA* 547ᵃ.
[22] Athen. 87d–e.   [23] Plin. *HN* 9. 138 (my italics).

do not see why I am called sober wool." '[24] The wordplay is ready-made: amethyst-coloured fabrics are obtained by dipping wool (or silk) already coloured amethyst into another vat of 'Tyrian' dye, that is, murex-purple. But the Greek term is *amethustos*, 'not intoxicated', which was originally used to denote the gemstone, and which has a Latin equivalent in *sobrius*.

The molluscs themselves also fit into the same 'dietary' pattern of themes, but in the perspective of 'the eater eaten'. It was Apollodorus of Athens, cited in *Deipnosophists*, who wondered about the point of the saying 'greedier than purple-shells': '[A]ccording to some authorities, it is derived from the dye; for whatever it touches it draws to itself, and produces the glint of its own colour in whatever is placed beside it. But others refer it to the animal itself . . .',[25] and he relies on a text of Aristotle describing the 'tongue', *glōtta*, which they use to feed with as they perforate the shells of other molluscs.[26] Their voracity is such that they even eat each other: like eats like, before it perishes, releasing the 'blood of its flower' in the vats of the dye-works, or being eaten alive in its turn. It is not improbable that the prohibition on the consumption of blood played a part in the laws excluding molluscs from the Jewish diet. Except for polemical purposes, this scruple did not affect Greek or Roman gourmets—quite the contrary. On the principle that 'whoever wears purple can eat purple-shells', murexes and whelks figured prominently on the most recherché menus. The Deipnosophists matched the deed to the word: they addressed the subject just as the slaves brought them the dish.

But how could distinguished guests enjoy food whose taste and nutritional value were by general consent mediocre, a view reinforced by quotations from dietitians and physicians? Was there interference of prestige between purple (colour) and purple (shellfish)? Undoubtedly. But none of our sources connects the two systems, dress and diet, to explain one in terms of the other. On the very rare occasions when the link is explicit, it takes the form of a rhetorical question whose function is to emphasize a scandalous paradox, a disgusting abuse. A human being who eats shellfish does not make a conscious association

---

[24] Mart. 14. 154, trans. D. R. Shackleton Bailey (Loeb edn.).
[25] Athen. 89a–b.
[26] Athen. 89b–c, citing Arist. *HA* 547[a]13 and [b]3; cf. Plin. *HN* 9. 128.

with the dye which they secrete. So one must look elsewhere, to other representations and other beliefs, for whatever might have caused the indigestible insipidity of purple-shells to be forgotten.

Athenaeus' Deipnosophists address the subject on three occasions and quote three comic fragments, one by Anaxandrides and two by Alexis. Here is Alexis on aphrodisiacs: 'Pinnas, crayfish, bulbs, snails, buccina, eggs, extremities, and all that. If anyone in love with a girl shall find any drugs more useful than these . . .'[27] Even clearer is a very long fragment of Anaxandrides which mocks the accumulation of foods served by the rustic Thracian king Cotys at his daughter's wedding feast: the menu, a real rag-bag, comprises no less than ninety-six different dishes, a sign of the man's burlesque munificence. Among them are octopuses and crabs, but in addition: '. . . bulbs, cauliflowers, silphium, vinegar, fennel, eggs, lentils, grasshoppers, rennet, cress, sesame, periwinkles, salt, pinnas, limpets, mussels, oysters, scallops, tunny . . .'[28] In this display of bad taste, the culinary tirade ends with an obscene joke which is not out of keeping with the rest. In another fragment of Alexis we find an even more explicit list: 'What is better for a man in love, Cteson, than the things which I have brought with me here? There are periwinkles, scallops, bulbs, a large polyp, and fine large fish.'[29] In each of these texts chaotically enumerating all kinds of dish, the context is that of a wedding feast, in the ordering of which there figure products, raw or cooked, which are aphrodisiac. Whelks fall into this category. But why does the murex not belong to it?

PHARMAKON AND *VENENUM*

Erōs and *kērux*, the humble whelk, maintained close and constant links. Where did this association originate? What was it based on? Why did the whelk for once supplant the murex, in a hierarchy which usually affirmed the supremacy of the latter? It is reasonable to suggest that this was a matter of 'actual fact', and that it

---

[27] Athen. 63e (= *PCG* 281). Gulick states (note ad loc.) that the bulbs in question are the roots of an edible iris.

[28] Athen. 131a–f for the whole passage (= *PCG* 42), and 131e for the lines quoted.

[29] Athen. 356e–f, citing Alexis' *Pamphilē* (= *PCG* 175).

was possible to draw up empirically a list of recognized aphrodisiacs, a list whose authority remained intact over a long period
of time. Such 'certainties' attaching to the efficacy of particular
substances are found in all periods, and the belief persists, in spite
of all learned evidence to the contrary.[30] When whelks were
served to him, the Syracusan Charmus greeted them with the
Homeric apostrophe of 'heralds [i.e. *kērukes*], messengers of
Zeus'.[31] That must surely be an allusion to the love life of the
most ardent of the gods: the link between sexuality and purple-
shells is so strong that certain courtesans adopted their names, to
judge from a line of Archippus: '*Kērux*, nursling of the sea, son of
purple-shell'.[32]

So the very names of purple-shells were enough to evoke
sexuality, whether venal or not: they connoted libido and eroti-
cism. Yet there is something of a paradox here: for the myth
recalls that the purple fluid is the most precious of dyes, a kind of
blood concealed in a 'shrine' hidden from view, and whose
'rampart' has to be broken; psychoanalysis would have no difficulty in seeing the relationship between this system of metaphors
and the flow of a girl's blood after intercourse. Achilles Tatius'
digression fits into the context of a wedding postponed because of
adverse omens; after the bride's father has given her a 'dress . . . all
of finest crimson cloth', the narrator explains that it was dyed
with the same purple as the *peplos* of Aphrodite.[33] But if purple
has to do with sexuality and marriage, it is also a poison, since the
dyeing fluid is called *venenum* in Latin, *pharmakon* in Greek.[34] The
basic meaning of both words has to do with 'drug', a preparation
which can both alter what it comes in contact with, and cure the

---

[30] There is no shortage of examples. It is enough to recall the preparations based on
mummy powder, which had their hour of glory in the West when Egyptology was all the
rage, or to think of the secret and lucrative traffic in rhinoceros horns in present-day
Africa.

[31] He was an inveterate user of quotations, which he had the knack of producing for
each dish: Athen. 4a. Here he quotes *Iliad* 1. 334.

[32] Athen. 86c (= *PCG* 25). In actual fact, one may well wonder how a courtesan, even
one nicknamed 'Periwinkle', could attract the description '*son* of purple', *kērux* being
always masculine in gender.

[33] Ach. Tat. *Leucippe and Clitophon* 2. 11. 2–4 (see n. 3 above).

[34] Chantraine (1968–80: 1177–9), s.v. φάρμακον (*pharmakon*), concludes that the problem of the word's etymology is 'insoluble in the present state of our knowledge'. He
rejects various proposed etymologies because they do not take into account the basic sense
of φάρμακον, namely '(medicinal) herb'. The meaning 'dye, colour, paint, make-up',
common in Attic writers, is regarded by C. as an extension of this original sense.

ailment it has provoked.[35] These veritable 'love poisons' would therefore have been capable of negating their own effects.[36] That may be the origin of the idea that the purple liquid secreted by the molluscs 'poisoned' the textile fibres which 'drank' it in the dyers' vats. In this respect, it is relevant to recall that the murex, which feeds on other shellfish, cannot serve as food for them. That which language has expressed is verified in practice: murex flesh is indeed toxic for organisms other than man and other mammals.[37]

The poets drew on this fact to produce obvious effects and images, which were the more convincing since fabrics and ivory, once dyed, could never recover their pristine state: purple represented a veritable 'tattooing', irreversible and spectacular, and super-luxurious when it was ivory that was dyed.[38] So we are concerned with concoctions which are their own antidote, and whose transforming power is irresistible—charms in the proper sense of the word. At once poison and love philtre, the purple-shell unites the power of Eros and the power of death in an association of opposites that Freud commented on in a remarkable essay.[39] 'Venerare laenas' and *pharmattein ta eria* are commonly used without necessarily meaning anything more than 'dyeing wool (purple)', at least in the speaker's clear field of consciousness, although the fabric is literally 'poisoned'. When

[35] A. Gell. 12. 9. 2: 'That *periculum* (trial), too, and *venenum* (drug) and *contagium* (contagion) were not used, as they are now, only in a bad sense, you may learn from many examples of that usage' (trans. John C. Rolfe, Loeb edn.). For these words incorporating opposite meanings, see Ernout and Meillet (1985), 719, s.v. *uenenum*.

[36] The 'philtre' drunk by Tristan and Isolde belongs to the same category of magic potions. But the lovers who succumb to it do not know the antidote.

[37] See ref. in n. 12 above.

[38] The image is common in Ovid's *Metamorphoses*. It is rather surprising to find this usage denounced as a perversion: ivory is said to be pleasing only if it remains perfectly white; dyeing it purple is a parvenu debasement, but it does at least protect it against yellowing (Ov. *Am.* 2. 5. 39–40).

[39] Sigmund Freud, 'The Antithetical Meaning of Primal Words' (1910), in *The Standard Edition of the Complete Psychological Works*, xi (London, 1957), 153–61. In 'Remarques sur la fonction du langage dans la découverte freudienne', in ch. 7 of Benveniste (1966), 75–87, Émile Benveniste vigorously rebuts 'the etymological speculations of Karl Abel which misled Freud' (79–80). Of *sacer* Benveniste observes that 'it was cultural conditions which determined two opposing attitudes towards the "sacred" object' (81). In the cases of φάρμακον and *venenum*, language has not confused poison and its antidote; on the contrary, it distinguishes between two paradoxical and contrary properties, empirically ascertained, of one and the same substance. (I owe the Benveniste reference to Pierre Vidal-Naquet.)

Aulus Gellius describes the prohibitions which affect the wife of
the priest of Jupiter ('they say that she observes other separate
[ceremonies]; for example, that she wears a dyed [*venenato*] robe,
and that she has a twig from a fruitful tree in her head-dress
[*rica*]'),[40] he gives absolutely no pejorative connotation to
'venenato'.

If the ancients classed purple-secreting molluscs among the
aphrodisiacs, this was not simply because they had observed their
stimulating properties empirically; for the original meaning of the
Greek and Latin terms denoting the fluid favoured such a representation. The whelk is an aphrodisiac, the murex a 'venereal'
shellfish. The former increases sexual potency. The latter is associated with Venus/Aphrodite/Astarte, a link which begins with
the etymology of *venenum*, which is related to the Latin name of
the goddess.[41]

Born from *aphros* (foam), Aphrodite is for her part the purple
goddess *par excellence*, created from the blood shed by Ouranos'
castration. She is not the fruit of love, but of the destruction of
the male principle; she has no mother, since she arises from the
Deep, Pontus, a masculine personification of the sea; and it is a
daughter, the goddess of feminine seduction, who results from
this union of like with like. Everything is paradoxical in this birth
which is no birth, and which has a profound determining effect
on the functions ascribed to the goddess, on her attributes, and on
the myths associated with her. The popular etymology which
Hesiod takes over in the *Theogony*[42] is perhaps, by the rigorous
standards of modern scholarship, invented; it may well be that
one should dissociate Aphrodite linguistically from her native
aphros; but the derivation remains none the less both an etymology and a genealogy. The important thing is not to know
whether the association is valid, but to observe that the whole
ancient world believed it, and to evaluate the consequences of
such a persistent belief. Aphrodite, then, is the purple goddess *par
excellence*, who touched land for the first time on the island of
Cythera, also called Porphyris. She has the epithet πορφυρῆ

---

[40] A. Gell. 10. 15. 26–9. The *rica*, a small, square, fringed cloak, was purple tinged with
orange, like the colours of a flame—the same shade, incidentally, as the orange veil with
which brides covered their heads.

[41] Ernout and Meillet (1985), 719 s.v. *uenenum*.

[42] Hes. *Th.* 190–8.

(*porphurē*) in Anacreon, while, almost a millennium later, Ausonius could write of Venus, goddess of the morning star and of the rose, that she 'bids both be clothed in the same purple hue'.[43]

But it is in a legend reported by Pliny that the link between Aphrodite and murex shells is most strikingly affirmed:

> Mucianus states that the murex is broader than the purple [*purpura*], and has a mouth that is not rough nor round and a beak that does not stick out into corners but shuts together on either side like a bivalve shell; and that owing to murexes clinging to the sides a ship was brought to a standstill when in full sail before the wind, carrying despatches from Periander ordering some noble youths to be castrated, and that the shellfish that rendered this service are worshipped in the shrine of Venus at Cnidus. Trebius Niger says that it is a foot long and four inches wide, and hinders ships, and moreover that when preserved in salt it has the power of drawing out gold that has fallen into the deepest wells when it is brought near them.[44]

In this fascinating text, the murex is distinguished from the *purpura*, even though the shell in question, according to Pliny himself, is one and the same, having become distinct from, and having lost the characteristics of, its species: it is no longer the spiny, masculine shell of the common murex, but rather the 'Venus shell', all roundness and femininity. These pseudo-murexes or, more precisely, hyper-murexes, are in fact non-murexes, for they no longer resemble the shellfish whose name they bear. All they retain is the symbolic charge, even in a predominantly historical episode like this one. The averted castration of the three hundred noble youths from Corcyra corresponds negatively to the fertile castration from which Aphrodite draws her origin; the murex, deprived of its spines and its 'blood', becomes a porcelain shell or a shell of the genus *Cypraea*, according to Cuvier.[45] What does it matter that this 'murex' is also and simultaneously a remora capable, it was believed, of arresting the forward motion of ships, a porcelain shell, and a murex? It is not

---

[43] Anac. *PMG* 357; Auson. *De ros. nasc.* 21–2.

[44] Plin. *HN* 9. 80. Herodotus (3. 48) describes the episode without mentioning the miraculous murex shells. The ship's destination was Sardis, and the Corinthians responsible for escorting the noble youths from Corcyra rescued them from their fate. See also Diog. Laert. 1. 95, who likewise passes over the role of the murex.

[45] See n. 1 (p. 125) by the Budé editor, E. de Saint-Denis, to Plin. *HN* 9. 80.

a matter of logic, but a discourse constructed on the logic of words and fable, on the truths of language and myth. It is this structured rationality which is at work in the elaborate representation of the aphrodisiac powers of whelks, as in the legend related by Mucianus. So in a way the whelk is a real aphrodisiac, while the murex is an aphrodisiac of the imagination.

When we enter the realm of strictly medical texts, does anything remain of this way of seeing things?

For lovers of good food, purple-shells were a commodity which could not possibly be served ungarnished. Their flavour was appreciated for reasons which Plutarch would have considered *para logon*, on account of the virtues which most people credited them with and which had no necessary relationship with verified knowledge. On the other hand, this mediocre food recovered its quality as a 'mixture' with unsuspected properties when dietitians and especially physicians reviewed its different pharmaceutical applications. The dyers' cooking was, as we pointed out, 'toxic' for wool plunged into the purple-vats. The cooks' cooking was aphrodisiac. In medicine, it is no surprise to find that the fluid remained the *pharmakon* or the *venenum* of the mythographers and dyers. The chain of words runs throughout the economic and literary networks where purple is found. It creates coherence and stability, always underpinned by a double polarity of contrary and complementary senses: a poison and its antidote. Yet, since nothing is mechanical in these subtle, modulated shifts, there is scope for examining the changes of direction and divisions by which the thought of the ancients created distinctions between the everyday realities of industry, the *haute cuisine* of the great, and the rational skill of the physician.

A *pharmakon* has by definition the capacity to produce contrary effects, depending on the mode of administration and the dosage. Hence the physicians of antiquity never used molluscs untreated. This is how Dioscorides describes the transformations to be carried out and the useful parts of the shellfish:

Calcined murex shell promotes desiccation, is abrasive for the teeth, purges wounds, and encourages scarring . . . Calcined whelks produce the same effects, being more caustic; if, having filled them with salts, you heat them for longer in an earthenware pot, they are good for cleaning teeth and, in unguents, for burns . . . The opercula of the murex cooked with oil and applied in layers stop hair loss. With vinegar, they suppress swelling of the spleen.[46]

So the different parts of the creature are separated, burnt, and ground, and the powder thus obtained is mixed with other substances to make pomades, ointments—in a word, *pharmaka*.

The common factor in these preparations is the attribution of the capacity to reduce, arrest, or diminish any excess due to sickness. This holds good even for the commonplace abrasion caused by toothpaste. To a certain extent, this representation of the reductive properties of the murex is in line with the legend which Pliny repeats from Mucianus. The introduction of purple-shells, in however small degree, allows the re-establishment of limits exceeded, the fighting of organic disorders, the return to a normality which had been disrupted.

But there is another text, this time by Galen, which deserves particular attention: '[. . . To bring about an inability to achieve erection.] Incinerate a whelk, and extinguish it with the urine of a castrated bull; use the mixture in food or drink; replace the remainder in a container.'[47] There follow five other preparations with the same properties. Arnould Locard, a nineteenth-century scholar working on purple, devoted a note to its uses in medicine. This is how he translates our text: 'Take a whelk, extinguish it in the flesh of a castrated calf, and put it in a potion.' In his commentary Locard adds, 'For men, Galen recommends this remedy *against* impotence.'[48] Thus he omits the heading and ignores the end of the sentence. The mistranslation is spectacular where such a straightforward text is concerned. Clearly the meaning is exactly the opposite: when reduced to ashes and mixed with a drink or with food, the whelk does not *counteract* male impotence, but *causes* it. The idea of bringing about this kind of disability seems so contrary to any conceivable

---

[46] Diosc. 2. 4. 1, 2. 7.

[47] Gal. xiv, pp. 486–7 Kühn: [. . .Πρὸς τὸ ἀνέντατόν τινα γενέσθαι.] Κήρυκα καύσας σβέσον οὔρῳ βοὸς τομίου καὶ λάμβανε ἀπὸ τούτου ἢ ἐν ποτῷ ἢ ἐν βρωτῷ.

[48] 'Chez les hommes, Galien recommande ce remède *contre* l'impuissance' (my italics): Locard (1884), a work printed in 150 copies.

therapeutic objective, at least in the context of his own time, that Locard is unable to accept it.[49] As '_venenum_', the whelk-based philtre induces _opposite_ effects to those one would expect from the mollusc itself, and which make it an obligatory dish at wedding banquets. In order to restrain _erōs_ this fiery principle must be 'extinguished', says Galen, with the urine of a castrated bull. The term belongs to the vocabulary of blacksmiths: the ash of the whelk is likened to the red-hot iron (first paradox) which, to reduce its incandescence, is plunged into cold water or into quicklime, itself often made from crushed murex shell (second paradox). One may reasonably speculate about the exact composition of this mixture and the method for administering it. The fact remains that this remarkable passage highlights the complexity of the relationship—sometimes identity, sometimes opposition—between sexuality and the whelk.

Divine Nuptials

Such a reversal is also found in representations of the world of the gods, which it is impossible to model directly on the world of mere mortals. Whereas eating purple-shells is commonplace among humans, the banquet of the gods can be real only in words: though sustained by nectar and ambrosia, they clearly do not _feed_. Their physiology is not subject to the constraints imposed on the human organism; they ignore considerations of diet. Nevertheless, they do feast, and Epicharmus ventured to describe the banquet of the immortals at the wedding of Heracles and Hebe. Here is their menu, as one of the guests presents it:

He brings all sorts of shell-fish—limpets, lobsters, _krabuzoi_, _kikibaloi_, _tēthunakia_ . . . barnacles, purple-shells, oysters tight-closed (to open them is no easy matter, but to eat them is easy enough), mussels, snails, periwinkles, and suckers (which are sweet to eat forthwith, but too acrid when preserved), and the long, round razor-fish; also the blackshell, to gather which brings fair profit to children; and on the other side are land-snails and sand-snails, which are held in poor esteem and are cheap,

[49] Who would want to resort to this strange medication, and with what aim? The texts are silent about the users. Since the context is medicine rather than magic, one would tend to think of socially recognized uses to do with artists and priests wanting to preserve their chastity without having to resort to infibulation, a practice current among singers in particular.

and which all mortals call *androphuktides* ('man-shy'), but we gods call *whites*.[50]

This is not the place to discuss the textual difficulties presented by the passage.[51] However, in the content there are elements relevant to our subject and requiring examination. Sixteen kinds of shell appear in the list. The speaker is apparently a god, since he contrasts the language of the immortals with that of humans. Moreover, besides easily identifiable molluscs, crustacea, testacea, land and sand snails, favoured by both gods and men, there occur *krabuzoi*, *kikibaloi*, and *tēthunakia*, which elude identification. Not surprisingly: what is being highlighted is the specificity of divine food, irreducible to human consumption or vocabulary. What is more, a man who ate it would not even realize the fact. The god makes that clear: on earth, a shell which the immortals find delicious is of interest only to children, and snails are dirt cheap among humans. The same food, changing in name and category, changes also in value and nature. What are we to think, from this perspective, of the 'whites' (in the dialect of the gods), which mortals call *androphuktides*, that is, 'avoiders of men'? Does that mean they make men (as opposed to women) flee, or that men flee *them*? In other words, is it an anaphrodisiac food, with that reputation among mortals? Certainly. But how can one imagine such a dish being served at the wedding feast *of Heracles*? From a literary point of view it would be burlesque or inconceivable for that to be the implicit meaning of the text. Athenaeus' commentator noted the paradox, and invoked the authority of Pliny, who stated that 'snails taken in food hasten delivery, and conception too if applied with saffron',[52] while Gesner remarked of *androphuktides* that they 'do not promote, but inhibit, desire'.[53] So the reversal of function and value which occurs for other reasons in medical texts is effected here by a change in vocabulary: purple becomes its own opposite.

[50] Athen. 85c–e.
[51] The third and eighth verses of the Greek text present important variants. I have followed Gulick's edition (cf. n. 13 above) and I am making use here of remarks in the *Animadversiones in Athenaei Deipnosophistas post Isaacum Casaubonum*, ii: *Animadvers. in lib. III et IV* (Strasbourg, 1802) of J. Schweighäuser.
[52] Plin. *HN* 30. 126.
[53] Cited by Schweighäuser on Athen. 85e.

Purple and Femininity

But a far more interesting distinction arises when medical texts address the question of the therapeutic effects of purple-shells on *female* physiology. One might expect those effects to be analogous to those which the shells allegedly have on men. Far from it: the properties of purple-based remedies vary according to the sex of the patient. Among the texts which deal with the subject, let us consider two, one by Dioscorides, the other by Galen.

The former writes, in connection with purple-shell opercula: 'When burnt for fumigation, they excite [the tissues of] women experiencing suffocation of the womb, and provoke the expulsion of the placenta.'[54] According to Galen:

Certain writers have stated that, in a potion with vinegar, purple-shell opercula will cure swelling of the spleen, and that in fumigation they are effective in the treatment of women experiencing suffocation of the womb, and facilitate the expulsion of the placenta in difficult births.[55]

In these texts, far from being either aphrodisiac or anaphrodisiac, murex shells and whelks no longer affect women's libido. Their function is to assist the process of pregnancy and to stem bleeding in pregnant women: though harmful to men, whose virility they now impair, they privilege motherhood.[56]

Being inhibitors of libido and promoters of conception, murex and whelk naturally affect the physiology of adolescents: they prevent the growth of hair at the onset of puberty, or reduce hirsutism.[57] Perhaps because puberty is a stage when sexuality still seems uncertain, remedies made from purple-shells for once serve women equally well: 'The breasts themselves are treated efficaciously by shells of murex or of whelks reduced to ash and combined with honey; by crabs too, river or sea, applied locally.

---

[54] Diosc. 2. 7.   [55] Gal. xii, p. 348 Kühn.

[56] Cf. Plin. *HN* 9. 79, on the remora or sucking-fish: '[A]nd for this reason it also has an evil reputation for supplying a love-charm and for acting as a spell to hinder litigation in the courts, which accusations it counterbalances only by its laudable property of stopping fluxes of the womb in pregnant women and holding back the offspring till the time of birth.'

[57] Gal. xii, p. 457 Kühn. According to Plin. *HN* 30. 41, slave traders sought to delay the growth of the body-hair of the adolescents they sold with an ointment based on 'blood that comes from the testicles of lambs when they are castrated. Applications of this blood after the hair has been pulled out also do away with the rank smell of the armpits.' The salve recalls the anaphrodisiac remedy intended to promote impotence.

The flesh of the murex if applied removes hair growing on the breasts.'[58] But, be it noted, in the last-mentioned remedy it is the molluscs' flesh, not their shells, which is used.

In gynaecology, the approved remedies draw their virtues from the inherent relationship, existing in the initial *muthos*, between shell and blood: the foetus in its placenta resembles the bloody creature living in its mineral envelope; the bleeding accompanying the premature expulsion of the child corresponds fairly well to the extraction of the mollusc, which also perishes in an effusion of blood. But the opposite applies when the same remedies are used on men: pregnancy is not involved, obviously; but if the analogy worked term for term, one might expect purple-shells to increase male fertility, for instance, or to favour procreation. Not so. The two networks coexist severally, each being constructed on the representation of the functions socially assigned to men and women.[59]

CONCLUSION

All this goes to show that, when one 'talked purple', one was far from making a mechanical application of an abstract rationality, resolutely turning one's back on the truths of myth and the meanings of the language out of which thought was elaborated. Fisherman, fishmonger, dyer, whelk-eater, god-guest, miscarrying woman, chaste man, physician, all depended on the same *muthos*, the clear awareness of which was lost when one moved away from the founding tale whose structures persisted down to Achilles Tatius' novel. Through various literary forms, remote from one another in space and time, and from one level of society to another, this myth operated unceasingly and latently in

---

[58] Plin. *HN* 32. 129.

[59] Symbolically, the purple carpet unrolled by Clytemnestra under the feet of Agamemnon, whom she is preparing to murder, brings together every level of significance. The 'purple road' is the one which leads from blood to blood: that is, from the blood of marriage to the blood of birth, then to the blood of Iphigenia's sacrifice, and finally to the blood of Agamemnon's murder. There is thus a union between *erōs* and death, the sacred and derision of the sacred, domestic virtues and their parody, since it was Clytemnestra who wove the dyed cloth: she is a kind of counter-Penelope, who hatches the fatal plot and dramatizes the return of the hated husband extravagantly, the better to deceive him.

the different categories of knowledge and in the most diverse realities of daily life. In whatever field of application, the myth was constructed according to a terminology powerfully charged with symbolism; what governed later representations was the meaning of words. Even in medicine, rationality depended on the truths established by the technical vocabulary to which dyers, writers, naturalists, and physicians were obliged to have recourse: there existed no other.

Marcel Detienne and Jean-Pierre Vernant have demonstrated, through the examples of the fox and the octopus, the remarkable persistence of the representation and vocabulary of *mētis*, 'cunning intelligence'.[60] The same goes for the powers attributed to purple-shells, beliefs rooted in the bedrock of the myth attaching to the discovery of the shell and its tinctorial virtues, and developed on the basis of a vocabulary which made it possible to refer to the mineral and organic parts of purple-shells. That is why the devising of remedies which seem to us to come close to pure superstition, and to resemble folklore and magic rather than scientific method, remains, in spite of everything, one might say, a rational form of mythic thinking. Ancient treatments based on murex shells and whelks seem to ignore the principle of contradiction, because they always rely on a universally held conviction: purple is a *pharmakon*, capable of producing an effect and its opposite. As *venenum*, it has on men's libido an effect which is sometimes positive, sometimes negative; on women's, none at all: the latter exist only in virtue of their menstrual cycle and their capacity for generation, that is, in their connection with blood. Purple literally slows down male functions, whereas it accelerates female biological processes, in relation to pregnancy. It is not surprising that its ability to unite contrary properties makes it into a substance endowed with superlative powers. Every part of the creature is used: the shell and the opercula which protect the shellfish, and the flesh itself, whether dry or forming the basis of

[60] (1978), ch. 2 ('The Fox and the Octopus'), 27–54. On p. 44 we read: 'How should we explain this stability of terminology and, through it, of the images, themes and models associated with *mētis*, and what is its significance? . . . [O]ne cannot fail to notice that, from Homer to Oppian, throughout a literary tradition which includes Hesiod, the lyric poets, the tragedians and Plato and Aristotle, some of the terms most closely associated with *mētis* seem to have a special application to the fields of hunting, fishing and also to warfare to the extent that this last activity is understood as analogous to the first two.' A similar 'stability of terminology' occurred in connection with purple-shells.

a broth. Murexes and whelks are used in the treatment of pretty well all ailments: pustules in the genital region, disorders of the ear, wrinkled and lined skin, and all kinds of tumour. But they are credited with therapeutic powers of a quite different order, the reason for which is not obvious at first sight: it turns on a belief *para logon*, devoid of any apparent rationality. Yet it has in fact its own peculiar logic.

A few examples will suffice to highlight the operation of this logic, which creates a link of symbolic causality, displacing the *muthos* into a *logos*. Aristotle asks why 'fishermen, divers for murex, and generally those whose work is on the sea, have red hair'?[61] According to Galen, shellfish can heal even the bites of rabid animals: *since* the purple-shell itself bites, it can heal deadly bites; it is the supreme antidote.[62] The purple-shell has a tongue like a lance which can perforate the shells of other marine creatures: *therefore* it has the power to extract gold hidden at the bottom of wells, and also arrows remaining lodged in open wounds.[63] When crushed (Pliny relates), the horny opercula 'which serve as doors for purple-shells' can unite severed sinews:[64] the operculum transfers to the damaged ligament its own ability to *close*, and can heal it by forming a scar. Far from being antagonistic, medicine and magic combine in one and the same representation of nature. There is nothing incoherent in this conception of illness and recovery: the purple-shell provides the *pharmakon* or *venenum par excellence*: 'the purple-fish too is a good antidote to poisons'.[65]

Because no dye could stand comparison with purple, and because it had required almost superhuman ingenuity to discover its secrets, the ancients retrospectively imagined the circumstances necessary for those secrets to be revealed to mortals by the gods. They constructed a beautiful myth, shared by the Greeks and the Romans, of a hero and his dog who, between them, made the discovery. Nor did the myth fade. Its basic elements infiltrated rational discourse, structuring its logic and directing its application, even down to the conception of the therapeutic virtues of

---

[61] Arist. *Prob.* 38. 2, trans. W. S. Hett (Loeb edn.). (In the Budé edn., Pierre Louis does not attribute this text to Aristotle himself.) The reader will recall (n. 7 above) that Pythagoras remembered having been a fisherman at Delos, with the name Pyrrhus ('red-haired').

[62] The remedy includes ten drachmas of calcined whelk; see Gal. xiii, p. 440 Kühn.

[63] Plin. *HN* 9. 80, 32. 125.   [64] Ibid. 32. 120.   [65] Ibid. 32. 65.

purple. This is not a case of the accidental and superficial interference of mythic thought in an area alien to it. To spell it out:
where purple was concerned, medicine and magic shaded into
each other. Murex shells and whelks would never have belonged
to the ancient pharmacopoeia if myth had conferred on them
nothing but an ordinary capacity for dyeing. They were magical,
and that is exactly why it was rational to use them. *Muthos* and
logos were one.[66]

[66] This paper has been translated by Michael Howarth and revised by the editor.

17

Mythical Production: Aspects of Myth and Technology in Antiquity

FRITZ GRAF

1

AMONG the dichotomies which the dichotomic theme of this volume inevitably generates is the opposition—all too easily posited—between the rational and the irrational. For the present paper I have taken a theme, the mythology of technology, which seems to bridge that opposition. Whatever Plato might have thought and said about it, *technē/ars* was, for most of antiquity, a procedure about which rational discourse was the rule. It is not surprising that in the late nineteenth century the development of technology in Greece was inscribed into the paradigm 'From Mythos to Logos': together with science, technology was seen as being emancipated from religion to constitute a new and independent field. In more recent times the process has been described by Jean-Pierre Vernant as a 'laïcisation des techniques': Vernant did not himself completely reject the older, 'From Mythos to Logos' view, but rather modified it, differentiating between the theoreticians with whom full rationality set in during, at the latest, the age of Aristotle, and the practitioners who worked by trial and error and were thus always exposed to a trace of irrationality and unpredictability.[1] In this article I shall not argue about Vernant's assessment (his concept of rationality is Platonic and might therefore not do full justice to all the facts). What I intend to do is more limited in scope: I shall concern myself with the intersection of myth and technology, more precisely that of myth and metallurgy.

We have no technical treatises on the subject of metallurgy:

[1] J.-P. Vernant, 'Some Remarks on the Forms and Limitations of Technological Thought among the Greeks', in Vernant (1983), 279–301, referring (n. 7) to Espinas (1897), esp. 6–7.

they may simply never have existed, or they may have failed to
survive for the same obvious reason that other treatises on many
other aspects of what the *banausoi* ('artisans') did for a living failed
to survive; Pliny, at least, mentions only books on *toreutica* (en-
graving in relief) and on *medicina metallica* (the use of remedies
from metals). Heron's trade is a different field, as is that of the
alchemists—the latter were engaged in a quest for spirituality,
while the former's interest in gadgets appealed to intellectuals.
Nevertheless, about certain aspects of ancient metallurgy we do
know something. There are descriptions of mining and metalworking in Nubia (in the gold-mines of the Ptolemies), in Etruria
and Elba (iron), in Spain (gold, silver, copper), and in Britain
(tin): Diodorus, fascinated by the subject, collected this information.[2] And there is the copious archaeological record of the
Laurium silver-mines. Any visitor to the extensive (though badly
tended) excavations at this site is bound to be impressed by the
skill and inventiveness with which the Athenian engineers and
workmen dealt with the crucial problem of the extraction process: they had to use a huge amount of water to wash out the
stones with the ore, in a region where water had always been a
very scarce commodity. The system of cisterns and ducts for
recycling rain water (the only water available there) still inspires
high admiration.[3]

2

Myth enters at the point where what is at issue is the inventing
(or rather discovery) of metals and metalworking; and there is
extensive, though somewhat monotonous evidence for it. In
order to avoid monotony, I start with another epoch and, seemingly, another culture.

'When the angels, the sons of heaven, saw the beautiful daughters of man, they lusted for them.' And after a solemn oath to
share the responsibility for what was nothing short of a revolt,
they went to earth, took them as their wives, and taught them
'concoctions and incantations and the digging up of roots, and

---

[2] Diod. Sic. 3. 12–14 (Nubia), 5. 13. 1 f. (Etruria and Elba), 5. 35–8 (Spain), 5. 22
(Britain).
[3] Conophagos (1980); Jones (1982); Vanhoeve (1994).

they showed them the plants'—in short, medicine. 'And the daughters of man gave birth to mighty giants who first ate up men's provisions, then began to eat the humans altogether. And earth was given over to lawlessness.'[4]

Thus chapters 6 and 7 of the apocryphal Jewish *Book of Enoch*—an account of a rebellion against God's established order. In its complete form, it is preserved in an Ethiopian translation from the Greek text (there are translations in other languages as well, but the Ethiopian one is the most important); its twenty-six manuscripts are dated between the fifteenth and the eighteenth century.[5] Its earliest stratum, the so-called 'Book of Watchers', was written in Hebrew, perhaps around 200 BCE; it elaborates and comments on the short account of the Fallen Angels in Genesis 5: 24.[6] We are dealing here not with metallurgy, but with the pharmacology and medicine whose powers could always be understood as a divine or demonic gift, despite the brave attempts of the early Hippocratics at a rational discourse.[7]

There is, however, a longer development of this same story, in the following chapter (ch. 8), which has to be understood as a later elaboration of the earlier version; it is dated as late as the second century CE. Its Greek version comes from the *History* of the Byzantine historian Georgius Syncellus (d. *c.*810) and from a papyrus fragment found in Gizeh (eighth–twelfth century): the texts agree in their essence, as does the Ethiopian text. It is this Greek (or later Latin) text of Enoch—or, rather, the several Greek (or Latin) versions of the text—which became influential in the Graeco-Roman world: the later translations into Ethiopian and Old Slavonic start out from the Greek or Latin text, and this text—and especially the part about the Fallen Angels—is frequently cited in the Christian writers, from Justin Martyr (d. *c.*167) to Augustine, who was the first to condemn the book as non-canonical.[8]

---

[4] Black (1970), chs. 6f. The crucial feature ('concoctions and incantations . . .'): φαρμακείας καὶ ἐπαοιδὰς καὶ ῥιζοτομίας, καὶ τὰς βοτάνας ἐδήλωσαν αὐταῖς.

[5] See F. Martin (1906); Knibb (1978); Uhlig (1984). There is also an extensive Slavonic version, for which see Böttrich (1995).

[6] For the stratigraphy and the earliest stratum, see Hanon (1977); Nickelsburg (1977); Knibb (1978). For a general introduction, see VanderKam (1995).

[7] See, among others, G. E. R. Lloyd (1987), esp. ch. 1.

[8] A (rather too extensive) list of echoes and citations in the Christian writers in F. Martin (1906), pp. cxii–cxxxvi.

This development of the original tale is a long list of what the Fallen Angels taught mankind, considerably longer than in the earlier version. 'Azael [one of their leaders] taught mankind how to make swords and weapons and shields and armour, and he showed them the metals and how to work them, and necklaces and ornaments and rings and cosmetics and precious stones and the dyeing of textiles.'[9] Other angels brought sorcery (*epōidai*, 'incantations'), exorcism ('the dissolving, undoing of incantations'), and different methods of astrological divination. 'They all began to reveal to their wives and their sons the secrets [*ta mustēria*]', Syncellus resumes,[10] while the Ethiopian text insists on the consequences: 'There came great and universal impiety into being; they committed adultery and all other errors and all their ways became corrupted.'[11]

The moralistic ring of the passage is unmistakable. What the angels gave to mankind is, on the one hand, herb-lore, sorcery, and divination—the exploitation of knowledge which belonged to the Divine, not to humans—and, on the other hand, metallurgy and chemistry, more specifically the chemistry of textile dyeing and of cosmetics. This results in warfare and, more emphatically, in female dissolution (*porneia*, 'prostitution', as the Greek text bluntly states); both technologies are rejected, as are sorcery, its corollary exorcism, and divination. It is a radical text, and it is a text written in a Jewish community. The two go together: the text condemns some fundamental intellectual and technological achievements of the dominating Hellenistic and Roman civilization, and, by lumping them together with sorcery and astrology, defines them as another transgression of the boundaries set to human knowledge. In order to do so, the text makes use of a traditional story which puts it into a universally accepted frame, the story of the Fallen Angels. The reaction to

---

[9] Enoch 8. 1 (Gizeh papyrus): μαχαίρας ποιεῖν καὶ ὅπλα καὶ ἀσπίδας καὶ θώρακας, διδάγματα ἀγγέλων, καὶ ὑπέδειξεν αὐτοῖς τὰ μέταλλα καὶ τὴν ἐργασίαν αὐτῶν, καὶ ψέλια καὶ κόσμους καὶ στίβεις καὶ τὸ καλλιβλέφαρον καὶ παντοίους λίθους ἐκλεκτοὺς καὶ τὰ βαφικά; cf. Syncell. *Chron.* 12 C (*Corp. Script. Hist. Byz.* (Bonn, 1829), p. 21): πρῶτος Ἀζαὴλ . . . ἐδίδαξε ποιεῖν μαχαίρας καὶ θώρακας καὶ πᾶν σκεῦος πολεμικὸν καὶ τὰ μέταλλα τῆς γῆς καὶ τὸ χρυσίον πῶς ἐργάσωνται, καὶ ποιήσωσιν αὐτὰ κόσμια ταῖς γυναιξίν, καὶ τὸν ἄργυρον. ἔδειξε δὲ αὐτοῖς καὶ τὸ στίλβειν καὶ τὸ καλλωπίζειν καὶ τοὺς ἐκλεκτοὺς λίθους καὶ τὰ βαφικά (substantially repeated in Cedren. *Hist. compend.* 10 B = *Corp. Script. Hist. Byz.* (Bonn, 1838), 19f.).
[10] Syncell. *Chron.* 13 A (p. 22).   [11] Enoch 8. 2.

technology, in this original context, is the reaction of fundamentalists who see their lifestyle threatened by the overpowering knowledge of a dominant culture.

But this text was also received outside Judaism, by the early Christian writers. Their attitude towards Graeco-Roman culture changed over time, from a position of defence, with the Apologists of the second and third centuries, to a position of integration, with the Fathers of the later fourth century. Even so, the text is considerably more radical than some of them, from early on, wished it to be. This shows in the way the Christian writers took up its main topics: the condemnation of technology, which is so prominent, was only rarely followed up. Justin expands the text into a story of how paganism with idolatry and sacrifice came about as a consequence of what the Fallen Angels had brought: besides identifying magic and divination with 'unclean pagan practices', he takes up a clue in *1 Enoch* 19. 1, where it is stated that the angels 'made men unclean and will lead them astray so that they sacrifice to demons as gods'.[12] The Pseudo-Clementine *Homily 8* concurs, starting with a list which is very close to the one in Syncellus and the Ethiopic text, but then focusing on precious metals and female finery, and giving the story a quaint twist: through their intercourse with human women, the Fallen Angels lost their ability to regain their angelic form, which had so impressed the women; in order not to lose their favours, the Angels compensated the women with luxurious finery.[13] Tertullian uses the story twice in order to curb female behaviour—first in his treatise about 'The Adorning of Women' (about 200 CE), then later in 'On the Veiling of Virgins'.[14] Other Christians, far from rejecting key elements of their contemporary civilization, used the Enoch story in order to explain and condemn magic and divination alone as the gift of the 'angeli refugae',[15] rituals which they, together with the Christian

---

[12] *Apol.* 2. 161.

[13] Ps.-Clem. *Hom.* 8. 12–18. Pagan worship resulted later from the worship of the giants born to the Angels by the women.

[14] Tert. *Cult. fem.* 1. 2; *Virg. vel.* 7.

[15] Origen, *in Numeros hom.* 13: 'magorum ministri angeli sunt refugae et spiritus maligni et daemonia immunda'; Tert. *Idol.* 9 (astrology); Euseb. *Praep. ev.* 7. 8. 16: γοητείας καὶ τῆς ἄλλης κακοτρόπου μαγγανείας ἐπιτεχνήματα. Iordan. *Get.* 121 f. even makes the Huns the children of the Fallen Angels and 'magae mulieres'. See Maenchen-Helfen (1944/5), esp. 245–8.

emperors, assailed vehemently. Thus, the (ultra-)orthodox rejection of the dominating Graeco-Roman culture from outside was
toned down by the Christians, who selected details which fitted
their moralistic and anti-pagan rather than anti-technical aims—
they were very soon on their way to integration into the Graeco-
Roman world.

   Inside that world, there existed a debate on those same issues,
and it made use of mythical expressions. Several items in the
Enoch story have close and good Greek or Roman parallels,
especially the linking of iron and gold, of weaponry and jewellery
as the reason for moral subversion, and the combination of
metallurgy and sorcery.[16]

3

Dyeing (*bapheia*) and metallurgy had been singled out for censure
by pagan moralists as well. In *Elegy* 1. 10, Tibullus curses whoever invented the art of making iron weapons, or the gold which
perverted this invention into a cause for all human unhappiness.[17]
To Ovid, the mining of iron and gold ('nocens ferrum ferroque
nocentius aurum', 'baneful iron, and gold more baneful than
iron') is the ultimate violation of earth, one of the evil achievements of Iron Mankind, together with the use of poison:
pharmaka and *metalla*.[18] Virgil's naturally ('sponte sua') red, yellow,
and purple sheep of *Eclogue* 4 are a sign that Nature benignly
acknowledges man's need for luxury and produces the luxury
goods themselves, thus preventing man's transgression on to her
rights: it is an ingenious way of solving the problem of
Kulturkritik without a radical denunciation of luxury.[19] In any
event, all three Romans purport to distance themselves from
contemporary culture—Virgil and Tibullus in a utopian vein
which acquires its seriousness from the sombre background of the
Civil Wars which both had just lived through, Ovid in a masterly
intertextual play with Hesiod. Like Enoch, Virgil and Ovid state
their case in the medium of *fabula*, of myth, referring to the

---

[16] This does not mean that I follow the thesis of Nickelsburg (1977) of a purely Greek
origin of these details; the eastern Mediterranean literary Koine is too complex for
simplistic derivations.
[17] Tib. 1. 10. 1–16. For full discussion, see Graf (1996).
[18] Ov. *Met.* 1. 138 ff.   [19] Verg. *Ecl.* 4. 42 ff.

Hesiodic tradition (in Ovid's case), to the Sibylline prophecies (in Virgil's). In the background there might be some Hellenistic theory;[20] but it is difficult to tell whose it was and what the intentions of its author were.

Tibullus in his turn draws on another tradition, that of the *prōtos heuretēs*.[21] Catalogues of these 'first finders' (like the ones in Pliny or Diogenes Laertius) mix categories: gods and heroes stand side by side with what we would call historical figures. Their categories are not ours, or rather, some discoveries (the first prediction of a solar eclipse, or the first map of the earth and sea[22]) are more recent than others; the preponderance of divine or heroic discoverers, furthermore, shows a distressing lack of interest in human inventiveness.[23] As to metallurgy, Pliny gives a long list which draws partly upon Aristotle and Theophrastus, but also upon Hesiod.[24] The only figure who sounds historical is a certain Midacritus, who first imported lead from the Tin Islands: to judge from his name, he might be an East Greek trader of the Archaic age, mentioned in some logographic account. All the rest—the discovery of gold, silver, and iron, and of the blending of bronze—is ascribed either to shadowy figures (the blending of bronze either to a Phrygian Delas or a Lydian Scythes[25]) or to outright mythical ones, from Helios (one of the discoverers of gold) and the Cyclopes (inventors of the working of bronze and iron) to Cadmus the Phoenician (another discoverer of gold).[26]

But foremost among the discoverers of metals and inventors of metalworking, especially of iron, are the Dactyls or the Telchines. Pliny, in his catalogue, refers to Hesiod for the Idaean Dactyls, who discovered iron in Crete.[27] From the same Archaic epoch dates the passage in the epic poem *Phoronis* which describes the Dactyls—'the wizards from Phrygian Ida, men of the wilderness, Celmis, great Damnameneus and mighty Acmon, well-talented

[20] See, for Ovid, Spoerri (1959).
[21] Essential: Kleingünther (1933); Thraede (1962).
[22] Eclipse predicted by Thales, Diog. Laert. 1. 23; map invented by Anaximander, Diog. Laert. 2. 2.
[23] G. E. R. Lloyd (1987), 51–2.
[24] Plin. *HN* 7. 197, after Arist. fr. 602 Rose; Hes. fr. 282 Merkelbach-West.
[25] Clem. *Strom.* 1. 16. 75 (and, following him, Euseb. *Praep. ev.* 10. 6. 5) calls Delas an Idaean Dactyl and refers the tradition about Scythes to Hesiod.
[26] Plin. *HN* 7. 197.
[27] Plin. *HN* 7. 197; Hes. fr. 282 Περὶ τῶν Ἰδαίων Δακτύλων.

servants of Adrasteia of the Mountains, who were the first to find, with the skills of Hephaestus, in the fiery valleys the blue-coloured iron, to carry it into fire, and to work a marvellous deed'.[28] Other sources—Sophocles, Pherecydes, Hellanicus, the Marmor Parium—agree.[29] The only difference to be found is between the *Phoronis*, where the Dactyls belong to Phrygian Ida, and Hesiod, where it is its Cretan namesake.

Thus not only do the Dactyls combine the crafts of blacksmiths and wizards, but they are also regularly servants of one of the forms of the Great Goddess—either Cretan Rhea or Phrygian Cybele, the Lady of the Mountain.[30] From a fragment of Sophocles' satyr-play *Kōphoi* ('The Dullards') we get a glimpse of a relevant narrative: Rhea arrived in Crete, looking for a place to hide with her baby, and the Dactyls offered her shelter, all but Celmis. Here, the text ends: the inhospitable brother must have been punished, and, since in this text he stands for the hardest iron, he was presumably turned into this substance which corresponded to his innermost disposition, in a mode of metamorphosis often adopted by Ovid.[31] The story makes use of known patterns: cultural invention and mythical arrivals often go together, and perhaps the Mother brought mankind iron, as Demeter brought cereals, and Dionysus wine.[32] The accounts which replace the Dactyls by the Telchines agree in the other details: the Telchines too were wizards and discoverers of iron and iron-working;[33] a late account has their names as Chrusos ('Gold'), Arguros ('Silver'), and Chalkos ('Bronze').[34]

The Dactyls or Telchines (or even, though rarely, the Curetes) as the inventors of metallurgy (or iron-working) stand out from the rest of the 'finders'-catalogues in two respects. First, with the exception of the Cyclopes, with whom they share the iron-

---

[28] *Phoronis* fr. 2 *PEG* = schol. Ap. Rh. 1. 1126/31b. It is, incidentally, the first mention of that enigmatic figure, the *goēs* ('wizard'); see Johnston (forthcoming).

[29] The first three in schol. Ap. Rh. 1. 1129 (= Pherecyd. *FGrHist* 3 F 47; Hellanic. *FGrHist* 4 F 89; Soph. fr. 364 *TrGF*); Marmor Parium, *FGrHist* 239, 11; see also Strab. 10. 3. 22, p. 473 C (including ref. to Soph. fr. 366 *TrGF*).

[30] Her Phrygian title is *matar kubeleija*: Brixhe (1979). The same tradition is in Strab. 10. 3. 22, p. 473 C.

[31] Zenob. 4. 80 (= Soph. fr. 365 *TrGF*).

[32] See Flückiger-Guggenheim (1984).

[33] Diod. Sic. 5. 55. 1–3.

[34] Eustath. *ad Il.* 9. 529 (p. 772); in Nonnus (*Dion.* 14. 39 ff.) they are Scelmis, Damnameneus, and Lycus, names ordinarily given to the Dactyls.

working, they are the only *group* of mythical beings to figure in the catalogues. Secondly, despite the interchangeability among the groups, the tradition which combines metalworking, sorcery, and the Mother is surprisingly stable, from the Archaic *Phoronis* to Nonnus and the Byzantines.

This stability has called for explanations; not all have been convincing. R. F. Forbes, the learned author of the invaluable *Studies in Ancient Technology*, believed that '[t]he legends of the Telchines and the Dactyloi . . . probably belong to these ancient mining centres in Phrygia and Lycia', while the parallel Cretan localization must be 'untrue': this argument is self-defeating, even if one generously allows for the shifting of the actual iron-mines in Bithynia and Pontus to Phrygia and Lycia.[35] Others are less euhemeristic and prefer to talk about 'ancient (presumably Phrygian) traditions';[36] but this still does not explain much. The combination of metalworker and sorcerer stimulated other explanations. It has ethnographic parallels, as Georges Dumézil and Mircea Eliade pointed out—parallels that seem to reflect the social position of blacksmiths in Archaic societies as marginal beings who retain a specialist wisdom to which outsiders had no access.[37] And the association of mythical blacksmiths with the Great Mother might point to ritual realities: in Mycenaean Pylos, it was one of the Potniai who presided over blacksmiths; in Archaic Sardis, the goldsmiths worked in a precinct of Meter-Cybele; in Archaic Cyprus, another goddess protected the bronzesmiths.[38] The *Phoronis* might thus hint at ritual and professional realities in Archaic Greece.

But one has to be more careful than that. Whether or not these realities existed in the Archaic age of Greece, they were certainly no longer actual in the society of Classical and later Greece and Rome. Lest we should believe in survivals, it must be stressed that Archaic social facts do not explain the surprising stability of the tradition. Not to mention the other aspect of this stability: the

[35] Forbes (1964), 183, cf. 257–9.
[36] Thraede (1962), 1197.
[37] Dumézil (1948), 208–46; Eliade (1977); see also J.-P. Vernant, 'Work and Nature in Ancient Greece', in Vernant (1983), 248–70, esp. 255.
[38] Pylos: PY Jn 431, ka-ke-we po-ti-ni-ja-we-jo = χαλκέϝες ποτνι-άρϝειοι, for which see A. Hurst, *Atti e memorie del 1° Congresso Internazionale di Micenologia* (Rome, 1968), ii. 1015. Sardis: Gusmani (1969); A. Ramage in Hanfmann and Waldbaum (1970), 16 f., 20.

326 Fritz Graf

combination of sorcery and metalworking (iron, gold, silver) turns up in the latest stratum of Enoch as well. Besides, the 'finders'-catalogues do not talk about miners and blacksmiths; they talk rather about the discovery of iron (*ferrum* in Pliny) and of its technology ('ferri fabricam'): the world of Archaic blacksmiths does not concern them.[39] Instead, they offer a discourse on iron technology and its place in their own culture. Iron, its mining, smelting, and working, have to do with the geographical and social margins of the Greek or Roman world: iron comes from abroad, from Crete or Phrygia (in fact, it comes from the south-eastern shore of the Black Sea and from Etruria), and its discoverers are beings of mountains and wilderness. As sorcerers, they are marginal beings of ambivalent power: according to Pherecydes, some Dactyls practise magical binding, others loosen it; some of Enoch's Angels bring incantations, others the means to undo them.[40] The protectress of iron is the ambivalent deity who is the 'Mother of the Gods', a divinity at the root of the present order of things, and who protects those foreign, ecstatic, ambivalent, and marginal worshippers of hers, the Galli and Metragyrtae.

Ambivalent power is what characterizes iron, and not only in Tibullus. 'Iron is an excellent or a detrimental instrument for human life, according to the use we put it to,' says Pliny;[41] in his account, 'medicina metallica' is more important than iron weapons. The feeling is widespread, and even the Qur'ān expresses it;[42] Diodorus repeats it for gold.[43] In his account of the Iron Age, Ovid takes sides in this ambiguity, focusing on its destructive aspects, and condemning them—as does the unknown author of the latest stratum of Enoch.

Without doubt, all this is not *logos* supplanting *muthos*. Rather, both forms of discourse coexisted during the whole of

[39] See Vernant (1983) (cf. n. 37 above).
[40] Pherecyd. *FGrHist* 3 F 47: ἀριστεροὶ μέν, ὥς φησι Φερεκύδης, οἱ γόητες αὐτῶν [sc. Dactylorum], οἱ δὲ ἀναλύοντες δεξιοί. I Enoch 8. 3: Semiazas taught ἐπαοιδὰς καὶ ῥιζοτομίας, Armarus ἐπαοιδῶν λυτήριον. For ἀναλύειν (and λυτήριον) as technical terms, see Magnes, *Ludoi* fr. 4 PCG (= Poll. 7. 188: ὀνειροκρίταισιν, ἀναλύταις); *Suda* α 1950 = Phot. α 1548: ἀναλυθῆναι· τὸ καθαρμῷ τινι χρήσασθαι φαρμάκων (= Men. *Herōs* fr. 5 Sandbach); Hesych. π 1722: περικαθαίρων· ἀναλύων τὸν πεφαρμακευμένον, ἢ τὸν γεγοητευμένον.
[41] Plin. *HN* 34. 138.
[42] Sūra 57. 25, cited in Forbes (1964), 175.
[43] Diod. Sic. 3. 14. 5.

antiquity—at least, it seems safe to assume that, together with our stories about the Dactyls and the Fallen Angels, a technical discourse on metallurgy continued as well. The 'finders'-literature retained its mythical information because that information provided concrete personal names (and obviously did not clash with the ideas which its authors, from Sophocles to Gellius and beyond, had about what iron meant to society); the Roman poets clung to it because it gave their criticism a voice which carried conviction, at least inside the poets' world; the Jewish sects who relied on Enoch used it as a voice of real authority. Myth, with its appeal to tradition, offered itself as a potent vehicle of cultural criticism and dissent.

But there is a further dimension to the question of why metallurgy was singled out. One might think it had something to do with the traces of irrationality contained in this technology: the process of smelting iron ore depends on mastering tricky fire. One would thus arrive at an explanatory model akin to the one Malinowski proposed for Trobriand magic: magic concerns only those technical processes whose outcome is not entirely foreseeable.[44] But the myths about iron technology do not fit into this pattern. On the one hand, another craft which has to rely on tricky fire is pottery, and here the irrationality is expressed: among the remains of late Archaic poetry, we even possess an imprecation to the demons of the kiln—but the inventors are non-marginal Greeks like the Athenian Coroebus.[45] On the other hand, iron (or metals in general) goes together with the entirely rational technology of dyeing wool, both in Enoch and in Virgil; other sources ascribe the dyeing of wool to the Lydians,[46] the dyeing of hair (perhaps not surprisingly) to the equally foreign and ambivalent Medea.[47] The ambivalence of iron technology has nothing to do with the use of fire.

Malinowski is thus of no avail. Another solution imposes itself. These technologies all transform and radically change natural substances (as their direct continuation, alchemy, claimed to do):

[44] Malinowski (1925); Malinowski (1935), but see S. J. Tambiah, 'The Magical Power of Words', in Tambiah (1985), 17–59.

[45] Plin. *HN* 7. 198: 'figlinas Coroebus Atheniensis, in iis orbem Anacharsis Scythes, ut alii Hyperbius Corinthius.' See Critias 88 [81] B 2, 12 ff. (DK = West).

[46] Plin. *HN* 7. 196: 'inficere lanas Sardibus Lydi (invenerunt)'; cf. Hyg. *Fab.* 274. 17: 'Lydi Sardibus lanam infecerunt.'

[47] Clem. *Strom.* 1. 16. 76.

dull stones into shining metal, white wool (or hair) into luscious purple or flamboyant blond. Crafts like these confound the categories in terms of which the sensible world is ordered, the homely oppositions of stone vs. metal, white vs. coloured, old age vs. youth. By doing so, they generate anxiety, which in turn calls for rejection. It is no accident that the technology which in the contemporary world provokes a comparable emotional response has just the same function: genetic engineering promises to create new plants and animals, beyond the secure network of our categories, even confounding the elementary dichotomy of natural and artificial. Or can anyone securely tell whether a genetically manipulated tomato is a natural fruit or a work of art?

Bibliography

AALDERS, G. J. D., H. WZN. (1986), *Historische periodisering in de oudheid* (Mededelingen der koninkl. Nederlandse Akad. van Wetenschappen, Afdeling Letterkunde, NR 49. 6; Amsterdam).

ADAM, J. (1963), *The Republic of Plato*, 2nd edn. (Cambridge).

ALCOFF, L., and POTTER, E. (1993) (eds.), *Feminist Epistemologies* (London).

AMES, R. T. (1983), *The Art of Rulership: A Study in Ancient Chinese Political Thought* (Honolulu).

ANNAS, J. (1981), *An Introduction to Plato's Republic* (Oxford).

—— (1982), 'Plato's Myths of Judgement', *Phronesis*, 27: 119–43.

APPADURAI, A. (1986), 'Commodities and the Politics of Value' in A. Appadurai (ed.), *The Social Life of Things: Commodities in Cultural Perspective* (Cambridge), 3–63.

ASSMANN, J. (1977), 'Die Verborgenheit des Mythos in Ägypten', *Göttinger Miszellen*, 25: 7–43.

AUERBACH, E. (1953), *Mimesis: The Representation of Reality in Western Literature* (Princeton; orig. *Mimesis: Dargestellte Wirklichkeit in der abendländischen Literatur* (Berne, 1946)).

AUSTIN, C. (1973), *Comicorum graecorum fragmenta in papyris reperta* (Berlin).

BADIAN, E. (1981), 'The Deification of Alexander the Great', in H. J. Dell (ed.), *Ancient Macedonian Studies in Honor of Charles F. Edson* (Institute for Balkan Studies, 158; Thessaloniki), 27–71.

—— (1996), 'Alexander the Great between Two Thrones and Heaven: Variations on an Old Theme', in A. Small (ed.), *Subject and Ruler: The Cult of the Ruling Power in Classical Antiquity* (*JRA* Suppl. 17; Ann Arbor), 11–26.

BALTES, M. (1976–8), *Die Weltentstehung des platonischen Timaios nach den antiken Interpreten*, i–ii (Leiden).

BARNES, J. (1979), *The Presocratic Philosophers*, i: *Thales to Zeno* (London).

—— (1980), 'Aristotle and the Methods of Ethics', *RIPh* 34, nos. 131–4: 490–511.

—— (1987), *Early Greek Philosophy* (Harmondsworth).

BAUDY, G. J. (1983), 'Hierarchie, oder, die Verteilung des Fleisches', in B. Gladigow and H. G. Kippenberg (eds.), *Neue Ansätze in der Religionswissenschaft* (Munich), 131–74.

BAUMGARTEN, A. I. (1981), *The 'Phoenician History' of Philo of Byblos: A Commentary* (Leiden).

BÄUMLER, A. (1926), *Das mythische Weltalter: Bachofens romantische Deutung des Altertums* (Munich).

BELOCH, K. J. (1927), *Griechische Geschichte*, iv. 2, 2nd edn. (Berlin).

BENJAMIN, W. (1970), *Illuminations* (London).

BENVENISTE, E. (1966), *Problèmes de linguistique générale* (Paris).

BERTHIAUME, G. (1982), *Les Rôles du mágeiros: Étude sur la boucherie, la cuisine et le sacrifice dans la Grèce ancienne* (Leiden).

BICKEL, S. (1994), *La Cosmogonie égyptienne avant le Nouvel Empire* (Fribourg).

BIDERMAN, S., and SCHARFSTEIN, B.-A. (1989), *Rationality in Question: On Eastern and Western Views of Rationality* (Leiden).

BILDE, P., ENGBERG-PEDERSEN, T., HANNESTAD, L., and ZAHLE, J. (1997) (eds.), *Conventional Values of the Hellenistic Greeks* (Aarhus).

BINGEN, J., CAMBIER, G., and NACHTERGAEL, G. (1975) (eds.), *Le Monde grec: Pensée, littérature, histoire, documents. Hommages à Claire Préaux* (Brussels).

BIRRELL, A. (1993), *Chinese Mythology: An Introduction* (Baltimore).

—— (1993–4), 'Studies on Chinese Myth Since 1970: An Appraisal, Part 1', *HR* 33: 380–93.

—— (1994–5), 'Studies on Chinese Myth Since 1970: An Appraisal, Part 2', *HR* 34: 70–94.

BISCHOF, N. (1996), *Das Kraftfeld der Mythen* (Munich).

BLACK, M. (1970) (ed.), *Apocalypsis Henochi Graece* (Pseudepigrapha Veteris Testamenti Graece, 3; Leiden).

BLUMENBERG, H. (1979), *Arbeit am Mythos* (Frankfurt a. M.).

BODDE, D. (1961), 'Myths in Ancient China', in S. N. Kramer (ed.), *Mythologies of the Ancient World* (New York), 369–408.

BOEDEKER, D. (1987) (ed.), *Herodotus and the Invention of History* (= *Arethusa*, 20; Buffalo).

—— and SIDER, D. (1996) (eds.), *The New Simonides* (= *Arethusa*, 29/2; Baltimore).

BOLTZ, W. G. (1981), 'Kung Kung and the Flood: Reverse Euhemerism in the *Yao Tien*', *T'oung Pao*, 67: 141–53.

BONITZ, H. (1870), *Index Aristotelicus* (Berlin).

BONNECHERE, P. (1993), 'Les Indices archéologiques du sacrifice humain grec en question: Compléments à une publication récente', *Kernos*, 6: 23–55.

—— (1994), *Le Sacrifice humain en Grèce ancienne* (*Kernos*, Suppl. 3; Athens).

——(1995), 'Le Sacrifice humain en Grèce ancienne: Bilans et perspectives', *CH* 15: 5–25.

BOREL, M.-J., GRIZE, J.-B., and MIÉVILLE, D. (1983), *Essai de logique naturelle* (Berne).

BORGEAUD, P. (1988), *The Cult of Pan in Ancient Greece* (Chicago; orig. *Recherches sur le dieu Pan* (Rome, 1979)).

BORGOLTE, M. (1997), 'Selbstverständnis und "Mentalitäten": Mittelalterliche Menschen im Verständnis moderner Historiker', *AKG* 79: 189–210.

BOTTÉRO, J. (1985), *Mythes et rites de Babylone* (Paris).

——(1987), *Mésopotamie: L'Écriture, la raison et les dieux* (Paris).

——and KRAMER, S. N. (1989), *Lorsque les dieux faisaient l' homme: Mythologie mésopotamienne* (Paris).

BÖTTRICH, C. (1995), *Das slavische Henochbuch* (Jüdische Schriften aus hellenistisch-römischer Zeit, V: Apokalypsen, 7; Gütersloh).

BOULOGNE, J. (1996), 'Pensée scientifique et pensée mythique en Grèce ancienne', *LEC* 64: 213–26.

BOURDIEU, P. (1977), *Outline of a Theory of Practice* (Cambridge; orig. *Esquisse d'une théorie de la pratique* (Geneva, 1972)).

BOUVIER, D. (1997), 'Mythe ou histoire: Le Choix de Platon', in M. Guglielmo and G. F. Gianotti (eds.), *Filosofia, storia, immaginario mitologico* (Alessandria), 41–64.

BOZONNET, J.-P. (1992), *Des monts et des mythes: L'Imaginaire social de la montagne* (Grenoble).

BRANDT, M. (1986), *Alpes valaisannes III: Du Col Collon au Theodulpass* (Lausanne).

BREGLIA PULCI DORIA, L. (1994), 'Le sirene di Pitagora', *AION (filol.)* 16: 55–77.

BRELICH, A. (1958), *Gli eroi greci* (Rome).

BREMMER, J. N. (1983), 'Scapegoat Rituals in Ancient Greece', *HSCP* 87: 299–320.

——(1987) (ed.), *Interpretations of Greek Mythology* (London).

——(1992), 'Symbols of Marginality from Early Pythagoreans to Late Antique Monks', *G&R* 39: 205–14.

——(1994), *Greek Religion* (Oxford).

——(1995), 'Religious Secrets and Secrecy in Classical Greece', in H. G. Kippenberg and G. G. Stroumsa (eds.), *Secrecy and Concealment: Studies in the History of Mediterranean and Near Eastern Religions* (Leiden), 61–78.

——(1997), 'Jokes, Jokers and Jokebooks in Ancient Greek Culture', in J. N. Bremmer and H. Roodenburg (eds.), *A Cultural History of Humour* (Cambridge), 11–28.

——and HORSFALL, N. M. (1987), *Roman Myth and Mythography* (*BICS*, Suppl. 52; London).

BRISSON, L. (1992/1995), 'Le Corps "dionysiaque"', in: ΣΟΦΙΗΣ ΜΑΙΗΤΟΡΕΣ: *Hommage à Jean Pépin* (Paris, 1992), 481–99 (= Brisson (1995), no. VII; same pagination).

——(1994), *Platon: Les Mots et les mythes*, 2nd edn. (Paris).

——(1995), *Orphée et l'orphisme dans l'antiquité gréco-romaine* (Aldershot).

——(1996), *Introduction à la philosophie du mythe*, i: *Sauver les mythes* (Paris).

BRIXHE, C. (1979), 'Le Nom de Cybèle', *Die Sprache*, 25: 40–5.

BROOKS, E. B. (1993–), Papers of the Warring States Working Group (University of Massachusetts, Amherst, privately circulated).

BROWN, W. L. (1960), *The Etruscan Lion* (Oxford).

BRUBAKER, R. (1984), *The Limits of Rationality: An Essay on the Social and Moral Thought of Max Weber* (London).

BRUIT ZAIDMAN, L., and SCHMITT PANTEL, P. (1992), *Religion in the Ancient Greek City* (Cambridge; orig. *La Religion grecque* (Paris, 1989)).

BRULÉ, P. (1987), *La Fille d'Athènes. La Religion des filles à Athènes à l'époque classique: Mythes, cultes et société* (Paris).

BRUNSCHWIG, J., and LLOYD, G. E. R. (1996) (eds.), *Le Savoir grec* (Paris).

BULLOCH, A. W., GRUEN, E. S., LONG, A. A., and STEWART, A. (1994) (eds.), *Images and Ideologies: Self-Definition in the Hellenistic World* (Berkeley and Los Angeles).

BURKERT, W. (1963), 'Iranisches bei Anaximandros', *RhM* 106: 97–134.

——(1972), *Lore and Science in Ancient Pythagoreanism* (Cambridge, Mass.; orig. *Weisheit und Wissenschaft: Studien zu Pythagoras, Philolaos und Platon* (Nuremberg, 1962)).

——(1979), *Structure and History in Greek Mythology and Ritual* (Berkeley and Los Angeles).

——(1980), 'Griechische Mythologie und die Geistesgeschichte der Moderne', in W. den Boer *et al.*, *Les Études classiques aux XIXᵉ et XXᵉ siècles: Leur place dans l'histoire des idées* (Entretiens sur l'Antiquité Classique, 26; Vandœuvres-Geneva), 159–207.

——(1982), 'Craft versus Sect: The Problem of Orphics and Pythagoreans', in B. F. Meyer and E. P. Sanders (eds.), *Jewish and Christian Self-Definition*, iii: *Self-Definition in the Graeco-Roman World* (London), 1–22.

——(1985), *Greek Religion, Archaic and Classical* (Oxford; orig. *Griechische Religion der archaischen und klassischen Epoche* (Stuttgart, 1977)).

——(1987), *Ancient Mystery Cults* (Cambridge, Mass.).

——(1991), 'Homerstudien und Orient', in J. Latacz (ed.), *Zweihundert Jahre Homer-Forschung* (Colloquium Rauricum, 2; Stuttgart), 155–81.

—— (1992), *The Orientalizing Revolution: Near Eastern Influence on Greek Culture in the Early Archaic Age* (Cambridge, Mass.).

—— (1994), 'Orientalische und griechische Weltmodelle von Assur bis Anaximandros', *WSt* 107: 179–86.

—— (1996), *Creation of the Sacred: Tracks of Biology in Early Religions* (Cambridge, Mass.).

—— and HORSTMANN, A. (1984), 'Mythos, Mythologie', in J. Ritter and K. Gründer (eds.), *Historisches Wörterbuch der Philosophie*, vi (Basle), 282–318.

BURNET, J. (1911), *Plato's Phaedo, Edited with Introduction and Notes* (Oxford).

BURNYEAT, M. F. (1986), 'Good Repute', *London Review of Books*, Nov. 6: 11–12.

—— (1992), 'Utopia and Fantasy: The Practicability of Plato's Ideally Just City', in J. Hopkins and A. Savile (eds.), *Psychoanalysis, Mind and Art: Perspectives on Richard Wollheim* (Oxford), 175–87.

BUXTON, R. (1994), *Imaginary Greece: The Contexts of Mythology* (Cambridge).

CAIRNS, F. (1992), 'Theocritus, *Idyll* 26', *PCPhS* 38: 1–38.

CALAME, C. (1991*a*), '"Mythe" et "rite" en Grèce: Des catégories indigènes?', *Kernos*, 4: 179–204.

—— (1991*b*), 'Quand dire c'est faire voir: L'Évidence dans la rhétorique antique', *EL* Oct.–Dec.: 3–22.

—— (1995), *The Craft of Poetic Speech in Ancient Greece* (Ithaca, NY; orig. *Le Récit en Grèce ancienne: Énonciations et représentations de poètes* (Paris, 1986)).

—— (1996*a*), *Mythe et histoire dans l'Antiquité grecque* (Lausanne).

—— (1996*b*), *Thésée et l'imaginaire athénien*, 2nd edn. (Lausanne).

—— (1998), 'Mémoire collective et temporalités en contact: Somare et Hérodote', *Revue de l'histoire des religions*, 215: 341–67.

CALASSO, R. (1988), *Le nozze di Cadmo e Armonia* (Milan).

CANFORA, L. (1995), 'Mito e storiografia greca: Minosse, Odisseo, Eraclidi', in M. Rossi Cittadini (ed.), *Presenze classiche nelle letterature occidentali* (Perugia), 109–23.

CARPENTER, R. (1946), *Folktale, Fiction and Saga in the Homeric Epics* (Berkeley and Los Angeles).

CARPENTER, T. H., and FARAONE, C. A. (1993) (eds.), *Masks of Dionysus* (Ithaca, NY).

CARTLEDGE, P. (1993), *The Greeks: A Portrait of Self and Others* (Oxford).

CASSIRER, E. (1925), *Philosophie der symbolischen Formen*; ii: *Das mythische Denken* (Berlin).

—— (1994), *Wesen und Wirkung des Symbolbegriffs*, 8th edn. (Darmstadt).

—— (1995), *Zur Metaphysik der symbolischen Formen*, ed. J. M.

Krois = *Nachgelassene Manuskripte und Texte*, ed. J. M. Krois and
O. Schwemmer, i (Hamburg).

CÉARD, J. (1977), *La Nature et les prodiges: L'Insolite au XVIe siècle en
France* (Geneva).

CERRI, G. (1996), *Platone sociologo della comunicazione*, 2nd edn.
(Lecce).

CHANTRAINE, P. (1968–80), *Dictionnaire étymologique de la langue grecque:
Histoire des mots* (Paris).

CHIODI, S. M. (1994), 'Le concezioni dell'oltretomba presso i Sumeri',
*Atti dell'Accademia Nazionale dei Lincei: classe di scienze morali, storiche e
filologiche. Memorie*, IX 4. 5 (Rome), 359–71.

CHRYSOSTOMOU, P. (1991), "Η Θεσσαλική θεά Εν(ν)οδία. Η Φεραία
θεά" (diss. Thessaloniki).

CLAY, D. (1992), 'Plato's First Words', *YCS* 29: 113–29.

CONOPHAGOS, C. E. (1980), *Le Laurium antique et la technique grecque de
la production de l'argent* (Athens).

COOK, E. F. (1995), *The Odyssey in Athens: Myths of Cultural Origins*
(Ithaca, NY).

COULOUBARITSIS, L. (1994), *Aux Origines de la philosophie européenne: De
la pensée archaïque au néoplatonisme*, 2nd edn. (Brussels).

CRANE, G. (1996), *The Blinded Eye: Thucydides and the New Written Word*
(Lanham, Md.).

CRETTAZ, B. (1993), *La Beauté du reste: Confession d'un conservateur
de musée sur la perfection et l'enfermement de la Suisse et des Alpes*
(Geneva).

CREUZER, G. F. (1810–12), *Symbolik und Mythologie der alten Völker,
besonders der Griechen*, i–iv (Leipzig).

CROMBIE, A. C. (1979), *Augustine to Galileo*, 2nd edn. (London; orig.
pub. 1952, 2 vols; rev. edns. 1959, 1970.)

CULLEN, C. (1976), 'A Chinese Eratosthenes of the Flat Earth: A Study
of a Fragment of a Cosmology in *Huai Nan-Tzu*', *Bulletin of the School
of Oriental and African Studies* 39: 106–27.

DALLEY, S. (1989), *Myths from Mesopotamia: Creation, The Flood,
Gilgamesh, and Others* (Oxford).

DARBO-PESCHANSKI, C. (1987), *Le Discours du particulier: Essai sur
l'enquête hérodotéenne* (Paris).

DASEN, V. (1993), *Dwarfs in Ancient Egypt and Greece* (Oxford).

DAVIES, M. (1988), *Epicorum Graecorum Fragmenta* (Göttingen).

DE CERTEAU, M. (1975), *L'Écriture de l'histoire* (Paris).

DELCOURT, M. (1938), *Stérilités mystérieuses et naissances maléfiques dans
l'Antiquité classique* (Liège; repr. Paris, 1986).

DEMISCH, H. (1977), *Die Sphinx: Geschichte ihrer Darstellung von den
Anfängen bis zur Gegenwart* (Stuttgart).

DE MOOR, J. C. (1987), *An Anthology of Religious Texts from Ugarit* (Leiden).

DEN BOER, W. (1979), *Private Morality in Greece and Rome: Some Historical Aspects* (Leiden).

DETIENNE, M. (1977), *The Gardens of Adonis: Spices in Greek Mythology* (Hassocks; orig. *Les Jardins d'Adonis: La Mythologie des aromates en Grèce* (Paris, 1972)).

——(1981), *L'Invention de la mythologie* (Paris). (The Eng. trans. is not recommended.)

——(1989), *Dionysos at Large* (Cambridge, Mass.; orig. *Dionysos à ciel ouvert* (Paris, 1986)).

——(1994), *Les Maîtres de vérité en Grèce archaïque*, 2nd edn. (Paris; Eng. trans. *The Masters of Truth in Archaic Greece* (New York, 1996)).

——(1998), *Apollon: Le Bel Homicide de Delphes* (Paris).

——and VERNANT, J.-P. (1978), *Cunning Intelligence in Greek Culture and Society* (Hassocks; orig. *Les Ruses de l'intelligence: La Mètis des Grecs* (Paris, 1974)).

DE VOGEL, C. J. (1966), *Pythagoras and Early Pythagoreanism: An Interpretation of Neglected Evidence on the Philosopher Pythagoras* (Assen).

DI BENEDETTO, V. (1957), 'Teocrito, XXVI 29–30', *PP* 12: 271–4.

DICKIE, M. W. (1990), 'Talos Bewitched. Magic, Atomic Theory and Paradoxography in Apollonius, *Argonautica* 4. 1638–88', in F. Cairns and M. Heath (eds.), *Papers of the Leeds International Latin Seminar*, 6 (Leeds), 267–96.

——(1995), 'The Dionysiac Mysteries in Pella', *ZPE* 109: 81–6.

DIELS, H., and KRANZ, W. (1951–2), *Die Fragmente der Vorsokratiker*, 6th edn. (Berlin).

DIERAUER, U. (1977), *Tier und Mensch im Denken der Antike: Studien zur Tierpsychologie, Anthropologie und Ethik* (Amsterdam).

DIHLE, A. (1994), *A History of Greek Literature: From Homer to the Hellenistic Period* (London; orig. *Griechische Literaturgeschichte* (Stuttgart, 1967)).

DILLER, H., and SCHALK, F. (1972), *Studien zur Periodisierung und zum Epochebegriff*, *AAWM* 4: 139–76.

DODDS, E. R. (1951), *The Greeks and the Irrational* (Berkeley and Los Angeles).

DOUGLAS, M. (1966), *Purity and Danger* (London).

DOVER, K. J. (1988), *The Greeks and their Legacy. Collected Papers*, ii: *Prose Literature, History, Society, Transmission, Influence* (Oxford).

DOWDEN, K. (1989), *Death and the Maiden: Girls' Initiation Rites in Greek Mythology* (London).

——(1992), *The Uses of Greek Mythology* (London).

DUBOIS, L. (1996), *Inscriptions grecques dialectales d'Olbia du Pont* (Geneva).

DUMÉZIL, G. (1948), *Tarpeia: Essais de philologie comparative indo-européenne* (Paris).

——(1985), *L'Oubli de l'homme et l'honneur des dieux et autres essais: Vingt-cinq esquisses de mythologie, (51–75)* (Paris).

DUNAND, F. (1986), 'Les Associations dionysiaques au service du pouvoir lagide (IIIe s. av. J.-C.)', in *L'Association dionysiaque dans les sociétés anciennes* (Collection de l'École Française de Rome, 89; Rome), 85–104.

DUPONT-ROC, R., and LALLOT, J. (1980), *Aristote: La Poétique* (Paris).

EASTERLING, P. E., and MUIR, J. V. (1985), *Greek Religion and Society* (Cambridge).

EBERT, J. (1975), *Griechische Epigramme auf Sieger an gymnischen und hippischen Agonen* (Berlin).

EDER, W. (1995) (ed.), *Die athenische Demokratie im 4. Jahrhundert v. Chr.: Vollendung oder Verfall einer Verfassungsform?* (Stuttgart).

EDMUNDS, L. (1990) (ed.), *Approaches to Greek Myth* (Baltimore).

EHRENBERG, V. (1931), 'Athenische Hymnus auf Demetrius Poliorcetes', *Die Antike*, 7: 279–97 (trans. in Ehrenberg, *Aspects of the Ancient World: Essays and Reviews* (Oxford, 1946), 179–98).

——(1965), *Polis und Imperium: Beiträge zur Alten Geschichte* (Zürich).

EHRHARDT, E. (1986), 'The Word of the Muses (Plato, *Rep.* 8.546)', *CQ* 36/2: 407–20.

ELIADE, M. (1968), *Myth and Reality* (New York).

——(1977), *Forgerons et alchimistes*, 2nd edn. (Paris).

——*et al.* (1987) (eds.), *The Encyclopedia of Religion*, x (New York).

ERBSE, H. (1992), *Studien zum Verständnis Herodots* (Berlin).

ERNOUT, A., and MEILLET, A. (1985), *Dictionnaire étymologique de la langue latine: Histoire des mots*, 4th edn. (Paris).

ESPINAS, A. (1897), *Les Origines de la technologie* (Paris).

EUCKEN, C. (1983), *Isokrates: Seine Positionen in der Auseinandersetzung mit den zeitgenössischen Philosophen* (Berlin).

EVANS-PRITCHARD, E. E. (1965), *Theories of Primitive Religion* (Oxford).

EYBEN, E. (1980/1), 'Family Planning in Graeco-Roman Antiquity', *AncSoc* 11/12: 5–82.

FARAONE, C. A. (1992), *Talismans and Trojan Horses: Guardian Statues in Ancient Greek Myth and Ritual* (Oxford).

FARNELL, L. R. (1896), *The Cults of the Greek States*, i (Oxford).

FEHLING, D. (1989), *Herodotus and His 'Sources': Citation, Invention and Narrative Art* (Leeds).

FELDMAN, B., and RICHARDSON, R. D. (1972), *The Rise of Modern Mythology* 1680–1860 (Bloomington, Ind.).

FERRARI, G. R. F. (1987), *Listening to the Cicadas: A Study of Plato's Phaedrus* (Cambridge).

FEYERABEND, P. (1975), *Against Method: Outline of an Anarchic Theory of Knowledge* (London).

—— (1987), *Farewell to Reason* (London).

FINLEY, M. I. (1965), 'Myth, Memory and History', *History and Theory*, 4: 281–302 (repr. with revisions in Finley (1975), 11–33).

—— (1975), *The Use and Abuse of History* (London).

—— (1985), *Ancient History: Evidence and Models* (London).

FISCHER, J.-L. (1991), *Monstres: Histoire du corps et de ses défauts* (Paris).

FLACELIÈRE, R. (1937), *Les Aitoliens à Delphes: Contribution à l'histoire de la Grèce centrale au IIIe siècle av. J.-C.* (Paris).

FLÜCKIGER-GUGGENHEIM, D. (1984), *Göttliche Gäste: Die Einkehr von Göttern und Heroen in der griechischen Mythologie* (Berne).

FONTENROSE, J. (1968), 'The Hero as Athlete', *CSCA* 1: 73–104.

—— (1978), *The Delphic Oracle: Its Responses and Operations, with a Catalogue of Responses* (Berkeley and Los Angeles).

FORBES, R. F. (1964), *Studies in Ancient Technology*, ix (Leiden).

FOUCAULT, M. (1966), *Les Mots et les choses: Une archéologie des sciences humaines* (Paris).

FOWLER, R. L. (1996), 'Herodotos and his Contemporaries', *JHS* 116: 62–87.

FRASER, P. M. (1972), *Ptolemaic Alexandria* (Oxford).

FREDE, M., and STRIKER, G. (1996) (eds.), *Rationality in Greek Thought* (Oxford).

FREL, J. (1994), 'Una nuova laminella "orfica"', *Eirene*, 30: 183–4.

FRIEDMAN, J. B. (1981), *The Monstrous Races in Medieval Art and Thought* (Cambridge).

FUHRMANN, M. (1971) (ed.), *Terror und Spiel: Probleme der Mythenrezeption* (Poetik und Hermeneutik, 4; Munich).

FUSILLO, M. (1986), '"Mythos" aristotelico e "récit" narratologico', *Strumenti critici* NS 1: 381–92.

GANTZ, T. (1993), *Early Greek Myth: A Guide to Literary and Artistic Sources* (Baltimore).

GEERTZ, C. (1973), *The Interpretation of Cultures: Selected Essays* (New York).

GEFFCKEN, J. (1912), 'Euhemerism', in J. Hastings (ed.), *Encyclopaedia of Religion and Ethics* (Edinburgh) v. 572–3.

GENTILI, B., and CERRI, G. (1983), *Storia e biografia nel pensiero antico* (Rome).

GERMAIN, L. R. F. (1995), 'L'Exposition des enfants nouveau-nés dans la Grèce ancienne: Aspects sociologiques', *Recueils Jean Bodin*, 35: 211–46.

GERNET, L. (1917), *Recherches sur le développement de la pensée juridique et morale en Grèce. (Étude sémantique)* (Paris).

——(1924), 'Sur l'exécution capitale: A propos d'un ouvrage récent', *REG* 37: 261–93.

——(1968), *Anthropologie de la Grèce antique* (Paris; Eng. trans. Baltimore, 1981).

——(1983), *Les Grecs sans miracle: Textes réunis et présentés par Riccardo di Donato* (Paris).

GIANGIULIO, M. (1989), *Ricerche su Crotone arcaica* (Pisa).

——(1994), 'Sapienza pitagorica e religiosità apollinea: Tra cultura della città e orizzonti panellenici', *AION (filol.)* 16: 9–27.

GILL, C. (1993), 'Plato on Falsehood—Not Fiction', in C. Gill and T. P. Wiseman (1993), 38–87.

——and WISEMAN, T. P. (1993) (eds.), *Lies and Fiction in the Ancient World* (Exeter).

GIRARDOT, N. J. (1975–6), 'The Problem of Creation Mythology in the Study of Chinese Religion', *HR* 15: 289–318.

GLASER, O. (1937), 'Skythenkönige als Wächter beim heiligen Golde (Herodot IV. 7)', *ARW* 34: 277–93.

GOODY, J. (1977), *The Domestication of the Savage Mind* (Cambridge).

GORDON, R. L. (1981) (ed.), *Myth, Religion and Society: Structuralist Essays by M. Detienne, L. Gernet, J.-P. Vernant and P. Vidal-Naquet; With an Introduction by R. G. A. Buxton* (Cambridge).

GOULD, J. (1989), *Herodotus* (London).

——(unpublished), '. . . and tell sad stories of the death of kings', Corbett Lecture, Cambridge, May 1991.

GOW, A. S. F. (1952), *Theocritus*, 2nd edn. (Cambridge).

GRAF, F. (1985), *Nordionische Kulte: Religionsgeschichtliche und epigraphische Untersuchungen zu den Kulten von Chios, Erythrai, Klazomenai und Phokaia* (Bibliotheca Helvetica Romana, 21; Rome).

——(1993*a*), *Greek Mythology: An Introduction* (Baltimore; orig. *Griechische Mythologie: Eine Einführung* (Munich, 1985)).

——(1993*b*) (ed.), *Mythos in mythenloser Gesellschaft: Das Paradigma Roms* (Colloquium Rauricum, 3; Stuttgart).

——(1996), 'Mythos, Natur und Technik in den frühen Hochkulturen', in K. Gloy (ed.), *Natur- und Technikbegriffe: Historische und systematische Aspekte: Von der Antike bis zur ökologischen Krise, von der Physik bis zur Ästhetik* (Abhandlungen zur Philosophie, Psychologie und Pädagogik, 242; Bonn), 1–18.

——(1998) (ed.), *Ansichten griechischer Rituale: Geburtstags-Symposium für Walter Burkert* (Stuttgart).

GRAHAM, A. C. (1981), *Chuang-tzu: The Seven Inner Chapters and Other Writings from the Book Chuang-tzu* (London).

——(1989), *Disputers of the Tao: Philosophical Argument in Ancient China* (La Salle, Ill.).

GRAVES, R. (1957), *The Greek Myths* (Harmondsworth).

GREEN, P. (1970), *The Year of Salamis, 480–479 B.C.* (London).

GREGORY, C. A. (1982), *Gifts and Commodities* (London).

GRIFFITHS, J. G. (1960), *The Conflict of Horus and Seth from Egyptian and Classical Sources: A Study in Ancient Mythology* (Liverpool).

GRIZE, J. B. (1990), *Logique et langage* (Paris).

GRMEK, M. D. (1983), *Les Maladies à l'aube de la civilisation occidentale* (Paris).

GROSS, P. R., LEVITT, N., and LEWIS, M. W. (1997) (eds.), *The Flight from Science and Reason* (Baltimore).

GRUPPE, O. (1921), *Geschichte der klassischen Mythologie und Religionsgeschichte während des Mittelalters im Abendland und während der Neuzeit* (= W. H. Roscher, *Ausführliches Lexikon der griechischen und römischen Mythologie*, Suppl. 4; Leipzig).

GUNKEL, H. (1895), *Schöpfung und Chaos in Urzeit und Endzeit: Eine religionsgeschichtliche Untersuchung über Gen. 1 und Ap. Joh. 12* (Göttingen).

GUSMANI, M. R. (1969), 'Der lydische Name der Kybele', *Kadmos*, 8: 158–61.

GUTHRIE, W. K. C. (1953), *'Myth and Reason'. Oration Delivered at the London School of Economics and Political Science on Friday, 12 December, 1952* (London).

——(1962–81), *A History of Greek Philosophy*, 6 vols. (Cambridge).

HABICHT, C. (1970), *Gottmenschentum und griechische Städte*, 2nd edn. (Munich).

——(1995), *Athen: Die Geschichte der Stadt in hellenistischer Zeit* (Munich).

HALL, E. (1989), *Inventing the Barbarian: Greek Self-Definition through Tragedy* (Oxford).

HALLIWELL, S. (1988), *Plato: Republic 10* (Warminster).

HANFMANN, G. M. A., and WALDBAUM, J. C. (1970), 'The Eleventh and Twelfth Campaigns at Sardis (1968, 1969)', *BASO* 199: 7–58.

HANSEN, W. (1995), 'The Theft of the Thunderweapon: A Greek Myth in its International Context', *C&M* 46: 5–24.

HANSON, P. D. (1977), 'Rebellion in Heaven, Azazel, and the Euhemeristic Heroes in 1 Enoch 6–11', *JBL* 96: 195–233.

HARDER, A. (1985), *Euripides' Kresphontes and Archelaos: Introduction, Text and Commentary* (Leiden).

HARRISON, J. E. (1890), *Mythology and Monuments of Ancient Athens* (London).
——(1903), *Prolegomena to the Study of Greek Religion* (Cambridge).
——(1912), *Themis: A Study of the Social Origins of Greek Religion* (Cambridge).
——(1921), *Epilegomena to the Study of Greek Religion* (Cambridge).
HARTOG, F. (1988), *The Mirror of Herodotus: The Representation of the Other in the Writing of History* (Berkeley and Los Angeles; orig. *Le Miroir d'Hérodote: Essai sur la représentation de l'autre*, Paris, 1980; rev. edn. 1991).
——(1990), 'Ecritures, généalogies, archives, histoires en Grèce ancienne', in M.-M. Mactoux and E. Geny (eds.), *Mélanges Pierre Lévêque, v: Anthropologie et société* (Paris), 177–88.
HEATH, T. L. (1926), *The Thirteen Books of Euclid's Elements* (Cambridge).
HEDRICK, C. W., JR. (1994), 'Writing, Reading, and Democracy', in R. Osborne and S. Hornblower (eds.), *Ritual, Finance, Politics: Athenian Democratic Accounts Presented to David Lewis* (Oxford), 157–74.
HEIDEL, A. (1951), *The Babylonian Genesis: The Story of the Creation*, 2nd edn. (Chicago).
HENRICHS, A. (1975*a*), 'Philodems De Pietate als mythographische Quelle', *Cronache Ercolanesi*, 5: 5–38.
——(1975*b*), 'Two Doxographical Notes: Democritus and Prodicus on Religion', *HSCP* 79: 93–123.
——(1976), 'The Atheism of Prodicus', *Cronache Ercolanesi*, 6: 15–21.
——(1981), 'Human Sacrifice in Greek Religion: Three Case Studies', in J. Rudhardt and O. Reverdin (eds.), *Le Sacrifice dans l'antiquité* (Entretiens sur l'Antiquité Classique, 27; Vandœuvres-Geneva), 195–235.
——(1982), 'Changing Dionysiac Identities', in B. F. Meyer and E. P. Sanders (eds.), *Jewish and Christian Self-Definition, iii: Self-Definition in the Graeco-Roman World* (London), 137–60, 213–36.
——(1984*a*), 'Loss of Self, Suffering, Violence: The Modern View of Dionysus from Nietzsche to Girard', *HSCP* 88: 205–40.
——(1984*b*), 'The Sophists and Hellenistic Religion: Prodicus as the Spiritual Father of the Isis Aretalogies', *HSCP* 88: 139–58.
——(forthcoming), 'Wie ein Rind zur Schlachtbank: Zur Problematisierung der Opferthematik in der griechischen Tragödie', in R. Schlesier (ed.), *Mythos und Interpretation*.
HERINGTON, J. (1991), 'The Poem of Herodotus', *Arion*, 3rd ser. 1/3: 5–16.
HERMANN, G. (1819), *Über das Wesen und die Behandlung der Mythologie: Ein Brief an Herrn Hofrath Creuzer* (Leipzig).

——(1827), 'De mythologia Graecorum antiquissima dissertatio', in *Opuscula*, ii (Leipzig), 167–94.

——and CREUZER, F. (1818), *Briefe über Homer und Hesiodus vorzüglich über die Theogonie* (Heidelberg).

HOFFMANN, H. (1997), *Sotades: Symbols of Immortality on Greek Vases* (Oxford).

HOFFNER, H. A., and BECKMAN, G. M. (1991), *Hittite Myths* (Atlanta).

HOLLIS, M. (1996), *Reason in Action: Essays in the Philosophy of Social Science* (Cambridge).

——and LUKES, S. (1982) (eds.), *Rationality and Relativism* (Oxford).

HÖLSCHER, U. (1953), 'Anaximander und der Anfang der Philosophie', *Hermes*, 81: 257–77, 385–418.

——(1968), *Anfängliches Fragen: Studien zur frühen griechischen Philosophie* (Göttingen).

HORKHEIMER, M., and ADORNO, T. W. (1947), *Dialektik der Aufklärung: Philosophische Fragmente* (Amsterdam).

HORNBLOWER, S. (1992), 'The Religious Dimension to the Peloponnesian War, or, What Thucydides Does Not Tell Us', *HSCP* 94: 169–97.

——(1995), 'The Fourth-century and Hellenistic Reception of Thucydides', *JHS* 115: 47–68.

HORSTMANN, A. E. A. (1972), 'Mythologie und Altertumswissenschaft: Der Mythosbegriff bei Christian Gottlob Heyne', *ABG* 16: 60–85.

——(1979), 'Der Mythos-Begriff vom frühen Christentum bis zur Gegenwart', *ABG* 23: 7–54, 197–245.

HORTON, R. (1967), 'African Traditional Thought and Western Science', *Africa*, 37: 50–71 and 155–87.

——(1990), *La Pensée métisse: Croyances africaines et rationalité occidentale en questions* (Paris).

——and FINNEGAN, R. (1973) (eds.), *Modes of Thought: Essays on Thinking in Western and Non-Western Societies* (London).

HOWALD, E. (1926) (ed.), *Der Kampf um Creuzers Symbolik: Eine Auswahl von Dokumenten* (Tübingen).

HSIA, R. PO-CHIA (1989), *Social Discipline in the Reformation: Central Europe 1550–1750* (London).

HÜBNER, K. (1985), *Die Wahrheit des Mythos* (Munich).

HUDSON, W. S. (1988), 'The Weber Thesis Reexamined', *ChHist* 57, Suppl.: 56–67.

HUGHES, D. D. (1991), *Human Sacrifice in Ancient Greece* (London).

HUMPHREYS, S. C. (1978), *Anthropology and the Greeks* (London).

——(1983), *The Family, Women and Death* (London).

——(1984), review of Eng. trans. of Gernet (1968), in *Man*, NS 19: 177.

HUNTER, V. (1982), *Past and Process in Herodotus and Thucydides* (Princeton).

JACKSON, S. B. (1995), *Myrsilus of Methymna, Hellenistic Paradoxographer* (Amsterdam).

JACOB, C. (1994), 'L'Ordre généalogique entre le mythe et l'histoire', in M. Detienne (ed.), *Transcrire les mythologies: Tradition, écriture, historicité* (Paris), 169–202.

JEFFERY, L. H. and MORPURGO-DAVIES, A. (1970), "Ποινικαστάς and ποινικάζεν: BM 1969.4–2.1, a New Archaic Inscription from Crete", *Kadmos*, 9: 118–54.

JOHNSTON, S. I. (forthcoming), 'Songs for the Ghosts: Magical Solutions for Deadly Problems'.

JONES, J. E. (1982), 'The Laurion Silver Mines: A Review of Recent Researches and Results', *G&R* 29: 169–83.

JOUANNA, J. (1992), *Hippocrate* (Paris).

JOWETT, B. (1953), *The Dialogues of Plato Translated into English with Analyses and Introductions*, 4th edn. (Oxford).

JULLIEN, F. (1985), *La Valeur allusive: Des catégories originales de l'interprétation poétique dans la tradition chinoise: contribution à une réflexion sur l'altérité interculturelle* (Paris).

KAHN, C. H. (1963), 'Plato's Funeral Oration: The Motive of the *Menexenus*', *CPh* 58: 220–34.

—— (1996), *Plato and the Socratic Dialogue: The Philosophical Use of a Literary Form* (Cambridge).

KALINOWSKI, M. (1996), 'Mythe, cosmogénèse et théogonie dans la Chine ancienne', *L'Homme*, 137: 41–60.

KALLET-MARX, L. (1993), *Money, Expense and Naval Power in Thucydides' History* 1–5. 24 (Oxford).

—— (1994), 'Money Talks: Rhetor, Demos and the Resources of the Athenian Empire', in R. Osborne and S. Hornblower (eds.), *Ritual, Finance, Politics: Athenian Democratic Accounts Presented to David Lewis* (Oxford), 227–51.

—— (forthcoming), 'Parallel Devastation: Athenian Finance and the Massacre at Mycalessos' (to appear in *TAPhA*).

KAMERBEEK, J., JR. (1964), 'Geschiedenis en problematiek van het begrip "tijdgeest"', *Forum der Letteren*, 5: 191–215.

KAUTZSCH, E. (1900), *Die Apokryphen und Pseudepigraphen des Alten Testaments*, ii (Tübingen).

KENNY, A. (1994), *The Oxford Illustrated History of Western Philosophy* (Oxford).

KERÉNYI, K. (1976), *Dionysos: Archetypal Image of Indestructible Life* (London).

KERN, O. (1922), *Orphicorum Fragmenta* (Berlin).

KERSCHENSTEINER, J. (1962), *Kosmos: Quellenkritische Untersuchungen zu den Vorsokratikern* (Munich).

KILANI, M. (1984), 'Les Images de la montagne au passé et au présent: L'Exemple des Alpes valaisannes', *Arch. suisses trad. pop.* 1: 27–55 (repr. in M. Kilani, *L'Invention de l'autre: Essais sur le discours anthropologique* (Lausanne, 1994), 137–65).

KINGSLEY, P. (1995), *Ancient Philosophy, Mystery, and Magic: Empedocles and Pythagorean Tradition* (Oxford).

KIPPENBERG, H. (1989), 'Intellektuellen-Religion', in P. Antes and D. Pahnke (eds.), *Die Religion von Oberschichten* (Marburg), 181–201.

——(1991), *Die vorderasiatischen Erlösungsreligionen in ihrem Zusammenhang mit der antiken Stadtherrschaft* (Frankfurt a. M.).

KIRK, G. S., RAVEN, J. E., and SCHOFIELD, M. (1983), *The Presocratic Philosophers*, 2nd edn. (Cambridge).

KLAGGE, J. C., and SMITH, N. D. (1992) (eds.), *Methods of Interpreting Plato and the Dialogues* (Oxford).

KLEINGÜNTHER, A. (1933), Πρῶτος εὑρετής: *Untersuchungen zur Geschichte einer Fragestellung* (*Philologus*, Suppl. 26/1; Leipzig).

KNIBB, M. A. (1978), *The Ethiopic Book of Enoch: A New Edition in the Light of the Aramaic Dead Sea Fragments* (Oxford).

KOSSMANN, E. H. (1995), *Vergankelijkheid en continuïteit: Opstellen over geschiedenis* (Amsterdam).

KUHLEMANN, F.-M. (1996), 'Mentalitätsgeschichte: Theoretische und methodische Überlegungen am Beispiel der Religion im 19. und 20. Jahrhundert', in W. Hardtwig and H.-U. Wehler (eds.), *Kulturgeschichte Heute* (Göttingen), 182–211.

KUHN, T. (1962), *The Structure of Scientific Revolutions*, 2nd edn. (Chicago).

KURKE, L. (1991), *The Traffic in Praise* (Ithaca, NY).

——(1992), 'The Politics of ἁβροσύνη in Archaic Greece', *ClAnt* 11: 91–120.

——(1993), 'The Economy of *kudos*', in C. Dougherty and L. Kurke (eds.), *Cultural Poetics in Archaic Greece: Cult, Performance, Politics* (Cambridge), 131–63.

——(1995), 'Herodotus and the Language of Metals', *Helios*, 22: 36–64.

LAKS, A., and MOST, G. W. (1997) (eds.), *Studies on the Derveni Papyrus* (Oxford).

LAMBERT, W. G., and PARKER, S. B. (1967), *Enuma elish: The Babylonian Epic of Creation. The Cuneiform Text* (Oxford).

LANE FOX, R. (1986), *Pagans and Christians* (London).

LANG, B. (1985) (ed.), *Anthropological Approaches to the Old Testament* (Philadelphia).

LATEINER, D. (1989), *The Historical Method of Herodotus* (Toronto).

LeBlanc, C. (1985), *Huai-Nan Tzu: Philosophical Synthesis in Early Han Thought* (Hong Kong).

Lehmann, H., and Roth, G. (1993) (eds.), *Weber's Protestant Ethic: Origins, Evidence, Contexts* (Cambridge).

Leichty, E. (1970), *The Omen Series šumma izbu* (*Texts from Cuneiform Sources*, iv) (New York).

Lemmen, M. M. W. (1977), *De godsdienstsociologie van Max Weber* (Nimwegen).

Lenfant, D. (1991), 'Milieu naturel et différences ethniques dans la pensée grecque classique', *Ktèma*, 16: 111–22.

——(1995), 'L'Inde de Ctésias: Des sources aux représentations', *Topoi*, 5: 309–36.

——(1996), 'Ctésias et Hérodote ou les réécritures de l'histoire dans la Perse achéménide', *REG* 109: 348–80.

Lévêque, P., and Vidal-Naquet, P. (1964), *Clisthène l'Athénien* (Paris).

Lévy, E. (1992), 'Hérodote *philobarbaros* ou la vision du barbare chez Hérodote', in R. Lonis (ed.), *L'Étranger dans le monde grec*, ii (Nancy), 193–244.

Lévy-Bruhl, L. (1922), *La Mentalité primitive* (Paris).

Lincoln, B. (1996), 'Gendered Discourses: The Early History of *Mythos* and *Logos*', *HR* 36: 1–12.

Lippold, G. (1911), 'Das Bildnis des Heraklit', *MDAI(A)* 36: 153–6.

Livingstone, A. (1986), *Mystical and Mythological Explanatory Works of Assyrian and Babylonian Scholars* (Oxford).

Lloyd, A. B. (1975–88), *Herodotus: Book 2* (Leiden).

Lloyd, Genevieve (1984), *The Man of Reason: 'Male' and 'Female' in Western Philosophy* (London).

Lloyd, G. E. R. (1966), *Polarity and Analogy: Two Types of Argumentation in Early Greek Thought* (Cambridge).

——(1979), *Magic, Reason and Experience: Studies in the Origin and Development of Greek Science* (Cambridge).

——(1987), *The Revolutions of Wisdom: Studies in the Claims and Practice of Ancient Greek Science* (Berkeley and Los Angeles).

——(1990), *Demystifying Mentalities* (Cambridge).

——(1994), 'Adversaries and Authorities', *PCPhS* 40: 27–48.

——(1996), *Adversaries and Authorities: Investigations into Ancient Greek and Chinese Science* (Cambridge).

Lloyd-Jones, H. (1983), 'Artemis and Iphigeneia', *JHS* 103: 87–102.

——(1990), *Greek Comedy, Hellenistic Literature, Greek Religion, and Miscellanea* (Oxford).

Lobeck, C. A. (1812), review of F. Creuzer, *Symbolik*, in *Allgemeine Jenaische Literatur-Zeitung*, Apr. 1812: 41–59 (signed 'G. St.').

——(1829), *Aglaophamus sive de theologiae mysticae Graecorum causis libri tres* (Königsberg).

LOCARD, A. (1884), *Histoire des mollusques dans l'antiquité* (Paris).

LOEWE, M. (1993) (ed.), *Early Chinese Texts: A Bibliographical Guide* (Berkeley and Los Angeles).

——(1994), *Divination, Mythology and Monarchy in Han China* (Cambridge).

LONG, T. (1987), *Repetition and Variation in the Short Stories of Herodotus* (Frankfurt a. M.).

LONGRIGG, J. (1993), *Greek Rational Medicine: Philosophy and Medicine from Alcmaeon to the Alexandrians* (London).

LORAUX, N. (1986), *The Invention of Athens: The Funeral Oration in the Classical City* (Cambridge, Mass.; orig. *L'Invention d'Athènes: Histoire de l'oraison funèbre dans la 'cité classique'* (Paris, 1981; rev. edn. 1993)).

——(1993), *The Children of Athena: Athenian Ideas about Citizenship and the Division between the Sexes* (Princeton; orig. *Les Enfants d'Athéna: Idées athéniennes sur la citoyenneté et la division des sexes* (Paris, 1981)).

LORENZ, G. (1984), *Snorri Sturluson, Gylfaginning: Texte, Übersetzung, Kommentar* (Darmstadt).

——(1990), 'Seelenwanderungslehre und Lebensführung in Oberschichten: Griechenland und Indien', *Theologische Literaturzeitung*, 115: 409–16.

LOSEMANN, V. (1977), *Nationalsozialismus und Antike: Studien zur Entwicklung des Faches Alte Geschichte 1933–1945* (Hamburg).

LUGINBÜHL, M. (1992), *Menschenschöpfungsmythen: Ein Vergleich zwischen Griechenland und dem Alten Orient* (Berne).

LUMPE, A. (1955), 'Der Terminus "Prinzip" (ἀρχή) von den Vorsokratikern bis auf Aristoteles', *ABG* 1: 104–16.

LUTHER, W. (1961), 'Die Schwäche des geschriebenen Logos', *Gymnasium*, 68: 526–48.

MAAS, P. (1924), 'Ein Exzerpt aus Ktesias Ἰνδικά bei Michel Psellos', *ZVS* 52: 303–6.

MACAN, R. W. (1908), *Herodotus: The Seventh, Eighth and Ninth Books* (London).

McCABE, M. M. (1994), *Plato's Individuals* (Princeton).

MacDOWELL, D. M. (1978), *The Law in Classical Athens* (London).

McGEE, M. C. (1980), 'The Ideograph: A Link between Rhetoric and Ideology', *Quarterly Journal of Speech*, 66: 1–16.

MACK, J. E. (1994), *Abduction: Human Encounters with Aliens* (New York).

MAENCHEN-HELFEN, O. (1944/5), 'The Legend of the Origin of the Huns', *Byzantion*, 17: 244–51.

MAJOR, J. S. (1993), *Heaven and Earth in Early Han Thought: Chapters Three, Four and Five of the Huainanzi* (Albany, NY).

MALINOWSKI, B. (1925), *Magic, Science, and Religion, and Other Essays* (Boston; repr. 1948).

MALINOWSKI, B. (1935), *Coral Gardens and their Magic: A Study of the Methods of Tilling the Soil and of Agricultural Rites in the Trobriand Islands* (New York).

MALKIN, I. (1987), *Religion and Colonization in Ancient Greece* (Leiden).

MANSFELD, J. (1990), *Studies in the Historiography of Greek Philosophy* (Assen).

MANSION, S. (1961) (ed.), *Aristote et les problèmes de méthode: Papers of the Second Symposium Aristotelicum* (Louvain).

MARCOVICH, M. (1988), *Studies in Graeco-Roman Religions and Gnosticism* (Leiden).

MARIN, L. (1981), *Le Portrait du roi* (Paris).

MARINATOS, N. (1981), *Thucydides and Religion* (Königstein).

MARTIN, F. (1906) (ed.), *Le Livre d'Hénoch, traduit sur le texte éthiopien* (Paris; repr. 1975).

MARTIN, R. P. (1989), *The Language of the Heroes: Speech and Performance in the Iliad* (Ithaca, NY).

MATHIEU, G. (1966), *Les Idées politiques d'Isocrate* (Paris).

MATTÉI, J.-F. (1990) (ed.), *La Naissance de la raison grecque* (Paris).

MAUSS, M. (1914), 'L'Origine de la notion de monnaie', *Anthropologie*, 25: 14–19.

—— (1924), 'Gift, Gift', in *Mélanges offerts à Charles Andler par ses amis et ses élèves* (Strasbourg), 243–7.

—— (1925), *Essai sur le don* (Paris).

—— (1968), *Œuvres*, ed. V. Karady (Paris).

MAZZARINO, S. (1947), *Fra oriente e occidente: Ricerche di storia greca arcaica* (Florence).

MEDAGLIA, S. M., and CORCELLA, A. (1993) (eds.), *Erodoto: Le storie, Libro IV* (Milan).

MEIJER, P. A. (1981), 'De Pythagoreïsche (leef)regels', *Hermeneus*, 53: 121–37.

MERKELBACH, R. (1988), *Die Hirten des Dionysos* (Stuttgart).

MEYERSON, I. (1948), *Les Fonctions psychologiques et les œuvres* (Paris).

MOMIGLIANO, A. D. (1966), *Studies in Historiography* (London).

—— (1990), *The Classical Foundations of Modern Historiography* (Berkeley and Los Angeles).

MORAVCSIK, J., and TEMKO, P. (1982) (eds.), *Plato on Beauty, Wisdom and the Arts* (Totowa, NJ).

MOREAU, A. (1997), 'Pour une apologie de la transgression? Esquisse d'une typologie', *Kernos*, 10: 97–110.

MORITZ, K. P. (1791), *Götterlehre oder mythologische Dichtungen der Alten* (Berlin).

MORRIS, B. (1987), *Anthropological Studies of Religion: An Introductory Text* (Cambridge).

MORRIS, I. (1996), 'The Strong Principle of Equality and the Archaic Origins of Greek Democracy', in J. Ober and C. Hedrick (eds.), *Dēmokratia: A Conversation on Democracies, Ancient and Modern* (Princeton), 19–48.

MOST, G. W. (1989), 'The Second Homeric Renaissance: Allegoresis and Genius in Early Modern Poetics', in P. Murray (ed.), *Genius: The History of an Idea* (Oxford), 54–75.

—— (1993), 'Die früheste erhaltene griechische Dichterallegorese', *RhM* 136: 209–12.

—— (1997), 'One Hundred Years of Fractiousness: Disciplining Polemics in Nineteenth-Century German Classical Scholarship', *TAPhA* 127: 349–61.

MÜLLER, K. O. (1820–4), *Geschichte hellenischer Stämme und Städte* (Breslau).

—— (1821), review of 2nd edn. of F. Creuzer, *Symbolik*, in *Göttingische Gelehrte Anzeigen*, 2: 940–60 (= *Kleine deutsche Schriften*, ii (Breslau, 1848), 3–20).

—— (1825), *Prolegomena zu einer wissenschaftlichen Mythologie* (Göttingen).

MÜLLER, M. (1856), *Comparative Mythology* (London).

—— (1869), *Essays*, ii (Leipzig).

—— (1873), *Introduction to the Science of Religion: With Two Essays on False Analogies and the Science of Mythology* (London).

—— (1897), *Contributions to the Science of Mythology* (London).

MURRAY, A. (1978), *Reason and Society in the Middle Ages* (Oxford).

MURRAY, O. (1972), 'Herodotus and Hellenistic Culture', *CQ* NS 22: 200–13.

NAGLER, M. (1980–1), 'Entretiens avec Tirésias', *CW* 74: 89–106.

NAGY, G. (1990), *Pindar's Homer: The Lyric Possession of an Epic Past* (Baltimore).

NENCI, G. (1990) (ed.), *Hérodote et les peuples non grecs* (Entretiens sur l'Antiquité Classique, 35; Vandœuvres-Geneva).

NESTLE, R. (1965) (ed.), *Bibliographie Wilhelm Nestle (16.4.1865–18.4.1959)* (Stuttgart).

NESTLE, W. (1940), *Vom Mythos zum Logos: Die Selbstentfaltung des griechischen Denkens von Homer bis auf die Sophistik und Sokrates* (Stuttgart).

NEUGEBAUER, O. (1975), *A History of Ancient Mathematical Astronomy*, 3 vols. (Berlin).

NEUMANN, J. N. (1995), 'La Malformation de l'homme: Son interprétation dans la cosmologie de l'Antiquité et du début du Moyen Age', *Ethique*, 16: 45–54.

NICKELSBURG, G. W. E. (1977), 'Apocalyptic and Myth in 1 Enoch 6–11', *JBL* 96: 383–405.

NIGHTINGALE, A. (1995), *Genres in Dialogue: Plato and the Construct of Philosophy* (Cambridge).

NILSSON, M. P. (1961), *Geschichte der griechischen Religion*, ii: *Die hellenistische und römische Zeit*, 2nd edn. (Munich).

—— (1967), *Geschichte der griechischen Religion*, i: *Die Religion Griechenlands bis auf die griechische Weltherrschaft*, 3rd edn. (Munich).

NOCK, A. D. (1972), *Essays on Religion and the Ancient World* (Oxford).

NOUHAUD, M. (1982), *L'Utilisation de l'histoire par les orateurs attiques* (Paris).

NUSSBAUM, M. C. (1978), *Aristotle's De motu animalium: Text with Translation, Commentary, and Interpretive Essays* (Princeton).

—— (1986), *The Fragility of Goodness: Luck and Ethics in Greek Tragedy and Philosophy* (Cambridge).

OBBINK, D. (1988), 'The Origin of Greek Sacrifice: Theophrastus on Religion and Cultural History', in W. W. Fortenbaugh and R. W. Sharples (eds.), *Theophrastean Studies on Natural Science, Physics, Metaphysics, Ethics, Religion and Rhetoric* (New Brunswick, NJ), 272–95.

—— (1996), *Philodemus on Piety: Critical Text with Commentary* (Oxford).

OLERUD, A. (1951), *L'Idée de macrocosmos et de microcosmos dans le Timée de Platon* (Uppsala).

OSBORNE, R. (1993), 'Women and Sacrifice', *CQ* NS 43: 392–405.

—— and HORNBLOWER, S. (1994) (eds.), *Ritual, Finance, Politics: Athenian Democratic Accounts Presented to David Lewis* (Oxford).

—— (1996), *Greece in the Making, 1200–479 BC* (London).

OSMUN, G. F. (1956), 'Palaephatus: Pragmatic Mythographer', *CJ* 52: 131–7.

OTTO, W. F. (1929), *Die Götter Griechenlands* (Bonn).

—— (1955), *Die Gestalt und das Sein: Gesammelte Abhandlungen über den Mythos und seine Bedeutung für die Menschheit* (Darmstadt).

—— (1963), *Mythos und Welt* (Darmstadt).

—— (1965), *Dionysus: Myth and Cult* (Bloomington, Ind.; orig. *Dionysos, Mythos und Kultus* (Frankfurt a. M., 1933)).

OWEN, G. E. L. (1986), *Logic, Science and Dialectic: Collected Papers in Greek Philosophy*, ed. M. Nussbaum (London).

PADEL, R. (1992), *In and Out of the Mind: Greek Images of the Tragic Self* (Princeton).

PAGE, D. L. (1955), *The Homeric Odyssey* (Oxford).

PAILLER, J.-M. (1988), *Bacchanalia: La Répression de 186 av. J.-C. à Rome et en Italie: Vestiges, images, tradition* (Bibliothèque des Écoles Françaises d'Athènes et de Rome, 270; Rome).

PARKER, R. (1983), *Miasma: Pollution and Purification in Early Greek Religion* (Oxford).

——(1995), 'Early Orphism', in A. Powell (ed.), *The Greek World* (London), 483–510.

——(1996), *Athenian Religion: A History* (Oxford).

PARRY, J., and BLOCH, M. (1989) (eds.), *Money and the Morality of Exchange* (Cambridge).

PASSERON, J.-C. (1994), 'La Rationalité et les types de l'action sociale chez Max Weber', *Revue européenne des sciences sociales*, 32, no. 98: 5–44.

PAYEN, P. (1997), *Les Iles nomades: Conquérir et résister dans l'Enquête d'Hérodote* (Paris).

PELLING, C. B. R. (1988), *Plutarch: Life of Antony* (Cambridge).

PIKE, K. L. (1967), *Language in Relation to a Unified Theory of the Structure of Human Behavior*, 2nd edn. (The Hague).

PINKWART, D. (1965), *Das Relief des Archelaos von Priene und die 'Musen des Philiskos'* (Kallmünz).

POLLITT, J. J. (1986), *Art in the Hellenistic Age* (Cambridge).

POUILLOUX, J. (1960), *Choix d'inscriptions grecques: Textes, traductions et notes* (Paris).

PRELLER, L. (1838), 'Friedrich Creuzer, charakterisiert nach seinen Werken', in *Hallische Jahrbücher für deutsche Wissenschaft und Kunst*, 1: 801–4, 809–11, 817–44.

PRINZ, F. (1979), *Gründungsmythen und Sagenchronologie* (Munich).

PRITCHETT, W. K. (1993), *The Liar School of Herodotus* (Amsterdam).

PUCCI, P. (1987), *Odysseus Polutropos: Intertextual Readings in the Odyssey and the Iliad* (Ithaca, NY).

PUGLIESE CARRATELLI, G. (1993), *Le lamine d'oro 'orfiche'* (Milan).

PUTTKAMMER, F. (1912), *Quo modo Graeci victimarum carnes distribuerint* (diss. Königsberg).

RADWIN, G. E., and D'ATTILIO, A. (1976) (eds.), *Murex Shells of the World: An Illustrated Guide to the Muricidae* (Stanford, Calif.).

REARDON, B. P. (1989) (ed.), *Collected Ancient Greek Novels* (Berkeley and Los Angeles).

REICHLER, C. (1994), 'Science et sublime dans la découverte des Alpes', *Rev. géogr. alpine*, 82. 3: 11–29.

REINHOLD, M. (1970), *History of Purple as a Status Symbol in Antiquity* (Coll. Latomus, 116; Brussels).

RICE, E. E. (1983), *The Grand Procession of Ptolemy Philadelphus* (Oxford).

RICHARDSON, N. J. (1974), *The Homeric Hymn to Demeter* (Oxford).

RIEDWEG, C. (1995), 'Orphisches bei Empedokles', *A&A* 41: 34–59.

——(1997), ' "Pythagoras hinterliess keine einzige Schrift"—ein Irrtum? Anmerkungen zu einer alten Streitfrage', *MH* 54: 65–92.

RIU, X. (1989), 'Dionís a la religió grega: cap a una lectura de les *Bacants*', *Itaca. Quaderns Catalans de Cultura Clàssica*, 5: 23–60.

ROBERT, C. (1915), *Oidipus: Geschichte eines poetischen Stoffs in griechischen Altertum* (Berlin).

ROBERT, L. (1938), *Études épigraphiques et philologiques* (Paris).

ROPER, L. (1994), *Oedipus and the Devil: Witchcraft, Sexuality and Religion in Early Modern Europe* (London).

ROSSELLINI, M., and SAÏD, S. (1978), 'Usages de femmes et autres nomoi chez les "sauvages" d'Hérodote: Essai de lecture structurale', *ASNP* 8: 949–1005.

ROSSI, L. (1996), 'Il testamento di Posidippo e le laminette auree di Pella', *ZPE* 112: 59–65.

ROTH, H. D. (1992), *The Textual History of the Huai-Nan Tzu* (Ann Arbor).

ROUSSEL, P. (1943), 'L'Exposition des enfants à Sparte', *REA* 45: 5–17.

ROWE, C. J. (1993a), *Plato: Phaedo* (Cambridge).

——(1993b), 'Philosophy and Literature: The Arguments of Plato's *Phaedo*', in *Proceedings of the Boston Area Colloquium in Ancient Philosophy*, vii, 1991: 159–81.

——(1997): 'Why is the Ideal Athens of the *Timaeus-Critias* not Ruled by Philosophers?', *Méthexis*, 10: 51–7.

RUDHARDT, J. (1982), 'De l'inceste dans la mythologie grecque', *Revue française de psychanalyse*, 46: 731–63.

RUSTEN, J. S. (1982), *Dionysius Scytobrachion* (Papyrologica Coloniensia, 10; Opladen).

RUTHERFORD, R. (1995), *The Art of Plato: Ten Essays in Platonic Interpretation* (London).

SAÏD, S. (1993), *Approches de la mythologie* (Paris).

——TRÉDÉ, M., and LE BOULLUEC, A. (1997), *Histoire de la littérature grecque* (Paris).

SAINT-HILAIRE, I. GEOFFROY (1837), *Traité de tératologie* (Brussels).

SARTON, G. (1959), *A History of Science: Hellenistic Science and Culture in the Last Three Centuries B. C.* (Cambridge, Mass.).

SAUNERON, S., and YOYOTTE, Y. (1959), 'La Naissance du monde selon l'Égypte ancienne', in *Sources orientales*, i: *La Naissance du monde* (Paris), 19–91.

SCHIBLI, H. S. (1990), *Pherekydes of Syros* (Oxford).

SCHLESIER, R. (1992), 'Ritual und Mythos: Zur Anthropologie der Antike heute', in R. Faber and B. Kytzler (eds.), *Antike heute* (Würzburg), 93–109.

SCHLUCHTER, W. (1979), *Die Entwicklung des okzidentalen Rationalismus: Eine Analyse von Max Webers Gesellschaftsgeschichte* (Tübingen).

——(1981) (ed.), *Max Webers Studie über das antike Judentum: Interpretation und Kritik* (Frankfurt a. M.).

SCOTT, K. (1928), 'The Deification of Demetrius Poliorcetes', *AJP* 49: 137–66 and 217–39.

SEAFORD, R. (1984), *Euripides: Cyclops* (Oxford).

——(1994), *Reciprocity and Ritual: Homer and Tragedy in the Developing City-State* (Oxford).

——(1996), *Euripides: Bacchae* (Warminster).

SEGAL, C. (1978), ' "The Myth Was Saved": Reflections on Homer and the Mythology of Plato's *Republic*', *Hermes*, 106: 315–36.

SHAPIN, S. (1996), *The Scientific Revolution* (Chicago).

SIEWERT, P. (1972), *Der Eid von Plataiai* (Munich).

SILK, M. S. (1996) (ed.), *Tragedy and the Tragic: Greek Theatre and Beyond* (Oxford).

SIVIN, N. (1995*a*), 'Text and Experience in Classical Chinese Medicine', in D. Bates (ed.), *Knowledge and the Scholarly Medical Traditions* (Cambridge), 177–204.

——(1995*b*), 'State, Cosmos and Body in the Last Three Centuries BC', *Harvard Journal of Asiatic Studies*, 55: 5–37.

——(1995*c*), *Medicine, Philosophy and Religion in Ancient China: Researches and Reflections* (Aldershot).

SMITH, J. E. (1985), 'Plato's Myths as "Likely Accounts", Worthy of Belief', *Apeiron*, 19: 24–42.

——(1986), 'Plato's Use of Myth in the Education of Philosophic Man', *Phoenix*, 40: 20–34.

SMITH, R. R. R. (1991), 'A New Portrait of Pythagoras', in R. R. R. Smith and K. T. Erim (eds.), *Aphrodisias Papers*, ii: *The Theatre, A Sculptor's Workshop, Philosophers and Coin-types* (Ann Arbor), 159–67.

SNELL, B. (1953), *The Discovery of the Mind: The Greek Origins of European Thought* (Oxford; orig. *Die Entdeckung des Geistes: Studien zur Entstehung des europäischen Denkens bei den Griechen* (4th edn.; Göttingen, 1975)).

SOURVINOU-INWOOD, C. (1995), *'Reading' Greek Death: To the End of the Classical Period* (Oxford).

SPADEA, R. (1994), 'Il tesoro di Hera', *Bolletino d'arte*, fasc. 88: 1–34.

——(1996), *Il tesoro di Hera: Scoperte nel santuario di Hera Lacinia a Capo Colonna di Crotone* (Milan).

SPOERRI, W. (1959), *Späthellenistische Berichte über Welt, Kultur und Götter* (Schweizerische Beiträge zur Altertumswissenschaft, 9; Basle).

STAUDACHER, W. (1942), *Die Trennung von Himmel und Erde* (Tübingen; repr. 1968).

STEIN, P. (1909), ΤΕΡΑΣ (diss. Marburg).

STEINER, G. (1959), *Der Sukzessionsmythos in Hesiods Theogonie und ihren orientalischen Parallelen* (diss. Hamburg).

STEPHENS, S. A., and WINKLER, J. J. (1995), *Ancient Greek Novels: The Fragments. Introduction, Text, Translation, and Commentary* (Princeton).

STERN, J. (1996), *Palaephatus, Peri Apiston: On Unbelievable Tales, Translation, Introduction and Commentary* (Wauconda, Ill.).

STEWART, A. F. (1990), *Greek Sculpture: An Exploration* (New Haven).

STRATHERN, M. (1992), 'Qualified Value: The Perspective of Gift Exchange', in C. Humphrey and S. Hugh-Jones (eds.), *Barter, Exchange and Value: An Anthropological Approach* (Cambridge), 169–91.

STRENSKI, I. (1987), *Four Theories of Myth in Twentieth-Century History: Cassirer, Eliade, Lévi-Strauss and Malinowski* (London).

STROCKA, V. M. (1992), 'Orpheus und Pythagoras in Sparta', in H. Froning *et al.* (eds.), *Kotinos: Festschrift für Erika Simon* (Mainz), 276–83.

TAMBIAH, S. J. (1985), *Culture, Thought, and Social Action: An Anthropological Perspective* (Cambridge, Mass.).

——(1990), *Magic, Science, Religion and the Scope of Rationality* (Cambridge).

TAYLOR, C. (1991), *Plato: Protagoras*, 2nd edn. (Oxford).

TEDLOCK, D. (1985), *Popol Vuh: The Definitive Edition of the Mayan Book of the Dawn of Life and the Glories of Gods and Kings* (New York).

TE VELDE, H. (1967), *Seth, God of Confusion: A Study of his Role in Egyptian Mythology and Religion* (Leiden).

THOMAS, R. (1989), *Oral Tradition and Written Record in Classical Athens* (Cambridge).

——(1995), 'Written in Stone? Liberty, Equality, Orality, and the Codification of Law', *BICS* 40: 59–74.

THRAEDE, K. (1962), 'Erfinder II (geistesgeschichtlich)', in *Reallexikon für Antike und Christentum* (Stuttgart), v. 1191–1278.

TONDRIAU, J. (1946), 'Les Thiases dionysiaques royaux de la cour ptolémaïque', *Chronique d'Égypte*, 41: 149–71.

TOTTI, M. (1985), *Ausgewählte Texte der Isis- und Sarapis-Religion* (Hildesheim).

TOULMIN, S., and GOODFIELD, J. (1965), *The Discovery of Time* (London).

TRENDALL, A. D. (1994), *A Passion for Antiquities: Ancient Art from the Collection of Barbara and Lawrence Fleischmann* (Malibu, Calif.).

TURNBULL, C. M. (1961), *The Forest People* (London).

UHLIG, S. (1984), *Das äthiopische Henochbuch* (Jüdische Schriften aus hellenistisch-römischer Zeit, V: Apokalypsen, 6; Gütersloh).

VALERI, M. (1997), 'Religion, Discipline, and the Economy in Calvin's Geneva', *The Sixteenth Century Journal*, 28: 123–42.

VAN DER HORST, P. W., and MUSSIES, G. (1990), *Studies on the Hellenistic Background of the New Testament* (Utrecht).

VANDERKAM, J. C. (1995), *Enoch: A Man for All Generations* (Columbia, SC).

VANDERMEERSCH, L. (1980), *Wangdao: ou, la voie royale: Recherches sur l'esprit des institutions de la Chine archaïque* (Paris).

VAN DER WAERDEN, B. L. (1961), *Science Awakening*, i, 2nd edn. (New York).

VAN DÜLMEN, R. (1988), 'Protestantismus und Kapitalismus: Max Webers These im Licht der neueren Sozialgeschichte', in C. Gneuss and J. Kocka (eds.), *Max Weber: Ein Symposion* (Munich), 88–101.

VANHOEVE, D. (1994), 'The Laurion Revisited', in H. Mussche (ed.), *Studies in South Attica*, ii (Ghent), 30–75.

VAN STRATEN, F. T. (1995), *Hierà kalá: Images of Animal Sacrifice in Archaic and Classical Greece* (Leiden).

VEGETTI, M. (1994), 'Quand la science parle à vide: Procédés dialectiques et métaphoriques chez Aristote', in V. de Coorebyter (ed.), *Rhétoriques de la science* (Paris), 7–32.

VERNANT, J.-P., *et al.* (1974), *Divination et rationalité* (Paris).

——(1980), *Myth and Society in Ancient Greece* (Hassocks; orig. *Mythe et société en Grèce ancienne* (Paris, 1974)).

——(1982), *The Origins of Greek Thought* (Ithaca, NY; orig. *Les Origines de la pensée grecque* (Paris, 1962; 2nd edn. 1992)).

——(1983), *Myth and Thought among the Greeks* (London; orig. *Mythe et pensée chez les Grecs* (Paris, 1965; 2nd edn. 1985)).

——(1995), *Passé et présent: Contributions à une psychologie historique réunies par Riccardo di Donato* (Rome).

——(1996), *Entre mythe et politique* (Paris).

——and VIDAL-NAQUET, P. (1988), *Myth and Tragedy in Ancient Greece* (New York; orig. *Mythe et tragédie en Grèce ancienne*, 2 vols. (Paris, 1972–86)).

VEYNE, P. (1988), *Did the Greeks Believe in their Myths? An Essay on the Constitutive Imagination* (Chicago; orig. *Les Grecs ont-ils cru a leurs mythes? Essai sur l'imagination constituante* (Paris, 1983)).

VIDAL-NAQUET, P. (1986), *The Black Hunter: Forms of Thought and Forms of Society in the Greek World* (Baltimore; orig. *Le Chasseur noir: Formes de pensée et formes de société dans le monde grec* (Paris, 1981)).

VON REDEN, S. (1995), *Exchange in Ancient Greece* (London).

——(1997), 'Money, Law and Exchange: Coinage in the Greek Polis', *JHS* 117: 154–76.

VON STADEN, H. (1992), 'The Mind and the Skin of Heracles: Heroic Diseases', in D. Gourevitch (ed.), *Maladie et maladies: Histoire et conceptualisation. Mélanges Mirko Grmek* (Geneva), 131–50.

VYSE, S. A. (1997), *Believing in Magic. The Psychology of Superstition* (New York).

WARDMAN, A. E. (1960), 'Myth in Greek Historiography', *Historia*, 9: 403–13.

WASCHKIES, H. J. (1989), *Anfänge der Arithmetik im Alten Orient und bei den Griechen* (Amsterdam).

WATKINS, C. (1995), *How to Kill a Dragon: Aspects of Indo-European Poetics* (Oxford).

WEBER, G. (1993), *Dichtung und höfische Gesellschaft: Die Rezeption von Zeitgeschichte am Hof der ersten drei Ptolemäer* (*Hermes* Einzelschr. 62; Stuttgart).

WEBER, M. (1920), *Gesammelte Aufsätze zur Religionssoziologie*, i (Tübingen).

——(1956), *Wirtschaft und Gesellschaft*, 4th edn. (Tübingen).

WEHRLI, F. (1969), *Phainias von Eresos, Chamaileon, Praxiphanes* (*Die Schule des Aristoteles*, ix), 2nd edn. (Basle).

WEINREICH, O. (1926), 'Antikes Gottmenschentum', *Neue Jahrbücher für Wissenschaft und Jugendbildung*, 2: 633–51 (= *Ausgewählte Schriften*, ii (Amsterdam, 1973), 171–97).

WERBLOWSKY, R. J. Z., and WIGODER, G. (1997) (eds.), *The Oxford Dictionary of the Jewish Religion* (New York).

WEST, M. L. (1966), *Hesiod, Theogony: Edited with Prolegomena and Commentary* (Oxford).

——(1971), *Early Greek Philosophy and the Orient* (Oxford).

——(1982), *Greek Metre* (Oxford).

——(1983), *The Orphic Poems* (Oxford).

——(1985), *The Hesiodic Catalogue of Women* (Oxford).

——(1986), 'Early Greek Philosophy', in J. Boardman, J. Griffin, and O. Murray (eds.), *The Oxford History of the Classical World* (Oxford), 113–23.

——(1994), 'Ab ovo: Orpheus, Sanchuniathon, and the Origins of the Ionian World Model', *CQ* NS 44: 289–307.

WESTFALL, R. S. (1980), *Never at Rest: A Biography of Isaac Newton* (Cambridge).

WHITE, H. (1978), *Tropics of Discourse: Essays in Cultural Criticism* (Baltimore).

WILAMOWITZ-MOELLENDORFF, U. VON (1881), *Antigonos von Karystos* (Berlin).

——(1895), *Euripides: Herakles*, 2nd edn. (Berlin).

——(1959), *Der Glaube der Hellenen*, i, 3rd edn. (Darmstadt).

WILLIAMS, B. (1993), *Shame and Necessity* (Berkeley and Los Angeles).

WILSON, B. R. (1970) (ed.), *Rationality* (Oxford).

WINCKELMANN, J. (1980), 'Die Herkunft von Max Webers "Entzauberungs"-Konzeption: Zugleich ein Beitrag zu der Frage, wie gut wir das Werk Max Webers kennen können', *Kölner Zeitschrift für Soziologie und Sozialpsychologie*, 32: 12–53.

WIPPRECHT, F. (1902), *Zur Entwicklung der Rationalistischen Mythendeutung* (Tübingen).

WITTKOWER, R. (1942), 'Marvels of the East: A Study in the History of Monsters', *JWI* 5: 159–97.

YUAN KE (1986*a*), *Zhongguo shenhua chuanshuo cidian* (Hong Kong).

——(1986*b*), *Zhongguo shenhua chuanshuo* (Beijing).

——(1991), *Zhongguo shenhuashi* (Taibei).

——and ZHOU MING (1985), *Zhongguo shenhua ziliao cuibian* (Chengdu).

ZANKER, G. (1981), 'Enargeia in the Ancient Criticism of Poetry', *RhM* 124: 297–311.

ZANKER, P. (1988), *The Power of Images in the Age of Augustus* (Ann Arbor; orig. *Augustus und die Macht der Bilder* (Munich, 1987)).

ZHMUD, L. (1997), *Wissenschaft, Philosophie und Religion im frühen Pythagoreismus* (Berlin).

ZUMBRUNNEN, D. (1996), 'Hérodote et l'Athènes de Périclès (Hdt. 9. 26–28)' (unpubl. diss. Lausanne).

ZUNTZ, G. (1963), 'Once More the So-called "Edict of Philopator on the Dionysiac Mysteries" (BGU 1211)', *Hermes*, 91: 228–39 (repr. in G. Zuntz, *Opuscula Selecta* (Manchester, 1972), 88–101).

92 - Anaxm - infinite

Anaxagoras - Together were
all things

Index

This index covers names and topics referred to in the book, with two main exceptions, namely (a) the terms 'myth', 'reason', 'rationality', muthos, and logos, which recur passim, and (b) the names of ancient and modern authors and works when these appear in footnotes as brief citations only.

Apollonia 170–1, 175, 176
Apollonius (of Rhodes) 5
Apsu 91–2
Aquinas, Thomas 11
Archelaus (of Priene), sculpture by
      225–6
archē ('beginning'):
   see cosmogony
Archidamus (Spartan king) 126, 132
Archimedes 6
Archippus (comic poet), on purple 304
Ares 133
Argo, the 110
Argos 132, 133
Arion, and dolphin 181
Aristophanes 115
Aristotle 2, 4, 6, 18, 29, 75, 97, 153,
      193, 230, 317
   archē-philosophy discussed in 88, 89,
      93, 96
   logic in 123, 124, 126, 139, 140 n.
      34
   metallurgy and 323
   metaphor in 141 n. 35, 157
   mētis in 314 n. 60
   money and 65, 67
   on monsters 198, 199, 200, 201,
      204, 205, 207, 213
   muthoi in 19–20, 279–91
   on *muthologoi* 154–5, 184
   Palaephatus and 215, 216
   on poetry 129
   on purple 299 n. 11, 302, 315
   on rhetoric 130, 133 n. 21
Artayctes 192
Artemis 219
Asius (Samian poet) 74
Aspasia 180, 274, 276
Astarte 306
Astraios 95
astrology 320
Atalanta 218, 219
Athena 62 n. 24, 113, 188, 189, 220,
      231, 245, 263 n. 2
Athenaeus, on fish 299–300, 301, 302,
      303
Athens 216, 288 n. 17, 299, 318
   children exposed at 201
   coinage at 65 n. 33
   Demetrius and 242–6
   Epimenides at 173
   in Eur. *Ion* 108, 113

finance at 66–8
human sacrifice at 229–37
Minos and 175 n. 23
mythical past of 131–6, 242
Neoplatonism at 89
Orphism at 82
depicted in Plato 263, 272–7
torture at 209 n. 83
Atlantis 255, 260, 272, 273, 276, 277
Atlas 285–7, 290
Atreus, house of 54
Atthidographers 242
Auerbach, E. 178 n. 34
Augustine:
   on Fallen Angels 319
   on monstrous races 214 n. 106
Augustus (Octavian) 247, 248
Ausonius, on purple 307
Autolycus 172
Autonoe 238
Azael 320
Azande, the 11

Baal 98, 99
Babylonia:
   astronomy in 151
   cosmogony in 89–92, 95–7, 99–103
   monsters in 203
Bacis, oracle of 189 n. 16
Barnes, J. 2, 124, 291 n. 24
Bélis, M. 20
Bellerophon 113, 173 n. 18
Benjamin, W. 115 n. 14
biography 61, 187
Birrell, A. 147, 148, 159
bittacos (monstrous bird) 211, 212
blacksmiths 310, 324, 325, 326
blindness, literal and metaphorical 171,
      172, 174, 176, 189
Blumenberg, H. 42
Bonitz, H., on *muthos* in Aristotle 280
Bonnechere, P. 229, 235
Boreas 125, 289
Bourdieu, P. 69
Brelich, A. 8
Bremmer, J. N. 15, 17
Brisson, L. 101
bronze 5, 81, 93, 180, 323, 324
Burkert, W. 9, 16, 74, 76, 77
Burnet, J. 261 n. 24, 266 n. 7
Burnyeat, M. 269 n. 17, 288
Buxton, R. G. A. 72, 212, 246–7

Warburg, A. 41
water:
 primeval, myths compared to 26,
  28, 47
 in cosmogony 92, 93, 96
 see also sea
Weber, M. 11, 15, 72–7, 82, 83
West, M. L. 98
whelks 295–316 *passim*
White, H. 12–13
Whitely, W. H. 14
Wilamowitz-Moellendorff, U. von
 216
Wise Men, Seven:
 see Sages, Seven
witchcraft:
 see magic
Wolf, F. A. 179
wolves 170–1, 284
women:
 in Eur. *Ion* 113
 in Pl. *Rep.* 268
 myth-tellers 252
 Orphic 82
 purple and 312–13
 superstitious 227

Xenophanes 3 n. 12, 32, 78, 81, 83,
 96, 219, 287 n. 16
Xerxes 131, 133, 181, 192

Yijing (Book of Changes) 159
Ymir 100
Yuan Ke 147

Zaleucus 174 with n. 21
Zarathustra 41
Zethus 221
Zeus:
 in Derveni papyrus 80, 81, 96, 97
 of Dodona 181
 in Eur. *Ba.* 220
 in Eur. *Hipp.* 112
 in Eur. *Ion* 113
 in Hes. *Theog.* 9, 103, 104
 in Hom. *Il.* 91, 180
 Homer sculpted in manner of 225
 in Isocrates 127, 135 n. 23
 Lycaeus 177 n. 29
 Palaephatus on 218, 219
 in Pl. *Rep.* 252
 Prodicus on 240
 and Ptolemy I: 241
 in Soph. *Ant.* 110, 111
 fights Titans 101
 kills Typhon 99
 and whelks 304
Zhuan Xu 150
Zhuangzi 148, 149, 156, 157, 158
zoology, Aristotelian 4
Zuo zhuan 148